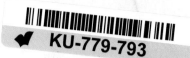

Training Interventions

Skills Devt.

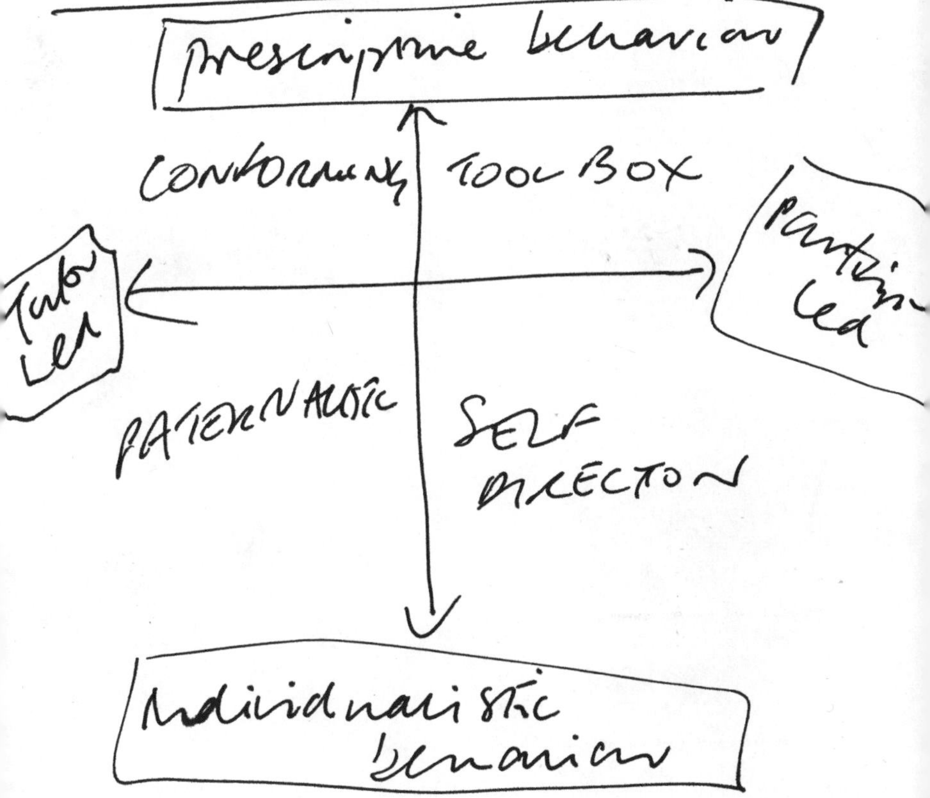

Training Interventions

John Kenney
and
Margaret Anne Reid

Second edition

INSTITUTE OF PERSONNEL MANAGEMENT

For Maureen

First published 1986
Second edition 1988
Reprinted 1989, 1990 and 1991

Cover design by Craig Dodd

Phototypeset by Auckland Litho Limited, 5-25 Burr Road, Wandsworth, SW18 4SG
Printed in Great Britain by
Dotesios Ltd.,
Trowbridge, Wiltshire

British Library Cataloguing Publication Data

Kenney, John.
Training interventions– 2nd ed.
1. Great Britain. Industrial training.
Management aspects.
I. Title II. Reid, Margaret
658.3'124'0941

ISBN 0-85292-409-7

Contents

List of figures

Foreword

Training should be an integral part of the work and development of any company or organization, large or small. After all, a company's human resources are among its most important assets and the skills and motivation of its workers can be crucial to success. We all need to recognize that training is not a luxury, but a necessity.

As *Training Interventions* outlines as part of its historical perspective, many United Kingdom employers, in contrast to its overseas competitors, have for too long placed a low value on training. The result has been shortages of skills employers need and a workforce not able to adapt to rapidly changing technology as quickly as we would hope. Although there are many exceptions and examples of good training practice, the attitudes of the majority of senior managers, who have a crucial influence on training decisions, still give much cause for concern. This was highlighted in the report prepared by Coopers and Lybrand Associates for the Manpower Services Commission and the National Economic Development Office, published in December 1985, which pinpointed indifference and complacency by senior managers as one of the most important factors inhibiting investment in training. I would like to see training elevated to a subject of board-level importance in every company and treated as an essential part of business planning from the early stages, rather than as an optional extra.

The great bulk of training activity will continue to be carried out by managers in collaboration with training professionals. It is to these professionals in their student years that *Training Interventions* is primarily addressed. I believe trainers can play an important role in influencing companies' attitudes towards training. The book's comprehensive and structured analysis of training policy and practice should be a helpful tool for them. The clear examples cited should be of direct practical assistance as well as being a useful source of reference.

The Government has made good progress in taking forward its strategic training objectives. The new two-year YTS to be introduced in April 1986, the pilot Technical and Vocational Education Initiative which is now stimulating the development of a better technical and vocational curriculum for 14 – 18 year olds in 500 schools and colleges, and the Review of Vocational Qualifications, which should result in a clearer and simpler structure of vocational qualifications of benefit to employers and students, are all significant achievements. But much remains to be done and employers, individuals and trade unions can all contribute to the recognition and exploitation of the advantages training can bring. *Training Interventions* will, I hope, contribute to both the debate on training and the national effort to achieve better quality training.

Lord Young of Graffham
Secretary of State for Employment
April 1986

Preface

This book is based upon and replaces the Institute of Personnel Management's publication *Manpower Training and Development*, which was first published in 1972. Our initial intention was to update the revised (1979) manuscript but the magnitude of the changes which have taken place in the training and development field made this inappropriate.

For centuries after the enactment of the Statute of Artificers in 1563, training philosophies and practices evolved at a very slow pace. The last 20 years, however, have seen a dramatic and fundamental acceleration in new thinking, approaches and practices in response to the rapidly changing scene of working life. As in all technological change, these advances have not occurred simultaneously on every front: they have had an irregular impact on organizations and individuals. Now, as at no time in the past, there is a sharper distinction between the old and the new. Training philosophies and strategies particularly appropriate for a rapidly changing environment include continuing development, self-managed learning, and innovatory delivery systems. On the other hand, where the required skills and knowledge can be defined, or emphasis is on the permanence of jobs, analytical skills and more formal instructional techniques are still appropriate.

Aware of the dangers of throwing out the baby with the bath water, we consider it necessary to provide a blend of the old and the new, and to look backwards as well as forwards. Professional trainers need to be equally aware of traditional and contemporary approaches, and competent to apply them appropriately.

In Chapter 5, we explain our view that an organization is a learning environment; its climate, culture and practices having a powerful influence on its members. Training is therefore seen as a deliberate intervention into an on-going process — hence our title. The spectrum of training interventions extends from informal giving and receiving of advice at one end, to more formal activity such as job rotation or providing other planned experience, to organizing and attending courses at the far extreme.

We have assumed that readers will be studying training and development as part of their professional careers, and some will therefore probably have limited knowledge or experience of training. We have tried to keep a balance between theory and practice, although we are conscious that our enthusiasm for the subject may at times have led us to be evangelistic! In offering guidance for further reading we have, wherever possible, quoted references in journals and books which are most likely to be available, to make it as easy as possible for students to pursue their studies. Literature on training abounds but the necessity to understand the context in which it was written has increased with the years as philosophies and practices have been developed and modified. At times, therefore, we have adopted an historical approach to provide an appropriate background.

The book has been planned to follow a logical order. Beginning with a consideration of the nature of training and its organizational role, it continues with the assessment of organization and individual needs, to the choice of strategy and the planning and evaluation of interventions. In the final chapter, we consider national interventions as they affect both the organization and the individual.

In recognition of the fact that there are probably as many women as men studying to become personnel professionals, we have used the pronouns 'he' and 'she' in alternate chapters.

We are greatly indebted to Eugene Donnelly, Stuart Dalziel, Pat Armstrong and Bernard Baron for their helpful advice and thoughtful criticisms of our drafts. The views expressed in the book are, of course, our own. We are also most grateful to the authors and publishers who have given us permission to quote their work. Acknowledgements are made, as appropriate, in the text. We thank Sylvia Seeker for permitting us to print the extract in Chapter 2 from *The Ragged-trousered Philanthropists*. Extracts from the *Glossary of Training Terms* are reproduced with the kind permission of the Controller of Her Majesty's Stationery Office.

John Kenney
Margaret Reid

November, 1985

Preface to second edition

We referred, in the 1986 edition, to the 'dramatic and fundamental acceleration in new thinking in the field of training and development'. Although it was, and still is, necessary to look back in order to understand what has already been achieved, we stressed the need to keep abreast of current developments which embody this new thinking.

Trains of thought had been initiated leading to concepts such as: learning to learn, core competencies, continuous development, the management of own learning, to name but a few. Following these ideas to their logical conclusion leads to new practices, new criteria and standards, new terminology both at organization and national level. Many of these changes, in their early stages in 1986, have progressed further on the way. National issues have changed in emphasis. Some, like skills shortages, arouse feelings of *déjà vu*, others, such as the decline in numbers of young people leaving school, are likely to affect the employment and training policies of many organizations. Even since 1988, there have been radical changes in national training provision in Britain (the Manpower Services Commission, for example, has changed its name twice). It has not been possible to update the whole of this book, but the main new developments have been outlined in Chapter 11. Readers particularly interested in the national scene are advised to turn there before proceeding to the main body of the text.

We should like to acknowledge our thanks to Harry Barrington, Eugene Donnelly, Rick Holden and Mike Long for their assistance with this chapter.

M.A.R.
July 1989

1: *What is training?*

INTRODUCTION

In this chapter we describe the role that training and development interventions can play in helping individuals and organizations adapt to the demands of a rapidly changing, technological society. We consider, in a work context, the differences and similarities between education and training. We demonstrate the benefits of a planned approach to training and the different ways in which planned training is used. Finally, we outline different philosophies of training.

MANPOWER AS A RESOURCE

- Investment in vocational education and training is an essential ingredient of a successful economy.
- The aggregate investment in training and development made by UK employers is inadequate in quantity and in quality, and this is especially so in times of economic recession.
- The country's training and retraining systems lack the capacity to respond quickly enough to the demands for new skills and knowledge created by rapid technological change.
- In many of the UK's growth industries there is an imbalance between the skills and qualifications required by employers and those available in the nation's workforce.

These four statements, set against a background of socially and politically unacceptable levels of unemployment, help to explain why there has been a marked increase in Government-led initiatives and investment in training, retraining and vocational education in the UK.

Progress towards a sustained economic recovery has been thwarted by mismatches between the 'competence profile' of the UK workforce and the needs of the labour market. Too often the skills and competencies that the unemployed can offer are obsolete and relate to the requirements of past rather than today's labour markets. The critical role that training and retraining must play in assisting national economic recovery is expressed in the Manpower Services Commission's (1981) consultative document, *A New Training Initiative* :

> The new markets and technologies require a more highly skilled, better educated and more mobile workforce in which a much larger number of professional and technical staff are supported by a range of more or less highly trained workers who perform a range of tasks and who are involved in a process rather than the repetitive assembly or manufacture of a part or specific product.

The contribution of training and development to improved efficiency is made largely at the level of the organization. Commercial, industrial and public sector organizations operate in a dynamic environment (see McIlwee 1982). Market, technological, personnel, political and other changes have far-reaching effects on an organization and unless it is prepared, and able, to move with the times its efficiency is eroded and its opportunities for growth curtailed. However, as Burns and Stalker (1966) point out, organizations often find it difficult to adjust to change. One of managers' key responsibilities is to develop their organizations to meet the challenge of the future. This responsibility is exercised by assessing the resources and opportunities available, defining objectives and efficiently managing the resources allocated to meet these goals.

One of the most important resources available to an organization, and many would say the most important, is its employees. Their competence and commitment largely determine the objectives that an enterprise can set for itself and its success in achieving them. This fact of working life is not new but since the Second World War labour market conditions have forced employers to pay particular attention to their personnel policies and practices. The rapid evolution of personnel management as a major function is itself a direct result of employers' growing concern for the more effective use and development of their human resources (see Armstrong and Dawson 1983).

For many years, especially in areas of full employment, most employers recognized that it made good sense to have progressive personnel policies. This recognition embraced welfare, remuneration, recruitment and industrial relations. It did not extend to training and development, except in relatively few organizations and it was this unsatisfactory situation which led to the 1964 Industrial Training Act (see Chapter 10). While more organizations have, since the mid-1960s, incorporated planned training (see page 14) within their manpower policies, others have not and this is an issue to which we shall return on many occasions in later chapters.

The terms 'education', 'training' and 'development' are open to differing interpretations. In this book we use the definitions contained in the Manpower Services Commission's *Glossary of Training Terms* (1981):

- Education is defined as 'activities which aim at developing the knowledge, skills, moral values and understanding required in all aspects of life rather than a knowledge and skill relating to only a limited field of activity. The purpose of education is to provide the conditions essential to young people and adults to develop an understanding of the traditions and ideas influencing the society in which they live and to enable them to make a contribution to it. It involves study of their own cultures and of the laws of nature, as well as the acquisition of linguistic and other skills which are basic to learning, personal development, creativity and communication'.

- Training is 'a planned process to modify attitude, knowledge or skill behaviour through learning experience to achieve effective performance in an activity or range of activities. Its purpose, in the work situation, is to develop the abilities of the individual and to satisfy the current and future manpower needs of the organization'.

- Development is defined as 'the growth or realisation of a person's ability, through conscious or unconscious learning. Development programmes usually include elements of planned study and experience, and are frequently supported by a coaching or counselling facility'.

Both training and development are achieved by creating conditions in which the necessary attitude, skill and knowledge can be effectively acquired by a learner who, as a result, becomes more confident of his abilities. It is important to understand that the learner's confidence is central to his ability to transfer his learning to novel situations – in a very real sense, it is the trainee's confidence which enables learning to transfer.

In considering these definitions, the reader should bear in mind that much of the training that took place in the past was of the 'autocratic' or 'telling people what to do' kind. The training officer's role in that context was comparable to that of a school teacher or instructor who ran training courses. Teaching and instruction still have their place in the training process but greater emphasis is now being given to encouraging self-learning, i.e. individuals are given more responsibility for identifying their own training and development needs and are given greater opportunities to plan and manage their own learning (see Lathrope 1985). In this context the role of the training officer is more appropriately described as a provider of flexible training services: he organizes learning opportunities by, for example, establishing open access resource centres, by intervening to remove structural and cultural barriers to learning, as well as running training courses (see Chapter 2).

EDUCATION AND TRAINING

A number of writers, including Stringfellow (1968), Tannehill (1970), and Stammers and Patrick (1975), have discussed the nature of education and training in a work context and have drawn attention to the problems which arise from the different meanings attributed to these two terms. The word education, for example, is at times narrowly used to mean the formal process of studying a subject syllabus, which has traditionally required attendance at an educational institution, a requirement which is lessened by the development of distance learning opportunities. It is also used in the very much broader sense of 'life itself is the best educator', where the idea conveyed is that of developing an individual's personality, attitudes and self-knowledge, largely or wholly independently of institutionalized education. Similarly, the word 'training' is used both as a synonym for education and, more appropriately, in the rather restricted sense of learning behaviour which is usually capable of being defined with greater precision in a specific job context.

Distinguishing between the purposes and methods of education and those of training is not always possible, as the two overlap. However, as we shall see later, there are differences which are of more than academic and semantic interest. Indeed, the assumptions that some employers and employees make about the nature of education and of training – what each aims to achieve, and by what means – have led to costly mistakes. A classic example of this was the incorrect assumption made by many companies both about the value of a university education as a preparation for a management career in business, and about the preparation that young graduates should be given to help them on their 'fast track' path to senior management positions. The formerly fashionable approach which these companies adopted to 'growing' their own potential senior executives was to recruit graduates fresh from university and give them a year or eighteen months' 'tour' of the company. The graduates typically spent a few months in the production unit, a month ot two in the accounts department, a spell with the sales division staff, and so on, in every case watching how experienced employees did their work and taking copious notes of the paperwork and procedures involved: a classic case of 'exposure' training.

This approach generally proved to be a singularly unsuccessful strategy for developing potential executives. It had been believed that, as graduates, the trainees would be able to learn the company's business quickly, be appointed to junior management jobs on completion of their 'training' and subsequently rise rapidly in the management hierarchy. There were three main reasons for the failure of this pragmatic approach. First, the companies had set too high a premium on the graduates' educational achievements and incorrectly assumed that they would correlate strongly with success in business. The graduates' training needs had not been correctly identified. Secondly, the 'tour' approach to training graduates was not strictly training at all, but rather an in-company educational programme. Thus inappropriate training strategies had been used (see Chapter 7). A similar conclusion is drawn by Stewart and Smith (1984) in their review of the National Health Service's national administrative training scheme: the trainees learnt a great deal about the organization but acquired little practical experience in accepting and exercising responsibility. They did not learn how to manage! Thirdly, there was a high turnover of some of the more able and ambitious trainees. They became impatient and/or disenchanted with the seemingly endless and boring collection of information when what they wanted was to do an actual job of work. Other trainees, on completion of their programme, found that they were ill prepared to be managers and either left the company, or remained but never achieved a senior post. There was inadequate monitoring of the 'training' while it was in progress. Thus only a small proportion of the intake of graduate trainees made the grade – and these did so almost in spite of the 'training' they had received.

The quite unrealistic expectations which many employers have of those staff members who have just attended a short training course provides another common example of this failure to appreciate the limited advantages that a brief training experience can provide. Some employers believe that attendance on a fortnight's course is sufficient to convert a clerk into an office supervisor, or to turn a research chemist into a leader of a research team. Such confidence is sadly misplaced. Appropriate training courses may be a useful way of providing some of the attitudes, knowledge and techniques which a newly appointed manager may require. What he also needs is supportive on-the-job training, possibly over a long period of time, to fit him for his new responsibilities.

The conflicting views of many employers and educationalists as to the role and content of secondary school curricula also illustrates the differing expectations that people can have from a learning process. Some critics of the present arrangements argue that curricula should be more explicitly designed to prepare children for the 'world of work' and provide them with those attitudes, skills and knowledge which employers demand, thus enabling young people to secure employment more readily – an argument which is particularly persuasive in times of high unemployment of school leavers. This school of thought supports the Manpower Services Commission's Technical and Vocational Education Initiative (TVEI) (see Chapter 8), which is a significant training intervention into what was essentially an educational environment. It can also be viewed as a strategy by industry to transfer some of the costs of training to the national education budget. However, others take the view that secondary education should prepare young people in a general way for work, for example, through the emphasis on the three Rs. But it should not do so at the expense of wider educational aims, such as the development of physical education interests and a general appreciation of literature and the arts. This latter view is strengthened by the argument that young people leaving school today will in the future probably have more time for leisure pursuits than has ever been the case in the past.

Bearing these examples in mind, and remembering also that both education and training are concerned with promoting and guiding learning and assisting in the achievement of goals, which gives the trained person confidence to apply his learning, we can now consider how education and training differ and yet can complement each other. They differ, in the degree to which their objectives can be specified in behavioural terms, in the time normally needed to achieve these objectives, in their methods of learning, in the learning material involved, and in the context in which learning materials are used.

A characteristic feature of a training objective in many situations is that it is capable of being expressed in behavioural terms (but see Chapter 7). It can and should normally specify the work behaviour required of the trainee at the end of his training, i.e. the criterion behaviour (see page 185). Another characteristic of a training objective in a work setting is that it is 'job' rather than 'person' orientated and this often implies a uniformity of job behaviour.

In contrast, educational objectives are less amenable to definition in behavioural terms because, as Glaser (1965) argues, 'they are too complex or because the behaviours that result in successful accomplishments in many instances are not known'. In an educational context, where behavioural outcomes are much less predictable, objectives have to be couched in more general or abstract terms. Such objectives may seek to provide the learner with the basic understanding which is considered necessary. He is then expected to interpret and apply this understanding in his own way to specific situations. Educational objectives seek to stimulate personal development and so can be thought of as 'person' rather than 'job' orientated. This holds true for both vocational and general education.

The following examples illustrate the differences between educational, training and development objectives. The training requirements for sewing-machine operators will specify the hand movements, etc. which trainee operators must learn and the output level which they must reach before they can be regarded as trained. In contrast, the (educational) objectives of a Master of Business Administration (MBA) degree course can only be expressed in general terms. For example, by studying behavioural science, computing, accountancy, economics and other business-related subjects, students will learn the relevance of these disciplines both to general and particular business situations. The satisfactory completion of an MBA course means that the students have demonstrated their ability to apply certain principles and techniques in solving examination problems. Their improved grasp of the business world should help them to be more successful managers in practice as well as in theory, but the former cannot be guaranteed.

The second point of difference between education and training lies in the time needed to achieve their respective objectives. A training objective can normally be reached in a relatively short period, while it may often take many years to accomplish educational aims. For example, young people starting work in an office can be trained to touch-type in a matter of months but it has taken 10 or more years of schooling to develop an acceptable standard of education and level of maturity.

Some approaches to learning are more appropriate to education than to training, and it is useful to refer to Tannehill's (1970) distinction between mechanistic and organic learning. Mechanistic learning is achieved as a result of stimuli and responses, reinforced by practice. Many industrial training programmes, in contrast to educational programmes, are designed with the assumption that mechanistic learning is involved. Organic learning, on the other hand, involves a change in the individual rather than in what he can do, and thus is much less amenable to external direction, with the outcome being very difficult to predict.

There is also a difference in the learning content of training and of educational programmes. As we have seen, training provides the learner with the attitude, knowledge and skills necessary to carry out specific work tasks. It is geared directly to this end and is essentially practical and relevant to the job. Much if not all of the material to be learnt, such as detailed work methods, techniques and procedures are derived from within the organization. In contrast, educational programmes contain theoretical and conceptual material aimed at stimulating an individual's analytical and critical faculties. Detail, although important, is included to illustrate principles and relationships. Moreover, the content of an educational programme is broadly based and frequently derived from different sources and disciplines.

Finally, Baron (1981) makes the point that the distinction between education and training is at times a function of the context of use. He quotes as an example the study of the principles of employment law, which can be a part of an educational programme in legal studies for undergraduate law students but equally a part of a training course for managers.

These various differences, although significant, should not obscure the reality that learning is the common factor linking education and training and that both are concerned with the development of human potential or talent. Education and training should be seen as complementary parts of the same process, and it is difficult to imagine any training which does not have some educational effect and vice versa. In short, some of each exists in both.

This interdependence of education and training has been stressed by the former Central Training Council (1966), (see page 275):

> The increasingly complex industrial environment, the rapid pace of technological change, and the intense international competition demand a workforce which is both highly trained and educated. In recent years, it has therefore become generally recognized that a programme combining education and training is essential if people in industry are to be equipped to carry out their work effectively as well as to have the opportunity to advance to more demanding and responsible work.

The sanguine view expressed by the Central Training Council has not materialized in practice and the extent to which a formal educational element is included in training programmes is far from general. This element figures prominently in what are sometimes called career programmes, where employees, such as trainee accountants or technologists, are prepared over an extended period of time for responsible positions within the organization. Typically, such trainees are given day or block release to follow an appropriate course at college and a similar arrangement is made for craft and technician trainees. In contrast, preparation for semi-skilled jobs, with their shorter term objectives and emphasis on specific behaviour change, has traditionally included no formal educational component. While in some cases this practice can be appropriate, in many others the failure to provide an integrated learning programme causes longer term problems for both the employees and their employers (see Chapter 5). This is especially true in the case of young people whose early preparation for employment should have given them the capacity to develop and adapt their actual and potential skills throughout their working lives. It is this philosophy of training and educating school leavers for work in an integrated manner that is embodied in the Youth Training Scheme (YTS), introduced in 1983 by the MSC (see Chapter 8).

Other important developments in the UK which are having the effect of blurring the historical differences between education and training are: the wider acceptance of the philosophy of 'continuing education', for which 'learning to learn' is a prerequisite (see page 261); the applied nature of the 'educational' courses validated by the Business and Technician Education Council (BTEC); the TVEI programme in secondary schools, mentioned above; and the view that in times of rapid technological – and therefore job – change, training, especially that provided for young people, should no longer be exclusively related to the specific work requirements of a particular job or employer. On the contrary, it is argued that initial training objectives should be broader in scope than has been the case in the past (i.e. they should have more of an educational flavour) and should provide the trainee with ownership of his skills. Hence the notion of 'portable skills', that is skills that equip a trainee both to carry out the work required in his current employment and provide him with a foundation of knowledge, skills and attitudes which will facilitate learning in subsequent jobs.

Historical differences between education and training in the UK are, in part at least, due to the long established practice of British governments to have separate Departments of State for the two fields. Hence, despite the considerable overlap in interests between the two ministries, there is a Department of Employment and a Department of Education and Science. This structure has been unhelpful in the context of industrial training. It has led to unnecessary divisions of interest, resulting in a lower level of integration of national policies and, at times, harmful competition rather than co-operation.

Whatever may be the theoretical relationships between education and training, in practice, as Jenkins (1983) has remarked, the word 'education' (like the word 'welfare') has become unpopular in industry and something of an embarrassment to trainers. While 20 years ago many trainers had the title 'education officers' or 'education and training officers', today the preferred title is simply 'training officer' or 'training manager'.

CHANGES IN ATTITUDES TO TRAINING AND DEVELOPMENT

Prior to the introduction of the Industrial Training Act in 1964, as noted above, successive governments and most employers had a *laissez-faire* approach to the training and developing of their employees. Whilst some organizations provided excellent training opportunities, most saw no advantages in spending money for this purpose. Why should they? With the exception of providing for skilled apprenticeships in certain industries, employers appeared to have no need to train. Much of the work that they wanted from their employees was of an unskilled or semi-skilled nature and had traditionally been learnt by watching and imitating other workers. An employee who did not learn to do the job satisfactorily would be replaced. Such an attitude was understandable, at least in economic terms, when there was a plentiful supply of labour in the marketplace capable of doing the work required by employers.

However, during the period of relatively full employment from the 1950s until the early 1970s the attitude of many employers towards training was modified. This was partly because it became clear that the traditional, *laissez-faire* approach consistently failed to provide adequate numbers of skilled and otherwise qualified staff, partly because staff shortages led to higher manpower costs, and partly to avoid the financial penalties inherent in the levy and grant policies of the Industrial Training Boards (see Kenney, Donnelly and Reid 1979). Another important factor was the changing attitudes of employees and their trade unions who increasingly expected organizations to provide more and better training and development opportunities.

Wellens (1968), writing early in this period, argued optimistically that changes in managements' attitudes to training were both predictable and permanent and that they depended primarily upon the state of technology in society. He considered that the increasing complexity of business and industry in the UK had reached a stage where only by pursuing a policy of training could employers ensure that their staffs' skills kept pace with technological progress. Add to this the impact of contemporary legislation (the Industrial Training Act 1964) and a better understanding by many managers of what planned training can offer a business, and the training function qualifies, as Wellens puts it 'for a place in the mainstream of management'.

Some employers did much more than pay lip service to the requirements of their Industry Training Board and decided, notwithstanding the levy-grant situation, that they could no longer afford to maintain a *laissez-faire* approach to this aspect of their business. They invested in training and development by appointing people of calibre to head the function, by laying down policies which integrated the work of this function with the objectives and operations of the organization, and above all by top management themselves taking overall responsibility for the efficient training and development of their employees. The experiences of these organizations and developments elsewhere in training and education circles, were leading to changes in the conceptual framework of training and to a reappraisal of its role in a rapidly changing industrial society.

The oil crisis in the early 1970s, the increasing impact of new technologies notably in product design and manufacture, the related decline in the international competitiveness of British firms, the growth in unemployment, and the considerable dissatisfaction expressed by business with the Industrial Training Board system, were the major factors which brought about this reappraisal.

Before the beginning of the current recession, the Training Services Agency (1977) (see Chapter 10) had stressed that:

> The whole environment in which training and the trainer has to operate has changed rapidly and in all probability will continue to change, e.g. the increasing stimulus and direction from the Training Services Agency and the MSC; increasing external demands through legislation; development of levy-grant policies from ITBs; availability of investment monies; inflation; competition in the market; and increasingly important, unemployment and the changing values and expectations of the work force, especially among young people.

These changes were not, of course, confined to the UK and the effect of technology on training had been highlighted in the EEC *Preliminary Guidelines on Social Policy* (1971):

> Progress is itself gradually raising the general level of skills; the faster rate of progress is tending to blur the nature of these skills by the swift and radical change in machinery, materials, methods of work and organization. Knowledge, know-how, techniques and acquired attitudes are quickly left behind and re-adaptation, which was recently the exception, is becoming the rule. As a result, occupational skills can no longer be defined by reference to the job and the nature

of the occupation involved. They are now seen as the permanent ability to adapt to the technical pattern of work.

However, this perception of the increasingly important role of training and development in modern society is not shared by many employers: in times of economic recession and high unemployment, the financial logic of the 'bottom line' of the balance sheet is much more compelling. Any expenditure which can be cut without apparently damaging the survival of the business, (and much training and development is still perceived to be in this category) is eliminated. In the short term, investment in training can be cut without apparent adverse repercussions. The failure to invest, for example in management development or in training for craft skills, will, in the longer term, create difficulties.

Thus some employers view training as an activity capable of making a cost effective contribution to the achievement of the company's objectives, (see Cannon 1979). In a far larger number of organizations the traditional, *laissez-faire* attitude persists and training is unplanned. In these latter organizations training has the following features:

- It is not an integral part of the organization's operations.
- It has a low priority and is, at best, a peripheral management responsibility.
- Employees are largely responsible for their own training. For example, managers are appointed on the basis of their technical abilities, and are expected to acquire their managerial skills with little or no formal help.
- Management development is practically non-existent and the training officer, if there is one, does not have the status or authority to advise on, or take any active part in, the training of management-level staff.
- Management take the view that, whilst properly organized training costs money, unplanned training, which relies on informal assistance from fellow employees, is inexpensive.
- The organization probably has no training department. If there is such a department it has a low status and staff of only limited calibre.

PLANNED TRAINING INTERVENTIONS

Planned training, which as we shall see may take many different forms, is a deliberate intervention aimed at achieving the learning necessary for improved job performance. Planned training (see Figure 1.1) can be defined as the processes involved in:

- deciding whether training can help to resolve or prevent a problem, and if so determining whether training is the most cost effective approach;
- identifying what learning is needed and setting learning objectives;
- deciding which training strategy or strategies to adopt and planning appropriate training programmes and arrangements to meet this need (see Chapter 7);

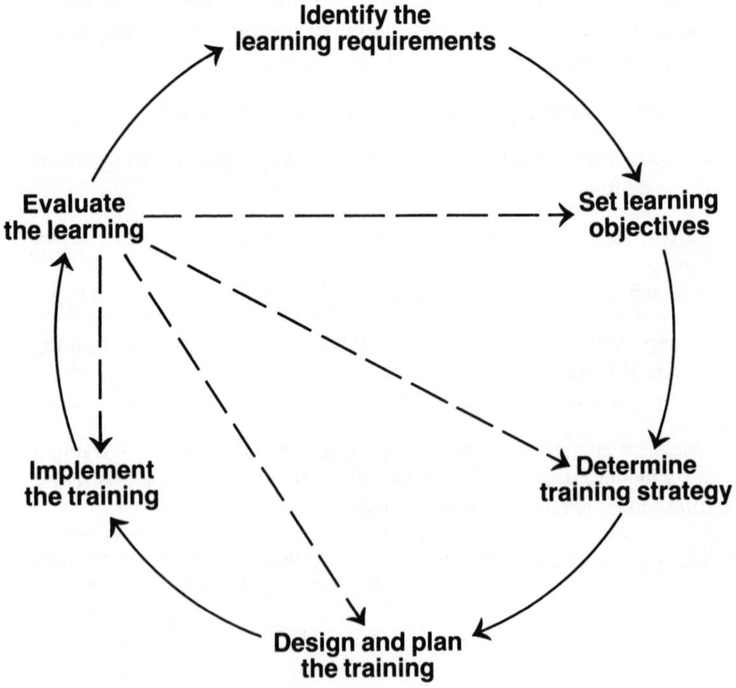

Figure 1.1
Planned training

- implementing the training and ensuring that employees are assisted to acquire the skills, knowledge and attitudes they require;
- evaluating the effectiveness of the learning at appropriate times during and after the training; and
- satisfying any residual learning requirements.

Planned training can be applied at the level of the organization, the department or section, the specific job, e.g. technician or clerk, or to individuals at any level in the organization, from school-leaver to chief executive, and whether newly appointed or with long service. The Industrial Training Boards (ITBs), established under the 1964 Industrial Training Act, were mainly responsible for disseminating and encouraging the adoption of an early form of planned training called 'systematic training'. This approach was widely adopted in the UK and was based on a simple, four-stage model expressed as follows: first, identify and specify the training need, then design a training programme, next implement the training, and finally, evaluate it. If the evaluation showed that further training was needed, then the four stages would be repeated, as necessary – hence the phrase the 'training cycle'.

This form of planned training provided a disciplined approach which was helpful especially to the many training officers appointed by their companies with only minimal training in the 1960s, largely in response to the levy-grant arrangements made by the ITBs. However, for a number of reasons, the 'systematic training' approach acquired a somewhat tarnished reputation.

First, the model was often poorly understood by trainers. Many companies were committed to maximizing ITB grant rather than training and were unwilling to pay competitive managerial salaries in order to recruit professional trainers. Typically, such a company appointed as its training officer one of its craft apprentice instructors or a manager who had been less than successful elsewhere in the organization. These appointees lacked the authority, competence and often the support from within the organization, to apply the 'systematic training' model. For example, they were incapable of deciding what to analyse, in what depth, when identifying training needs. This often led to either an inadequate analysis being undertaken or, much more frequently, to an extraordinary amount of quite unnecessary and confusing job analysis data being amassed. In both cases inadequate training resulted.

Secondly, a major aim of the ITBs in the 1960s and 1970s was the improvement of training arrangements for skilled and semi-skilled work and it was in these areas that 'systematic training' was widely applied. Although many of these applications were successful – compared with the sitting-next-to-Nelly approach which they displaced – nonetheless some companies began to question whether the time and other resources spent in this way were justified, particularly in operator training where traditionally there had been no apparent expenditure on training. Thus 'systematic training' began to be regarded as making a mountain out of a molehill and a spurious justification for the continued employment of the training officer.

Thirdly, and most importantly, the four-stage 'systematic training' model has inherent limitations. These became clear to trainers, especially those who had attempted to apply the model other than in a manual skills context. Even in what may appear to be a straight-forward case, training is a complex set of processes which are not adequately accommodated by the four stages of the model. These complexities can arise both within and between each of the four stages of the cycle and thus a more sophisticated model is required.

It is important to realize that, although it was frequently misapplied, the 'systematic training' concept represented a significant and perhaps necessary development in the evolution of best practice in industrial training.

An illustration of a planned training intervention

The following simplified example describes the stages in applying a planned training approach, in this case using the strategy option of an internal course (see Chapter 7), for the training of new employees. It also illustrates the roles played by line managers and the training specialists.

The works manager of a successful electronics manufacturing business has decided to meet an increasing demand for his company's products by introducing shiftwork. New employees are to be recruited to undertake the specialized work involved. It is assumed that relevant job specifications and training programmes are not available in the company. The sequence would be as follows:

Stage 1: Can training help prevent or resolve the problem, and if so, is it the most cost effective solution?
The work involved is specialized and high standards of quality are essential. There is little chance of recruiting new employees with the required skills, i.e. the skills cannot be bought in. The work methods and machines cannot be altered for use by unskilled labour, i.e. no deskilling of the tasks is possible. In view of the strong demand for the company's products, there is only a short 'lead time' for the new shiftworkers to acquire the necessary skills and knowledge, i.e. the company cannot risk loss of orders through failure to meet delivery dates. The company has the necessary training resources. Thus the answer to the question is 'yes', training is judged to be the most cost effective way of resolving the problem.

Stage 2: Identify the training requirements
With the co-operation of the departmental manager, his staff and the trade union representative, the training officer carries out a training analysis of the work to define precisely what the new staff will be expected to do. In particular he will identify those parts of the job which the trainees are likely to find difficult to learn and where work errors would be costly.

Stage 3: Set learning objectives
The training analysis clarifies the performance standards to which the new staff must be trained and so provides the behavioural objectives for the training programme. For example, 'to construct 20 A-type units per hour with a maximum reject rate of three per cent'.

The training officer then compares the trainees' anticipated (or present) levels of competence with the required levels of competence. Any difference between what the recruits have to be able to do and what they can already do, can be thought of as a 'learning gap'. A training programme must then be designed to bridge the gap between the trainees' present levels of skill and knowledge and those of experienced staff.

Stage 4: Decide the training strategy and plan the training programme
Having identified what training the recruits require, the training officer recommends to the departmental manager how this training need will be met, bearing in mind relevant company policies, resources, time available, and other constraints. In this case an off-the-job training course is agreed to be most effective strategy.

The training programme will specify: the training objectives, where possible in behavioural terms; the skills and knowledge required; when and where it will take place; what evaluation will be undertaken and by whom; the timetable for the training sessions and who will be responsible for them; and the resources needed. In helping to prepare the programme the training officer uses his specialist knowledge and experience to keep costs to the minimum compatible with efficient training.

Stage 5: Implement and monitor the training
The training is then carried out according to the agreed programme, with adjustments being made, where necessary, to suit the learning rates of individuals. Training times will therefore vary depending on the trainees' abilities to reach the required standard. Instruction is given by trained staff in the training area or school (off-the-job, or vestibule, training) and subsequently in the workplace (on-the-job training).

Records are kept of each of the trainees' progress for immediate control purposes, such as rearranging the programme to cater for recruits finding certain parts more difficult to learn and others easier than had been anticipated, and to provide information on the effectiveness of the training.

The training is reviewed at intervals during and on completion of the programme by the training officer, the line management and in many cases by the trainees themselves. Any lessons that can be learnt from these reviews, such as changes in the training methods or the training times, are built into future programmes. In this way experience is used to improve the efficiency of training in the company. See Chapter 7 for a discussion of the ways in which the effectiveness of training programmes can be tested.

Stage 6: The final evaluation of the effectiveness of the completed training
If the training has been successful, its outcome should be demonstrated in the competent job performance of the 'trainees'. However, if the training was inadequate, for example if the off-the-job course was not properly designed, then the trainees may experience problems in transferring their learning to the actual job situation. The trainees' performance immediately after the training therefore needs to be monitored and, if necessary, remedial training provided.

In this illustration of a planned training approach, the training officer decided that a 'course strategy' was the most appropriate form for the training intervention. However, we would stress that planned training can take many different forms apart from a 'traditional' course, e.g. job rotation, individual or group project work, or following a self-learning computer based programme. A detailed discussion of the range of planned training options is contained in Chapter 7.

Other approaches to planned training and development

In the above application of planned training the learning objectives were not difficult to set because the skilled performance required of the recruits could be readily specified. However, this does not apply in all cases. For example, while some of the results of a management development programme can be anticipated (increased knowledge of the organization's policies) and so planned for in the manner described above, other outcomes (such as a manager realizing during the programme that his interpersonal skills are not well regarded by his colleagues) are unpredictable and so cannot be predetermined. Moreover, the latter may turn out to be of greater significance than the former. Thus while in some training situations the trainer may be working to achieve a rigorously specified set of objectives, in others he may have to adopt a contingency approach, that is he has to be able to capitalize upon unforeseen but positive developments as they arise during a programme.

It is important to appreciate that there is no single approach to a training or development problem that will guarantee a satisfactory and cost effective solution (see Jones 1983). On the contrary, there are many different approaches and, in a given context, the one that is chosen will depend upon a complex set of interactions in which four variables are critical. These are the organization's culture and values; its goals and priorities; the responsiveness of the organization and of its training systems; and the perceptions and abilities of trainers and trainees.

Variable number one : organization culture and values. We have already described how organizations have very different implicit or explicit policies for human resource management and in particular for training and development. For example, top management's views (and degree of tolerance) concerning which grades of employee should have access to training, the quality and quantity of learning resources provided, and the training techniques which are acceptable or not acceptable, form the backcloth against which the trainer can operate (see Chapter 2).

Variable number two : organization goals and priorities. How an organization expects these to be achieved, and the role of its training and development function in this process (see Chapter 2) create contraints and opportunities for the trainer, as the following example shows.

A medium-sized manufacturing company decided to introduce new technology into its production processes and viewed this investment primarily as a technical and financial matter. Top management set up a project team but did not consider it necessary to consult or involve their personnel and training officer in the planning of the new plant. It was only when the technical and engineering problems had apparently been solved and the plant was about to be commissioned that the company began to think about the 'people' implications of the investment and formally involved the personnel department. Personnel policies were hurriedly made to meet the rapidly approaching commissioning date, e.g. whether to retrain existing personnel or to recruit employees with the new skills, what enhanced pay and conditions of employment should be negotiated with the trade unions for those employees working the new plant? Even at this late stage the company seriously underestimated the importance of the 'people' aspect in determining the success of the project. For nearly 18 months the operation of the plant was plagued with 'people' problems, which could have been minimized or avoided by appropriate planning and investment in personnel as well as plant.

In this case study, the personnel and training officer's contribution to his organization's goal (the successful operation of the new plant) was severely restricted. He could only react to major decisions that had already been implemented and which he had minimal opportunity to alter. He was limited to doing his best to apply the 'fit the men to the job' approach rather than 'fitting the job to the men'. Had he been a member of the project team, his specialist knowledge and skills could have been used much more effectively by helping to design the needs of the employees into the work system of the new plant.

Variable number three : the ability of individuals and work groups in the organization to accept change, to learn and adopt the different behaviours required, is of great importance in planning a training intervention to assist organizational change. For example, the Engineering ITB (1983) reported that:

> the research into changing technology at the Science Policy Research Unit, University of Sussex, has shown that the probable rapid diffusion of CAD (computer assisted design) interactive graphics systems requires a rethink about the training of draughtsmen; it also shows that management adjustment to the new systems takes much longer than the operators take to learn them.

Variable number four : the perceptions and abilities of the trainer and the trainee. Boydell (1983), quoting an unpublished work of Megginson, has described how the trainer's technical or professional background tends to influence both the type of training problem that he identifies, his preferred approaches and the related training activities. An example of this was the 'skills training' emphasis which, in the past, typified the work of training officers in many engineering companies – training was almost exclusively focused on skill development for craft and technician trainees. Boydell describes how different mixes of these factors can be identified in the 'systematic training' model (see page 15) and in the following commonly found approaches to training and development.

- The *Organization Development* (OD) approach which tends to be adopted by trainers with a behavioural science background. They apply behavioural science training techniques to stimulate organization change, and their perception of training needs includes assisting people in their relationships with others, especially in the context of group and intergroup dynamics.
- The *welfare approach*, which is characterized by trainers whose background is in a non-profit making organization. Their view of training is that it is less to do with organizational effectiveness but concerned more with the provision of courses for the individual to gain qualifications and so improve career prospects.
- The *administrative approach*. Here the trainer typically has a bureaucratic background. He sees his function as meeting the needs of the organization's formal system by implementing training procedures and courses laid down by senior management rather than proactively identifying training needs. The trainer places great emphasis on the efficiency of his administration, the quality of his office's paperwork and on the quantity of trainees who have attended his courses. Indeed, 'administrative convenience' generally takes priority over other factors.

- The *political approach*. This is adopted by the status seeking 'empire builder', whose psychological needs (e.g. for prestige) and whose personal goals dominate his role as a trainer. He concentrates on meeting those training needs within the organization which will bring 'kudos' to him and will extend the influence of his department. He is 'visible' to top management and appears to be doing a good job even though his selective strategy may not be meeting many of his clients' training needs. This approach, in a less extreme form, is used by all politically aware trainers at some stage in their careers. (See page 24.)

Before concluding this discussion we will consider two contrasting approaches to planned training: one which attempts to achieve a holistic view (the systems approach) and the other which deliberately takes a narrower, very selective perspective (the problem-centred approach).

A systems approach to planned training

There is no one single 'systems' approach to training, indeed Goldstein (1980) has noted that there are almost as many different 'systems' approaches to training as there are authors on the subject! A systems approach has been defined as the process of

> identifying inputs, outputs, components and sub-systems, and then seeking to identify the contribution that training can make to improving the operation by enhancing the contribution of the human components (people) as opposed to machinery and operational procedures. The systems approach is next applied to the training design, where the components are learning strategies and people, and the objectives are in terms of learning. Finally, the systems approach is applied to the interaction between training and the operation to produce a feedback which can be used to improve subsequent training. (Manpower Services Commission 1981.)

A systems approach is very useful to the training officer for a number of reasons. First, and perhaps most importantly, because it encourages him to think widely about his objectives and about the opportunities and difficulties he might encounter in identifying and in resolving priority training issues. In using a systems approach the training officer initially looks at a number of feasible options which he then evaluates before choosing the strategy that he judges to be the most appropriate in the circumstances. It is worth noting that a possible outcome of the use of a systems model is that a problem which had been presented as having a training solution is in fact better handled in another way, for example by better selection methods or changing the technology used, i.e. training is one of a number of possible options.

Secondly, in using a systems approach the training officer (working with his colleagues) seeks to take account of all the relevant variables in a given context. He acquires an overall view of the system and of the relationships between its component parts and so he can help predict the probable outcomes of a postulated change. Since these outcomes include when and where potential problems are likely to occur, decisions can be taken at the appropriate time which enable the changes in the system to be managed effectively. The following example illustrates this point.

A local council wanted to reduce its workforce and so introduced an attractive voluntary early retirement scheme. The scheme achieved its purpose and as anticipated resulted in a loss of some of the older office supervisors. The central personnel department had anticipated this and took early action to arrange for the selection and training of internal replacements. Thus the impact of a change in one part of the local council's manpower system – its retirement policy – led to planned action in another part – the promotion and training of the replacement staff, with a minimum of disruption in the work of the council.

Thirdly, this approach to training is helpful in that it is flexible and can be applied at many different levels. For example, it can be usefully applied to the training of an individual (e.g. the off-the-job training of a sales representative), or to a group of people (such as all the supervisors in a department), or at the level of an organization (all its employees), or at a national level (a training programme of the Manpower Services Commission, such as the Youth Training Scheme), or at an international level, (the European Economic Community's training support for the unemployed in Member States (see Blachere 1980).

Another way of viewing the application of a systems model in training is to appreciate that systems may be either 'open' or 'closed'. The former has many interactions with its environment (as in the case of the EEC example above) and as a result is a more complex model. A closed systems model, as its name implies, has few external links, it has well defined boundaries and is consequently less complex. The new plant commissioning case study, described on page 20, would probably have had a quite different ending if the company had adopted an open systems approach in planning the introduction of the new plant.

Planned training – a problem-centred approach

This is a pragmatic approach in which the training officer deliberately concentrates on a specific problem, notwithstanding the fact that there may be other, although less critical, training needs. This strategy is often very acceptable to an organization and helpful to a trainer seeking credibility because such a training intervention is seen to produce quick and apparently cost-effective results. However, the success of this approach depends on the correct identification of a priority training need and to achieve this can require a much greater amount of analysis than is apparent from the perhaps small amount of training that eventually takes place. Failure to diagnose a training need correctly can lead to a misuse of training resources and a loss of credibility for the trainer. An example of this was the action taken by a newly recruited training officer who was told by a number of line managers that he ought to 'do something' about the low output from the company's audio-typing pool. Keen to make his mark in the company and relying over-much on the evidence of the line managers, the training officer organized a short refresher course for the typists. As the course proceeded it became embarrassingly obvious to the training officer that he had incorrectly identified the cause of the output problem and that he was training the wrong people: the typists were competent – it was the managers who lacked the skills to use the audio equipment correctly.

PHILOSOPHIES OF TRAINING

The rights and obligations which society, employers and employees are considered to have concerning preparation for employment are central to any 'philosophy of work'. For this reason it is appropriate for us to consider the different 'philosophies of training' which underlie and inform attitudes and practices in the field of employee development.

A complex range of influences account for the philosophies of training that may exist in a society and in a work organization. Among the more important of these are the political ideologies of governments, employers and employees, the expectations of employees with regard to access to training, the degree to which receipt of training carries with it an obligation to the provider, the traditions and power of the trade unions in regulating access and conferring status, the ratio of the broad categories of unskilled to skilled work in the society, the variety of skilled occupations in the workforce, whether technologies are relatively stable or are undergoing significant change, the stock of skilled personnel relative to the demand for skills in the short and longer term, and the scale of unemployment in the country.

As we shall show in the following paragraphs, different philosophies of training reflect the range and mix of responses to such questions as who is considered responsible for funding training (the employee, the employer or the government or a mix of these), whether the training that is provided is narrowly focused (e.g. single skilled) or broadly based and transferrable (e.g. multi-skilled), the degree and pace of technological development, who takes the responsibility for initiating training (the individual, the employer or government), whether training is regarded as essentially an investment (for the future) or a cost (to be avoided), whether there should be priority provision for the training of certain groups within society (the disabled, the young, the unemployed, women, ethnic minorities) and if so at what stage or stages in their lives this training should be provided, should national or industry standards of training be set and monitored (e.g. for craft trainees as well as for airline pilots), to what extent does training to a standard automatically confer status on the trainee?

Thus a philosophy of training has its foundations in the cultural, economic, social and other values and experiences of the individual, organization or nation and it tends to be permanent, while the purpose of training is to achieve change. It is this potential or actual conflict which underlies many of the more intractable issues facing training and development at all levels in society.

Traditionalism

This philosophy of training can, of course, take many forms and has its roots in long established patterns of provision and applications of training which are seen to have served a country well and so have remained essentially unaltered over many years. For example, in a country where traditional craft skills reflect the degree of technological advance and where the great majority of the workforce engage in unskilled or semi-skilled work, the tradition may well be that training is considered essential for the high status work (the craft and administrative jobs) but unnecessary for the rest of the working population. Today this expression of traditionalism is associated with third world countries which have undergone only limited industrialization.

A similar philosophy of training (with voluntarism) was dominant in the UK throughout the industrial revolution and persisted, inappropriately, well into the twentieth century – despite changing technologies and the increasing demands for new and higher order skills (see Perry 1976). In the UK, the traditional training philosophy was expressed in restricted access to the 'high status' fields of employment, trainees were expected to pay for the privilege of being trained, the training was typically uni-craft based (or the equivalent), and the methods of training remained unaltered for centuries. A particular feature of the training was that it was 'front loaded', i.e. provided only at the beginning of a career, since work and skills do not change in a stable technological environment – hence retraining or updating of skills and knowledge are irrelevant.

Voluntarism

A *laissez-faire* philosophy of training assumes that requirements for skilled and professional staff will be produced as a result of initiatives taken by individuals and or by employers, as and when these seem to be appropriate. A *laissez-faire* philosophy places much of the onus for initiating and paying for training on the individual as, for example, in the USA, although Federal Government training programmes have been instituted. One important outcome of this philosophy of training is that the skills and knowledge provided by employers tend not to be 'portable', at least at the manual skill level: training is typically specific to a job in a particular firm and therefore has limited application elsewhere.

Interventionism

The belief that voluntarism is an inefficient and inadequate approach to providing a country's training requirements leads some to argue that the State has a responsibility for training which should be expressed through legislation to achieve control of a country's training systems. The degree of control may be considerable, as in the 1964 Industrial Training Act (see Chapter 10). Social imperatives, such as the current very high levels of youth unemployment in EEC countries, can, it is argued, be more effectively ameliorated by national interventions in training arrangements. For example, there were dramatic increases in the numbers of young people receiving some form of training or vocational education, following co-ordinated interventions by EEC member countries in 1978 (see Sellin 1983).

Continuing development

The Central Policy Review Staff Report (1980) argues that one of the major weaknesses in the UK's training provision is 'the concentration on initial training at the expense of updating and retraining provision later in life'. It is still widely assumed in this country that a young person acquires the skills and knowledge necessary to secure employment for the rest of his working life at school and during the first year or so after starting work. This 'front loading' model of education and training may have been adequate in times of full employment and limited technological change but it is a grossly inadequate approach in today's society with its rapidily changing technologies and persistently high unemployment.

There are some indications that both government and progressive employers in the UK are coming to the view that all people of working age, whether currently employed or unemployed, must be given frequent opportunities to update their existing skills and, should their jobs become obsolete, given help to acquire new work skills and knowledge. This is the philosophy of continuing development or as it is referred to in mainland Europe 'permanent education' (see Janne and Schwartz 1980). An interesting example of continuing development in the professions is the Law Society's scheme for the continuing education of newly admitted solicitors. Under this scheme solicitors are required to attend for updating tuition within three years of admission to the Law Society.

Continuing development, an established concept on the continent, is the latest philosophy of training to gain attention in this country. It poses a major challenge to traditional thinking and practices on training matters for individuals, trade unions, employers, educationalists and government. The Institute of Personnel Management's Code of Continuous Development (1984) – we prefer the word 'continuing' – reflects this new and radical philosophy which shares the responsibility for identifying and proposing training with all members of an organization and, by extension, with society as a whole. This philosophy which is as much concerned with cost effectiveness as with humanitarianism, places great emphasis on the need to be able to 'learn how to learn' especially in the work context, and to accept that learning has become a prerequisite for individual, organizational and national economic prosperity (see Chapters 7 and 9).

In this chapter we have stressed the valuable contributions that planned training can make at different levels in a society. But training is not a panacea and it is necessary to adopt a balanced view of what it can and cannot achieve. The limitations of training are well expressed by Miller (1979):

> an environment which cannot use the skills the trainee acquires in training; an environment which will not permit performance of the behaviours acquired in training; a change in behaviour which cannot be measured; employees who are unmotivated to meet performance standards though they are capable of doing so; established organizational goals which can be accomplished more effectively through other means; resources required to complete training are non existent or insufficient.

Our aim in this chapter has been to set the scene for the rest of the book. We have outlined some of the approaches that the training officer may use in his work and we have stressed that he must be sensitive to the attitudes and traditions towards training which prevail in his organization and industry. He must be competent in the flexible use of diagnostic and problem solving skills. His success will in large measure depend upon his interpersonal skills for in his work he will be dealing with complex issues concerning people in the context of organizational effectiveness.

BIBLIOGRAPHY

ARMSTRONG P, and DAWSON C. *People in organizations*. Kings Repton, Cambridge, Elm Publications, 1983.

BARON B in *Managing human resources*, eds, Cowling A G and Mailer C J B. London, Arnold, 1981.

BLACHERE M. *Role of training in setting up new economic and social activities*. 2nd edition. European Centre for the Development of Vocational Training (CEDEFOP), Berlin, 1980.

BOYDELL T H. *A guide to the identification of training needs*. London, British Association for Commercial and Industrial Education, 1983.

BURNS T and STALKER G N. *The management of innovation*. London. Tavistock Publications, 1966.

CANNON J. *Cost effective decisions*. London. Institute of Personnel Management, 1979.

CENTRAL POLICY REVIEW STAFF. *Education, training and industrial performance*. London. Report by the Central Policy Review Staff, 1980.

CENTRAL TRAINING COUNCIL. *Industrial training and further education*. London. HMSO, 1966.

ENGINEERING INDUSTRY TRAINING BOARD. Summary of annual report 1982/3. *Watford, Engineering Industry Training Board*.

EUROPEAN ECONOMIC COMMISSION. *Preliminary guidelines for a community social policy programme*. Brussels, Sec (71), 6000 Final, 17th March, 1971.

GLASER R. *Training research and education*. New York, Wiley & Sons, 1965.

GOLDSTEIN I L. Training in work organizations. *Annual Review of Psychology*. 31:229-72, 1980.

INSTITUTE OF PERSONNEL MANAGEMENT. *Continuous development: people at work*. London, Institute of Personnel Management, 1984.

JANNE H and SCHWARTZ B. *The development of permanent education in Europe*. Brussels, Commission of the European Communities, 1980.

JENKINS D in *A textbook of techniques and strategies in personnel management*, eds Guest D and Kenny T. London, Institute of Personnel Management, 1983.

JONES J A G. *Training intervention strategies – making more effective training interventions*. ITS Monograph No. 2. London, Industrial Training Service Ltd, 1983.

KENNEY J P J, DONNELLY E L, and REID M. *Manpower training and development*, London, Institute of Personnel Management, 1979.

LATHROPE K. Stop your workforce standing still. *Personnel Management*, October, 1985.

MANPOWER SERVICES COMMISSION. *A New Training Initiative*. Sheffield, Manpower Services Commission, 1981.

MANPOWER SERVICES COMMISSION. *Glossary of training terms*. Manpower Services Commission, HMSO, 1981.

McILWEE T. *Personnel management in context, the 1980s*. Kings Repton, Cambridge, Elm Publications, 1982.

MILLER V A. *The guide book for international trainers in business and industry*. Wokingham, Van Nostrand Reinhold/American Society for Training and Development, 1979.

PERRY P J C. *The evolution of British manpower policy from the Statute of Artificers 1563 to the Industrial Training Act 1964*. London, British Association for Commercial and Industrial Education, 1976.

SELLIN B. *Youth unemployment and vocational training*. Berlin, European Centre for the Development of Vocational Training (CEDEFOP), 1983.

STAMMERS R and PATRICK J. *The psychology of training*. London, Methuen, 1975.

STEWART R and SMITH P. *Review of the national administrative training scheme*. National Health Service. Oxford, Oxford Centre for Management Studies, 1984.

STRINGFELLOW C D. 'Education and training'. *Industrial Training International*, 3, 2, 1968.

TANNEHILL R E. *Motivation and management development*. London, Butterworths, 1970.

TRAINING SERVICES AGENCY. *An approach to the training of staff with training officer roles*. Sheffield, Training Services Agency, 1977.

WELLENS J. 'The exploitation of human resources'. *The Times*, 26th August, 1968.

2: *The training function in organizations*

INTRODUCTION

In this chapter we examine the nature of the training function within organizations, the responsibilities of management for training, and the typical 'locations' and lines of accountability which top management have established for the function. The changing roles and activities of the training officer are considered and, finally, we review the general benefits and costs of undertaking training.

THE TRAINING FUNCTION

The word 'function' comes from the Latin verb 'to perform or to act', and a useful definition of the training function (based on that contained in the Manpower Services Commission's *Glossary of Training Terms*, is 'the purposes, structure and specialized activity of training and its relationships with other activities within a working organization' (1981).

The reader should appreciate that the training function is a recent addition to UK organization structures compared, for example, with production, accounting or sales. Donnelly (1984), in his review of the evolution of training as a specialist function, draws attention to the fact that prior to the 1960s training activities were very restricted and diffused within organizations. Not surprisingly, therefore, there was an almost complete absence of any objective analysis into the job demands of the training officer and the nature of company training activities did not justify the status of a function. As Donnelly expresses it:

> Training took its first faltering steps as an economic and professional activity within organizations through the work done by consultants such as Seymour (1954), Taylor (1966) and King (1964).

We are then dealing with what is a recent feature of organizational life and one moreover which, often from a zero base, enjoyed a spectacular but often ephemeral growth.

Primarily in response to the stimulus of the 1964 legislation (see Chapter 10), numerous training departments were created but in many cases they had failed to consolidate their position when some years later the legislative support was withdrawn. As might be anticipated there were great variations in the ways in which training functions developed, in what they perceived to be their achievements and in the extent to which these were valued and accepted within organizations. At one end of the spectrum the function had no real impact but existed as a token presence to satisfy minimal internal needs, and perhaps more importantly, to qualify for an ITB grant. At the other extreme training functions were developed which enjoyed a high status internally and came to be embedded within the mainstream activities of the organization.

Bearing in mind the very limited 'stock' of training expertise that was available, the low calibre staff frequently appointed to the training department and the limited training that they were given, the expectations which organizations had of their training function at that time were often unrealistically high. A warning note about the range of activities of training officers was sounded by Rodger, Morgan and Guest (1971). In their study, carried out in the mid-1960s, they sought to clarify the function of the training officer and the limits of that function and commented that:

> Training is a means of making better use of human resources in the organization by developing people to meet the requirements of the job to be done. It should be viewed as one of a series of methods, which includes: re-structuring of jobs or work group, changes in equipment or system design. Any attempts to extend the expertise of training officers into broader human resource specialist roles is to change the trainer into – in the majority of instances – a more exotic role that would be beyond the aspiration of all but a small minority of training officers.

This quotation should not be taken to mean that training *per se* has no part in organization change and the creation of a flexible workforce. On the contrary, it is a primary vehicle for these developments. But their achievement demands the exercise of a high order of training expertise, and this was in short supply at that time.

The economic recessions of the 1970s and 1980s provided the *coup de grace* for the weak departments, typically resulting in the cessation of planned training activities in the host organization. Other training departments lost their independent functional status and the responsibility for the activities which survived cost cutting was dispersed to other functions. Thus in many organizations the training function which had enjoyed a departmental status in its own right regressed to its pre-1964 state.

A study of training departments which survived, and in some cases flourished, through the extremely difficult periods of recession provides guidance as to the conditions which a training function must meet if it is to secure its place within an organization. Apart from the general requirement that training should be planned (see Chapter 1), three further conditions have to be satisfied. These are that: the management team accept responsibility for training; the function is appropriately structured within the organization; and the training staff are effective, professionally-trained and the roles expected of them are clearly defined. These prerequisites for success are discussed in the following sections.

MANAGEMENT'S RESPONSIBILITY FOR TRAINING

Although, as we shall see, there are different types of managerial responsibility for training, all managers without exception ought to accept personal responsibility for the training and development of their own staff. This involves taking an active interest in their careers, providing opportunities to improve and extend their abilities, especially by using day-to-day work tasks, and above all, by encouraging them to continue learning (see Singer 1979). An organization should ensure that each of its managers accepts the importance of this personal role when contributing to the corporate training effort and that their success in exercising this responsibility will have a bearing on their own career prospects. Unlike other training responsibilities, this cannot be delegated.

These assertions of good practice, however, are not universally accepted by managers. 'More urgent tasks have to be given priority' and 'general pressure of work' are the usual reasons given by managers for not being more involved in developing their staff. While not discounting these reasons, it is true to say that a critical aspect of the management process is concerned with identifying and dealing with priority tasks, and for many managers training and development is simply not perceived to be a priority. We have drawn two conclusions from numerous discussions we have had with senior, middle and junior managers attending our management development programmes. First, a significant obstacle to progress in exercising this responsibility is that, for many managers, the task is (correctly) perceived as being difficult to carry out and so is avoided. Secondly, and perhaps for the same reason, it is unusual for managers to be assessed on this aspect of their work. In reviewing the training needs of managers an evaluation should be made of their expertise in training and development and provision made to remedy any shortfall.

The nature of the responsibility for training and how it is exercised varies with the level of management and the culture and size of the organization. Top management have four major responsibilities as follows:

- They bear much of the burden for creating and sustaining a positive attitude towards human resource development throughout their organization.

- They determine the organization's policies for training and development and ensure that they are supported with the necessary resources (see Chapter 4).

- To a greater extent than they often realize, top management by their personal involvement in training and by taking a consistent interest in training decisions and interventions, provide the environmental 'energy' which gives the training function much of its corporate vitality.

- The quality of an organization's management training and development is critically dependent on the personal commitment of its top management (see, for example, Lathrope 1985).

Middle and junior managers are responsible for implementing the organization's training policy within their own spheres of influence. There are certain aspects which require their personal attention, such as encouraging their staff to engage in continuing development activities. Other aspects they normally delegate: for example, much of the detailed work involved in the day-to-day analysis of departmental training requirements and in the preparation of programmes, is dealt with by the training officer, with the help and co-operation of line management.

STRUCTURING THE TRAINING FUNCTION

The responsibilities for training in small organizations rests with the owner or manager, but in medium sized and large organizations it is often necessary to establish a training department to provide line management with the necessary specialist service.

There is no one correct way of 'positioning' the training department within an organization and different structures have been evolved which have been equally successful in meeting their requirements. For example, the extent to which the function should be centralized or decentralized. Whatever form of structure is adopted, the main criterion to be satisfied is that the department contributes effectively to the running of the organization. How this is achieved will depend on the particular circumstances.

Apart from a limited number of organizations with a full-time training specialist at director level, the training department is usually organized so that its manager reports to a senior executive with wider responsibilities than training alone. In practice, as the following structures illustrate, the head of the training function is normally accountable to one of the three senior managers: the personnel manager, the chief executive, or the relevant line manager (where training is restricted to a group of employees in the company) e.g. the sales manager.

The training officer within the personnel department

We have already demonstrated that training is an essential part of an organization's human resource function and that its effectiveness is reduced if it is isolated from related activities such as recruitment and selection. In general, therefore, the more closely training is integrated within the personnel function the more effective it is likely to be. This is not to suggest that the training officer should invariably report to the personnel manager; where the personnel department has a dynamic and progressive outlook and is successfully led by professional staff, the function will usually be part of it. On the other hand, where a personnel department has only a limited development and influence, a dependent training function is unlikely to prosper and the training officer may be more effective if made directly responsible to the chief executive or to a senior line manager.

Traditionally, the responsibilities of personnel departments have included the training function, and the advantages of this structure will be considered briefly under the following headings.

Line management expectations of the personnel function

Communications will tend to be more effective and a better professional service result if line managers have only one internal source to contact for advice and help on any human resource management problem.

Human resource planning

An organization's estimated requirements for various categories of employee have direct implications for training specialists. They need to know the numbers and types of future training programmes required for new and existing staff, and for retraining where jobs change or become obsolete (see Chapter 3). Such data will be available from the corporate manpower plan, although it should be noted that not all organizations have a formal plan for their human resource function.

Recruitment

The contribution of a training department in this important area will largely depend on the extent to which the organization's recruitment policy is to engage ready-trained employees or to develop its own. The traditional role of the training officer in recruitment has been restricted to helping select junior staff, i.e. operatives and craft trainees. However, if the role of the department is wider than that of simply responding to the demands for the training of new staff, it will also influence recruitment policy. For example, the training officer of a large department store carried out an analysis of its long-term training requirements and highlighted the fact that the age structure of its management was skewed. This would lead in six years time to a high loss of senior staff through retirement. There were insufficient employees with appropriate experience in the right age range to succeed the present key staff. The training officer, therefore, recommended that future recruitment must compensate for this imbalance.

Selection procedures

The feedback on the progress of new recruits during training helps validate recruitment and selection procedures.

Remuneration

An organization's remuneration policy and practice should recognize the enhanced market value of the employee who has successfully completed training. This can be overlooked if personnel and training staff are not working closely together.

Staff development

A system of staff appraisal indicates the strengths and weaknesses of individual employees, and at the same time identifies how training can help improve work performance (see Chapter 6). Appraisal and training must be recognized as part of the same process of staff development.

Career planning

Career plans for staff at all levels in the organization invariably have training connotations. In some cases the training required is limited, in others an anticipated promotion may necessitate the grooming of an employee over a period of months or years. Planning an employee's promotion, deliberately increasing her responsibilities, assisting her where necessary with training and matching her improved performance with increased pay, are all part of the same process and are best dealt with as such.

Personnel records

Personnel records contain employee's work histories and, more important in many cases, details of staff training and development plans. A central and up-to-date source of this information is a basic requirement for effective personnel practice. Decentralization of record keeping to various sub-functions leads to duplication, which apart from being expensive presents problems in keeping several sets of records up to date and increases the potential misuse of confidential information. The utility of computer-based personnel record systems is enhanced for all authorized users if the data held in the computer is as comprehensive as possible.

This list indicates the major advantages that an organization gains from having a high-level personnel department co-ordinating training and other human resource activities in a single personnel system. However, for the reasons given at the beginning of this section, placing training under the wing of the personnel department is not necessarily desirable, and other structures may be more appropriate.

The training officer reporting to the chief executive

This arrangement is found where the chief executive has a personal interest in training matters or wishes to demonstrate to the organization that she considers training to be a sufficiently important function to justify its head reporting direct to top management. This type of structure is common in medium-sized and in some very large organizations, where the importance of the training function makes it necessary for the training officer to have direct access to the chief executive. A training officer in this situation, by 'having the ear' of the chief executive, will almost certainly acquire a great deal of informal authority within the organization. If the chief executive gives personal support, then the training officer is less likely to meet 'political' difficulties in the day-to-day implementation of training. But this structure also has its limitations. Chief executives are busy people and may not always be able to devote adequate time to training matters. Decisions may be delayed or made without their implications being fully appreciated.

The training officer reporting to a line manager

In an organization where formal training is essentially restricted to one category of employee, the training officer is usually responsible to the departmental manager concerned. A common example is the sales trainer who reports direct to the sales manager. In this structure, training can be closely related to the needs of the department and it may be the most suitable, temporary arrangement where training is restricted within the organization. Should planned training be introduced into other parts of the firm the need for a co-ordinated training effort may become apparent and one of the previously mentioned structures could then be more appropriate.

TRAINING STAFF: THEIR ROLES AND THEIR TRAINING

The roles of training staff

We have selected and will describe aspects of two studies which are helpful in illuminating the activities of training staff. For further information the reader is referred to the Local Government Training Board (1976), the Training Services Agency (1977), Jones (1983), and Bennett and Leduchowicz (1983).

The first study, carried out by Rodger, Morgan and Guest (1971), demonstrated that training officers have no common single role or set of roles but undertake a very wide variety of activities in response to variables such as:

- the status and importance of the training function in the organization as expressed by top management's interest and support;
- the extent to which there is a need and demand for training in the organization;
- the natural development of training in the firm which can change the role of the training specialist over quite short periods of time;
- the managerial calibre of the training officer, the postholder's seniority in the organization's hierarchy and her acceptability (as a person) to other managers.

Various combinations of these factors result in a wide spectrum of training practice. At one end is the senior training specialist who is deeply involved in the policy making processes, and her role is that of consultant to the board of directors and senior management. Her major responsibility is to help identify and achieve the organizational changes necessary to reach corporate objectives and she assists in the diagnosis of problems which appear to have training solutions. She is actively concerned with management training and development.

Reddin (1968) has described a training specialist with this top level responsibility as:

> a manager of organizational development ... [whose] ... client is not the individual alone but, in addition, the department and the organization. He is interested in training's contribution to overall effectiveness, not simply to individual effectiveness.

Few training specialists in this country have this corporate training role but Jones (1983) has drawn attention to the trend for more training officers to adopt an interventionist role than has traditionally been the case. He argues that the traditional assumptions on which training activities have taken place in the UK are that the training officer has a primary contract with the individual trainee and a secondary (weaker) contract with the organization. Jones suggests that different assumptions are needed if a training officer is to play a greater role in influencing more efficient and relevant training. Her primary contract should be with the organization and this will be achieved by 'becoming involved in mainstream organizational processes and problems'. The outcome of this greater organizational involvement will enable the trainer to 'cause learning to happen in a wide variety of ways – not only by providing a specialist 'teaching' service' (see Chapter 7).

At the other end of the spectrum is the training officer working in an organization where the function is little developed. She has junior management status, limited authority and the legitimacy of her role is questioned. She is in no position to influence organizational development in the way described by Reddin, and her responsibilities typically are the training of junior staff and the maintenance of training records. Her contact with management training is probably limited to making administrative arrangements for managers to attend external courses. Between these two extreme role types, there are of course many others, intermediate in their authority, status and in the tasks for which they are responsible.

The second study, by Pettigrew, Jones and Reason, (1981, 1982), has provided interesting data about training and development roles and the factors which influence effectiveness in these roles. They selected a sample of training officers in the UK chemical industry using company size and type of job (training manager, training officer and advisor) and using semi-structured interviews collected data on: the relational aspects of the trainers' jobs, the activities which they performed or felt they ought to be performing; the degree of job satisfaction they achieved, and the ways in which they influenced decisions. The research underlined the importance of congruence between three variables: the role of training officer, the culture of the organization in which he or she worked, and the person concerned.

Pettigrew and his co-authors identified the following five types, or perspectives, of training officer roles and associated behaviour, stressing that these perspectives, or role interpretations, should not be considered as watertight categories but as broad descriptions and that no judgemental assumptions should be made that one role type is better or worse than another.

The provider – has a generally accepted although limited role in offering training expertise geared towards the maintenance and development of the organizational performance but not with organization change. She works within the current culture in a manner which is congruent with its expectations, i.e. she operates in the standard ways expected of a training officer in that organization.

The training manager – concentrates her efforts on the management and performance of her training staff and on the development of the function. She sees herself as a manager, not a trainer, and is likely to be concerned with policy development and co-ordination issues.

The change agent – this is the classic organization development consultant and is the antithesis of the provider role. As the title indicates, the change agent is concerned with the definition of organizational problems and helping others to resolve these problems through changing the organizational culture. The role is very difficult and demanding and its legitimacy is uncertain.

The passive provider – this role is similar to that of the provider i.e. it is concerned with contributing to the maintenance, rather than the reform, of the organization and as such the role is seen to be legitimate. However, a passive provider has low influence within the organization due, Pettigrew, Jones and Reason argue, to personal difficulties which she has in managing her social position as a training officer. She tends not to take initiatives, is low in self-esteem, is not 'politically' skilled in securing support. She is not good at putting across a clear image of her role and/or in articulating what distinctive services she can offer potential clients. Thus in the latters' minds she creates uncertainty.

The role in transition – here the training officer has developed a wider view of her role and of the contribution she believes she can make and is in the process of moving from being a provider to being a change agent or advisor. She may not have a clear understanding of what the new role entails and there may be very considerable opposition to such a move from those with whom she works. The role therefore has some characteristics of the provider and others of the change agent.

Pettigrew, Jones and Reason (1982) identified two key issues from their research. First, that successful training activities depend upon the training officer's personal effectiveness which itself is a function of the degree of 'fit' or 'congruence' between the organization culture, the personality and style of the training officer and the role she assumes. A training officer therefore needs to recognize that there may be a choice of roles that she can play, to select the most appropriate one (for her in the particular context), and then to be able to meet the expectations of that role. Secondly, they considered questions of influence and survival 'resulting from the way the trainer, on an on-going basis, manages the boundary between his activity and the rest of the organization'.

These writers examined the essential but largely ignored theme of role relationships in training through the concepts of power resources, legitimacy, and boundary management ('the system of exchanges a function, activity, or a role, has with its environment'). This part of their study was concerned with five major requirements, that is how the training officer:

- acquires resources and disposes of outputs;
- exercises influence;
- builds relationships and activates her image;
- protects her territorial integrity, and
- co-ordinates her activities with other roles and units of the organization.

Pettigrew and his co-authors considered the training officer's 'power bases' and 'cultural identification' (expertise at using aspects of the organization's culture) to be central to the effective functioning of her job. They developed the theme of the power resources available to her e.g. political access, cultural identification, credibility and access to information, and argued that successful boundary management and cultural identification are much more important than technical competence.

Providers and passive providers were not active in 'boundary management' but tended to be dominated by administration, analyses and courses. Change agents, those whose role was in transition, and training managers were aware of the importance of 'boundary management' and had to a greater or lesser degree developed a strategy to increase their power bases. They were more inclined to accentuate the image-building side of their jobs through activities such as counselling, organizational diagnosis and the influencing of human resource decisions.

While the main contribution of the work of Pettigrew, Jones and Reason is that it offers a much needed theoretical framework for the analysis and understanding of training officer roles in the context of power and relationships, it is necessary to appreciate that the sample was relatively small and that the study relates to the perceptions of training officers. Nonetheless, the research provides an important basis for the further conceptual analysis of the relational context of training officers' jobs in the industrial context and in non-profit making organizations.

ROLE DESIGNATIONS

Training director

In very large organizations the importance of the training function may be such that it is controlled by a full-time training director. As we have seen, relatively few organizations have appointed full-time training directors, hence this responsibility at board level is usually carried as an additional, partial responsibility by the director of another function, such as personnel or production. The requirement is that there is an individual at this level to oversee the function in terms of overall policies and objectives.

Group training manager

This title is used in two different ways. It may refer to the senior training specialist in a multi-company organization who is responsible for the training function at group or holding company level. The 'group training manager' in this sense advises the group board of directors on training matters and through a staff role influences the work of training officers in the constituent companies of the group.

The term 'group training manager' can also refer to the training specialist in charge of a 'group training scheme'. Small companies, because of their limited facilities, often lack the expertise and breadth of training opportunities necessary for effective training of their employees. One solution to this problem is for such companies with similar training needs to form a training group. Member companies benefit by pooling training resources and sharing the services of the group training manager appointed to co-ordinate and develop the group. She is normally assisted by part-time and sometimes full-time training instructors. The larger group training schemes also employ specialist training officers.

Company or general training officer

The training needs of organizations employing between five hundred and a thousand staff are often sufficient to justify a full-time training officer. Such a person is normally responsible, to a greater or lesser extent, for all types of training and may be assisted by full-time and part-time instructors.

Specialist training officer

In organizations with large numbers of employees requiring specialized (e.g. technical) training, it may be necessary to appoint specialist training officers. They may be specialists in a specific aspect of training, e.g. management development, youth training, craft training.

Training advisor

An advisory or consultant role may be undertaken either by an employee of the organization or, on an *ad hoc* basis, an external specialist e.g. an organization development consultant (change agent).

The part-time training officer

Where the amount of training required is perceived as limited – as in most small companies – a line manager may act as a part-time training officer. In some companies the personnel officer includes training among her responsibilities but often it is the company secretary, the work study, sales or production manager, who is in charge of training.

Instructor

An instructor is employed in situations where the training role is primarily concerned with face-to-face instruction at the place of work or in an off-the-job training centre.

THE CHANGING ROLES OF TRAINING STAFF

The current economic recession dominates many of the decisions relating to the training function but training officers' jobs are being affected by four significant and related trends, which may have an even greater impact on the nature of training officer roles in the longer term:

- changes in the structure of the workforce;
- changes in the perception of the role of training;
- the application of the new technologies to learning;
- the direct and indirect outcomes of the increasingly powerful interventions of the Manpower Services Commission.

Each of these trends may present a challenge, and perhaps a threat, to the training officer: all offer opportunities to adapt to changing demands.

The changes in the structure of the workforce and the resultant implications for the training function are succinctly expressed in the Institute of Personnel Management's policy statement on training and development (1983):

> The nature of work has changed and continues to change: white collar jobs now outnumber blue collar, reflecting in part the decline of job opportunities in the manufacturing sector, the growth in service industries and the introduction of modern technology. Less skilled work is fast diminishing, leaving unqualified school leavers and the more elderly unskilled and semi-skilled workers particularly vulnerable to unemployment. There is an increasing demand for technical skills of a type or in a combination not anticipated a decade ago. Thus continuous change should be expected and people should be prepared to face it. Clearly the acquisition of skills and knowledge through training and development is becoming more important as a prerequisite for entry into the productive workforce, and skills once acquired are likely to need updating or modifying to match changing

> requirements. Both equity and necessity that every individual should make the maximum contribution to society requires that training should be available to all. A period of initial training no longer provides a sufficient skills base (if it ever did): continuous development is necessary. Training must match the changing needs of industry, commerce and public sector, and so our traditional educational and training systems must adapt and change.

Training specialists have the opportunity to propose and implement cost effective initiatives to help reform the national systems and to bring about the changes required by their own organizations. While some funding, for what is considered more appropriate initial training and for retraining, will come from government (and some companies have made good use of such funds to contribute towards their training department's overheads), the bulk of the resources will come from employers and the actual training will take place under the aegis of their training functions (see Chapter 9).

We noted in Chapter 1 that the traditional philosophy of training in the UK (a 'front loaded' model) is beginning to give place to the 'continuing development' concept and that there is a growing recognition that more effective training is often achieved when less emphasis is placed on formal instruction and trainees are given responsibility for their own learning. It is increasingly recognized that the training officer's contribution to individual and organizational effectiveness cannot be achieved merely through providing courses. Her interventions need to take different forms such as arranging meetings of managers with the aim of removing barriers to learning, setting up an open access learning centre, or utilizing of existing computer terminals for computer-based training applications. This new thinking about learning and training cannot simply be dismissed as a change in emphasis. It raises fundamental questions for employers and employees about policies for employee development, the *raison d'etre* of traditional forms and activities of the training function, and therefore about the future roles of training staff. Changing views on training and its provision include the important, and as yet unresolved, issue of who should pay for training (see page 6).

Increasing numbers of senior managers have benefited from the expansion of management and technical education and training provision which began in the 1960s. They are familiar with the training and development concept and have, for example, been involved in helping to supervise project work. They expect, as a routine support for their work, that they will receive a high quality professional service from the training function. This attitude is often found in the newer industries but is less well established in the older traditional industries where top management has often learned primarily from experience or 'exposure'.

New technologies applied to learning in a work context have far-reaching implications for the management and administration of training, for the methods of delivering and monitoring training, and for obtaining information about the training packages and programmes available. New technologies have already had a substantial impact on the roles of many trainers. For example, open and distance learning are not new concepts but their relevance and acceptability to many more learners has led to an increase in the availability of high quality training packages incorporating an imaginative use of sound and video tape, and computer-based learning, including interactive video programmes (see, for example, Crofts 1985). These applications are permeating many levels and functions within organizations and opening up a range of opportunities for training staff. To take advantage of these opportunities requires investment and the ability of the training officer to argue successfully the case for such investment: it also requires trainers to develop different relationships with their clients. Increasingly, a key role for the training officer will be to act as a provider of flexible training services.

Some of the Manpower Services Commission's policies, in particular those stemming from its *New Training Initiative* (1981) (together with the finance which the Commission is making available to support them) are having profound effects on the training function in many organizations, e.g. the Youth Training Scheme (YTS) and the Open Tech Programme. In some instances these initiatives are resulting in company training staff working wholly or in part to meet national rather than company training needs. The MSC's other policies have longer term implications for training staff, e.g. the further reform of skill training, the Technical and Vocational Education Initiative (TVEI), the special funding of training programmes for the disadvantaged, and the closer control which the MSC has over the budget for non-advanced vocational further education (see Nicholson 1985).

Organizations are reacting, more or less effectively, to these 'winds of change'. Some training departments, for example, Austin Rover's Open Tech project and the Lloyds Bank multi-million pound investment in interactive video for staff training, responded proactively to the changes and harnessed the new opportunities to provide novel and cost effective solutions to training needs. In contrast, the response to the MSC's YTS initiative by some training departments – facing the problem of underemployed apprentice instructors and declining numbers of apprentices – has been disappointing. In such situations YTS trainees were recruited partly to provide a solution to an internal problem, at times with very unsatisfactory results. The apprentice instructors were skilled at training well-qualified and highly-motivated craft trainees but were quite unfamiliar with the very different approaches to training appropriate for many YTS recruits who had different abilities and motivations. The lesson to be drawn from this latter experience is that trainers themselves require training to achieve competence in their developing roles.

The training of training staff

From the above discussion of the many roles that training staff undertake it follows that the skills and knowledge required for effective performance will vary from individual to individual, and will be subject to change in response to developments such as those outlined in the previous section. There is no one set of abilities needed by all trainers – contrary to the assumption which had underlain the concept of the Introductory Training Officers' Courses, introduced at the time of the dramatic increase in the number of training officers appointed following the 1964 Act.

The Manpower Services Commission (1978) published a report *Training of Trainers* which aimed to improve the quality, quantity, relevance and effectiveness of the training of those who have responsibilities for organizing, managing or advising on training. The report led to the replacement of the Introductory Training Officers' Courses by an approach to the training of training staff which focused on 'core competencies'. A further report, *Direct Trainers*, (MSC 1980), provided recommendations for the training of:

> all individuals who have specific responsibility for directly helping people to acquire, develop and apply the knowledge and skills they need in order to perform effectively and also in order to meet new and changing problems and opportunities.

This report also recommended the 'core competency' approach to meeting the variety of training needs of direct trainers.

The core competency framework detailed in the MSC report of 1978 recognizes that there are some 'common areas of know-how' of which all trainers need to have a practical understanding and, in addition, there are 'areas of specific knowledge and skills' which each trainer will require to carry out her particular role. For a list of typical activities undertaken by training officers, see Appendix 2.

The common areas of know-how are:

- the organization and its business;
- the training function and the training specialist's roles;
- learning and the design of learning;
- diagnosis and problem solving;
- people in organizations.

All holders of training specialist roles at any level need a practical understanding of these areas so that they may be able more effectively to:

- ensure that training activities are geared to the real needs and circumstances of the organization and its work force;
- identify and overcome obstacles to training and learning which may exist;
- bring to bear on problems an appropriate specialist understanding of training and learning;
- interact across the many boundaries of their roles with those of others inside and outside the organization.

In the context of specific knowledge and skill requirements the MSC identified 'four 'role elements' which in one combination or another are present in training manager, training adviser or training officer types of posts'. The specific knowledge and skills are grouped under the role elements of: direct training; planning and organizing; determining or managing; consulting and advising.

The application of this approach to a newly appointed training officer might take the following form (adapted from the Local Government Training Board 1976):

Induction training: the training officer should take part in a foundation course which covers the 'common areas of know-how' and special courses to cover the specific areas of knowledge and skills in which she is required to be competent. This should be followed by an initial programme of job-centred practical training. The initial programme for a completely inexperienced training officer is unlikely to span less than 12 months.

Further development: planned developments of the training officer should continue while she is in post and she should have an individual training and development programme which is regularly reviewed and up-dated. This can include short courses, guided reading, secondments and attachments, visits, participation in committees, and project work.

Career development and professional qualifications: if she sees her long-term career in the training function and aspires to a post concerned with the management of training, she should be encouraged to become professionally qualified by taking the examinations of the Institute of Personnel Management or of the Institute of Training and Development. In some cases the need may be for a more general management qualification in which case a Diploma in Management Studies would be appropriate.

THE BENEFITS AND COSTS OF TRAINING

We saw in Chapter 1 that some employers tend to perceive expenditure on training as an unnecessary cost which should be avoided, others see it as an investment in developing their organization's human resources, while the position of the majority of employers lies somewhere between these two extremes.

Investments of all kinds, including training, contain an element of uncertainty. Prudent management, whether in the public or the private sector, demands that before an investment proposal is sanctioned, a convincing case has to be made showing that the expected return on the expenditure will be forthcoming. For example, British Airways decided to set an upper age limit of 47.5 years in selecting pilots to train to fly Concorde. This was partly because the special training involved costs £100,000 per trainee and the airline wants seven and a half years of service from a pilot before he or she reaches the retirement age of 55, and partly because a quarter of the senior pilots entered for Concorde training had failed to reach the required standard. Compared with conventional aircraft, faster reactions on the part of the pilot are required to fly Concorde (see Preston 1985). Moreover, alternative strategies, i.e. non-training solutions, must be demonstrated to be less appropriate. The 'best value for money' argument and the extent to which the risks involved in a particular investment can be planned for and so minimized, apply just as much to training as to any other investment decision.

Thus from the employer's point of view, planned training can be regarded as a sound investment only after the proposal has been subjected to an appropriate cost benefit appraisal. This requires answers to two questions. What benefits can the organization obtain from investing in training, and what costs are involved in the proposed training ?

What benefits can an organization obtain from investing in training ?

For reasons discussed below, it is usually difficult to identify the precise contribution that training – one of many variables – may have made in a work context. This may help explain one result of a survey carried out by the Industrial Society (1985), which showed that two thirds of the UK organizations surveyed spent less than 0.5 per cent of their annual turnover on training their employees. Nonetheless, in general terms the following benefits may be anticipated:

- Training helps employees to learn their jobs quickly and effectively, thus minimizing learning costs.

- Existing staff can be helped by training to improve their work performance and to keep up-to-date in their specialist fields. The present and future standards of work required by the organization is more likely to be achieved and maintained if employees are well trained.

- A greater volume of work can be expected from trained staff, partly because they work more rapidly and partly because they make fewer mistakes.

- A reduction in work errors benefits an organization in two other ways. First, management can spend more time on planning and development activities instead of correcting mistakes. Secondly, costs of correcting errors are eliminated.

- Labour turnover among new staff, if caused by ineffective learning and inadequate training, can be reduced. Staff who are helped by induction, and other training, to learn their jobs rapidly are more likely to achieve a high level of job satisfaction soon after joining the company and so tend to remain longer (see Jones and Moxham 1969, Fowler 1983).
- Retention of staff is an advantage to an organization only so long as their skills and knowledge contribute to its operation. By retraining staff, new abilities replace obsolescent ones.
- Training in safe working practices reduces accidents, resulting in social and financial benefits to employers, employees and society.
- An organization with a reputation for providing good training tends to attract better applicants for its vacancies.
- Employees are less likely to become frustrated and leave if training and development opportunities are available for furthering their careers with their present employer.
- An organization needs a flexible workforce to operate efficiently when staff are absent through sickness or on holiday. Training increases employees' versatility by extending their range of expertise to include related jobs.
- The general morale of an organization is enhanced by effective organization development (OD) and individual employee training interventions. Taken together these approaches can improve an organization's ability to accept and implement change, to become more proactive and so be able to take greater advantage of new opportunities.

To this list of reasons why employers are advised to consider the 'training option' should be added the personal and wider social benefits which can result from training. The successful acquisition of a skill or knowledge wanted by employers increases the value of an individual in the labour market and this usually provides both her and her family with a higher standard of living. There are also important non-financial benefits which trained people enjoy. These include enhanced status, greater job security (trained staff are a valuable asset which employers are loathe to lose), improved chances of obtaining another job if made redundant, better promotion prospects, and, because their work talents are fully used, greater job satisfaction.

The advantages to society of a well trained national workforce are of fundamental importance. Without such expertise in its working population, the relatively high standard of living of technology-based societies, such as that of the UK, would not be possible. It is the dearth of a well-educated and trained workforce, as well as a shortage of financial and other resources, which mark developing countries.

While the various benefits which can flow from planned training are desirable and impressive, a training intervention – if it is not compatible with the policies and operations of the organization – may solve some problems but create others. It is insufficient to provide first-class training opportunities without also recognizing that training adds to their employees' market value, as many employers have found to their cost. In particular, employers who have a 'unitarist' view of their organizations can seriously misjudge the extent of an employee's loyalty by assuming, especially if significant resources have been used in training the individual, that there is in consequence a greater staff commitment and forget that, in reality, loyalty may be defined by the period of notice in the contract of employment. It is therefore important that attention is paid to the broader context of a firm's personnel and operating policies if the benefits of training are to accrue to the organization bearing the cost of the training and not to another employer. For example, remuneration, staff development, quality of management and general conditions of work must be at least comparable to those offered by competitors if investment in training is to pay dividends in the longer term.

What costs are involved in training?

The list of advantages noted above may well convince an employer that investment in training is worth serious consideration, even after taking into account the practical difficulties involved in assessing the benefits of training in a particular case. These advantages can only become of interest in cost-benefit terms when they are considered in relation to the resources needed to achieve them.

What then does training cost an employer? One possible approach to training costs is that adopted by economists, who argue that the actual cost to an organization of training is not the financial expenditure incurred (i.e. the money costs), but the opportunity costs involved. Garbutt (1969) argues:

> The opportunity which a firm foregoes may be a better measure of its cost than its accountancy procedure. In other words we may spend a £100 on training but if in doing so we lose the opportunity to make £200 then the opportunity cost of training is £200.

However, as Garbutt continues:

> Measures of opportunity cost are hard to establish and even harder to agree between conflicting interests.

The opportunity cost approach is, therefore, not usually a practical one for a training officer to adopt in trying to identify training costs except where the level of investment in training is high.

An alternative approach is to consider the costs that an organization is forced to incur as a direct result of employees having to learn their jobs (learning costs) and then determining how these costs can be minimized by expenditure on training (training costs). Talbot and Ellis (1969) have pointed out that learning costs are unavoidable and will be incurred by an organization whenever learning is taking place, whether or not the employee is being formally trained.

The following are examples of learning costs:

- payments made to employees when first learning their jobs or when undergoing refresher training;
- the cost of materials wasted, sales lost or incorrect decisions made as learners acquire competence;
- the cost of reduced output caused by the deleterious effect which learners can have on those with whom they are working;
- costs resulting from employees leaving the organization because they find the work too difficult;
- costs attributed to accidents caused by inexperience or ignorance.

Training costs are defined as those deliberately incurred by an organization to facilitate learning and with the intention of reducing learning costs. Training costs are of two kinds: fixed costs, that is those that do not change with the amount of training that takes place (e.g. the rates that have to be paid to the local council for the training centre building, or the salaries of the permanent staff of the training department); and variable costs, that is costs which vary directly with the amount of training undertaken (e.g. the cost of materials used or the fees charged by a consultant lecturer).

The following are examples of training costs:

The capital and running costs of a training centre building:

- the building itself and its furnishing, initial, maintenance and depreciation costs
- heating
- lighting
- cleaning
- rates
- apportionment of general company overheads

'People' costs:

- part of managers' salary for the time they spend in coaching staff
- the salary/wages other emoluments and expenses of training officers, instructors and their supporting technical, secretarial, clerical, and manual staff
- payments of fees to consultants, guest speakers, colleges and other outside bodies
- travel, overnight accommodation, meals and associated expenses incurred by trainers and trainees

Equipment costs

- telephone and postage
- typewriters, photocopiers and other office equipment
- training aids such as micro computers, closed-circuit television, and overhead, video and 35 mm projectors
- training equipment such as plant, simulators
- depreciation, maintenance and insurance of equipment

Material costs

- paper and office consumables
- distance learning packages
- films and tapes
- practice materials

- protective clothing
- books and journals

Ideally, the relationship between learning costs and training costs should be such that both are minimized, since expenditure on training is only justified if it reduces the costs of learning. However, since learning costs are to some extent unavoidable there must be an upper limit to the amount of training expenditure which is appropriate in any context. Incurring additional training costs beyond this point would not further reduce the costs of learning.

In reality, organizations can rarely exercise the fine degree of control needed to optimize their training expenditure in this way because decisions normally have to be made on incomplete information. Anderson and Tobbell (1983), for example, in a survey of the costs of training centres, found that their respondents (managers) were generally ill-informed about the costs of their training centres. Senior managers and accountants do not necessarily appreciate, or accept, the wider significance of learning and training costs and so do not give these items due prominence in their costing systems. As a result, many organizations lack the financial information necessary to identify and control accurately these two sets of costs. For example, certain items of training expenditure, such as the salaries of training staff, can be readily identified. Other costs, such as those arising from mistakes made by an inadequately trained invoice clerk (delays in receiving settlements, loss of goodwill, overtime work needed to amend and send out correct invoices, etc.) or the loss of overhead recovery from a plant under-utilized through shortage of skilled staff, typically remain hidden in the general operating costs of a business.

In theory, any cost incurred by an organization can be identified but the process of collecting and analysing data costs money and can only be justified if the value of the information produced makes the process worthwhile. A sophisticated system of costing learning/training activities is unnecessary in small companies but becomes increasingly important in larger organizations where expenditure can be considerable. Whatever the size of the organization the important point is that its management recognizes the relationship between the learning and training costs being incurred and is aware of their relative order of magnitude. It is then a matter of management policy to decide the degree of detailed information necessary for the effective control of these costs.

In practical terms a useful starting point in finding out what training costs an organization incurs is to examine the training budget, as this might be expected to provide information on the type and amount of approved expenditure on training. However, such an approach is not always very illuminating for two main reasons. First, organizations do not necessarily have a separate budget for training. Their expenditure in this area may be limited and included under other budget headings. Secondly, even if an organization has a training budget, many of its training costs are incurred in the day-to-day running of the business. These costs are difficult to identify and are, therefore, not itemized in financial statements.

The costs and benefits resulting from a training investment can be analysed by means of what is technically termed a cost benefit analysis approach. Cost benefit analysis is:

> a systematic comparison between the cost of carrying out a service or activity and the value of that service or activity, quantifying as far as possible in terms of money. All costs and benefits (direct and indirect, financial and social) are taken into account. (Manpower Services Commission 1981.)

This approach has been developed by economists in an attempt to produce information (ultimately expressed in financial terms) which defines the net benefit or net cost of a particular investment decision. Cost benefit analysis is an analytical tool used particularly in circumstances where major investment proposals/decisions, with significant social overtones, have to be made, e.g. the siting of a nuclear power station.

Very useful data can result from the application of a cost-benefit study – using the term in the strict technical sense – and in theory this approach could be used routinely to evaluate and compare training proposals and practices within organizations (see Woodward 1976). But there are several reasons why rigorous cost-benefit studies are not undertaken:

- There are the difficulties of scientifically attributing specific outcomes (benefits) exclusively to specific inputs (costs), see the Birmingham sales training case study, on page 59.

- While it may be relatively easy to identify the broad headings of putative costs and benefits for a proposed investment, putting numbers to these components, especially the social costs and benefits, is a very difficult process. It depends to a significant degree upon making 'reasonable assumptions' and the use of 'soft' data derived from comparisons, 'expert' opinion and value judgements. Recommendations derived from such data are at best approximations, not certainties, and open to criticism.

- There is a difficulty in choosing an appropriate time horizon over which the benefits resulting from the investment can be expected to accrue to the organization, e.g. will the trainees still be using their expertise in two, four or six years time or will their skills and knowledge be obsolete? Will some or all of the trainees have left the company in six months or three years time?
- A further problem is to determine what discount factor to apply to the costs and the benefits of training which extends over a number of years.
- The process of developing a model, collecting and analysing the quantitative and qualitative information, and drawing conclusions costs money and has to be justified.
- The expertise required to undertake a study is usually not available.

However, for details of ways in which a cost-benefit analysis approach can be used as a decision-taking tool in organizational analysis and the problems generated by its application, see Hall (1976), Cannon (1979), Bridge (1981).

We have already stressed that it is often difficult to quantify the benefits which unequivocally result from a particular investment in training. This is primarily because many variables affect an organization's activities and it is frequently impossible to isolate and measure the precise contribution made by any one of these, e.g. training. In a number of situations, however, improved performance can, with certainty, be attributed directly to training. Such examples are usually drawn from operative training where there can be fewer, identifiable, variables (see Seymour 1966). The following example illustrates the more general case both in terms of the complexity of training evaluation and of the attitude which management typically adopts towards it.

As part of its expansion programme, a Birmingham manufacturing company decided to recruit additional sales staff and give them a thorough training. This was the first time the company had run training programmes for its new representatives. On completion of training, and after several months in the field, the new sales staff proved to be extremely successful, with their sales results being very much better than had been anticipated. But to what extent could this success be attributed to the training given to the representatives? Many other factors could have combined to produce this satisfactory outcome. The recruits may have been of above average calibre. Production or distribution difficulties may have put competitors at a disadvantage during the period which benefited the new sales staff; the advertising support for the company's products may have been more effective; special price or discount arrangements may have given the sales representatives an additional advantage over their competitors; the quality of sales management may have been improved, and so on.

The company could have carried out a detailed review of the sales training programme, including a comparison of the costs incurred with the benefits gained. This would have provided structured information about the relative importance of the variables influencing the final results. In the event no such analysis was carried out since the cost and effort required to investigate these issues were not considered to be justified. In the directors' opinion the training programme had made a useful contribution, at a reasonable cost, and that was the end of the matter, even though their opinion was based entirely on value judgements.

The problem of identifying the contribution made by one of many variables in a work context is not restricted to training. It occurs in a similar form in other important business activities such as industrial relations and advertising. For example, a company which enjoys good industrial relations may attribute this achievement, in part, to its joint management and union consultative machinery. While this may be a reasonable view to take, it remains more a matter of judgement than a proven fact in the absence of a systematic attempt to isolate the effect of this one variable in a complex set of activities. Again, while, in principle, it is considered sound business practice to assist the sales effort with advertising support – resting on the general argument that a company failing to advertise its products is likely to face falling sales – it is a much more difficult task to specify the precise benefits of advertising expenditure.

Similarly, it is common sense to help people to learn their jobs: employers who do not train their staff forego the benefits which planned training would have brought. However, to rely solely upon the common sense argument to justify a proposed investment in training is a poor substitute for an 'order of magnitude' assessment of the costs and benefits that are likely to result (or have resulted).

The more factual data that is available, difficult though it may be to produce, the less dependence needs to be placed on the value judgements as to worth of a training programme, be it that of the trainer, the trainee or the senior management.

'Best practice' in the financial management and control of the training function is achieved by applying a responsible cost-benefit approach to all its major activities. Here we use the phrase cost-benefit not in its rigorous technical sense but to indicate that the training officer ought to have a full awareness of how and why her resources are deployed and with what results. Awareness should extend to being able to respond competently and readily to top management requests to provide financial justification for any significant programme or other expenditure on training. This requires the training officer to plan and determine a resource budget (people, equipment, materials and building services) for each major programme, and to record both the actual resources used and an assessment of the outcomes of the training. (Training evaluation is considered further in Chapter 7.) For examples of this kind of cost-benefit applied to training, see Cannon (1979), Kearsley (1982), Pepper (1984).

Some training officers may be concerned with a further, and in certain cases very important, aspect of financial management. This relates to sources of income generated as a result of carrying out training activities for third parties. One widespread example is the income from the Manpower Services Commission which the training function receives for undertaking a Youth Training Scheme programme. Another example is the training department which is expected to sell its expertise within the company and is in competition with external providers, such as consultants or colleges. It is expected to recoup its costs, i.e. achieve income by providing training services on a commercial basis to other departments. This approach raises the important question, who should pay for training?

WHO SHOULD PAY FOR TRAINING?

One very clear answer to this question is given in the following extract from Tressell's classic book, *The Ragged-Trousered Philanthropists*, which describes the lives of working-class people in Hastings at the beginning of this century:

> Bert, who was their only child and not very robust, had shown a talent for drawing, so when his father died ....his mother readily assented when the boy said that he wished to become a decorator... Resolving to give the boy the best possible chance, she decided, if possible, to place him at Rushton's, that being one of the leading firms in the town. At first Mr. Rushton demanded £10 as a premium, the boy to be bound for five years, no wages the first year, two shillings a week the second, and a rise of one shilling every year for the remainder of the term. Afterwards, as a special favour – a matter of charity in fact as she was a very poor woman – he agreed to accept five pounds. This sum represented the thrifty savings of years, but the poor woman parted with it willingly in order that the boy should become a skilled workman. So Bert was apprenticed – bound for five years to Rushton & Co.

The expectation that trainees (together with their families) should pay an 'employer' for the privilege to be trained has long since ceased to be normal practice. However, the notion that a lower wage is appropriate for a person undergoing training persists, although it is resisted by unions (especially in the case of adults undergoing retraining) and is ignored by employers when there are difficulties in recruiting trainees. The economic justification for the approach is that in employing an untrained person, the employer incurs additional (i.e. learning) costs and some contribution towards this cost ought to be made by the beneficiary of the training. This view became an issue of some contention when the YTS scheme was introduced in 1983 and the Government insisted that YTS trainees should receive a 'training allowance' from the MSC, i.e. a sum less than a young person's wage.

While employees no longer have to pay for their in-house training (other than by receiving lower wages), if they follow a course of vocational education, they are often expected to fund, wholly or in part, their college fees and provide their own books, etc. There are three main reasons for this. First, as we explain in Chapter 10, there is no tradition of UK employers funding vocational education. Secondly, even in the 'prosperous' 1960s and early 1970s when many organizations adopted a more enlightened approach and encouraged, with various financial incentives, certain categories of younger employees to acquire vocational qualifications, this policy was not open-ended. In times of economic recession, a typical employer's view is that adults (variously defined as aged 18, 21 or 25) should pay for their own further or higher education. Thirdly, much vocational education and training gives the employee skills and knowledge which are transferable or 'portable', e.g. professional business qualifications, and therefore the risk of a poor return on the investment is high. Some employers have a 'half-way' policy of funding college and associated fees for employees attending approved external courses, subject to the employee remaining with the organization for an agreed period of time. Should she leave after receiving financial support, she has to refund a proportion of that support.

A change in the balance between what an employer and what an employee have traditionally 'paid' for training is one outcome of the application of new technologies to training. Indeed, one of the attractive selling points made by producers of distance learning packages is that if the studying is undertaken in the trainee's own time, significant training costs are shifted to the learner, while other costs normally incurred by an organization in running a face-to-face mode of training can be reduced or eliminated, e.g. travel time and costs, hotel costs. It remains to be seen how cost effective these alternative approaches will prove to be.

The State's role in paying for training has expanded dramatically in the last decade with the funding of a range of training programmes for school leavers and, to a lesser extent, adults (see Chapters 8 and 9). There remains, however, an unknown number of people, e.g. the self employed, who want to acquire new skills and qualifications but are either ineligible for existing State funded programmes or who, because of family or other commitments, cannot afford to pay for the often long period of training which is required. One approach to this problem is for the State to make it easier for adults to pay for their own development by means of training loans (see Department of Employment 1984 and the White Paper *Training for Jobs* HMSO 1984).

Few would disagree in principle with the Institute of Personnel Management's (1983) view that:

> The costs of learning should be shared by its beneficiaries – the individual, the organization and the State – in appropriate proportions depending upon the status of the learner (young person, adult, employed or unemployed).

However, what constitutes 'appropriate proportions' remains in practice a matter of debate and policy.

A caveat

In this chapter we have considered the training function mainly from the management perspective. We have examined the roles of training staff and indicated how an organization can gain maximum benefit from its investment in training and development. What must not be forgotten is that employees' attitudes to training are varied and certainly do not necessarily coincide with those of their employer – no matter how well intentioned the latter may be. These differences in perception can give rise to tensions and misunderstandings which need to be managed with sensitivity by those with responsibility for training.

Some attitudes to training:

- The 'self-made' manager who left school at 15 and learnt her job in the school of hard experience aided by years of evening class study; is it surprising that she is intolerant of the policy which gives day release to graduate trainees?
- The bright school-leaver who sees training as a means of achieving her career ambition and therefore tries to find a job in an organization which will offer her quality training.
- What to the personnel manager are clear advantages (of a more streamlined apprentice scheme) are to the trade union official a threat to the *status quo* since the change would cause an over-supply of skilled labour.
- I am too old to learn how to use a word processor!
- The chief executive decides that her company should contribute to the national Youth Training Scheme programme and offers training places which are spurned by local school leavers.
- Some of the different reactions from people invited to attend a training course: 'it will confer status', 'it will be a holiday from work', 'it is a reward for past services', 'what is wrong with the way I do my work?'

From the learner's point of view, and especially if job security or potential promotion is at stake, training is at times neither an enjoyable nor an easy experience: it may therefore be viewed with considerable apprehension. Great efforts may have to be made by the learner to achieve even modest results, personal weaknesses can be revealed, while self doubt and a sense of failure can seriously impede learning. Flexible, open learning methods can help reduce such apprehensions but those responsible for training should never underestimate the significance of these barriers to effective learning.

BIBLIOGRAPHY

ANDERSON A and TOBBELL G. *Costing training centres.* IMS Report No 72. Brighton, Institute of Manpower Studies, 1983.

BENNETT R and LEDUCHOWICZ T. *What makes for an effective trainer?* Bradford, MCB University Press Ltd, 1983.

BRIDGE J. *Economics in personnel management.* London, Institute of Personnel Management, 1981.

CANNON J. *Cost effective personnel decisions.* London, Institute of Personnel Management, 1979.

CROFTS P. 'Distance learning's broader horizons'. *Personnel Management*, March, 1985.

DEPARTMENT OF EMPLOYMENT. *Training loans. A proposal from the Secretary of State for Employment for an experimental training loans scheme for adults.* London, Department of Employment, 1984.

DONNELLY E L. *Training as a specialist function – an historical perspective.* Working Paper Number 9, Faculty of Business Studies and Management. London, Middlesex Polytechnic, 1984.

FOWLER A. *Getting off to a good start – successful employee induction.* London, Institute of Personnel Management, 1983.

GARBUTT D. *Training costs with reference to the Industrial Training Act.* Gee and Company Ltd, 1969.

HALL N. *Cost effective analysis in industrial training.* Manchester Monographs No. 6. Manchester, University of Manchester, 1976.

HMSO. White Paper *Training for jobs.* HMSO, 1984.

INDUSTRIAL SOCIETY. *Survey of training costs.* New Series No.1. London, The Industrial Society, 1985.

INSTITUTE OF PERSONNEL MANAGEMENT. *A positive policy for training and development.* London, Institute of Personnel Management, 1983.

JONES J A G and Moxham J. 'Costing the benefits of training'. *Personnel Management*. Vol 1. No. 4, 1969.

JONES J A G. *Training intervention strategies – making more effective training interventions*. ITS Research Monograph No. 2. London, Industrial Training Service Ltd., 1983.

KEARSLEY G. *Costs, benefits & productivity in training systems*. London, Addison-Wesley, 1982.

KING D. *Training within the organization*. London, Tavistock Publications, 1964.

LATHROPE K. 'Stop your workforce standing still'. *Personnel Management*, October, 1985.

LOCAL GOVERNMENT TRAINING BOARD. *Training and development of training officers*. Training recommendation No. 17. Luton, Local Government Training Board, 1976.

MANPOWER SERVICES COMMISSION. *Training of trainers. First report of the Training of Trainers Committee*. London, HMSO, 1978.

MANPOWER SERVICES COMMISSION. *Direct trainers. Second report of the Training of Trainers Committee*. London, HMSO, 1980.

MANPOWER SERVICES COMMISSION. *Glossary of Training Terms*. 3rd edition. London, HMSO, 1981.

MANPOWER SERVICES COMMISSION. *A new training initiative: an agenda for action*. Sheffield, Manpower Services Commission, 1981.

NICHOLSON B. 'Managing change in education and training'. British Association for Commercial and Industrial Education Journal. March/April, 1985.

PEPPER A D. *Managing the training and development function*. Aldershot, Gower, 1984.

PETTIGREW A M, JONES G R, and REASON P W. *Organizational and behavioural aspects of the role of the training officer in the UK chemical industry : a research study in two phases*. Chemical and Allied Products Industry Training Board, 1981.

PETTIGREW A M, JONES G R, and REASON P W. *Training and development roles in their organizational setting*. Sheffield, Manpower Services Commission. 1982.

PRESTON F. *The Times*. 6th March, 1985.

REDDIN W J. 'Training and organizational change'. *British Association for Commercial and Industrial Education Journal*, March, Vol. 2, No. 1. 1968.

RODGER A, MORGAN T, and GUEST D. *A study of the work of industrial training officers*. Staines, Air Transport and Travel Industry Training Board, 1971.

SEYMOUR W D. *Industrial training for manual operatives*. London, Pitman, 1954.

SEYMOUR W D. *Skills analysis training*. London, Pitman, 1966.

SINGER E J. *Effective management coaching*. London, Institute of Personnel Management, 1979.

TALBOT J P and ELLIS C D. *Analysis and costing of company training*. Aldershot, Gower, 1969.

TAYLOR N. *Selecting and training the training officer*. London, Institute of Personnel Management, 1966.

TRAINING SERVICES AGENCY. *An approach to the training of staff with training officer roles*. Sheffield, Training Services Agency, 1977.

TRESSELL R. *The ragged-trousered philanthropists*. London, Panther Books, 1984.

WOODWARD N. 'A cost benefit analysis of supervisor training'. *Industrial Relations Journal*, Summer Vol. 6, No. 2, 1976.

3: Assessing organizational training needs

INTRODUCTION

If an organization is to achieve its goals it must have sufficient numbers of people with the appropriate expertise. The training function's strategic contribution to corporate goals is to help provide these 'vital' skills, knowledge and attitudes. In this chapter we explain how training needs analysis at a corporate or organizational level is a critical step in this process. We show that training needs exist at different levels within organizations and we consider a variety of approaches to identifying organizational training needs. We give examples of the reasons why top management decide to investigate training needs at a corporate level, and we illustrate the stages in carrying out an organization-wide training needs review. As Jones (1983) has pointed out, carrying out such an analysis is a form of training intervention which may be welcomed by some parts of the organization and resisted by others.

TRAINING NEEDS

A retailing company suffered bad publicity due to press and TV coverage of unfortunate incidents in some of its branches. In a number of cases the company's employees were alleged to have had a very poor attitude towards customers' requests for after-sales service. The chairman called for an urgent investigation. The subsequent report accepted the criticisms but showed that in almost every case the employees concerned were of a reasonable standard.

They were achieving sales targets but due to work pressures in the branches the employees were giving a low priority to after-sales problems. The chairman recognized that as an organization there had been insufficient attention paid to the importance of after-sales service and that this weakness must, as a matter of priority, be addressed both by management directives and training. The training officer was instructed to take immediate action. He worked with line management in reviewing and amending, as necessary, the job specifications of staff, and then provided training for those employees who were assessed by their managers to require it.

This case illustrates that training needs, as Boydell (1983) has suggested, can be said to exist:

- *at the organizational level*; there was an identified general weakness in the way in which the organization had perceived its priorities (after-sales service was inadequate) which training could ameliorate: the organization needed to improve its standard of customer service.
- *at the job or occupational level*; there was recognition that the company needed certain groups of employees to achieve improved performance: a number of jobs had to be redefined in terms of skills, knowledge and attitudes required to meet the new standards set by the chairman.
- *at the individual employee level*; the present abilities (skills, knowledge and attitudes) of each member of staff concerned with customer service had to be assessed against the higher standards now needed to carry out their work satisfactorily, and any shortfall remedied through training.

In Chapter 6 we explain that when applying a planned training approach to an individual or to a group of employees it is very important first to identify the standards of skills, knowledge and attitude required in a job and then to assess where present competence falls short of that required, i.e. clarify the training 'gap'. These two processes should be carried out as accurately as possible because the results provide the data from which the training programme is developed. The subsequent training can be no better than the quality of the analysis permits. In Chapter 6 we describe the techniques available for analysing jobs for training purposes (typically the first step in many training interventions) and for assessing the training needs of individuals: this same logic applies when seeking to identify needs, at a sectional, a departmental or organizational level.

TRAINING NEEDS – ORGANIZATIONAL REVIEWS

Alternative approaches

For many companies their first involvement with training-needs identification stemmed from contact with their Industry Training Board. The latter provided its in-scope companies with a preferred method of determining what training was needed: this was usually supplied through a global approach. Applied in its extreme form, the training officer, in a somewhat mechanistic way, would analyse every job category in the organization from the least skilled to (in theory) that of the managing director and record on training specification forms the skill, knowledge and attitude requirements. The logic behind the exercise was that in an organization unfamiliar with the benefits of planned training every job could, in principle, be performed more effectively if the standard of performance and the skill, knowledge and attitude required to achieve this standard were specified. Each employee could be assessed against this specification, and training provided where a shortfall was identified. Thus the organization's efficiency would be, it was argued, improved.

The commercial logic of adopting a global approach may have seemed to be persuasive to some companies, particularly in the context of the levy-grant arrangements introduced under the Industrial Training Act 1964, but in many cases the approach was pursued without adequate discrimination. This resulted in the production of a mass of paperwork much of which was never used, partly because training resources were not available but more importantly because the assumption that training would bring about significant improvement in the work performance of every employee was not always valid. Moreover, the cost of undertaking such an exhaustive exercise was very considerable, especially in larger organizations.

These criticisms should not be taken to mean that a global approach is never an appropriate strategy for an organization to adopt in identifying its training needs, although it is very difficult to imagine circumstances in which the excessively mechanistic approach described above could be justified. A global approach, if used with discretion, can be a necessary strategy to obtain data about training needs when, for example, introducing or re-introducing planned training into an organization. The reader should note that the approach may be used differentially, that is, applied in a very detailed way in one section or department and not at all in others. For this reason and because the processes involved provide a good illustration of 'the most difficult case', we describe below the stages in a global training-needs investigation.

An alternative and often more appropriate strategy is the 'critical incident' or 'priority problem' approach, illustrated by the retailing company case quoted above. In this model the objective is not to produce a comprehensive list of every possible training need but to identify and document those problems which have a training solution and which have emerged as priorities when viewed from an organizational standpoint. The whole process, and in particular the determination of priorities, is constrained by realistic cost and budget considerations.

It should be noted that, in practice, the scope and effectiveness of a needs analysis is determined largely by the level of support it receives from management. The reader should also appreciate that differing types of review require different authority status and technical competence. For example, the analytical and interpersonal skills, and the level of authority necessary to identify the training requirements of semi-skilled work arrangements to be changed as a result of a modified production process would normally be within the competence of a junior training officer. An organization-wide review of management training needs could only be undertaken by a training officer who is a member of the senior management team and who has access to confidential information, including performance appraisal details and promotion plans.

The diagnosis of training needs on an organizational scale requires high order analytical, evaluation and communication skills. Talbot and Ellis (1969) make the point that:

> the provision of mere routine training answers to traditional problems will not be sufficient. The requirement is for a much more extensive diagnostic skill which looks beyond the learning processes of individuals and of groups and assesses the impact of this on the business needs for growth and adjustment.

Over and above the routine techniques described later, the training officer must know how and when to enlist the help of other specialists, such as manpower planners or systems analysts, in predicting training and retraining needs. He must also be able to take a fresh view of the organization and see what effect its structure, policies and practices have on the optimum use of its employees' abilities. To what extent, for example, does the organization provide promotion plans, career paths or job opportunities within and across departments, and what training is, or should be, available to help staff move along these paths? He must be able to propose training priorities and assist in the development of policies which are likely to make the best use of the organization's human resources (see Chapter 4). He must be sensitive to possible differences between his and other managers' perceptions of problems and recognize that opposition to his proposals may be both covert and overt. In addition to being technically competent the training officer has to be acceptable as a person to top management and to the management hierarchy in general. Without this, he would lack the personal authority necessary to complete the review satisfactorily and the chances of his recommendations being implemented would be reduced.

The training officer must be prepared to handle difficulties which he will from time to time uncover when carrying out a review. Internal politics, personality clashes between managers, bad discipline in a department, are examples of problems which may not have training solutions but do have implications for the trainer. As we explain in Chapter 5, training activities are interventions in a continuing learning process that takes place in all organizations, and for training to be effective, account must be taken of the organizational climate. There is no one way of handling these types of situations but the training officer is advised to keep to his brief impartially and diplomatically. At the same time he must not ignore the fact that these problems exist and that they may create a hostile attitude to training.

REASONS FOR ORGANIZATIONAL REVIEWS

The following examples illustrate the occasions when training needs have to be identified at the level of a section, a department or a whole organization.

Establishment of a training department

An organization which has appointed a training officer for the first time will be aware of some of its training requirements; it rarely possesses all the information necessary to formulate an appropriate training policy and plan of action (see Chapter 4). In these circumstances the new training officer would expect to carry out a training audit to assess the strengths and weaknesses of the present training policies and activities and to find out how training can be more effective. Whether the review is organization-wide or limited to, say, the production departments (if they are considered by top management to be the top priority), will in practice depend on the training officer's terms of reference. If he has responsibility for training throughout the organization, an overall assessment is likely to be necessary although it may be completed over a period of time. For the training officer with a more restricted responsibility, this initial assessment would be correspondingly less comprehensive.

As we shall see later, in carrying out an organizational review the training officer will discuss a range of issues with line and other staff managers. This review gives him an opportunity to explain and clarify his roles and responsibilities. Similar comments can apply when a new training officer is appointed to an existing department.

In general, the new training department's priorities are to meet immediate training needs. When these are under control, the department can turn its attention from the present training needs to those of the future.

Corporate planning and longer term training needs

Organizations monitor trends in the demand for their goods or services and attempt to forecast possible threats and opportunities which would affect their survival or growth. These forecasts should take account of critical factors such as economic conditions, government policies including possible legislation, financial constraints, anticipated market changes, competitors' activities, technological developments, investment programmes, new products or services planned, and personnel issues. Data from these sources are used to construct possible future operating scenarios which the top management evaluate in deciding the organization's future policies and strategies. Human resource planning ('a strategy for the acquisition, utilization, improvement and retention of an enterprise's human resources', Manpower Services Commission 1981), should play an important part in these processes, although the reader should be aware that there is often a considerable gap between what should happen in theory and what actually happens in practice.

Human resources specialists help to develop the scenarios and offer advice to top management when the organization's strategies are being formulated. The staffing implications of the agreed policies and strategies have to be translated into operational plans by the training and personnel officers working in consultation with line managers. The organization's anticipated manpower profile, expressed in numbers of staff by occupational category and by skills and knowledge required, is then compared with the existing workforce, and after making adjustments for retirement and other anticipated staff losses, surpluses and shortages of staff are identified. This is the first step in developing a comprehensive human resource plan for the organization which, by co-ordinating recruitment and training, retraining, career development and other personnel responsibilities, will help to ensure that appropriately trained and experienced staff are available when required. For a detailed discussion of human resource planning, see Bramham (1982).

Preparing the training budget and plan

A training officer reviews the organization's training requirements annually in order to prepare his proposed budget and training plan for the following year. The preparation process will include a problem-solving approach to the identification of training needs which is achieved by discussions with the directors and the heads of all departments.

Working within the financial guidelines for preparing the next year's budget, the training officer uses the results of his review to produce a draft training plan. This is a statement of intent which shows how his department, in co-operation with others, proposes to meet the specific training objectives required by the company's manpower plan. The draft will specify what has to be achieved, how it will be done, whom it will affect, what benefits will accrue to whom, and what financial expenditure will be required (see Chapter 4).

A major change in an organization's activities

Training plays a major organizational role in preparing people to be more ready to accept change and, when a specific change is on its way, to equip the staff concerned with the expertise they will need to do the new work expected of them.

Profound changes or discontinuities which affect the whole of an organization present formidable challenges to the training function as, for example, in the case of the privatization of a nationalized industry. A lower order but still powerful challenge is presented by a major change to the way part of an organization operates, for example when a decentralized computer-based management information system is introduced.

Another example of a major operational change and its training implications is when an airline decides to buy a new type of aircraft. New skills, knowledge and perhaps attitudes will be needed by some of its pilots, navigators, maintenance engineers, marketing and sales staff and, in varying degrees, by other employees. The successful introduction of the new aircraft will depend in part upon all the staff concerned being trained to undertake the new tasks required of them. The training implications which flow from the decision to buy the new aircraft have to be identified if the changeover problems are to be minimized and if the benefits of the decision are to be gained at the earliest possible stage. Policies, priorities, costs, and schedules of training must be determined and co-ordinated at an organizational level and, eventually, detailed training programmes prepared. In tackling this kind of problem there are advantages to be gained by adopting a systems perspective of training, as described in Chapter 1, i.e. the airline is viewed as a total system and as a series of sub-systems which interact with each other. Working with and using data obtained from planning and senior line management, the training officer examines in turn the list of the activities which will be undertaken by each function, how each function will interact with other parts of the airline (the boundaries of the sub-systems) and with the external environment. The training officer clarifies where specific and common training will be needed and prepares a schedule of priorities, sequences of training programmes, costings, etc.

Training audits

An audit of existing staff's knowledge, attitudes or skills in a particular facet of their work is another example of an organization-wide training-needs analysis. Such an analysis may be undertaken for a variety of reasons such as an industrial relations audit (Jennings and Undy 1984) or a discrimination audit (see page 179).

'Displaced' training needs

Problems which stem from inadequate training can often be attributed to other causes and not recognized by management as training needs. For example, an investigation into the backlog of work in the accounts department of a rapidly-expanding company showed that the root of the trouble was not, as the chief accountant had claimed, a shortage of staff, but a deterioration in the calibre of accounts clerks which the company had employed. Previously, the recruitment position in the area had been favourable and new employees had not needed formal training. When the labour market was tighter less able staff were recruited and still no attempt was made to train them. The newcomers were eventually able to learn how to do the work (without training) but this took time and in the process they made many more mistakes than their predecessors.

As a further illustration, newsagents were frequently complaining that they did not receive delivery of an evening newspaper in time to sell all the copies. An investigation found that the delay was due to the editorial department being so keen to have their news hot from the press that they only released copy to the composing room at the very last minute and the paper was therefore late in leaving the printers. The problem was resolved by the editorial staff having some work experience in the composing room, so enabling them to understand the compositors' difficulties.

Incorrectly-identified training needs

A training officer should approach an assessment objectively and with an open mind. He should not be unduly influenced by the assumptions which management and others may make about the cause of a problem and how it should be solved. On occasions he will find that a difficulty which was presented to him as being caused by lack of training is in fact not a training problem. For example, the training officer in a civil engineering company was asked to prepare a training programme for supervisors in the sub-contracting department. On investigation he found that the supervisors' apparently inadequate performance was caused by the irregular flow of work into the department. The problem was an organizational one and could not be solved by supervisory training.

In Chapter 5, we argue that training may be likened to a game of skittles in that aiming at one target can lead to repercussions elsewhere. For example, as mentioned above, apparent poor performance by one group of people may indicate training needs in an entirely different part of the organization. It is therefore necessary to obtain and analyse all relevant facts; hasty conclusions leading to incorrect training priorities could make the situation worse by frustrating those who are already working under difficulties beyond their control.

Partial training needs

A training officer's help is often sought in tackling such problems as reducing customers' complaints about the quality of goods or removing bottlenecks in a production department: the assumptions being that the employees concerned have not been trained to do their jobs correctly. While this could be the case, an investigation might show that inadequate training is only partly responsible for the poor quality of work or slow working: the major causes may be poor supervision, discontent over pay, or recruitment of unsuitable employees. The training officer has to distinguish between those problems which are wholly or partly due to ineffective training and are therefore likely to have training solutions, and those which result from non-training factors for which other answers must be found.

Satisfying statutory requirements

Organizations, their executives and employees are variously affected by both new and long-standing statutory obligations. Ignorance of the law is no defence for failure to comply with it. Nor are an organization's legal obligations necessarily met by a once and for all training intervention. For example, Donnelly and Barrett (1981), in a survey of the effects of the Health and Safety at Work etc. Act, found that although substantial safety training had taken place in the companies surveyed, 'some managers and employees were reluctant to tolerate safety training where it was deemed to endanger profitability'. It is clear that the training function has a continuing role to play in helping to ensure improved compliance with legislation and this can be achieved by the training officer having a checklist of statutory responsibilities which he uses in reviewing training needs for a department or for the organization as a whole. Such a list would include the following areas: health and safety; industrial relations; worker participation; race relations; and sex discrimination.

Health and safety. The Health and Safety at Work etc. Act 1974, specifies that it is the duty of every employer to provide:

> such information, instruction, training and supervision as necessary to ensure, as far as is reasonably practicable, the health and safety at work of his employees (Part I Section 2).

Subsequent sections of the Act are concerned with a written statement of policy on health and safety and the 'arrangements' (which presumably include training) for its implementation, together with the appointment in 'prescribed cases' of employee representatives and safety committees. The philosophy of the Act is clearly supportive of employee participation and consultation and this has training implications. For a more detailed discussion of the training implications of this Act, see Howells and Barrett (1975).

It must be emphasized that Part I Section 2 of this Act (quoted above) mentions the provision of supervision. It is generally recognized that safety training must be an integral part of a company's training schemes and must be included in programmes for supervisors and managers as well as in induction courses and in operator training. School leavers are particularly at risk and require special attention. The problems associated with Youth Training Scheme trainees are relevant here. (For an excellent publication on safety training, see Iron & Steel Industry Training Board 1976.)

Industrial relations. The inept handling of relatively minor problems by supervisors and managers unaware of the law can lead to major industrial relations issues. Furthermore, if a case is brought against an organization at an industrial tribunal, it is extremely damaging if top management cannot support the actions of their subordinates. Similarly, bad publicity for an employer results from cases of unfair dismissal which are often brought to tribunals, the former employee alleging that he was given inadequate training. In addition to a knowledge of the relevant laws, skill in devising the procedures necessary to comply with it and training in company policies and practices, as well as in union agreements, are necessities.

Worker participation. A policy of increasing worker participation within an organization has training implications of which the most obvious is the training of employee representatives. The Employment Protection (Consolidation) Act 1978 places the employer under a legal responsibility to allow trade union officers time off with pay during working hours to take part in industrial relations training relevant to their duties. There have been considerable developments in shop steward training, particularly that sponsored by the TUC. The large number of shop stewards and the comparatively high rate of turnover indicate the extent of this problem. Important as this training is, however, it is only one aspect of an enormous training need. Participation can only be truly successful where the organizational climate is suitable and in some cases this could be the consequence of a far-reaching programme of organization development in which training would play a most important role. Effective participation involves numerous managerial and supervisory skills and in some cases genuine attitude change, as well as a certain amount of education of the whole workforce so that they can make a fair appraisal of the work of their representatives. None of this can be achieved overnight. The training officer should be aware of these trends when considering organizational training needs.

Race relations. The harmful results of failure to deal effectively with major issues in this field are becoming increasingly apparent. Training will not solve such problems in an organization but it has an important contribution to make. Awareness of the special needs of particular groups of workers is likely to be achieved most effectively when they are included as an integral part of the organization's training plans for managers, supervisors and other employees. There are obvious needs relating to job-centred training. The Race Relations Act, 1976, encourages positive action (it is not a legal requirement) to promote the entry of racial groups into new areas of work by stipulating that the employer or trade union can provide training facilities exclusively for a particular racial group to fit them for work in which they are under-represented. For examples of positive action projects in this field, see Prashar (1983). Another important aspect is induction to the organization and to the trade union, including knowledge of all relevant procedures. This training can help to prevent the painful consequences that may otherwise arise from later misunderstandings. Language teaching may be necessary and there is evidence that such programmes must be supported by the indigenous English-speaking population and related to shopfloor practices. For a discussion of the advantages and costs of language training, see Carby and Thakur (1977). Race relations audits have shown that ethnic minorities tend to be under-represented in more senior posts and point to the necessity for improved opportunities and training for career development.

Advice on problems ranging from provision of language training to courses for managers and shop stewards can be obtained from the Race Relations Employment Advisors at the Department of Employment's Regional Offices. The National Centre for Industrial Language Training has an information service, a centre with audio-visual materials and staff training programmes.

Sex discrimination. Organizations have a legal responsibility to comply with the requirements of the Sex Discrimination Act 1975. For example, discrimination (as defined in the Act) in recruitment or in the treatment of existing employees is unlawful. As in the case of the race relations legislation, an organization should ensure that its managers and supervisors understand their obligations in this field, and, where necessary, they should also ensure that appropriate training is provided.

CARRYING OUT AN ORGANIZATION-WIDE REVIEW

We have seen that the reason for reviewing an organization's training and development needs is to provide objective data about the training investments required, in the short and/or longer terms, to meet the corporate goals. Thus the review provides top management with professional advice on human resource development and enables them to decide the nature and extent of the role of training in the achievement of corporate objectives. Top management's decisions determine the operational training policies and plans for the organization.

The organization's corporate policies and plans set the context within which the review takes place. The review comprises:

- the identification, at all levels in the organization, of the certain and probable needs for training;
- a critical review of this data;
- the submission of a report which sets out the priority training and development issues and recommends action plans, supported by cost estimates.

Figure 3.1 shows the sequence which a training officer might follow in reviewing training needs at the level of an organization. The main stages are as follows.

Step 1
Preparation for the review

↓

Step 2
Collection of data and initial interpretation

↓

Step 3
Detailed interpretation of data and development of recommendations

↓

Step 4
Preparation for implementing the recommendations

Figure 3.1
Stages in identifying organisational training needs

Stage 1: preparation for the review

The importance of preparation as a key to the success of a training-needs investigation cannot be overstressed. The training officer must prepare himself by ensuring that he has a clear brief, specifying the precise objectives for the exercise. This brief should cover the scope, objectives, and the time horizon of the review, the degree to which it is confidential, the authority which the training officer is given for access to relevant information, when the results are required and the person to whom the final report is to be sent. In deciding what essential investment in training must be made, the training officer must constantly bear in mind the organization's goals.

When the objectives of the review have been clarified, the training officer's next step is to ensure that all employees who are likely to contribute to it are informed. This is necessary for three reasons. First, the training officer relies on the co-operation of managers and others to help him carry out the review. It is, therefore, important that the purpose of the investigation, and how and when he proposes to carry it out, are fully discussed in advance with the appropriate staff. He should, for example, make it clear that the review is *not* part of an organization and method or work measurement exercise. This initial activity has an important part to play in the formation of attitudes and will help determine the acceptability of any resultant training activities.

Secondly, during the investigation the training officer asks searching questions. These can cause adverse reactions from some employees who may adopt a less than co-operative attitude if, as can easily happen, they misconstrue the training officer's intentions. This is particularly likely if the organizational climate is unsettled. A review taking place soon after a company has been taken over, or during an industrial dispute, may well run into difficulties which are not of the training officer's own making. Even if the organizational climate is generally favourable, he should nonetheless explain the purpose of the review to the staff concerned and obtain their co-operation. Training needs are often weak spots in an organization and those concerned tend to be sensitive when questioned about them, especially if they regard the investigation as implied criticism.

A third reason for a training officer advising those involved of the impending review is that, given advance notice, they can collect the information which the training officer will require from them, for example up-dating job specifications or organization charts, where available, and by preparing labour turnover statistics. This can save everyone a great deal of time.

Finally in this first stage, the training officer has to decide where to initiate the investigation. The most appropriate starting point in any given case depends upon many variables, such as staff availability, the purpose of the investigation, the personal choice of the assessor and the degree to which line management is prepared to co-operate.

An organization chart showing the relationships of different departments and the formal lines of responsibility is a useful document for the training officer, but it is important to remember that these charts often show much less information than may at first be apparent. To be of value they must be up-to-date and indicate, where possible, the real areas of responsibility and lines of communication, not just those of the formal organization. If, as is often the case, no chart exists, the training officer may have to draw up his own as he progresses with the review. The data shown on such a chart must be continually cross-checked against the perceptions of other managers.

Stage 2: collection of data and its initial interpretation

Although, in theory, information has first to be collected before it is interpreted, in practice it is artificial to separate these two processes, as they tend to take place simultaneously. The training officer interprets the facts and opinions that he gathers about the organization as he records them, at times seeking more detail and at others deciding further information is not required. Later (Stage 3) he evaluates the data more critically in relation to the broader picture which has emerged.

In the process of collecting information for the review, the training officer will also receive comments on current and former training policies and interventions. Whether this feedback is agreeable to him or not, the perceptions which his clients have of the training department's services must be taken into consideration when helping to formulate the organization's training plan. The amount of support which line managers are prepared to give to the training function will certainly influence top management's decision as to the resources which will be made available for his department. Organizations are always faced with the problem of competing claims for limited resources. The training officer must secure as much support as he can for his function and the most effective way of achieving this is to argue a case which has wide support within the organization. His case must therefore be based on acknowledged training priorities, the rationale for these priorities must be explicitly expressed, and alternative strategies, for example job redesign or the recruitment of ready-trained employees, shown to be less cost-effective than training solutions.

Methods of collecting information

Depending on the focus of the investigation, the training officer might obtain information by:

- reference to policy statements on marketing, production, staffing, etc.;
- analysing minutes of management meetings;
- selecting data from departmental records such as personnel statistics, accident records, training reports, and staff appraisal forms;
- formal and informal interviewing;

- questionnaire surveys;
- discussions with the training committee, which can provide information on training requirements and the priority areas;
- direct observation of work as he proceeds with the review.

The training officer often has to ferret out information, since it is not necessarily available in the form in which he needs it. For example, job specifications prepared for recruitment purposes are useful but are, at best, only a starting point for any job training analysis (see Chapter 6).

Sources of information

There is no one correct sequence to follow in collecting relevant data. The following are likely to be the main information sources: external influences, top management, personnel department, other service departments, departmental managers and their staff and trade unions.

External influences

An organization's training needs are directly influenced by the external environment. The demand for its goods or services provides the *raison d'etre* for the organization's existence and any changes in demand can have a considerable impact on the training function. The reduction or discontinuation of apprentice recruitment in a recession can have a major effect on a training department, while a policy of non-replacement when staff leave eliminates the need for induction and initial job training. Conversely, an increase in demand for the organization's goods or services can lead to an expansion of training activities, especially if competitors' requirements for skilled staff are also increasing and the supply of skilled staff is limited.

Changes in technology can also have a profound influence on training activities, particularly if the organization has a policy of retraining its staff when jobs become redundant. For example, Holland (1984) has drawn attention to changes in job skills which can be expected when a company introduces a computer-integrated manufacturing system, (see Figure 3.2).

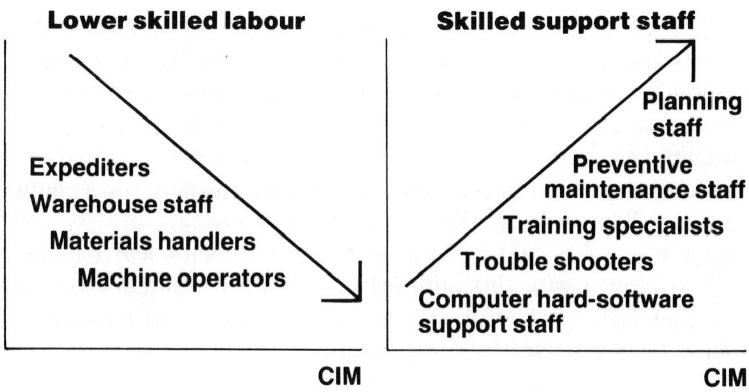

Figure 3.2
The effect that computer integrated manufacture will have on the nature of the workforce. (Reproduced, with permission, from Holland (1984).)

Top management

The training officer should begin the investigation by discussing with each of the directors their objectives and the human resource problems likely to emerge in meeting them. However, an organization's objectives are not always clearly defined nor will they necessarily be fully disclosed to the training officer. If senior management does not supply him with strategic information about the company's present and future operations, the validity of the review will be in doubt. Without this information the training officer would have no objective means of assessing the significance of the data collected, no certain basis for determining priorities and other training recommendations, and therefore no satisfactory way of measuring the standards and effectiveness of existing and future training.

Furthermore, if the organization's goals have not been clarified it is possible that the company's structure is inappropriate and that operating problems may occur because managers are unknowingly working to different ends. This can give rise to situations where training is apparently being applied successfully to remedy a problem: in reality it is only a palliative which treats the symptoms of a problem while its cause, for example an out-dated policy, remains unaltered.

The training officer must therefore obtain from top management indications of any anticipated variations in the business such as technical, product or market changes, future capital expenditure, or predicted adjustments in the labour force. These variations have training implications if they result in a demand for new expertise, or an increased requirement from existing staff categories, e.g. multi-skilling. The training officer records these changes in detail and notes when they will be implemented, their scope and estimated effect. Armed with this information, he will be able to assess the relevant factors when discussing training needs with managers of departments affected by these changes.

Personnel department

The training officer must be familiar with the organization's personnel policies, practices and plans. Recruitment, selection procedures, employee relations, remuneration, promotion policies and training are interdependent and therefore relevant to the investigation. A personnel department can supply valuable information, including job descriptions, job specifications, recruitment plans, the industrial relations climate, bonus payment and assessment systems and promotion policy. In addition, it can provide employee statistics of three main kinds: labour turnover, length of service of leavers, age distribution, all by department and section. These statistics are of great importance in an organization-wide review and are illustrated on page 88.

Labour turnover. Labour turnover statistics are of significance to the investigation because where there is a high turnover of new staff there is also likely to be a substantial need for induction and job training for recruits. An investigation of the reasons for high turnover of labour may reveal that it is caused by inadequate training or by non-training problems. The organization may need to solve some of the latter problems, such as low wages or inadequate supervision. If it fails to do so, a disproportionately heavy expenditure on training is the penalty.

Organizations sometimes find that the cause of a high labour turnover lies outside their control. An example of this is the employment of computer programmers in central London, where the demand for programmers is far greater than the supply. Thus, in spite of attractive salaries and work conditions, it is quite common for these staff to leave within a year. Faced with this situation, the training officer might recommend the introduction of training, having decided that the costs of providing it would be outweighed by the benefits. Staff turnover may not be significantly reduced by training new employees but it would help ensure that they would be more productive sooner. If the average length of service of the programmers was a year and, without formal training, they took three months to be fully productive, they would give on average only nine months' productive work before they left. If, with a planned training approach learning times were reduced to about a month, even though the new staff still left after approximately a year with the firm, then at least for 11 of these months they would be pulling their weight.

It should be noted that staff turnover as an index of labour instability is only valid if related to small, homogeneous groups of employees. When dealing with large numbers of staff, marked variations in labour turnover tend to be 'evened out' and their significance lost. Further caution is necessary in deciding what constitutes a 'high' or 'low' figure. Comparison should be made only with the same type of industry and area which have similar recruitment problems. For a helpful guide to the use of quantitative methods by managers, see Cuming (1984).

Length of service of leavers. As noted above, the absence or inadequacy of training in an organization can be a cause of labour turnover. An unstable workforce can be expected if staff are not trained correctly and find the work too difficult to learn unaided. The 'length of service of leavers' should be checked to determine whether, as in Figure 3.3, many staff have left within a short period of joining the firm. Even if the training officer finds this pattern in the figures, he should not automatically assume that inadequate training is to blame, as non-training reasons, such as poor selection or tight bonus times, may be the cause (see Laird 1978).

As with labour turnover figures, the training officer should initially regard leavers' length of service data as general indicators for further investigation. Finding out why employees leave is not easy. They are often reluctant to give the real reason and this kind of data can be misleading unless interpreted by experienced staff.

Age distribution. The purpose of an age distribution analysis, in this context, is twofold: to discover how many employees in a

	Length of service					
Job	Up to 3 months	4 to 8 months	9 to 23 months	2 to 5 years	Over 5 years	Total
Sales assistants	48	25	9	6	4	92
Section supervisors	–	3	2	2	1	8
Departmental heads	–	–	–	1	1	2
Buyers	–	1	–	2	4	7

Figure 3.3
'Length of service of leavers' data (takes over a one year period).

department or staff category fall within certain age groupings, and to interpret the training implications of any imbalances in the age structure.

A department may have a very young labour force, in which case both inexperience and staff mobility are likely to create considerable demands on training resources. Conversely, a department may be staffed largely by older employees, perhaps with a number of its key personnel approaching retirement. Figure 3.4 (office supervisors)

	Age range						
Job	Under 25	26-30	31-40	41-50	51-60	61-65	Total
Office supervisors	1	2	2	5	7	8	25
Senior clerks	–	3	3	2	1	–	9
Word processor operators	6	6	3	–	–	–	15
Typists	15	7	4	7	8	6	47
Clerks	32	26	20	17	18	15	128

Figure 3.4
Data showing 'Age distribution' by job category.

illustrates the latter position. The training officer should check that plans have been made to provide successors. An ageing workforce is not revealed by labour turnover statistics; on the contrary, a low staff turnover might appear to suggest that little training is required. The implications of continuing education may also be relevant. The training officer must therefore use both turnover and age distribution statistics in identifying an organization's training needs. A training officer normally has little difficulty in obtaining these various human resource statistics if the organization has a professional personnel department. His task is more difficult where no such department exists: the data have then to be extracted from pay and other records. This is much less satisfactory and usually results in incomplete and less useful information.

Other service departments

In medium and large companies there are usually other specialists from whom the training officer can obtain information. For example, the accounts, organization and methods, work study, quality control, and research and development departments all have data about the company's activities which can be of direct value to the training officer.

The accounts department may be able to provide such details as: training expenditure in the company, with a breakdown by department and the system of recording training costs (see Chapter 2). A review of company training, expressed in financial terms, provides the training officer with a valuable measure of the scale on which training is taking place. However, the level of expenditure must be carefully interpreted. For example, a department's high training costs may be due to either inefficient training or they may be fully justified; while low expenditure can either indicate inadequate training or little requirement for it.

The records in the organization and methods or the work study departments can be an important source of information for the review. Work procedures, job specifications and grades, training times and work standards all provide a clear picture of the structure and work of a department. Moreover, since these specialists are concerned with analysing existing work as well as implementing new systems, they can often suggest where training requirements already exist in the organization, and where in the future training is likely to be needed.

Similar help can be given by the quality control and research development departments. The former can provide quality standards for particular work and indicate where employees have difficulty in achieving these standards. Research and development staff will know of anticipated technological changes and when they are likely to be introduced in the company. They may also be able to predict some of the human resource implications of the proposed changes, such as the grades of employee that will be required in the future and the feasibility of retraining existing staff for new jobs, e.g. operators to undertake more highly skilled work associated with the introduction of higher technology.

The costs of unplanned training are often hidden but are usually well worth investigating, both to help 'sell' an improved scheme and to use as a yardstick in later evaluation. These costs can be expressed in inadequate equipment utilization, damage to equipment, high scrap levels, time taken by supervisors or others in instruction, lack of recruits and, as already mentioned, in staff turnover and length of training time.

Departmental managers and their staff

The training officer is by this stage well prepared to start the major part of the investigation: discussions with line management. Using the information already collected about the organization's current operations and its objectives he discusses the following questions with each departmental manager:

Present training arrangements in the department

- Who is responsible for training?
- What training has the nominee had to do this job?
- How much is training costing the department?
- What is the scope of the present training?
- What plans are there for training new and existing staff?
- Do these cover job and career training?
- Are these arrangements regarded as satisfactory?

Quality of present training

- Have training programmes been based on identified needs?

- Have training standards been established and, if so, on what basis?
- How are trainees assessed?
- What records of training are kept, and why?
- Are training resources adequate, and what is the basis for their allocation?

Departmental management's attitude to training

- Is the manager well-informed about the training in his department?
- Is he aware of the organization's training policies?
- Does he regard the policies as satisfactory?
- Has he developed his own departmental policy? For example, is it his practice to train staff to be able to do more than one job?
- Can senior management, or the training department, give him any further assistance?
- Are there any training problems which are particular to the department?

Future training requirements

- What future training needs have been recognized in the department?
- What plans have been evolved to meet them?
- Which requirements should have priority?
- What departmental and other resources will be required to meet these needs?

The training officer then interviews the junior managers and supervisors involved in day-to-day training who are therefore well-qualified to discuss the quality of existing arrangements and recommend improvements. The close involvement of junior managers and supervisors in training is vital. Their perception of training needs is often insightful and they are one of the organization's most important training resources. These discussions also give the training officer an opportunity to assess the managers' actual and potential performance as trainers.

Other employees who can help the training officer in his assessment are staff currently under training or who have recently completed their training. The consumer's point of view is often very illuminating!

Finally, the trade unions' attitude to and policies on training matters are important factors which must be considered by the training officer both during and after the review process.

Having collected data under these headings the training officer should have a comprehensive record for each department's present arrangements, its anticipated training needs and priorities and the resources required to meet them.

Stage 3: detailed interpretation of data and development of recommendations

At this stage in the identification of training needs, the training officer reviews the information he has collected and begins to analyse the results. He works through his assessment notes and assembles the material which is particularly relevant and disregards that which is now seen to be of marginal significance. At times, he will find gaps and discrepancies in his data necessitating a return to particular information sources. He attempts to weigh the relative importance of the training needs which have been identified, initially on a departmental basis and subsequently for the organization as a whole, bearing in mind that the only training which should be supported is that which is vital to help the organization achieve its objectives.

The ranking of training priorities is a difficult but important part of the review process. It is difficult because the training officer has to exercise judgement in deciding between different priorities although he is helped in his decisions by reference to criteria such as the terms of his brief, the organization's existing training policies, the availability of resources which particular training programmes will require and the benefits which they are expected to yield.

The ranking of training requirements is important because the organization's training budget is never large enough to meet every need. The training officer has, therefore, to synthesize his findings and express them as recommendations for action. His recommendations should satisfy the following criteria. They should be:

- clearly in support of the organization's objectives;
- consistent with the organization's training policies, or where policy changes are needed, reasons given;

- acceptable to senior management;
- justified, with supporting evidence of actual training needs listed in priority terms;
- feasible, in that the necessary resources are likely to be made available;
- costed and, if appropriate, they should indicate whether or not the proposed training is eligible for Manpower Services Commisson or other grant;
- practical and acceptable to those implementing and receiving the training;
- specific, in naming who would be responsible for implementing the training and when it is required.

These recommendations and the evidence on which they are based are normally contained in a report prepared by the training officer for top management. In writing the review report, the training officer bears in mind such points as: the initial and likely subsequent readers of his report; the use of confidential information collected during the review; how to express criticisms of managers who have apparently failed to train their staff; and the general principles of good report writing (see British Association for Commercial and Industrial Education 1981).

Stage 4: preparation for implementing the recommendations

When the review report is completed, the training officer still has two key tasks to perform. First, to follow up his recommendations and help to get them accepted within the company and, secondly, to see that they are implemented.

No experienced training officer assumes that all his assessment recommendations will be adopted. Some managers will accept the assessor's specialist advice enthusiastically and use the training department's services fully. Others will disagree with particular findings or recommendations, but will be open to persuasion if the training officer can substantiate his points with facts and figures. The apathetic manager, who superficially accepts the results of the assessment but takes no positive steps to implement them, is more difficult to win over.

The training officer should be prepared to spend a great deal of time discussing, persuading and marketing his services using the support of senior management, keen departmental managers, and the training committee. If the training officer does not carry his fellow managers with him, much of the value of a review will be lost. For further details on corporate training-needs identification, see Turrell (1980) and Walters (1983).

BIBLIOGRAPHY

BOYDELL T H. *A guide to the identification of training needs.* London, British Association for Commercial and Industrial Education, 1983.

BRAMHAM J. *Practical manpower planning.* London, Institute of Personnel Management, 1982.

BRITISH ASSOCIATION FOR COMMERCIAL AND INDUSTRIAL EDUCATION. *Report writing.* London, BACIE, 1981.

CARBY K and THAKUR M. *No problems here.* London, Institute of Personnel Management, 1977.

CUMING M. *A manager's guide to quantitative methods.* Kings Repton, Cambridge, Elm Publications, 1984.

DONNELLY E L and BARRETT B. 'Safety training since the Act'. *Personnel Management*, June, 1981.

HOWELLS R and BARRETT B. *The Health and Safety at Work Act, a guide for managers.* London, Institute of Personnel Management, 1975.

HOLLAND D. 'Strategic benefits from computer-integrated manufacture'. *The Production Engineer*, June, 1984.

IRON AND STEEL INDUSTRY TRAINING BOARD. *The management of health and safety.* Iron and Steel Industy Training Board, 1976.

JENNINGS S AND UNDY R. 'Auditing managers' IR training needs'. *Personnel Management*, February, 1984.

JONES J A G. *Training intervention strategies – making more effective training interventions.* ITS Research Monograph No. 2 London, Industrial Training Service Ltd, 1983.

LAIRD D. *Approaches to training and development*. Wokingham, Addison Wesley, 1978.

MANPOWER SERVICES COMMISSION. *Glossary of Training Terms*. Manpower Services Commission, HMSO, 1981.

PRASHAR U. 'Evening up the odds for black workers'. *Personnel Management*, June, 1983.

TALBOT J R and ELLIS C D. *Analysis and costing of company training*. Aldershot, Gower, 1969.

TURRELL M. *Training analysis: a guide to recognising training needs*. Plymouth. Macdonald and Evans, 1980.

WALTERS B in Guest D and Kenny T. eds, *A textbook of techniques and strategies in personnel management*. London, Institute of Personnel Management, 1983.

4: Training policies and resources

INTRODUCTION

In this chapter we consider the relationship between the training requirements of an organization and its training policies. We then examine how these two factors determine the content of a training plan and some of the typical resources that can be used to implement the plan.

TRAINING POLICIES

King (1964) has pointed out that the word 'policy' probably has its roots in the Greek word *polis*, meaning city – a term, which in classical times, conveyed notions of system, order and enforcement of laws. These ideas survive in our contemporary usage of the word 'police'. In a work context, a policy can be thought of as 'an expression of intention' which gives general guidance for the conduct of affairs. Thus an organization's policies for training and development establish the broad framework for its training plan. The plan in turn expresses the organization's priority training interventions and the strategies to be followed during a given period of time (see Chapter 7, and Guest and Kenny 1983).

An organization's philosophy towards the training and development of its employees is reflected in its policies: these policies govern the priorities, standards and scope of its training activities. All organizations have training and development policies: they may be explicit or implicit. Some policies are the outcome of a planned human resource management approach, others are reactive responses to requests and problems. Some are written, others not; some are regarded as being semi-confidential; others are promulgated to all staff. Some, where there is no organizational support for training, are negative; others a part of the reward system of the organization. Some apply only to certain job categories, others concern all employees. Some are enforced, others honoured more in the breach than in the observance.

Organizations develop training policies for four main reasons:

- to define the relationship between the organization's objectives and its commitment to the training function;
- to provide operational guidelines for management. For example, to state management's responsibilities for planning and implementing training and in particular to ensure that training resources are allocated to priority and statutory requirements (see Chapter 3);
- to provide information for employees. For example, to stress the performance standards expected, to indicate the organization's commitment to training and development, and to inform employees of opportunities for training and development;
- to enhance public relations. For example, to help attract high calibre recruits; to reassure clients and the public at large about the quality of the products (e.g. in pharmaceutical and food companies) or services (an airline's safety standards); or to project an image as a caring and progressive employer by taking part in government sponsored 'social' training programmes such as the Youth Training Scheme.

These four purposes overlap each other and are expressed in policy statements, in the organization's plans for training, and in the rules and procedures which govern training access and implementation.

A corporate policy statement which aims to influence the outside world tends to be couched in broad terms, such as 'We offer training as part of our equal opportunities programme' (see Equal Opportunities Commission 1985). Corporate policies which regulate internal action may be published as a 'free standing' policy document (see page 101) or included in the organization's training plan. Both typically include general statements of intent which set the corporate frame of reference for training and development activities, e.g. 'The Council will provide appropriate development opportunities for all its employees', and specific statements which define the organization's current priorities for training, for example,

'All managers and supervisors will attend a seminar on the Company's industrial relations procedures'.

Corporate training policies, applied at a department level, shape the line manager's action plan by specifying what training will be provided for which staff, when it will take place, and who will be responsible for ensuring its implementation. It is at this level that policy can form the important role of helping to ensure equality of opportunity as between employees working in different parts of the organization. For example, published policies such as 'Junior office staff should be encouraged to attend appropriate day release further education courses' or 'All employees within two years of retirement are entitled to attend pre-retirement courses' will limit the discretion which a manager might otherwise apply unfairly.

Before 1964, it was unusual for training policies to be written, let alone published (see King 1964). This was because management had not generally been sufficiently interested in planned training and because the expertise required to produce relevant policies was often lacking. Moreover, many top managements were cautious of 'publicly' committing themselves to policies which were untried and which they considered were better handled, at least initially, on a less formal basis. Many organizations produced written training and development policies as a result of Industrial Training Board requirements. Legislation, as we have noted in Chapter 3, obliges employers to provide a written policy on safety which, by implication, should include reference to training provisions.

Organizations have very different approaches to training. Some have policies designed to gain the maximum benefit from training; in contrast, many others have no planned training and do not accept significant responsibility for training. The majority lie somewhere between these two extremes, with policies which permit training which is variable in quality, limited in scope, and to a greater or lesser extent lacking in direction. In these circumstances priorities are determined on an *ad hoc* or reactive rather than a planned basis.

POLICY DEVELOPMENT

An organization's policies for training and development are influenced by variables such as:

- size, traditions and prevailing culture;

- products or services;
- economic and social objectives;
- obligations to provide professional updating (continuing) training, e.g. for nurses;
- top management's views on the value of training;
- availability of information about the organization's training needs;
- the labour market and the alternative means of acquiring skilled and qualified staff, other than by training;
- past and current training policies and practices;
- training experience of its managers;
- calibre of its specialist training staff;
- resources that can be allocated to training;
- expectations of employees and their representatives.

Training policies are more often determined by prevailing interest than principle and as such tend to be impermanent and susceptible to change. This applies whether or not an organization has adopted planned training. In the former situation, top management decide what contribution they want the training function to make in the achievement of the organization's objectives. Their decision provides the framework within which training policies and plans are determined.

In organizations where planned training has not been adopted, policies for training result from the unsystematic growth of decisions, rules and procedures introduced to deal with particular problems. These decisions are typically made on a piecemeal basis and, with the passage of time, may be accepted as precedents and become 'policy'. *Ad hoc* policy development of this kind can give rise to inappropriate emphases and inconsistencies in application in different parts of the same organization, particularly if changes in demand for skill and professional competencies occur over short periods of time. A thorough review of an organization's training policies is essential to assess the relevance of existing priorities, rules and procedures in relation to current organizational objectives.

Other reasons can prompt an organization to review its policies for training and development. These include: the availability of new methods of delivering training (see page 105); an unexpected demand for training caused, for example, by successful productivity bargaining (Chemical and Allied Products ITB 1970); new legislation (see page 77); the need for retraining stemming from fluctuations in trading; and changes in the work and role of particular groups of employees, e.g. maintenance engineering craftsmen (see Cross 1985).

An example of the effects on company manpower profiles, and therefore on their human resource policies, caused by competition and new technology is illustrated by manpower changes in the Scottish electronics industry described by Cassels (1985). While in the six years after 1978 the industry continued to employ broadly the same number of people, the relative proportions of those employed altered dramatically. There were increases of 94 per cent in the number of technologists and scientists in the industry, 26 per cent in the number of technicians, and 22 per cent in the number of managers. There were corresponding reductions in the numbers of craftsmen (9 per cent), administrative jobs (22 per cent), and of operators (18 per cent, but the greatest fall in absolute numbers). It can be seen that in a rapidly changing environment, training policies can quickly become out of date. Policy reviews are essential to ensure that training is helping to provide current and future skills and expertise required by the organization.

It is clearly essential for an organization to frame its policies so that they take account of potential problems and opportunities. Radical changes in organizational policies and objectives are more likely to secure wide suport and to cause minimal anxiety (for example, about job security) when an 'open' consultative approach is used.

Tavernier (1971) stresses the need for:

> any policy regarding training (to) be in harmony with the company's personnel policies on recruitment, salaries, promotion and security of employment.

Top management are responsible for deciding training policies, although the effectiveness of their decisions is likely to be increased if they have been based on consultation at all levels. The requirements of line management should be fully considered and, as we have argued in Chapter 2, the training officer should play an important part in this process. The trend in some organizations towards effective employee consultation and participation in top-level decision-making has led to the increased involvement of trade union and other employee representatives in the formulation of corporate training policies.

One of the achievements of the Industrial Training Boards was that they persuaded companies to develop and publish their training policy. Some training boards went further and required participation in the planning of training, e.g.

> the policy should contain provisions, appropriate to the company, for employees or their representatives to participate in formulating and evaluating training plans. (Clothing and Allied Products ITB 1977.)

There are obvious benefits in involving employees in this way, notably that top management's decisions are likely to be more effective if they are consonant with the values and expectations of the employees in the organization they direct.

For the reasons we have mentioned above, training policies vary with the approach and requirements of different organizations. The following is an example of a company's training policy statement:

> The Directors recognize the important contribution which training makes to the company's continuing efficiency and profitability. They further recognize that the prime responsibility for training rests with management. The Company Training Officer is responsible for advising and assisting all managers on training matters and is accountable to the Managing Director.
>
> The Company's training policy refers to all employees and aims to:

- provide induction training for new staff and for those transferred to new departments;
- ensure that appropriate training is available to enable individuals to reach and, through updating training, maintain satisfactory performance in their jobs;
- provide the training required by those selected for promotion so that they are appropriately prepared for their new responsibilities;
- provide information, instruction and training to ensure the health and safety of all employees.

There are a number of advantages to be gained from making the training policy widely known in the organization. This approach communicates top managements' intentions, defines the organization's responsibility for the development of the individual employee, helps those responsible for implementing training, clarifies the role and function of the training specialist, indicates in general terms the training opportunities available to employees and, if the contents are progressive, publication enhances employer – employee relationships. However, the success of a training policy is likely to be diminished if the 'public relations' element is overplayed or if the employees' expectations are not met. Employee resentment and, as a consequence, the possibility of more difficult problems, can result if an organization fails to honour the development opportunities promised in its published policies.

Writing a training policy is a task which requires considerable skill and attention to detail. The starting point is to clarify the reasons for introducing the policy and the objectives that the policy is designed to achieve. It is important that the staff categories to which the policy will apply are clearly stated. Account should be taken of any contingent precedents that may have been established either in a formal way or by custom and practice. Discussions with representatives of those who will be affected is an essential part of the process of drafting a policy statement. It is important that the policy is written in an acceptable style, that the statement is positive (avoid using negatives) and that it contains no ambiguities.

ANNUAL TRAINING PLAN

An organization's training plan should be a detailed and authoritative statement of the training which will be implemented over a given period. The plan results from a reconciliation of priority training needs, policies for training and development, and available resources, particularly budgets.

A range of requirements for training are identified prior to the preparation of the annual training budget and/or from a detailed investigation of the kind described in Chapter 3. These training needs should then be appraised against the criteria contained in the exisitng training policies: a process which may eliminate some requirements from the proposed plans. For example, a proposal from one departmental head for certain managers to attend a day-release Diploma in Management Studies course would not be included in the plan if there are to be no exemptions from a company's policy that staff over the age of 21 are not granted day release. In other cases, as we have seen above, it is the policies which have to be changed to meet the new conditions. Finally, training priorities have to be established by ranking, in order of importance, all the training requests received. The decision regarding what to include and what to exclude from the plan is made in the light of the resources available. For example, a company which has limited training resources but which is introducing an important new range of products in the coming year may have no option but to give a high priority to providing product training for its sales force, if necessary, at the expense of less urgent training in other fields, when such training can be postponed without serious repercussions.

A typical training plan should contain the following elements:

- Details on a calendar basis (monthly, quarterly, half yearly) of each department's training requirements by job classification and by number of employees involved, e.g. accounts department, four clerical staff (BTEC qualifications) and two supervisory staff (junior management course); laboratory, one technician (attachment to raw material supplier); production department, an estimated 25 operatives (induction and initial training) and four managers (computer applications course).
- Details on a monthly, quarterly, half yearly, etc. basis of the projected training for categories of staff not permanently allocated to a department (e.g. five Youth Training Scheme trainees, three graduate trainee managers).
- Specification, against each item of training, of the standard to be achieved, the person responsible for seeing that it is implemented, the training strategy to be used (e.g. self-development, on-the-job coaching, internal or external course), how much the training will cost, its duration, when it will take place, and its target completion date.
- A summary of the organization's and each department's budget allocation for training: this may be divided into training which is continuing and to which the organization is already committed, for example craft trainees who are part-way through their apprenticeships, and other training.

It should be noted that similar data can be collected and used to develop training plans of longer duration, e.g. two or three year rolling plans.

TRAINING RESOURCES

Managing learning resources

We explain in Chapter 7 that when a training officer recommends or chooses a training strategy to meet an identified need she strives to achieve the 'best fit' consistent with the learning objectives, the organization's policies, the trainee's preferences and the resources available. Training resources can be thought of as the input required to enable a training plan to be implemented. The range of resources that can be drawn upon by the training officer are considered later in this chapter and include people (e.g. the training officer herself), money (e.g. the training budget) and facilities (e.g. self-learning packages, a 'walk-in' open access resource centre, a training room). However, it is often not so much the resources themselves that achieve results but the skill with which they are managed.

Central to the success of a training officer is her function as a manager of learning resources. Her credibility and influence are enhanced when she is accepted as the focal point in the organization for advice and information about training activities (both internal and external), as the source of specialist knowledge and experience about learning in a work context; as the co-ordinator and monitor of the organization's training policies, plans and budgets, as a competent trainer; and as a successful (line) manager of the training department, its staff, the training centre and learning aids. It is through her contacts with top managers that the training officer benefits from the key resource of 'political' support for her activities. Thus a training officer depends upon a range of different kinds of resources.

For the reasons discussed in Chapters 1 and 2, the work of many training officers has been dominated by organizing and contributing to in-house courses and arranging attendance at external courses. The resources at their command are those required to carry out this restricted function, i.e. a limited training budget and a training room or area. As we indicate in Chapter 10, the Industrial Training Boards were responsible for encouraging the wider use of off-the-job training, but the pendulum swung too far and in recent years the benefits of structured on-the-job learning have been more widely recognized. This recognition has extended to both the techniques and, through the greater involvement of line managers, the range of resources which an organization can apply to planned training.

Work-based projects, job rotation, and coaching, are examples of activities which can result in effective learning of a kind which, by itself, classroom-based training cannot achieve.

The recognition that successful training does not have to take place in a training centre has been powerfully reinforced by the application of the new technologies to training and development. These technologies are having three main effects.

First, revolutionary methods of delivering training are being introduced as a result of the application of the new technologies to vocational training and education. Computers, video tape-recorders, interactive-video systems, and access to computerized data bases using modems and telephone lines, have greatly increased the choice and flexibility of learning systems available. Wherever there is a computer terminal there is a potential training resource.

Secondly, these applications of the new technologies are changing the perceptions which people have of training. As a result, effective training is no longer so widely perceived to be primarily a classroom-based activity and few would now hold the simplistic view that, to be trained, employees had to attend an in-house course. In the right circumstances the 'course strategy' (see page 204) remains a very important method of achieving training objectives.

Thirdly, the new technologies are opening up opportunities for employees who have in the past been 'disenfranchised' from training and educational programmes because they worked shifts (i.e. could not attend 'normal' courses on a regular basis), or worked in dispersed units or in small organizations, could not be released for training, or lived in an area without a local college. The new technologies have enabled the creation of sophisticated 'open learning' systems which make it possible for employees (and employers) to study at home, at work or wherever they wish; to embark on their studies when it is suitable for them (as opposed to the fixed enrolment date of an educational institution); to have access to a very wide range of courses, irrespective of where the learner happens to live, and to construct their own learning environment without having to cope with the 'going back to school' anxiety.

The trend to reduce what have come to be accepted as 'artificial' admission barriers to vocational education courses (for example, traditional and notional minimum or maximum age regulations) and the parallel trend to recognize that in some circumstances adults' 'life experience' and high motivation to learn can more than offset their not having 'A' levels, have also opened up training and development opportunities for the 'unqualified' person. This characteristic of open learning is of particular importance in helping less well qualified technical personnel to acquire improved qualifications in the context of serious shortages of skills in the new technology industries.

The Council for Educational Technology (1984) has pointed out that there is a wide variety of open learning systems. One of these is distance learning which, as its name indicates, enables the learner to acquire in a flexible way knowledge and skills which may or may not involve face-to-face tuition. Open learning systems have important implications for initial and updating training and for retraining of many categories of employee. The Open Tech Programme has concentrated its efforts in 'pump priming' open learning programmes for technicians and supervisors. Packages in export marketing and in management education and training, including masters degrees, are available via open and distance learning techniques.

Clearly the role and expertise of the training officer in influencing and evaluating these approaches to planned training are very different from those required for traditional in-house training activities. For example, the explosive increase in the number and variety of open learning programmes becoming available presents a major challenge for the training officer to give advice as to which is the most appropriate programme for a particular employee. The training officer has to be aware of, and able to access, information sources such as the Materials and Resources Information Service (MARIS), the computerized data base of open learning materials in areas related to the Open Tech's target users.

As we saw in Chapter 2, all training resources ultimately cost money and the training officer is responsible for advising on the best use of the available resources to facilitate learning. To do this she requires an up-to-date knowledge of the resources on which she can draw and how they can best be employed. In the remainder of this chapter we describe the three major categories of training resources: people, money and facilities.

People as a training resource

Line managers. We argue in Chapter 5, that line managers are probably an organization's most important training resource since most learning takes place in the day-to-day work situation.

Successful off-the-job training relies heavily upon the trainees being briefed by their managers prior to the training and being given support to transfer their learning to their work. Line managers' commitment to training is not only crucial to maximize the benefits of formal course training; it is also a powerful factor in creating and developing a climate which expects and supports training interventions as a normal part of organizational life. At an operational level, line managers, especially if they are good trainers, are an important source of lecturers for induction and other in-house programmes.

Training specialists. An experienced training officer is potentially one of the major contributors to her organization's training operation (see Chapter 2). The extent to which her skills and knowledge are put to profitable use depends in practice upon many variables, in particular upon her credibility, technical competence and the degree of co-operation which she receives from fellow managers.

Trainers. The role of trainers (or instructors) is discussed in Chapter 2. They act as the essential link between the learner and the training programme and include managers (when coaching their own staff), company tutors overseeing trainee technologists, craft apprentice supervisors and operator instructors.

Former trainees. Satisfied 'customers' are a training officer's best ambassadors in helping to create informed opinion about the training function. They can also be of great assistance in getting a new form of training accepted, such as adventure (outdoor) training (see Bank 1985), within an organization. Again, because of their experience of a former programme and in particular its subsequent value to them in their work, past 'trainees' can also often make helpful contributions as speakers or 'syndicate' leaders.

Money resources

Training budget. Many training activities depend upon the availability of finance: the preparation of a proposed expenditure budget is therefore a very important aspect of a training officer's job. An income budget will also have to be prepared where training services are provided for people outside the organization or where the training department receives income for undertaking projects such as those sponsored by the Manpower Services Commission (e.g. Open Tech) or the European Social Fund.

The content and size of the training budget depends on many factors. Of particular importance are how the organization views the training function, the level of its activity, and the training officer's tenacity in 'fighting her corner' when budgets are being finalized! The size of the budget varies from year to year, depending upon the profitability of the company or, in a public sector organization, upon government policy and funding. This is an added challenge for the training officer because training or retraining needs can be greatest when financial resources are at a premium. It is always necessary to plan well ahead and to assess the probable future requirements carefully so that whatever finance is available goes to the real, and acceptable, priorities.

While budgets vary from one organization to another, all require appropriate systems of forecasting the financial resources required for training and controlling the money which is allocated. Singer (1977) has specified certain main requirements of a budget and budgetary control in the training function. These are:

- adequate training plans;
- the expenses incurred in achieving the training plan must have been identified and estimated;
- the responsibility for items of expenditure must have been allocated between training specialists and other managers;
- account classifications must have been made so that expenditure can be allocated to specific cost areas;
- cost information must be recorded accurately and a mechanism for feeding back the collated information must be present so that individuals can take corrective action when required.

Internal training facilities

Off-the-job facilities. These include training centres or areas, which range from country mansions for management development programmes, to apprentice schools, to part of a shop, office or workshop set aside for training. The size and type of the facility depends on requirements and policy. We have already commented that self-learning training programmes which use computers (such as interactive video) can in principle take place wherever there is a terminal. Of increasing importance is the provision of in-house 'open access' learning centres where employees can, in work or in their own time, read, work through computer-based learning packages, watch videos, listen to tapes, etc.

Training aids. Writing in an Institute of Personnel Management booklet some 30 years ago, Davies (1956), urged speakers to use epidiascopes and lantern slides when addressing training courses! Technology has moved on in the intervening years and professional training staff must now be competent to use a wide range of learning aids such as: computers, closed-circuit television, overhead projectors and audio-visual materials. But as Powell (1981) has stressed, learning aids, if they are not to be regarded as gimmicks, must be chosen and used skilfully. For discussions on the changing fashions in training methods, see Huczynski (1984), and on the perceived validity of the choice of particular training methods, see Carroll (1972).

Company training information. An organization with a planned approach to employee development has a wide range of data covering its training operations, e.g. job descriptions and specifications, training programmes, employee's training histories, reports on training needs and training plans. This information bank is a useful asset in improving future programmes or reducing the time needed for job training analysis.

External training facilities

These can be grouped under six headings:

- private sector courses and consultants;
- group training schemes;
- professional associations;
- public sector education and training services;
- the Manpower Services Commission;
- trade union-run courses.

Private sector courses and consultants. Numerous organizations offer a wide and, at times, bewildering variety of courses on almost every aspect of training. Although these providers suffered during the recession, the reduction in the number and size of training departments has resulted in some cases in an increased demand for external courses. Selecting the right course is a difficult but important task for a training officer if her company is to benefit from what can be a very considerable financial outlay.

Nelson (1966) (see also page 196) has examined criteria for selecting training courses and proposes that an organization should ask the following questions when considering their use:

- Is it policy for the training need to be met by an external course?
- Is attending an external course acceptable to the trainee?
- Is the cost of the course related to its anticipated benefits?
- Has the course clearly defined objectives which can be realistically achieved in the time available?
- Do the instructional methods employed seem suitable to meet the objectives e.g. do they teach knowledge or skill?
- To what extent does the course content coincide with the organization's specific requirements?
- What experience and other qualifications do the course tutors possess?

Advice in choosing an appropriate course is also available from the information departments of organizations such as the Institute of Training and Development, the Institute of Personnel Management, the British Association for Commercial and Industrial Education, the British Institute of Management, and the Industrial Training Boards.

Consultants are a valuable source of expertise and organizations considering the use of training consultants should apply similar criteria to those used in selecting courses. An external consultant can often achieve results which would not be possible by using internal staff. It is not only the perhaps wider expertise that the external consultant can bring it is also the advantage of being unaffected by internal politics and value systems.

Group training schemes. These are formed by a group of employers, often in a similar industry, who join together to establish joint training facilities which individually they would be unable to afford. These schemes normally offer employers, particularly small employers, the facilities of a training officer, instructors, and an off-the-job training centre. Traditionally, group schemes were concentrated in the craft training area, particularly in first year off-the-job training but some schemes now cover the whole spectrum of training and may also assist with employee selection. The decline in the numbers of craft trainees has affected group training schemes but this has been partly offset by an increase in Youth Training Scheme work.

Professional associations. The growth of professionalism in many fields of employment in recent years has led to new professional bodies being formed. The training officer needs to be familiar with those professional associations relevant to her organization. They can supply detailed information on training courses and programmes which lead to membership qualifications, and of post-qualification short courses to assist their members to keep up to date in specialist fields – courses an organization could not normally afford to run internally.

Public sector education and training services. Polytechnics, Colleges of Higher Education and Further Education Colleges offer vocational courses in a wide variety of subjects and skills. Many of these courses are geared to national examination syllabuses but there is a trend for colleges to provide courses to meet specialized regional demands and the specific requirements of individual organizations. The availability of courses 'tailor-made' to meet an organization's specific training requirements is a well-established feature in management training, where it is closely associated with consultancy (Kenney and Marsh 1969). This aspect of college work has been extended to other disciplines, for example through the PICKUP scheme. Thus, in addition to their more traditional role as providers of standard courses, colleges are increasingly regarded by industry and the public sector employers as 'resource centres' from which they can commission research and consultancy and obtain specialist guest lecturers. Universities may also be able to provide courses and consultancy services.

The Manpower Services Commission (MSC). Skillcentres. These developed from Government Training Centres which were established during the Second World War and, whilst preserving the original functions of rehabilitation for the disabled and accelerated vocational training for craft and semi-skilled occupations, they underwent a major expansion in the 1970s. However, the fields of training in which the Skillcentres were best qualified were, by the mid-1980s, decreasingly those in demand by employers and a reduction in the number of Skillcentres took place. The Skillcentre Training Agency of the MSC provides training services in its

Skillcentres and wherever training needs arise through its mobile instructor force. These services are now provided on a cost recovery basis.

The MSC has, since its formation, established a very wide range of training programmes, some of which had relatively short life-cycles and others a more permanent role in the provision of training opportunities provided by the Commission. While in some cases employers do not have direct access to these programmes, they are nonetheless of importance to training specialists. Some programmes may involve employers in providing work experience, as in the case of the Youth Training Scheme, and others, such as the Technical and Vocational Education Initiative, will be used to initiate and develop work skills for school leavers (see Chapter 8). This in turn will require employers to change their approaches to induction and initial job training.

MSC initiatives in support of its Adult Training Strategy are being developed to meet the changing needs of the economy (see Chapters 9 and 10).

Industrial Training Boards are responsible to the Training Division of the MSC and the assistance they offer companies is described in Chapter 10.

Trade Unions. Employers should be aware that a wide diversity of training courses are run by trade unions for shop stewards and union officials. Some of these courses are sponsored jointly by employers' associations and trade unions and are usually orientated towards a particular industry; most, however, are arranged by the TUC or by trade unions, sometimes in conjunction with colleges. Some trade unions have been quick to apply new educational technology for the benefit of their members, for example the Electrical, Electronic, Telecommunication and Plumbing Union pioneered the use of video discs and micro-computers for technical retraining at their Union College at Cudham (Chapple 1984).

A training officer may wish to inform her directors of the possible consequences of their union representatives being better trained than their managers in the knowledge and skills of industrial relations!

BIBLIOGRAPHY

BANK J. *Outdoor training for managers*. Aldershot, Gower Press, 1985.

CARROLL S J. 'The relative effectiveness of training methods – expert opinion and research'. *Personnel Psychology*, Vol. 25 1972, pp 495-500.

CASSELS J. 'Education and training must be geared to match the demand for more skills in British industry today'. *The Times*, 13th June, 1985.

CHAPPLE F. 'A report on the Electrical, Electronic, Telecommunication and Plumbing Union's retraining programme'. *The Times*, 13th March, 1984.

CHEMICAL AND ALLIED PRODUCTS INDUSTRY TRAINING BOARD. Information paper on productivity agreements. Chemical and Allied Products ITB, 1970.

CLOTHING AND ALLIED PRODUCTS INDUSTRY TRAINING BOARD. *Levy exemptions and key training grants*. Clothing and Allied Products ITB, 1977.

COUNCIL FOR EDUCATIONAL TECHNOLOGY. *Open learning*. Information Sheet No. 5. Southampton, Council for Educational Technology, 1984.

CROSS M. *Towards the flexible craftsman*. London, The Technical Change Centre, 1985.

DAVIES A T. *Industrial training – an introduction*. London, Institute of Personnel Management, 1956.

EQUAL OPPORTUNITIES COMMISSION. *Code of practice for the elimination of sex and marriage discrimination and the promotion of equality of opportunity in employment*. London, Equal Opportunities Commission, 1985.

GUEST D and KENNY T. eds, *A textbook of techniques and strategies in personnel management*. London, Institute of Personnel Management, 1983.

HUCZYNSKI A. 'Training methods – fads and fancies?' *British Association for Commercial and Industrial Education Journal*, March/April, 1984.

KENNEY J P J and MARSH P J. 'Management schools and industrial training'. *Industrial and Commercial Training*. December, Vol. 1, No. 2, 1969.

KING D. *Training within the organization. A study of company policy and procedures for the systematic training of operators and supervisors.* London, Tavistock Publications, 1964.

NELSON J. 'The criteria inventory'. *Industrial Training International*, Vol. 1, No. 8, 1966.

POWELL L S. *A general guide to the use of visual aids*. London, British Association for Industrial and Commercial Education, 1981.

SINGER E. *Training in industry and commerce*. London, Institute of Personnel Management, 1977.

TAVERNIER G. *Industrial training systems and records*. Aldershot, Gower Press, 1971.

5: *Learning and training*

INTRODUCTION

Bass and Vaughan (1966) defined learning as a 'relatively permanent change in behaviour that occurs as a result of practice or experience'. While this definition is still true in its entirety, the aspect we would wish to emphasize today is that of learning from experience. People cannot be brought together into an organization to achieve any kind of common purpose without learning taking place. As a result they will change their behaviour in various ways. For instance, at the simplest level, they learn to use each other's names, technical terms and location of equipment, and at a more sophisticated level, they learn about the behaviour of their colleagues, supervisors and management and thus develop attitudes which can have complex effects on behaviour. The way in which a manager responds to a request for advice from a subordinate affects the subordinate's attitude and future behaviour. This in turn will confirm or alter the manager's attitude towards the subordinate. In other words the process is interactive, both are learning about each other and modifying their behaviour accordingly. People learn by imitating others, i.e. modelling, by perceiving and interpreting what happens in the organization and by the cumulative experience of trial and error. In this sense, therefore, as King (1964) has stressed, learning is an inevitable organizational activity.

In assessing training needs, as described in Chapters 3 and 6, we are therefore attempting to decide whether this natural learning process needs to be supplemented by some kind of planned training intervention. If we decide that this is the case, the next question is what specific form the intervention might take. Prior to examining the range of possibilities in Chapter 7, we first consider the ways in which the training strategy reflects the assumptions made by the trainer about the learning process. These assumptions may be explicit and well informed, on the basis of careful study and deliberation, or they may be implicit, the trainer relying solely on intuition, or purely anecdotal sources. The training officer should have a working knowledge of the processes with which he is involved before committing his organization to considerable expenditure.

This is no easy matter, because there is at present no all-embracing theory of learning which will cover all situations. The range of human learning ability is extremely wide, from psychomotor skills, such as operating a keyboard or styling a client's hair, to the negotiating skills of an industrial relations expert, the symbolic skills of a computer programmer, or the decision-making skills of a financier. The training officer searching for simple rules which adequately encompass such varied activity is going to be disappointed. Researchers have concentrated on different aspects of this complex process and have been able to demonstrate certain principles, but no one theory is in itself complete and none can claim to cover all eventualities. In addition, there is a basic difference between a theory of learning and a theory of training. As Annett (1974) pointed out:

> The aim of the former is to elucidate the processes underlying learning, ultimately (although this is denied by some) referring to the physiological processes of information storage and retrieval in the brain.

A theory of training on the other hand, is essentially concerned with what actually has to be done to bring about a change in the learner's behaviour. However, as we shall explain later in this chapter, there has been a gradual trend away from trainer-centred activities, focusing on the provision of courses and training events, towards a trainee-centred approach, concentrating on how people learn from experience, how they 'learn to learn' and how best they can continually develop themselves and update their talents. This has directed attention towards certain aspects of the learning process, so that although the distinction between learning and training continues to exist, it has been gradually modified. While trainers still prepare instructional material and provide courses, an increasingly important part of their function is to help people understand their own learning processes and to create conditions in which they can learn for themselves (see Chapter 2).

Learning theory is a detailed study in its own right and a comprehensive overview would be beyond the scope of this book. For this we would refer the reader to a psychology text such as Borger and Seaborne (1982), or the series *Essential Psychology*, edited by Herriot (in particular Stammers and Patrick 1975). Our aim in this chapter is rather to whet the reader's appetite to pursue more specialized texts, by demonstrating ways that learning theory can inform the trainer, and provide useful guidance. This will be done by discussing certain relevant aspects (in some instances by referring to experimental evidence, and in others by more general consideration) and relating them to training problems and to some of the training techniques which will be discussed in Chapter 7 and which are also mentioned in Appendix 3.

Initially four main theories of learning will be outlined, namely: reinforcement theories; cybernetics and information theories; cognitive theories and problem solving; and experiential learning theories. These have been chosen because we have found them most useful to trainers, and we shall briefly discuss their relevance to situations in an organization. This will be followed by an examination of six aspects of learning, selected because of their relevance to the design and management of training interventions. The final consideration will be the concept of the organization as a learning environment and its influence on the training function and policy.

REINFORCEMENT THEORIES

A very basic concept in learning is that of 'conditioning' or 'shaping' behaviour, the main exponent being Skinner (1965), who tested his theory by carrying out numerous experiments, the most famous of which concerned pigeons. By means of rewarding his experimental subjects with corn every time they made an appropriate movement, he was able to teach them many things, including how to play 'ping pong' with each other. Although behaviour in animal experiments cannot necessarily be considered as an accurate reflection of complicated and sophisticated human conduct, it has been claimed that conditioning is an essential ingredient in many types of learning. One example is provided by techniques of programmed learning and its current, more sophisticated development into computer assisted learning. The theory is that receiving a 'reward', which for humans is not corn, but being told that they have answered correctly, or 'done well', gives positive reinforcement to that response, and so motivates them to extend their learning.

Skinner regarded this reinforcement as so important that he designed programmes where the content was subdivided into small steps each followed by a question to which the learner should give the right answer. If the answers were wrong, the programme, not the learner was adjudged to be at fault, and was rewritten. Today it is widely held that questioning can also have a useful diagnostic purpose and programmes are devised to cope with incorrect answers by directing trainees to extra material to bring them up to standard, thus sparing those who answer correctly the tedium of working in small steps through material with which they are already familiar. The reinforcement principle, however, still holds good, and the 'user friendly' computer assisted learning programme gives messages such as 'Good', 'Your answer is correct', 'Well done', which both reinforce the learning which has taken place and provide encouragement to attempt the next section. The principle also applies to comments from trainers or managers, who, in their concern to ensure that a task is being carried out correctly, may direct their comments towards the trainee's or subordinate's errors, while omitting to commend, and thereby reinforce, the good aspects of performance.

Conditioning applied to social systems

Skinner (1976) extended the application of his theory from experimenter and subject, (trainer and trainee), to the whole area of the structure of social systems. In his novel, *Walden Two*, Skinner developed the concept of a society based on the use of positive reinforcement. He conceived systems which were designed to reward behaviour functional to the society. In other words, the citizens were not controlled by law but by the way in which the environment was designed. Other writers, e.g. Nord (1969), have attempted to apply Skinner's ideas to management through positive reinforcement, embracing items such as job design, compensation and rewards, organizational design and change. For instance, Nord suggests that annual merit interviews and salary increments are very inefficient development techniques, as the rewards are so delayed that they have little feedback value. He quotes Fleishman (1967) who found that human relations training programmes were only effective in producing on-the-job changes if the organizational climate was supportive of the content of the programme. Nord maintains:

> Those responses which are rewarded will persist; those responses which are not rewarded or are punished will decrease in frequency. If the organizational environment does not reward responses developed in a training programme, the programme will be at best a total waste of time and money.

Quoting Sykes (1962) as evidence, Nord maintains that, at worst, such a programme may be disruptive.

Skinnerian theory embraces a very elementary form of learning, which goes only a limited way to assisting understanding of the process by which human beings acquire their whole range of knowledge and skills. His theory of 'social engineering' by the provision of positive reinforcement, is not accepted in its entirety today, although it provides an important reminder of the need for feedback or knowledge of results, without which no desired learning will take place. Less frequently recognized is the proposition stated at the beginning of this chapter, that although not in quite the simplistic way postulated by Skinner, an organization is nevertheless a powerful learning environment.

Punishment or 'negative reinforcement'

In contrast to the encouragement of correct responses by reward or positive reinforcement, other researchers, e.g. Estes (1970), have investigated the effect of punishment in suppressing an inappropriate response. The principle involved in these experiments (which mainly involved administering electric shocks to rats), demonstrated that punishment will temporarily suppress a response, but will not extinguish it. After having been 'punished' for pressing a bar, the rats made fewer trials, but later after the punishment was withdrawn, they resumed their original behaviour patterns.

The principle carries an important implication for trainers, in that while positive feedback and reinforcement can bring about a more permanent learning outcome, negative feedback, or harsh criticism may be effective only as long as some threat appears imminent. This is particularly important in safety training, where it might be said that the trainee is being taught to avoid possible punishment (in the form of an accident or injury). Safety precautions are most likely to be heeded when the danger appears imminent, and to be ignored where it is not immediately apparent, for example in casual lifting of awkward objects. This is one of the major reasons why safety training is not always effective, and must be borne in mind when devising safety training programmes. For instance, the programme might be started with a film, or other material which brings home the imminence of danger, so that trainees approach the ensuing sessions with an appropriate mental set.

A second reason why safety training is often ineffective is that many accidents are the result of a chain of events, or a number of different conditions all coinciding at one fateful moment. Because these events do not normally all happen together, it may be possible to ignore certain safety precautions for a considerable time without necessarily meeting with an accident. If safety equipment is irksome to wear and a worker has managed to do without it and suffered no harm, this habit will be reinforced as thoughts of danger recede. An illustration is provided by car seat belts, which large sections of the population refused to wear for the sake of their own safety (largely because the habit of ignoring them had been reinforced – it was easier and no accident had 'happened to them'). It was not until the threat of prosecution became constantly imminent that the correct usage began to approach 100 per cent!

Learned helplessness

A development of reinforcement theory which has significance for those concerned with trainees who are suffering from depression, possibly as the result of a long spell of unemployment, is that of Seligman (1975). From his experiments he concludes that just as subjects can learn to perform certain behaviour for some kind of reward, they can also learn that certain situations are 'uncontrollable', i.e. that no behaviour they can display will produce any result. He claims that just as organisms can learn by positive reinforcement, when they are exposed to uncontrollable events, they can learn that responding is futile. This learning undermines motivation to respond and persists even when events actually become controllable. He argues that the fear of an organism faced with trauma is reduced, if it learns that it can take some action to control it but that if it learns that the trauma is uncontrollable, fear gives way to depression.

He relates his findings to chronic depression and to the situation of the long-term unemployed and racial minorities. He quotes the fact that the tested IQs of depressives have been found to drop during the disorder and suggests that this may explain the findings of Jensen (1976) that American blacks score 15 points lower than whites on culture fair IQ tests. The theory may well have a message for trainers of people who are disadvantaged in some way or have suffered long-term unemployment, or even some Youth Training Scheme trainees who, seeing the experience of their friends, have become convinced that they will be unable to find employment. They therefore may not display much motivation to learn and initially may not perform effectively. If, in addition they are constantly being told that their work is poor, the condition will be reinforced. A basic tenet of Seligman's theory is that the learning persists long after the situation has ceased to be uncontrollable. A very considerable 'unlearning' process has to take place before the subject will make any attempt to behave in a positive manner.

CYBERNETIC AND INFORMATION THEORIES

These theories concentrate on how information is received and monitored. Stammers and Patrick (1975), and Duncan and Kelly (1983) liken the way in which feedback can control human performance to the manner in which a thermostat controls a heating system. The temperature is monitored and regulated because information from the thermostat determines the level of power input to the system. See Figure 5.1 which is based on Stammers and Patrick's model.

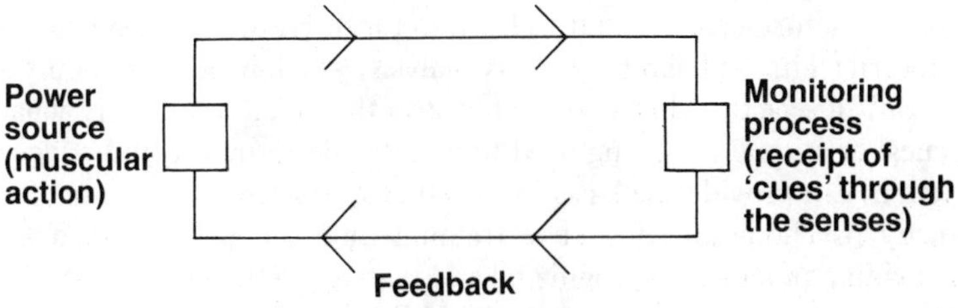

Figure 5.1
The monitoring and regulating process.

This monitoring is a constant process in all activities. For example, someone who is profoundly deaf may develop an unusual speaking voice because he cannot hear it and must monitor it in some other way, possibly by the feel of muscles in the mouth and throat. A machinist is receiving 'stimuli' from the environment, by which he monitors and regulates performance, or in other words, his input to the system. He receives these stimuli through the senses – touch, sight, hearing, smell, taste, kinaesthesis (the sense of muscular effort, or the 'feel' that one's limbs are in the correct position) and balance. For instance, he may interpret the sound of the machine, the pressure required by his foot to operate at the correct speed and appearance of the work in the machine. A cook or a wine taster may be relying on his sense of smell or taste to monitor performance.

In a training situation, the most usual form of feedback is provided by comments from an instructor, but sometimes it can be given by simulators, which act as artificial 'thermostats' and help the trainee monitor his performance. Before such artificial feedback is removed it is essential that the trainee is able to monitor his performance using the same senses and stimuli as those employed by a skilled worker.

An important part of skills analysis (see Chapter 6) is to determine by which 'cues' or 'stimuli' an experienced worker is being guided and by which of the senses they are being received. Probably the best known example is to be found in the job of a typist. Observation of a skilled performer reveals heavy reliance on kinaesthesis, or the 'feel' and positioning of the fingers on the keyboard. Left to his own devices, it is likely that the beginner would rely upon sight, looking intensely at the keyboard and using what has been described as the 'hunt and peck' method. Anyone who has taught himself in this way finds it notoriously difficult to learn to touch-type because he has to unlearn all his bad habits. A skills analysis, which includes not only a record of exactly what is done but also the details of exactly what 'cues' or stimuli are being used to monitor performance and trigger action, can provide the basis for an efficient training programme for many psychomotor jobs. The training time can be shortened by providing practice in recognizing and reacting to the stimuli used by those with experience, rather than allowing the learner to work unsupervised and thereby reinforcing less efficient habits (such as the 'hunt and peck' method).

Since recognizing stimuli is central to learning, a training officer should understand the process of perception. Training for inspection tasks, for instance, is largely a matter of organizing the perception to highlight certain stimuli or details and ignore others. For more detailed study, the reader is referred to Thomas (1962) and Wright and Taylor (1970). During the learning process this 'selectivity' of stimuli becomes automatic, and the experienced worker ceases to think consciously about it (in other words he 'sheds the perceptual load'). For example, when learning to ski, the beginner has to concentrate hard on cues which assist his balance, the correct position of the body in relation to the skis, how to traverse, how to turn or stop. After a number of painful experiences, he may look wistfully at the experienced performer, who seems to carry out all these operations naturally and apparently without thought, although possibly observing other matters such as the texture of the snow, or the position of other skiers on the piste. In other words, certain of the experienced skier's actions have been pre-programmed.

Seymour (1968) advocates training programmes where the tasks are subdivided into small parts so that the learner can concentrate on one item at a time (part analysis). Each part then becomes pre-programmed more quickly, the training period is shortened and fewer errors are made. For instance, the beginner can attend dry ski school and, wearing shorter skis which are easier to manage, can learn such skills as correct body position or how to carry out a 'kick turn'. On reaching the ski slopes, some pre-programming will already have taken place, a little of the perceptual load can be shed, and some of the discomfort taken out of learning! (See also Plateaux of Learning, page 134.)

Earlier in this chapter we discussed the difficulties of using the threat of punishment to persuade people to avoid accidents. Far more effective is the positive aspect of ensuring that from the beginning the trainee will always perform in a safe manner (compare the example of the use of car seat belts above). Consideration of safe working methods must therefore be a prime concern of those responsible for preparing training programmes. Kay (1983) gives a useful explanation of accidents as enforced changes from programmed to unprogrammed activity. For example, someone walking along a pavement is carrying out an activity which has been programmed since childhood, and therefore does not need to think consciously about it. If, however, his foot slips on a banana skin, the programmed activity will not suffice, and he has to concentrate rapidly on evasive action! Injury will result if he cannot think out and effect this action in time. Someone trained in the art of falling could probably manage this because his mind is pre-programmed, but most of us would likely fail.

A vital part of safety training, therefore, is to pre-programme trainees for possible hazard situations (e.g. training vehicle drivers on a skid pan), so that they can more rapidly recognize and interpret the stimuli they receive in the monitoring process (e.g. the first feel of the vehicle's wheels sliding), and because an appropriate response pattern to these stimuli has been pre-programmed, the trainees have an improved chance of avoiding an accident. This theory has a further implication for safety. Because learners have to concentrate on many items at once and cannot shed the perceptual load, they have less ability to anticipate potential hazards, and are therefore more prone to accidents. Trainers need to pay special attention to this fact. It is particularly important when dealing with young employees and school children or students undertaking organization placements, where not only is the trainee attempting to cope with cues and signals from the job itself but also has to become acclimatized to a whole new work environment, as opposed to the familiar background of school or college.

COGNITIVE THEORIES AND PROBLEM SOLVING

In direct contrast to reinforcement theories, which are concerned with the establishment of particular behaviour patterns, cognitive theories draw attention to aspects of behaviour which we might ordinarily describe as 'insight'. They reflect the way in which we learn to recognize and define problems, experiment to find solutions, whether by trial and error, by deductive reasoning, by seeking information or help, or by a combination of all three. The real learning comes when we conceptualize or 'internalize' the solution and methodology, so that we are able to extend their use and adapt them to future situations.

These theories are not new. In 1925, Kohler was experimenting with an ape which was required to solve the problem of retrieving a banana placed beyond its reach outside the cage. It first tried to grasp it by frantically stretching its arms through the bars but gave up after several unsuccessful attempts. After retreating to the back of the cage for some time, the ape returned to the bars, reached for a stick which was lying outside, and managed to poke the banana and pull it nearer the cage. The experiment was then repeated but this time the banana was further away and the ape had to use a short stick to pull in a longer stick before being able to reach the desired food (see Kohler 1973). Although this is a good illustration of insight, human problems are more complicated, and much attention has been devoted recently to human problem solving strategies (see, for instance, Jackson 1984).

This experiment demonstrates the close relationship between cognitive theories and the training technique called discovery learning.

> The trainee is presented with tasks which engage him in the search for, and selection of, stimuli on how to proceed. The effectiveness of the discovery method depends on the design of these tasks which have two aims: to provide an intrinsic means for unassisted learning and to provide the experience upon which insight into key relationships can be developed. Department of Employment (1971).

An example is provided by a model designed to illustrate the principles of electricity where by operating levers and watching the results, trainees can work out the principles for themselves in a safe situation. This example involves the use of a practical working model, but the technique is very versatile. For instance, depending upon the method of presentation, a case study can provide discovery learning.

This training method has the advantage of assisting transfer of learning to the job because the learning occurs in an applied manner (see also Learning Transfer, page 140). It does, however, require careful structuring of the situation to the learner's needs, as long periods spent in vain pursuit of a solution which is well beyond his current capability, can prove an extremely frustrating experience. In those circumstances anger and irritation are likely to be turned upon the trainer! As we have seen from reinforcement theory, however, finding the solution acts as a well-earned reward to reinforce the learning. Obviously it is usually quicker to tell the learner than to let him find out for himself and therefore discovery learning sessions tend to be time consuming, although by providing better learning transfer they may be more effective in the long term.

EXPERIENTIAL LEARNING

Kolb, Rubin and McIntyre (1974) conceive learning as a four-stage cycle, which is illustrated by means of the model in Figure 5.2 below.

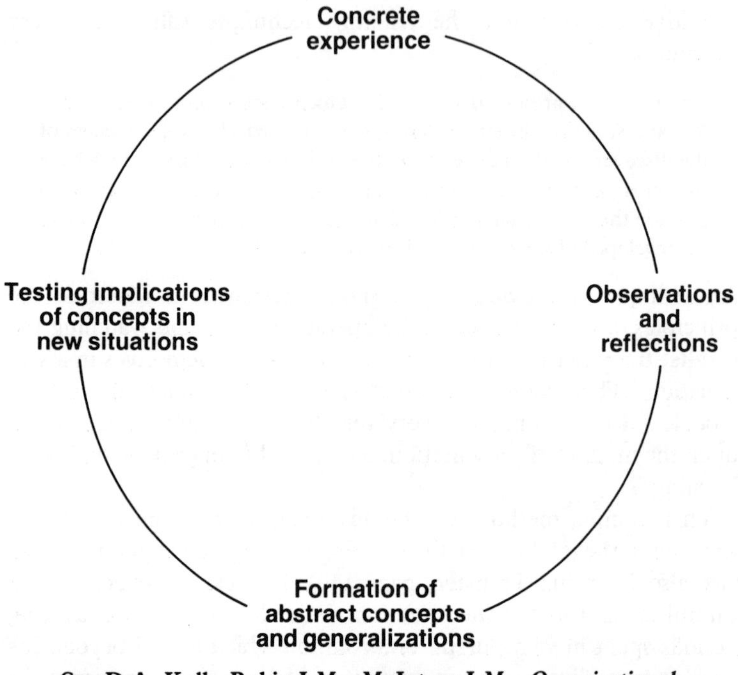

See D.A. Kolb, Rubin I.M., McIntyre J.M., *Organizational Psychology: A Book of Readings,* 2nd edn, p.28. Reprinted by permission of Prentice-Hall, Englewood Cliffs, NJ, 1974

Figure 5.2
The Kolb learning cycle.

Immediate experience of, for example, an unsatisfactory interview, leads to observing and reflecting as to what actually happened and what really went wrong. This is followed by generalizing and theorizing about possible implications for the future conduct of similar interviews. The 'theories' are then tested out in new situations, which result in further experience and a return to the beginning of the cycle. Kolb, Rubin and McIntyre (1974) claim that:

> as a result of our hereditary equipment, our particular life experience, and the demands of our present environment, most people develop learning styles that emphasize some learning abilities over others.

Kolb, Rubin and McIntyre suggest that a mathematician might give preference to abstract concepts, while a manager may have greater concern for concrete experience and the active application of ideas. This does not necessarily imply that, when required, each might not adopt the other approach, but rather that each has a preferred style.

In order to study styles further, Kolb, Rubin and McIntyre developed a Learning Style Inventory (LSI), based on self description. Using the LSI, they have established norms for different types of professions such as marketing, personnel management and finance. They identified four dominant types of learning styles, which they describe as follows.

- The converger who combines abstract conceptualization and active experimentation. He favours the practical application of ideas. Kolb *et al.* suggest that he responds best to situations where there is a single correct answer, that he prefers to deal with things rather than with people and that many engineers have this style.

- The diverger combines concrete experience and reflective observation, and can consider situations from many perspectives. He is imaginative, good at generating ideas and is interested in people. Kolb, Rubin and McIntyre have found that personnel managers tend to display this style.

- The assimilator combines abstract conceptualization and reflective observation and his strength is inductive reasoning and creating theoretical models. He is less concerned about the practical use of the theory than the logicality of its basis. This style tends to characterize those working in research and planning departments.

- The accommodator combines concrete experience and experimentation, and is a risk taker who excels in carrying out plans and experiments. At ease with people, he is often found in organization roles connected with marketing or sales.

Other writers, e.g. Honey and Mumford (1982, 1983), have refined these categories and used them in selecting the type of trainee (identified by learning style) most likely to benefit from a certain type of programme. Other classifications have been made, e.g. that of Pask (1976), who distinguished between 'serialists' who prefer to learn smaller pieces of information in detail, and 'holists' who prefer to gain an initial overview of the material to be learned.

The concept of learning styles is an important development because it helps to throw some light on how people actually learn. It indicates that there are varying approaches which relate to different training methods. In the example of the interview situation above, immediate experience requires a practical interview session (either 'for real' as part of the learner's daily work, or as a simulated exercise in a classroom situation); observing and reflecting might take place by individual thought, or by discussion with a coach or mentor, or observers and tutor in the case of the classroom exercise. Generalizing and theorizing might involve comparing his findings with relevant literature and formulating or re-examining his own principles and guidelines on, for example, the use of specific techniques and strategies. The next stage would be testing out these perceptions in a new situation and so back to concrete experience. This example demonstrates the need for all four stages. However, when planning internal programmes and selecting participants for external courses, it is wise to allow for the fact that some people learn better by one style than by another, and some may reject certain styles altogether.

It is also important for the trainer to realize that he has a natural learning/teaching style, and that in choosing appropriate techniques he should consider the trainees' preferred or desired learning style, as well as his own, insofar as it is practicable to do so. For example, personnel management students in a particular educational institution sometimes had difficulty in learning from lecturers who were professional accountants, and similarly accountancy students appeared to find problems in learning from staff who were basically behavioural scientists. It was considered that this was purely the nature of the subject but an unpublished pilot study (Reid 1976), threw a new light on the matter by demonstrating a statistically significant difference in learning styles between the two groups.

Considerable developmental work on learning styles has already taken place and there is now a wide range of literature. For example, Richardson and Bennett (1984) have examined the structural and cultural barriers to behaviour at each of the stages in the learning cycle. They suggest that one can think of the organization itself as having a preferred learning style, which influences those within it. Although further research and validation of this work is still necessary, it is important for the trainer to realize that his own natural learning/training style may be at variance with the culture of his organization. A traditional difficulty of group training activities is the effect of the composition or 'chemistry' of the group and the influence it can have upon individual learning. Although the concept of learning styles does not produce instant answers to this problem, it nevertheless contributes an explanation, and may help to promote useful discussion within the group and assist trainees' understanding. Furthermore, a learning style inventory provides the trainer with a measuring instrument which could ultimately yield data relating to the influence of different learning styles on group activity, thereby constituting a valuable guide in, for instance, determining an optimum composition of learning groups.

The importance of flexibility in the application of learning styles must be emphasized. The more the individual understands about his own learning processes, the more capable he is of learning for himself from experience and reaping the benefits of continuing development. Many managers have a preference for practical matters and little time for theory. It is likely, however, that the reflecting and conceptualization stages are those which assist transfer of learning to new situations and it would seem that the ability to use all four styles is of particular advantage.

In 1979, we wrote: 'Our cyclical economy and the speed of technical change suggest that 'learning to learn' is the central training problem of our time' (Kenney, Donnelly and Reid 1979), and we suggested the need for further research in this area. Attention has been gradually focused away from mechanistic formulation of objectives and the conditions which surround learning, to the activities of the learner, and the means of equipping him with strategies and a range of styles which are not only appropriate for present learning but which will transfer to future situations and enable learning from experience to take place. The emphasis has moved from activities largely controlled by the trainer, to the learning process, and where possible to self-directed and self-managed learning, using the opportunities provided by new technology such as computer-assisted programmes.

The implication for the training officer in this changing situation, is that in addition to being competent in analytical techniques, objective formulation and planning and implemention of programmes, he has to keep up to date with the latest knowledge of the nature of learning and the whole concept of continuing development (see page 262). If the UK is to have a flexible and adaptive workforce to cope with rapidly changing technology, it is vital to create training policies and a climate at both national and workplace level which not only enables employees to improve their current performance but also helps them to embark upon a process of constant updating and development so that they are alert to new situations and possibilities, instead of merely reacting to change. Writers such as Hayes, Anderson and Fonda (1984) have stressed that interest in continuous development is one of the main features which distinguishes workforces in countries such as Japan and USA, from those in the UK where the training emphasis tends to be placed more upon short-term considerations.

SELECTED ASPECTS OF LEARNING

We have shown how learning theories provide a background to help us plan the conditions in which learning takes place. We now discuss six aspects of particular relevance in the formulation of training interventions. These are:

- motivation
- knowledge of results
- attitude formation and change
- age factor
- memory
- learning transfer.

Motivation

The old saying that a horse can be led to water but cannot be made to drink holds an important lesson for the trainer. People learn if they accept the need for training and are committed to it. If their motivation is weak because, for example, they doubt their ability to learn or if they do not appreciate the need for training and fail to see what use it will serve, then no matter how well it is designed and implemented, its effectiveness will be limited. Motivation is a complex concept, and it is most important to recognize that people are multi-motivated. As McGehee and Thayer (1961) have noted:

> similar behaviour shown by different people may result from different underlying motives, and ...the trainer... must expect vacillation and indecision from people in the day-to-day work situation. The mere recognition of indecision and an attempt to discover the underlying cause may suggest solutions to the problem.

Otto and Glaser (1970) suggest a useful classification of motivation factors based on the kind of rewards which are involved in learning:

- achievement motivation, for which the reward is success (compare this with the principle underlying reinforcement theory);
- anxiety, for which the reward is the avoidance of failure;
- approval motivation, for which the reward is approval in its many forms;
- curiosity, for which the reward is increased opportunity to explore the environment and be exposed to novel stimuli;
- acquisitiveness, for which the reward is something tangible, such as money or material benefits.

None of these classification groups should be regarded as excluding the other; for instance, both achievement and anxiety motivation are possible in the same person at the same time. All the factors, however, are influenced by the immediate experience of the learner, and as motivation is a personal matter, the case for careful discussion of individual programmes is obvious. Frequently, however, a variety of people are undertaking the same programme and it is necessary to bear all the general motivation factors in mind. For instance, achievement motivation requires that learning should be a successful experience. This has implications for the size of the learning 'steps' in relation to the target population, for timing, for the provision of ample knowledge of results to trainer and trainee, and assistance in case of difficulty. If the training is lengthy and possibly daunting, the setting of intermediate targets can be a useful means of effecting a sense of achievement, as can the introduction of a competitive element for younger trainees, although older learners tend to react unfavourably to that type of atmosphere. Approval is also concerned with supplying knowledge of results, and psychological theory suggests that it is more effective to approve, and so reinforce correct actions, than to punish and ridicule incorrect ones (see page 119).

It is likely, however, that there is an optimum level of motivation. Trainees who are too eager can suffer from excessive anxiety, which may inhibit learning. This can apply particularly to older workers who may be anxious for financial reasons, for prestige, or because of domestic problems and a good trainer should watch for this and allay any fears. Either the learner wastes time worrying about failure, or he practises very hard. This is beneficial if he is practising the correct method, but if not, he may be reinforcing errors which may be difficult to eradicate. It is therefore not entirely true that 'practice makes perfect'.

Curiosity can be a very powerful motivator, as experience with small children will show. For this reason discovery methods (see page 125), are often very effective if they are so designed that the experience is ultimately successful. An example is given by the office supervisor who, upon receiving delivery of a new piece of technical equipment which he wanted all staff to learn to use, left it covered up in the office without mentioning it, and claimed that within two weeks every member of staff knew how to use it! Curiosity is an important part of discovery learning! It is also one of the trainer's most powerful allies and should be nurtured by using the learners' interests whenever it is reasonably practicable rather than destroying it by a rigorous insistence on logicality. For example, it was discovered that trainee sewing machinists appeared to have little interest in an initial off-the-job induction course because their main concern was to find out what using a machine was really like. The order of the programme was changed and they were allowed to go straight into the department and run a machine as fast as they could. Curiosity about employment conditions or other departments came at a later stage, and the new programme was much more successful.

There can be difficulties in establishing a direct link between the acquisitive instinct and successful completion of training. The relationship is probably at its most obvious in the field of operator training for pieceworkers, where a resultant increase in output will be reflected in a higher overall wage. In management development, however, the outcome is likely to be less clear, as exemplified by a survey of managers who had attended courses. The results demonstrated that not one of them thought that attending the course would lead to a pay rise (Marks Group 1985). The relationship is more likely to be indirect, in that if the training leads to better performance, an increase in salary or promotion may result but, as many factors contribute to improved managerial achievement, it can be extremely difficult to attribute cause and effect.

Knowledge of results

Knowledge of results is a form of reinforcement, without which it is difficult for learning to take place. This has important implications for the way learning situations are structured. Holding (1965) provides an excellent discussion on types of knowledge of results and the effect of timing. The more specific the reinforcement, the more effective it is likely to be, and this can involve setting criteria for adequate performance to act as sub-goals to final achievement. There is also an obvious relationship with continuous assessment of progress, behavioural objectives, target setting or goals in managerial jobs.

Extrinsic knowledge of results is provided artificially, for example by comment from the trainer or fellow trainees, or by information derived from a simulator such as a monitor screen in simulated pilot training.

Intrinsic knowledge of results relates to the monitoring and guidance the operator is able to gain from cues within the job itself. Unless the trainee can internalize knowledge of results, i.e. convert it from extrinsic to intrinsic, and know himself whether he is performing well or badly, the effects may not last after removal of the extrinsic provision, and may not transfer to the working situation. Success depends upon drawing attention and recognition to the intrinsic cues during training.

Learning curves depict the rate at which learning takes place, thus providing knowledge of results to trainer and trainee. Progress is plotted on a graph, with the vertical axis (ordinate) representing a measure of achievement, such as output per hour, and the horizontal axis (abscissa) denoting the time period or number of attempts made (see Figure 5.3).

The curvature can be described by the way the gains vary from trial to trial – in the case of sensorimotor skill the curves are most often of decreasing gains (the change in performance from the current trial to the next is frequently less than the change that took place on the previous trial): this is one reason why the learning of a skill is often discouraging. Sometimes it is practicable for trainees to plot their own learning curves and seeing their own progress can act as a motivator.

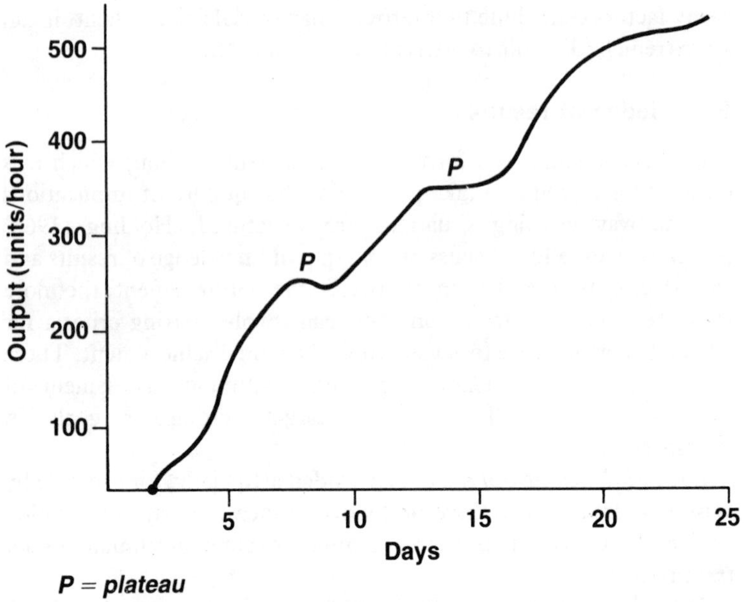

Figure 5.3
A learning curve.

Fleishman and Hempel (1955) have suggested that as the attainment of skill level in a task increases, the importance of certain ability dimensions can vary. For instance, having gained more competence in the task, the learner's further progress may be affected by his reaction time and rate of movement, while other abilities, such as spatial relations, may have a decreasing influence on performance improvement. The learning curve may therefore not be measuring the acquisition of one skill, but of different skills which are called in to use as the learning progresses. This may be one cause of a plateau of learning.

Plateaux of learning are periods of no improvement in the learning curve. They can sometimes be explained by a shift from a lower order of learning to a higher order (e.g. from letter habit in typing to word habit, i.e. learning to type or write familiar words as a single unit). A plateau is often followed by a rapid burst of progress. The trainer should attempt to discover the causes of plateaux, particularly those which occur regularly, in order to assist the trainees to overcome them. For instance, there may be certain stages when trainees become demotivated, indicating an alteration should be made to the training programme. They may need to concentrate more on one aspect, perhaps in the example above in learning to type particular combinations of letters where errors are most frequently made, or as Fleishman and Hempel maintain they may have reached a stage when they are dependent on a different type of ability which has not yet been adequately developed. The exponents of part analysis (see page 123) claim that by learning one small part of a job at a time and combining the parts gradually, learning plateaux may be minimized or avoided. (For a discussion of the use of learning curves, see James 1984.)

Attitude formation and change

Attitudinal aspects of training are extremely important as they predispose learners to action. The relationship betweeen attitudes and action is, however, by no means a simple one: there is a useful section in Krech, Crutchfield and Ballachey (1962), which gives a comprehensive discussion of the whole topic. In outline, we would state that attitudes are formed through our relationships with other people and are notoriously difficult to change. The concept of cognitive dissonance (Festinger 1957) provides one explanation based on the premise that we normally like our attitudes to be in harmony with each other. Admiring a superior who actively supports an organizational practice of which I strongly disapprove, I am left in an uncomfortable and dissonant state of internal inconsistency, in that someone whom I admire is supporting something I dislike. The problem can be resolved by modifying my attitude about my superior, or about the organizational practice, or by a decision that the practice is not very important anyway. Whatever the outcome, I shall have altered my attitude in some way. Cognitive dissonance can occur in role playing where, while acting to a brief, I may be required to give a convincing argument from a viewpoint other than my own (such as that of my subordinate). If this is done in public, I am left with an uncomfortable state of dissonance and may begin to move slightly nearer my subordinate's viewpoint. In other circumstances, however, it may cause me to reject new learning as unimportant, possibly even subconsciously, because it is inconsistent with my other firmly held attitudes. A useful discussion of this phenomenon in relation to management development is given by Mumford (1980).

Group discussion has been found to be one of the effective ways of attempting to modify attitudes. One example may be found in T Groups and a number of other forms of social skills and leadership training.

Another method of attitude change is by providing new information. For instance, attitudes towards certain medicinal drugs can change radically upon learning of research which indicates harmful consequences. This fact is particularly important in training as preparation for organizational change. If little or no information is given on important issues, people may develop attitudes to the change which may harden and be difficult to alter. When a particular attitude has been adopted, the natural tendency is to seek confirmation which reinforces it, unless there is extremely strong evidence to the contrary.

Age factor

The climate and the approach to teaching in schools is usually different from that in industry, and school leavers can experience considerable difficulty in adjusting to a different kind of learning situation. Trainers must take this into account when designing programmes if young people's natural enthusiasm is to be channelled in the right direction. Young trainees usually react favourably to intergroup competition and appreciate variety in their programmes. They prefer to keep within their original training groups, membership of which gives them confidence. Leaving school and looking for work is a big and worrying step for many young people and behaviour, such as over-confidence or shyness, often results from a feeling of insecurity. A patient and supportive trainer can do a great deal to help; this is particularly true with Youth Training Scheme trainees who may be discouraged if they see little hope of obtaining a permanent job. A perceived and desired outcome is an essential motivator, and YTS schemes include skills which are likely to transfer to a variety of jobs, as well as social and life skills. An important feature is that the trainees are consulted about their programmes, and are thus participating in training which is seen as interesting and relevant.

Gradually, as we become older, the reproduction of new cells to replace those which die, slows down and those which continue to reproduce start yielding a higher proportion of unhealthy offspring. The result is that speed of performance can decline. For example, as they grow older the majority of people will perform less well on a timed test. Welford (1962) found that the process of ageing impairs the central decision processes. This affects the time taken to reorganize information, monitor movements and deal with a number of matters at one time. Short term memory deteriorates, resulting in time increase and errors in complex cognitive tasks. On tasks involving number matrices, Welford's older subjects were unable to cope with a large amount of information arranged according to different criteria. This involved not only short-term memory but the reorganization of behaviour to shift from one aspect of the task to another. Because of these changes, researchers, e.g. Belbin (1969), have discovered that older learners may respond better to some training methods than to others (see page 205).

Vocabulary, comprehension and informational tests demonstrated an improvement with age, but reasoning and numerical sections of intelligence tests showed a decline for older people and therefore, although they were able to score as well, or possibly even better than in their youth, the marks were obtained in different ways. Bromley (1975) classified vocabulary and comprehension as attainments rather than basic abilities. Seen in this way, one could say that after maturity, ability starts to decrease, but attainments remain.

Bromley argues:

> The adult person's attainments show the maximum level reached by his intelligence, and as age advances, his capacity decreases, leaving some of his attainments as markers showing the highest level reached...

He also suggests that attainments remain, unless they 'fall into disuse' but the ability to formulate and use new ideas and concepts declines. It is, however, generally agreed that a number of factors are likely to affect achievement in later years and that age is by no means the sole determinant. The first of these is the original level of intelligence. Vernon (1960) gives evidence that the rate of decline is slowest among those whose original intelligence score was high, and greatest among those whose original score was low. There is therefore an accentuation of individual differences.

The second factor is stimulation and use of intellectual ability. A number of studies suggest a slow decline among those who make the greatest use of their intellectual ability and a more rapid decline in intelligence among those who do not. It is also possible that stimulation may have physical consequences for the brain. Evidence from animal studies shows that weight of cerebral cortex is affected by stimulation from the environment (Bromley 1975). Evidence was found by Vogt (1951) of slower deterioration in brain cells of those whose level of intellectual activity has been high. A third factor is education and training. A number of studies have thrown light on the effect of prior experience and training. Welford (1962) suggests that the manipulative, occupational, mental and social skills acquired through experience help to offset a decline in abilities as a result of the ageing process. Other important factors are state of health, age, and motivation.

Our knowledge of the ageing process is admitted to be imperfect, but there are a number of important implications for the trainer. First, if mental stimulation assists the retention of active cognitive processes, there is a very good argument for training even 'for training's sake', particularly in a rapidly changing environment, where an ageing workforce is required to be adaptive. Those least likely to be able to cope with new learning experiences are those who originally had a lower level of cognitive ability, and who have had little exposure to learning situations. This highlights the need for continuing development of staff – for example a liberal policy regarding employer support to attend courses, even although immediate relevance of specific items may not be instantly recognizable by the organization.

Secondly, if people are at their most receptive to learning in youth, and in later years draw upon their earlier attainments, it is essential that the young are given every opportunity to learn. Thirdly, if those with lower cognitive ability are likely to show greater deterioration than those with above average potential, it is extremely important to provide learning opportunities while they are in their prime. This can be a potent argument for attending to the training of *all* school leavers, not merely those who are selected by organizations for further training and development. Fourthly, as people may, in their working life, have to change types of job several times, it is important that a broadly-based training is given to young people, so that through vertical transfer (see page 140), they may find it easier to learn a variety of skills when they are older. These arguments provide a strong case for a scheme such as the Youth Training Scheme and supply a justification for the prevention, albeit at a high cost in financial terms, of a young unemployed (unemployable) labour force.

Memory

The *dual memory* theory distinguishes between short-term and long-term memory and postulates that rehearsal is necessary, if we wish to transfer material from short-term to long-term memory. The average number of discrete items that the human mind can take in at one time is about seven. This can be tested by looking up telephone numbers. When we look up a new number and dial it, it is in our short-term memory. If the line is engaged and we have to dial again, unless we have been repeating it (putting it into long-term memory), we may well have to look it up once more. We obviously can remember much more if we combine small items into larger 'bits'. For instance, it is only possible to remember about seven random letters of the alphabet but if we combine them into meaningful words or sentences we can remember many more. The implication for the trainer is that meaning assists memory. It is very difficult and time consuming to remember something we do not understand.

The two factors of long-term and short-term memory greatly affect the effectiveness of lecturing as a training technique. If the listeners do not understand they are unlikely to remember, and any matters they cannot recall shortly after the lecture are unlikely to have entered long-term memory and will probably not be retained. Two other phenomena are worth noting: sharpening and levelling. When material is recalled later, certain items are remembered for their peculiarity or particular interest (although they may not necessarily be the most important in terms of content). An example may well be the jokes or amusing stories which may be remembered long after the serious content of an address has been forgotten. Other items are glossed over and a 'levelling' process takes place. The material is remembered in very general terms, the only detail being that which has become 'sharpened'. From a trainer's point of view it is very necessary that he makes sure that the important items are 'sharpened' in the listeners' minds. One way of assisting this to happen is to plan the lecture logically – making sure that every point is clear and likely to be understood and to summarize succinctly at the end, in the hope that those points will be 'sharpened'. Other methods of assisting memory are mental imagery (see Chapter 7), appealing to more than one sense, e.g. using an overhead projector involves sight as well as hearing and helps to 'sharpen' the main points, and finally, overlearning (see page 143). A good account of the process of memory can be found in Hilgard, Atkinson and Atkinson (1983).

Learning transfer

Learning transfer can be 'positive' or 'negative', depending on whether the old learning assists or hinders the acquisition of new knowledge, skills or attitudes. Positive transfer can be either vertical or lateral. We shall discuss each of these types in turn.

Positive learning transfer is said to occur when learning which has already taken place on one task assists later learning on another. For example, having learned to use a typewriter makes it easier to operate a word processor. Duncan and Kelly (1983) comment that the components which can give rise to transfer may be very precise (such as removing nails with a claw hammer) or they can be much more generalized. They quote the example of 'marking out' and cutting to minimize waste in sheet metal working and suggest that there may well be transfer potential for this kind of skill within an industry but query how far it would be transferable to other industries, such as textiles. This has relevance to the concept of Occupational Training Families underlying the design of YTS programmes. (See Hayes *et al.* (1983) and Chapter 8.) For instance, one 'Family' is Manufacturing, and it is hoped that learning skills in one industry will provide transfer to what appear to be similar skills in another. So far there is insufficient empirical evidence to prove the validity of this approach.

Hayes *et al.* (1983) use the concept of 'Skill Ownership' in relation to YTS trainees. This they define as 'the ability to redeploy learned skills and knowledge in new and unfamiliar circumstances'. They suggest the addition of a new dimension to the acquisition of knowledge and skills, which involves the trainee in taking the conscious step of learning how to 'find out what he needs to know and be able to do'. In this way the potential for transfer to new situations is being built in to the original learning situation.

Vertical transfer occurs when one subject area acts as a basis for another. For example, a basic knowledge of mathematics can transfer vertically to make it easier to learn statistics. The justification for starting many training schemes with a basic foundation course, before allowing the learner to undertake specific modules, is that as well as providing an overview, the content will transfer vertically in a number of different ways. For example, the one year basic training devised by the Engineering Industry Training Board includes items such as the use of a wide variety of hand tools. This provides a necessary basis for later, more sophisticated modules, such as milling and grinding.

Lateral transfer occurs when items to be learned resemble each other because identical components are present in both. Training simulators are devices for teaching a skill which will transfer, usually laterally, to the real task. For example, a trainee pilot can practise in a 'safe' situation provided by a computer-controlled flight simulator which imitates the effect of using different controls but the extent of transfer obtained by the use of simulators is complex (see Annett 1974).

On- and off-the-job training. Off-the-job training relies upon lateral transfer to the working situation and was recommended, and in some cases demanded, by many of the Training Boards in preference to what was then termed a 'sitting with Nellie' approach. It can have many obvious advantages, including: the provision of conditions conducive to learning away from the noisy rush of the workplace; properly trained instructors; planned training methods; a carefully prepared programme at a pace governed by the trainees' needs rather than one dominated by the relentless requirements of production; the creation of safe and inexpensive situations in which to try out and practise newly acquired skills and techniques; use of a greater variety of training techniques (e.g. discovery learning, case studies, films, closed-circuit television); and the opportunity to emphasize all four stages of the Kolb learning cycle, particularly observation and conceptualization.

Learning undertaken in a specialized environment however, does not necessarily transfer to reality and the very absence of some of the 'adverse' factors may mean that the trainee is not learning to cope with the actual situation. For example, case studies are useful in the consideration of a variety of possible courses of action, and of principles and concepts, but they can be criticized on the grounds that in the 'real' world we frequently have to decide on one best course of action and undertake personal responsibility for the results. What is learned during leisurely contemplation of alternatives may well not transfer to a stress situation. Furthermore, if the on-the-job climate is not supportive of what has been learned in the training situation, it is unlikely to be transferred.

While it is generally agreed that off-the-job training can be beneficial, it is necessary to introduce factors from the 'real' world and on-the-job experience as it becomes appropriate. There has, for instance, been a progressive increase in the number of 'organizational placement periods' as an essential part of educational courses. There is a current trend to attempt to obtain the best of both worlds by a more systematic organization of on-the-job training. This is evidenced by the use of trained operator instructors, for example, in the Youth Training Scheme with its very specific on-the-job requirements (see also Core Analysis, page 161), and by on-the-job coaching and the use of mentors (see Clutterbuck 1985).

Negative transfer occurs when old learning hinders performance on a new task, that is when the same stimulus requires a different response – for example, when driving a new car, certain actions will be accomplished easily through positive transfer – while others, such as changing strange gears may be confusing because of past experience. Literature suggests that although negative transfer can interfere with positive transfer it quickly gives way to positive transfer and may actually result in more flexible performance in the long term (see Holding 1965 and Duncan and Kelly 1983).

In matters relating to safety (such as learning to drive abroad on the right hand side of the road), or where dangerous or expensive machinery is involved, early learning may be vital and it is necessary to overcome negative effects immediately. Duncan and Kelly (1983) indicate that the more similar the responses required in the two tasks, the greater is the likelihood of negative transfer: it increases with response similarity until the point is reached where the required responses are identical and transfer becomes positive. There is no guaranteed method of avoiding the problem; one precaution is to check the learner's previous experience of similar tasks and carefully point out the differences and the possible consequences of negative transfer. It is worth noting that negative transfer is most likely to occur when the learner's attention is distracted, for example by situational factors or new elements of the task, such as approaching a roundabout when driving abroad.

Factors which assist learning transfer. Transfer of knowledge and skills to new situations is essential for continuing development and the attainment of flexibiity. It is a complex area and there is no one set of infallible rules but the following points may be helpful:

Transfer of learning from one job to another, or to future tasks (unknown). Transfer occurs through the understanding of general principles and concepts rather than by concentration on one narrow application. It can be facilitated by discovery learning (see page 125). This technique of training can be time-consuming and the training officer must therefore decide whether the emphasis should be on achieving a more rapid standard of performance in training, or in later performance, when the learning is expected to transfer to a different setting. There are dangers in accepting good 'training performance' as a predictor of good on-the-job performance unless steps have been taken to ensure transferability. It is necessary both to understand the general principle and to be able to apply it under different conditions. For example, a knowledge of employment law is less likely to transfer to the working situation if the learner has had no practice in applying it to the actual employment procedures in an organization. Examples of training methods which might assist this process are case studies and histories, structured exercises, assignments and projects. Group discussions and any means of associating and integrating new learning with existing knowledge also help. The readers might also like to consider the relationship of learning transfer with the reflection and conceptualization stages of the Kolb learning cycle described above.

Overlearning (i.e. practising beyond the level of minimum competence) facilitates transfer. In situations where confusion could be caused by the acquisition of several similar skills, minimum negative transfer will occur if the learner obtains a really good grasp of the first step before proceeding to the others.

Association factors; the transfer of learning will be assisted if the trainee can associate and integrate new learning with other learning which has already taken place. Any structured exercises which help attain this aim are therefore useful.

Motivation and genuine interest are important prerequisites; material learned verbatim (i.e. rote learning), purely for test or examination purposes without really becoming part of the learner's thought process, is unlikely to transfer.

Skill loss can prevent the occurrence of positive transfer. Annett (1983) has produced a useful guide on this topic. He suggests that manual skills which depend on hand/eye co-ordination and body movement deteriorate less from lack of practice than those which are mainly dependent on knowledge. The thoroughness of the original training, the trainee's understanding of what he is doing and why, and the division of lengthy procedures into coherent sequences, are all important factors in skill retention. Systematic rehearsal and mental practice also assist in the maintenance of skills already acquired.

THE ORGANIZATION AS A LEARNING ENVIRONMENT

If we accept the link between experience and learning in Bass and Vaughan's (1966) definition of learning (quoted at the beginning of this chapter) and consider Nord's (1969) application of Skinnerian theory of reinforcement to organizations, we find a number of important implications for the training officer.

A continuing learning process

The first implication is that the training officer is really intervening in a continuing learning process, and therefore requires diagnostic and analytical skills of a far higher order than is commonly realized. People learn by example and reinforcement and the influence of a superior upon his subordinate is very powerful. It is particularly strong when the superior holds the key to what may be termed the rewards and punishments of the organization. Successful training requires active management support – ideally it should start at the top and filter down through the organization, each superior being involved in the training of his subordinate. McGregor (1960) maintains that:

> every encounter between a superior and subordinate involves learning of some kind for the subordinate (and should for the superior too). The attitudes, habits and expectations of the subordinate will be reinforced or modified to some degree as a result of every encounter with the boss.... Day by day experience is so much more powerful that it tends to overshadow what the individual may learn in other settings.

Range of training interventions

Secondly, formal training encompasses much more than the provision of courses and off-the-job training: it includes *any* activity which provides organizational experience relevant to training objectives. Such activities range from short periods of work in different organizations, jobs or roles, to problem solving discussion groups, projects and giving advice. Removing barriers to learning constitutes an important intervention and can include the provision of open learning facilities to counter practical difficulties such as shift work and geographical location, as well as attempting to overcome attitudinal constraints. A highly skilled training officer can extend his role by helping the whole organization to learn more effectively from its experience, for example by reviewing the group processes and conducting a meeting.

Influence of organization climate

Thirdly, off-the-job training requires reinforcement at the workplace: the attitude of the superior and the climate of the organization are both powerful influences in determining whether training is likely to be transferred to the working situation. For instance, it is difficult for a manager to put into practice what he has just learned about the adoption of a participative and democratic style if the organization structure and atmosphere is autocratic. During courses for supervisors, a common cry is 'It's our managers you ought to have here'. However, being realistic, it is not always possible to start at the top, as we shall discuss later.

Unexpected repercussions

The fourth implication is that training may be likened to a game of skittles, where aiming at one target may have repercussions in a variety of other areas. The 'skittle effect' suggests that it may be impossible to train one group of people efficiently without changing the behaviour of another group. For example, the early ITBs, for a variety of reasons, put their first efforts into operative or craft training but soon found that in order to gain the benefits from the trained operators it was necessary to start training the supervisors. What appeared to be inefficiencies on the part of one section of employees was caused by their attempts to cope with poor materials or poorly maintained equipment. Training can sometimes act as a catalyst in triggering change in other parts of the organization and can also have unexpected consequences: in one instance, a complete redefinition and reappraisal of the organization structure resulted from an in-house training course for managers.

Development of attitude to training

The fifth is that everyone in the organization, not least management, is learning something about training and formulating an attitude towards it. The advantages of planned training have to be 'sold' and clearly demonstrated; this is no easy task and because organizations are all different there is no one recipe for success. The credibility of the training officer is an important factor and may come originally from his personality, but can ultimately only be maintained by successful training results. The starting point is crucial and it needs little imagination to see why the recommendation that training should start at the top is not always practicable. It is a question of weighing up the situation and deciding whether to start where the most serious problems and priorities appear to be, or where success seems to be the most likely, or to begin in an idealistic and politically sensitive manner at the top.

Necessity for commitment

The sixth implication is expressed by McGregor (1960) who suggests that:

> knowledge cannot be pumped into human beings the way grease is forced into a fitting on a machine. The individual may learn; he is not taught. Programmes do not produce managers; we cannot produce managers as we do products – we can only grow them.

Skill and knowledge are required in the design of training programmes to meet specific needs, but the most difficult task is often that of gaining enthusiasm and whole-hearted co-operation because people will normally only learn if they want to do so. It is all too easy to pay lip service to training. We could extend McGregor's horticultural analogy a little further and suggest that a gardener will succeed in cultivating a delicate plant if he starts by allowing it to grow in appropriate conditions and encourages and feeds it to help it bloom. We must never lose sight of the fact that commitment comes from involvement and if we involve people we must attempt to use their suggestions, even if they do not accord with neat and tidy models of the training described in Chapter 1. It is necessary for a training officer to be fully conversant with planned methods so that he can adapt them to specific situations, and his capacity to determine how far and how fast he can move towards the attainment of training goals is of singular significance.

Organization development

The final implication is that people learn from the organization and that, as Greiner (1972) maintains, 'their behaviour tends to be determined primarily by previous events and experience, not by what lies ahead.

He extends this analogy to the organization itself and suggests that a company can become:

> frozen in its present state of evolution, or ultimately in failure, regardless of market opportunities...(because of)...the inability of management to understand its organization development problems. [He quotes an example:] 'Key executives of a retail chain store hold on to an organization structure long after it has served its purpose, because their power is derived from this structure. The company eventually goes into bankruptcy'.

A lengthy analysis of the relationship between organization development and training is inappropriate here but is discussed by Thakur, Bristow and Carby (1978). Learning processes (as defined by Bass and Vaughan (1966)) are involved in organization development and if we recognize that training can include group activities which might trigger organizational change, then there is a very close link between training and organization development. A somewhat sophisticated assessment of training needs would therefore include not only details of the future development of individuals but also a framework for discussion of the future potential of the organization and the changes in climate and structure which would be necessary to achieve it. The simplest example of this is to be found in the small established company which is owner-managed. It often appears that such an organization has no training needs: all employees know their jobs as the company has been running the same way for years. If, as a result of training, the owner-manager sees the potential of his company in a different light and installs new methods, then the company may require not only new skills but a new organization structure. Training and organization development needs can therefore arise at the second level when a fresh assessment may be required. The whole operation must be seen as a dynamic process, not as a once and for all event.

Our aim in this chapter has been to examine specific links between learning theory and training practice, and their implications for the design and implementation of training programmes. Learning has been shown to be an inevitable organization feature: training is therefore seen as a deliberate intervention into a continuous learning process.

BIBLIOGRAPHY

ANNETT J, in *Psychology at work*. Warr P, (ed.). Harmondsworth, Penguin Education, 1974.

ANNETT J. *Skill loss*. Sheffield, Manpower Services Commission, 1983.

BASS B M and VAUGHAN J A. *Training in industry – the management of learning*. London, Tavistock Publications, 1966.

BELBIN R M. *Employment of older workers*. No. 2, *Training methods*. Paris, OECD, 1969.

BORGER R and SEABORNE A E M. *The psychology of learning*. Harmondsworth, Penguin, 1982.

BROMLEY D B. *The psychology of human ageing*. Harmondsworth, Pelican, 1975.

CLUTTERBUCK D. *Everyone needs a mentor*. London, Institute of Personnel Management, 1985.

DEPARTMENT OF EMPLOYMENT. *Glossary of training terms*. London, HMSO, 1971.

DUNCAN K D and KELLY C J. *Task analysis, learning and the nature of transfer*. Sheffield, Manpower Services Commission, 1983.

ESTES W K. *Learning theory and mental development*. New York, New York Academic Press, 1970.

FESTINGER L. *A theory of cognitive dissonance*. Evanston, Ill. Row Peterson, 1957.

FLEISHMAN E A. 'A leadership climate, human relations training and supervisory behaviour'. *Studies in Personnel and Industrial Psychology*. Homewood, Ill., Dorsey, 1967.

FLEISHMAN E A and HEMPEL W E. 'The relationship between abilities and improvement with practice in a visual discrimination task'. *Journal of Experimental Psychology*, 49, 1955.

GREINER L E. 'Evolution and revolution as organizations grow'. *Harvard Business Review*, July-August, 1972.

HAYES C, ANDERSON A, and FONDA N. 'International competition and the role of competence'. *Personnel Management*, September, 1984.

HAYES C, FONDA N, POPE N, STUART R, and TOWNSEND K. *Training for skill ownership*. Brighton, Institute of Manpower Studies, 1983.

HILGARD E R, ATKINSON R C, and ATKINSON R L. *Introduction to psychology*. New York, Harcourt Brace Jovanovich, 1983.

HOLDING D H. *Principles of training*. Oxford, Pergamon Press, 1965.

HONEY P and MUMFORD A. *Manual of learning styles*. Maidenhead, Honey, 1982

HONEY P and MUMFORD A. *Using your learning styles*. Maidenhead, Honey, 1983.

JACKSON K F. *The art of solving problems*. Bulmershe-Comino Problem Solving Project, Reading, Bulmershe College of Higher Education, 1984.

JENSEN A R. *Educability and group differences*. London, Harper & Row, 1976.

JAMES R. 'The use of learning curves'. *Journal of European Industrial Training*, Vol. 8, No. 7, 1984.

KAY H. 'Accidents: some facts and theories', in *Psychology at work*, Warr P (ed.). Harmondsworth, Middx. Penguin Education, 1983.

KENNEY J P J, DONNELLY E L and REID M A, *Manpower training and development*. London, Institute of Personnel Management, 1979.

KING D. *Training within the organization*. London, Tavistock Publications, 1964.

KOHLER W. *The mentality of apes*, International Library of Psychology, Routledge, 1973.

KOLB D A, RUBIN I N and McINTYRE J M *Organizational psychology:* a book of readings, 2nd edn Englewood Cliffs, NJ Prentice Hall, 1974.

KOLB D A, RUBIN I M and McINTYRE J M. *Organisational psychology – an experiential approach*. Englewood Cliffs, NJ Prentice Hall, 1974.

KRECH D, CRUTCHFIELD R S and BALLACHEY E L. *Individual in society*. New Jersey, McGraw Hill Book Company Inc., 1962.

MARKS GROUP. 'Alfred Mark's group quarterly survey'. *Personnel Management*, August, 1985.

McGEHEE W and THAYER P W. *Training in business and industry*. Wiley, 1961.

McGREGOR D. *The human side of the enterprise*. Maidenhead, McGraw Hill, 1960.

MUMFORD A. *Making experience pay*. Maidenhead, McGraw Hill, 1980.

NORD W R. 'Beyond the teaching machine: the neglected area of operant conditioning in the theory and practice of management'. *Organizational behaviour and human performance*. Vol. 4, 1969.

OTTO C P and GLASER R O. *The management of training*. London, Addison Wesley, 1970.

PASK G. 'Styles and strategies of learning'. *British Journal of Educational Psychology*. 46, 1976.

REID M. Unpublished paper, 1976.

RICHARDSON J, and BENNETT B. *Applying learning techniques to on-the-job development*. Part 2, *Journal of European Industrial Training*, Vol. 8, No. 3, 1984.

SELIGMAN M E P. *Helplessness*. San Francisco, Freeman, 1975.

SEYMOUR W D. *Skills analysis training*. London, Pitman, 1968.

SKINNER B F. *Science and human behaviour*. New York, Free Press U S, 1965.

SKINNER B F. *Walden two*. Collier MacMillan, 1976.

STAMMERS R, and PATRICK J, *Psychology of training*. London, Methuen, 1975, (Essential Psychology Series, Heriot P, General Editor).

SYKES A J M. 'The effect of a supervisory training course in changing supervisors' perceptions and expectations of the role of management'. *Human Relations*, 15, 1962.

THAKUR M, BRISTOW J and CARBY K. *Personnel in change – organization development through the personnel function*. London, Institute of Personnel Management, 1978.

THOMAS L F. 'Perceptual organization in industrial inspectors'. *Ergonomics*, Vol. 5, 1962. Quoted in *Experimental psychology in industry*, Holding D H (ed.), Harmondsworth, Penguin, 1969.

VERNON P E. *Intelligence and attainment tests*. London University Press, 1960.

VOGT O. 'Study of the ageing of the nerve cells'. *Journal of Gerontology*, No. 6, 1951.

WELFORD A T. 'On changes in peformance with age'. *Lancet*, Part 1, 1962.

WRIGHT D S and TAYLOR A. *Introducing psychology – an experimental approach*. Harmondsworth, Penguin Education, 1970.

6: *Assessing training needs – the job and the individual*

INTRODUCTION

In Chapter 3, we distinguished between training needs at the organization level, at the job or occupational level and at the individual employee level. We demonstrated how an assessment of organization needs can isolate problems which may indicate the need for the training of groups of employees or of particular individuals. These needs may be job specific or broadly developmental and possibly educational in nature. For instance, courses run under the auspices of the National Examinations Board for Supervisory Studies (NEBSS) can provide a general background to a supervisor's overall career development. The employee may view her requirements in this broader perspective because her aim might well be to prepare herself for promotion, or to obtain a better position elsewhere. There is thus a potential conflict between the needs perceived by the individual and those of the organization.

For example, a number of employees were to be trained in computer programming and the chief executive was adamant that they should learn only those aspects which related directly to their jobs because, in her view, a fuller training would have been unnecessarily expensive and would have empowered the employees to demand higher salaries, or possibly to obtain appointments in other organizations. Despite the risks involved, meeting developmental needs can be a prudent investment by cultivating future potential both for the organization and the nation, and can increase job satisfaction and encourage able employees to stay. The distinction between the two viewpoints is not always clear cut, and it is often possible to find a compromise or 'best fit', which will benefit both employee and employer.

As we have shown in Chapter 3, a consideration of organizational problems will also reveal a variety of job-specific training needs, and it is with these that we are now concerned. In this case there are two questions to be considered:

- first, how to identify the detailed skill and knowledge requirements of a particular job or task;
- secondly, how to assess the existing competence and potential of the employee against these requirements.

We shall approach the first question by considering the different ways of analysing jobs for training purposes, some of the techniques which are commonly used, and we shall then proceed to the second question of how an individual's performance may be assessed.

JOB TRAINING ANALYSIS

The use of job analysis is not confined to purposes associated with training and we therefore use the term 'job training analysis' to distinguish it from analyses carried out for recruitment, work study, ergonomic or other reasons. Although the emphasis and the detailed information will vary, there is likely to be some overlap of the results of these different types of analysis; for example, a training officer might find that a work study or job evaluation 'breakdown' can provide a useful starting point. Conversely, a job training analysis might be an aid in recruitment and selection.

The development and use of the techniques of job training analysis

In order to understand the literature which abounded on this topic in the 1960s and 1970s, it is necessary to give very brief consideration to the ways in which techniques developed. Much of the training which existed prior to 1964 was based on the 'common skills' approach. It was assumed that certain skills, such as those relating to 'human relations' were common to many jobs and that there were certain principles and practices of management which could be taught generally. Training courses could then be designed around the classical literature on these topics. In the majority of organizations very little was provided in the way of training based on the specific needs of individuals.

Although Seymour (1954) had published his work on skills analysis and some forward-looking training officers were working along these lines, the common belief was still that the best way of learning manual skills was by watching and imitating another operator (or 'sitting with Nellie' as it was then termed). Craft training was of a five or even seven year period where the apprentices spent a considerable proportion of their time carrying out menial tasks in the workshop, gradually absorbing what was happening, and in time learning by imitating the skilled people around them. Many managements had a paternalistic attitude towards training, seeing it as a peripheral activity, with attendance at courses and individual programmes within the gift of the company. The idea of spending money on analysing a job, or even the effort involved, would have been at odds with this philosophy.

It was from this scene that what might be termed the 'analytical movement' emerged. Encouraged by the Industrial Training Boards and boosted by the considerable incentive of the levy-grant system, job training analysis became a prime concern of many training officers; in fact some were employed by companies primarily to 'do the paperwork' (mainly job analyses and the resultant programmes), to maximize grant returns from the ITB concerned. Contemporary research, for example Woodward (republished in 1980), supported the movement by demonstrating that every supervisor's job was different and by implication had different training needs, and the work of Seymour (1954) had shown that, by studying skilled performance in meticulous detail, it was possible to provide planned training programmes which offered dramatic reductions in time and cost compared with the haphazard methods of watching and imitating, i.e. 'exposure training'.

There is no doubt that this concentration on rigorous analysis had some very beneficial effects. A considerable amount of training had previously been based on vague and indeterminate assumptions which were now being challenged, allowing some important truths to surface. One of the most significant of these was that imparting knowledge does not necessarily bring about an improvement in the appropriate skill, and that, depending upon the precise definition of objectives, not only training content, but appropriate technique might vary. For instance, knowledge about interviewing might be conveyed by prescribed reading, a lecture, discussion, or a film. But while skill development necessitates knowledge it also requires demonstration, and especially supervised practice and feedback. Today, this may appear an obvious truth but at that time it was surprising how many interviewing courses were produced and marketed with no mention of their objectives! For this reason, as we shall see later, a distinction is made between knowledge requirements and necessary skill, during the process of job analysis, although it has never been disputed that the two are closely interlinked.

This emphasis on analysis undoubtedly made those responsible for training think very carefully about exactly what they were attempting to achieve but it also had a number of drawbacks:

- it was inward-looking towards the specific skills and knowledge of a particular job at a given time;
- minimum allowance was generally made for the 'interface' between jobs, for example the creation of teams or the incidence of role conflict;
- it was time consuming and because it was assumed that all aspects of the job had to be investigated, in the early days in particular, analysts sometimes became absorbed in aspects of the job where improvement would have only a minimal effect on overall performance. This difficulty was recognized by the Industrial Training Boards in their later recommendation of the definition of key tasks (see page 160).

For these reasons and because the present demand for a flexible workforce capable of responding to technological and organization change has focused attention more upon the learning process than the acquisition of knowledge and skills for one specific job, analysis is now seen in a somewhat different perspective, although it is still considered essential. The current national emphasis is on broadly based training which, it is assumed, will transfer to a variety of jobs and tasks, the best known example of this approach being the Youth Training Scheme (see page 223). The attention of various bodies, such as the Institute of Personnel Management, points towards continuing development and trainee-centred learning assisted by the provision of suitable facilities and opportunities in an appropriate organization climate. In such organizations, the training officer is seen as a provider of flexible learning resources, as well as an analyst of what should be learned, and the approach tends more towards 'do it yourself' – if one might use such a term to describe training! This is partly because new technology has enabled the provision of 'open access' schemes, (such as the open learning programmes available to all employees in Austin Rover (see page 194) and partly because the approach is considered to be cost effective in meeting the requirement for organizations and their employees to update and change (see pages 48 and 259).

It might appear that fashion has come round full circle and returned to 'common skills', but this is an oversimplification. Job training analysis is still an essential technique in the training officer's armoury of skills. Indeed it is even more valuable now than it was in the 1960s and 1970s because the pace of technological innovation necessitates more frequent reviews of the skills required. If an organization needs to make a sudden and speedy change, the shortest and most efficient training programmes will be based on careful analysis. Two opposing influences can be seen in the current situation. When the economy is depressed, the deeper the recession, the narrower will be the training regarded as essential and the shorter the training time which will be seen by employers as realistic. On the other hand, the necessity for change demands an adaptive and proactive workforce. In the former circumstance, job analysis is an essential tool to ensure that training programmes are directed towards the critical aspects of the job. In a changing situation, the broad training, such as that required by Youth Training Scheme or the foundation courses for craft trainees, must also be based on an analysis of the skills and knowledge which are common to a number of tasks to enable learning transfer to take place (see Core Analysis, page 162).

Many of the present training techniques, such as computer-assisted learning, must be based on detailed analysis. A computerized programme will only be as appropriate as the quality and relevance of its contents, which must be carefully pre-programmed by its authors. The trainee will frequently be totally dependent on the programme and instructions provided.

THE PROCESS OF JOB TRAINING ANALYSIS

As Boydell (1977) points out: 'Job analysis is a process of examining a job. Thus it is not a particular document, but rather gives rise to certain documents, the product of an analytical examination of the job'. A variety of documents can arise as a result of the analytical techniques; the main ones are as follows:

Job description is 'a broad statement of the purpose, scope, responsibilities and tasks which constitute a particular job' (Manpower Services Commission 1981). The description contains the job title, the department in which the job holder works, to whom she is responsible and for whom she has responsibility for, the purpose of the job, a list of the major tasks and, if appropriate, a brief description of any resources for which she is accountable. In a large organization, it may be advisable to add the hours and precise place of work, as it can provide useful information in determining availability and suitable timing for proposed training programmes. A job description helps to assess the importance of the job and clarifies its purpose and content for the job holder, her superior and others with whom she works. It is useful in recruitment and selection.

Job specification is 'a detailed statement, derived from the job analysis, of the knowledge and the physical and mental activities involved in the job and of the environment within which the job is performed' (Manpower Services Commission 1981). These activities are normally classified under the two headings of knowledge and skill and sometimes a third heading, 'attitudes', is used. In the case of a secretary's job, two of the tasks in the job description might be typing letters and answering the telephone. Two of the associated 'physical and mental activities' might be knowledge of organization style and format of letters, or interpersonal skills required in dealing with irate customers on the telephone.

Training specification is 'a detailed statement of what a trainee needs to learn, based on a comparison between the job specification and the individual's present level of competence' (Manpower Services Commission 1981). Methods of determining the latter may be by comparison with experienced worker's standard in the case of an operator, or in the case of a manager, by staff appraisal.

Task analyses give details of each of the tasks of the job, often in the form of Stages and Keypoints (see page 165). In the secretary's job an example might be the stages and important points to remember in using a piece of office equipment, such as a telephone switchboard.

Faults analyses give details of the faults which can occur in specific tasks (see page 166).

When a training officer begins an analysis she has a certain amount of the background information about the job but she should avoid being unduly influenced by, for example, the classification or title. Work classifications such as managerial, skilled or semi-skilled, are in themselves of little help beyond conveying a general idea of different types of work. Work categories are difficult to define, since there are no sharp boundaries between them and usage can vary from one industry to another and even between companies in the same industry. Moreover, the terms can be misleading. Work classified as 'semi-skilled' can require a high degree of skill in particular tasks, while the category 'unskilled' is a contradiction in terms because all work, no matter how menial, requires the application of some, albeit low order, skill.

Because of the analytical work carried out by the Industrial Training Boards, it is now often possible to find published documents of the type described above, relating to most kinds of jobs. While these can be extremely useful as a basis, it is important to ensure that they really do refer to similar work and that there are not important organization-specific requirements.

In practice, jobs are varied and have many facets. Some jobs consist of few tasks, others of many, some are relatively static and others subject to frequent changes, some require a high degree of discretion while others are mainly prescribed, some necessitate formal education, others none. Additional complications are caused by the wide variety of social and physical environments in which jobs are carried out. A helpful way forward is to view a job as consisting of the two components, knowledge and skill. This sub-division provides a useful framework in which to collect and organize information about the job and as we have already seen, the distinction is also necessary at the later stage of devising training programmes.

A wide variety of skills and knowledge may need to be analysed, for example job skills may be manual (psychomotor), diagnostic, interpersonal (face-to-face), or decision making. The knowledge component may be technical, procedural (what to do and when), or concerned with company organization. Moreover, jobs vary widely in the range, variety and degree of skills and knowledge needed to perform them (see Singleton 1978). With many different combinations of these components occurring in jobs, different analytical approaches and techniques are necessary.

Types of analysis

There are four main approaches to analysing jobs for training purposes: the comprehensive, the key task, the problem-centred, and the core analysis.

The comprehensive analysis

In this approach, all facets of the job are examined with the aim of producing a detailed record of every task in the job, and the skills, knowledge and attitudes required to carry out every one of these tasks. The training officer normally goes through certain stages. First, she checks that the approach is appropriate and that the time and costs incurred are justified: a less comprehensive and less expensive approach may often be adequate. The following criteria need to be satisfied before a comprehensive analysis is carried out:

- the majority of work tasks which the trainee will have to do are unfamiliar to her, difficult to learn and the cost of error unacceptable;
- time and other resources are available for a full analysis – the job is likely to remain basically unchanged and the resultant training programme used frequently by a number of trainees;
- the job is closely prescribed and the 'correct' method of doing it must be learnt;
- the need for analysis is accepted by management and, where relevant, by the trade union.

A situation in which an exhaustive analysis of this kind is necessary is where new plant is to be installed in a factory and, because unfamiliar operating skills are required, the staff concerned need retraining.

Secondly, having decided that a comprehensive analysis is justified, the training officer initially examines the job to gain an overall picture and to write a job description. The third step is to examine the job in depth to produce a job specification.

Examples of techniques used in a comprehensive analysis are described later in this chapter and while there is no single correct approach, a useful sequence is to identify the main responsibilities of the job holder and then to record the constituent tasks for each of these, together with the skills and knowledge involved in carrying them out. For example, the responsibilities of a garage forecourt attendant may include accepting new stock and receiving payment for goods sold. Taking the first of these, a number of separate tasks can be identified, such as the handling of petrol deliveries, or receiving a consignment of new tyres. Each task is then analysed to find out what knowledge and skill is necessary. In the case of the petrol delivery, the attendant must know the relevant fire precautions and understand their significance, the sequences to be followed in dipping petrol tanks, the paperwork procedures, etc.

On completion of the comprehensive analysis, the training officer will have specified for every task, its objectives, frequency, required standard of performance, and the skill and knowledge needed to achieve it. With this information she prepares a training syllabus and designs a training programme to meet the requirements of the employee (see Boydell 1977 and page 189).

Key task analysis

As its name suggests, this approach to job training analysis is concerned with the identification and detailed investigation of the key or central tasks within a job. Wellens (1970) has pointed out that job analysis as a means of determining training needs is at its most effective at the lower end of the organization; the discretionary and ever-changing nature of supervisory and managerial jobs means that they cannot be predetermined or prescribed accurately. Indeed, often the most important task facing a manager is to determine what in fact he or she ought to be doing and this can involve a complicated balance of priorities. Although a breakdown into tasks and their requisite knowledge and skills can be of some use at supervisory and middle management levels, a total analysis would be costly, cumbersome and likely to obscure the critical areas of the job. At management level, therefore, job descriptions and specifications are expressed in more general terms, concentrating on objectives, targets and key areas.

Key task analysis is appropriate for any type of job where the following conditions apply:

- the job consists of a large number of different tasks, not all of which are critical for effective performance; it is assumed that the job holder does not normally require training in minor or non-key tasks;
- the job is changing in emphasis or in content, resulting in a continuing need to establish priority tasks, standards of performance and the skills and knowledge required.

As in the case of comprehensive analysis, the key task approach yields a job description (and a limited job specification), in addition to details of the critical tasks in the job.

Problem-centred analysis

This approach differs from those described previously in that no attempt is made to produce a description or specification of either the whole job or all of its key tasks. In a problem-centred approach, analysis is limited to a difficulty considered to have a training solution, such as the chief chemist asking the training department to organize a report writing course for her technical staff because their reports were unclear and poorly structured. The training officer concentrates her analysis on this particular aspect of the technical staff's work and excludes others unless they are directly relevant to the specific problem. A problem-centred approach is appropriate when:

- the need for training is urgent but resources are not available for a more extensive analysis;
- a fuller analysis is unnecessary, for example, where an employee's work is satisfactory except in a specific area.

Warr and Bird (1968) have developed an approach to identifying the training needs of junior managers which is basically a problem-centred type of analysis. They call it 'training by exception', because the analysis concentrates on those issues which are exceptions to a supervisor's normally adequate performance.

Core analysis

The types of analysis so far described are applicable to specific jobs (or groups of jobs) within an organization. The training officer, however, may be involved in planning programmes under national schemes, mainly for young people with the status of trainee rather than employee. Here the intention is to provide broad training which might transfer to a variety of tasks, thereby presenting participants with enhanced opportunities of obtaining work within as wide a range of organizations as possible. Clearly this kind of programme must be based on a different type of analysis.

One method used is core analysis (see Mansfield 1985), where instead of describing a task in her own language and the terminology of a particular workplace, which would make interpretation in other organizations difficult, the analyst uses a generally recognized reference list of core skills. The Manpower Services Commission (1984) defines core skills as 'those skills which are common in a wide range of tasks and which are essential for competence in these tasks'. Each core skill is identified and described by a core key word in the form of an active verb such as 'interpret', 'measure' or 'find out'. It is suggested, by Mansfield (1985), that an adequate description of job competence must include more than a list of the core skills required. An example of this is two office workers, both of whom carry out similar tasks, such as filing, answering the telephone or making appointments. One of them, however, is a junior clerk and the other is personal secretary to a chief executive. It is not necessarily the tasks performed but the degree of responsibility, complexity or decision-making which distinguishes these two jobs. Mansfield therefore refers to 'three distinct skill components involved in applying knowledge and skill on the job':

- task-related skills: i.e. those used in carrying out the task;
- task management skills: i.e. those used to manage a number of tasks, including planning, problem solving and decision making;
- job/role environment skills which include working directly with people outside the workplace, working in a hazardous environment or one which can be critical in terms of cost, such as dealing with highly confidential work.

It is thus possible to make a more realistic analysis, with the task related skills 'supplying the 'bare minimum' competence and the other skill components describing how the tasks are implemented in a variety of work situations' (Mansfield 1985).

Core analysis was developed in the Youth Training Scheme but it is claimed to have far wider applications, as it provides a useful identification of competencies which could be used for many purposes such as: recruitment and selection, performance appraisal, career counselling, identification of training needs. Furthermore, this type of job breakdown is sufficiently straightforward to be understood by the younger trainee. Trainees and supervisors can share a non-technical document which might be regarded as a map, or itinerary for the training. This enables a more participative and learner-centred style than is usual with more traditional analyses, where the training officer and instructor normally retain the resultant documents entirely for their own use. Core analysis can also provide a basis for recording, discussing and assessing achievement, strengths and weaknesses, and identifying individual training needs. Using the detailed list of core skills it is possible to give more precise feedback and knowledge of results (see page 133, also Profiling page 233). As the list of core skills is widely recognized, it should provide a useful basis for determining exactly what training has been given to those who have taken part in YTS schemes. This will be of considerable help in assessing their residual needs should they undertake employment in different organizations.

In implementing any one of these main approaches, a training officer will use specific analytical techniques, her choice depending upon the job she is analysing. Commonly used techniques include stages and key points analysis, (a technique which originated in the government-sponsored Training Within Industry programme, and which was thus formerly termed TWI analysis), manual skills analysis, faults analysis, decisions analysis and interpersonal skills analysis. Some of these techniques are discussed later in this chapter.

ANALYTICAL TECHNIQUES

Many different techniques have been developed to enable the variety of job skills to be analysed and recorded; amongst the best known are the following: stages and key points analysis, manual skills analysis, faults analysis and interpersonal skills analysis.

Stages and key points analysis

This technique can be applied to any job for which the learning time is a matter of hours or days. It can also be applied to relatively simple tasks which are part of a more difficult job, but it is unsuitable for complex work. A stages and key points analysis is normally undertaken by a trained instructor, supervisor or senior operator.

The analyst watches and questions an operator at work and, using a stages and key points breakdown sheet (see Figure 6.1), records in the 'stage' column the different steps in the job. Most semi-skilled jobs are easily broken down into their constituent parts and a brief summary is made of what the operator does in carrying out each part. The analyst then examines the stages separately and for each one describes in the 'instruction' column against the appropriate stage, how the operator performs each task. The description of the operator's skill and knowledge is expressed in a few words. At the same time, the analyst notes in the 'key points' column of the breakdown sheet any special points such as quality standards or safety matters, which should be emphasized to a trainee learning the job. A 'stages and keypoints' breakdown sheet serves two purposes; it provides the *pro forma* which aids the analysis and, when completed, it is used as the instruction schedule. This is an efficient method of analysing relatively simple jobs. It is well proven and has been used widely since its introduction into the UK from the USA as part of the Training Within Industry programme (TWI) during the Second World War.

Manual skills analysis (MSA)

This is a technique derived from work study, and developed by Seymour (1966) to isolate the skills and knowledge employed by experienced workers performing tasks requiring a high degree of manual dexterity. It is used to analyse short-cycle repetitive operations, such as assembly tasks and other similar factory work. Its application, however, is not restricted to the factory nor to semi-skilled jobs. It can be used to analyse any task in which manual dexterity and perception are important features.

The hand, finger and other body movements of an experienced operative are observed and recorded in great detail as she carries out her work. This is a highly specialized technique and should be used selectively: those parts of the job which are relatively easy to learn are analysed in much less depth (a stages and key points approach may often be adequate), and a MSA is limited to those tasks (or parts of tasks) which involve unusual skills. These are the 'tricky' parts of a job, which, while presenting no difficulty to the experienced operative, have to be analysed in depth before they can be taught to trainees. In Figure 6.2 we give an example of a typical *pro forma* used in a MSA which illustrates the breakdown of the complex task of filleting raw fish in a food processing factory. It will be seen from this example that an experienced operative's hand movements are recorded in minute detail, together with the cues (vision and other senses) which the operative uses in performing the task (see page 122). Explanatory comments are added, where necessary, in the 'comments' column. Special training is needed to apply this level of analysis and, in particular, to identify the cues on which the operator

JOB TITLE: How to make a job breakdown

Stage (what to do in stages to advance the job)	*Instructions (how to perform each stage)*	*Key points (items to be emphasized)*
1 Draw-up table	Rule three columns. Allow space for column headings and job title	Use this sheet as example
2 Head the columns	On top line insert the title of job Insert: Column 1 (Stage) Column 2 (Instructions) Column 3 (Key Points)	Headings – summarize what worker needs to know to perform each job Watch for steps which are performed from habit
3 Follow through the job to be analysed	After each step, ask yourself – 'What did I just do?' Note places where the worker could go astray. Note items to be emphasized. Note hazards. Stress safety points	Write notes clearly and concisely Keep stages in order Ensure directions are complete – never assume they are
4 Fill in Columns 1, 2 and 3 as stage 3 above is performed	Make brief and to-the-point notes	Review and emphasize these 'Key Points' decisively
5 Number the stages	Follow the sequence a worker must follow when learning the job	
6 Follow the job through using directions in Columns 1 and 2	Follow the instructions exactly	
7 Check that all 'Key Points' are included	Record in Column 3 all points where the worker may be confused	

Figure 6.1

A 'stages' and 'key points' breakdown sheet. (Reproduced with acknowledgement to the former Ceramics, Glass and Mineral Products Industry Training Board.)

depends in both normal and abnormal work conditions, and the senses by which she receives them.

For further details of the analysis of manual skills, see Seymour (1968).

Faults analysis

When analysing a job, information is collected about the faults which commonly occur and especially those which are costly: 'the process of analysing the faults occurring in a procedure, product or service, specifying the symptoms, causes and remedies of each...' Manpower Services Commission (1981), is termed a faults analysis. The result of this analysis – a faults specification – provides a trainee with details of faults which she is likely to come across in her work, how she can recognize them, what causes them, what effects they have, who is responsible for them, what action the trainee should take when a particular fault occurs, and how a fault can be prevented from recurring. A faults specification is usually drawn up either in a tabular or 'logic tree' form (see Jones 1968), and is useful both for instruction purposes and as a memory aid for an employee after completion of training.

Interpersonal skills analysis

Interpersonal skills are sometimes referred to as interactive, face-to-face, or social skills. Some jobs, such as those of a sales assistant or a receptionist, contain tasks which involve dealing with the public and have a very obvious interpersonal skills content which can determine successful performance. These skills should be analysed if they are to be taught and learned systematically, but in practice, despite their importance, they are rarely analysed in any depth. They are often extremely complex and have proved very difficult to analyse in the absence of adequate tools and methods, but see Argyle (1983). Attempts have been made to identify the cues and responses which characterize the successful use of interpersonal skills and one approach, developed by the Food, Drink and Tobacco Industry Training Board (1972), is illustrated in Figure 6.3. While at first reading the example may be so obvious that it should be taken for granted, skills such as those described are very often conspicuous by their absence in day-to-day work situations.

In other types of jobs, e.g. managerial and supervisory positions, the need for interpersonal skills occurs at the 'interface', i.e. the

DEPARTMENT: Fish-filleting		TASK: Fillet/trim small plaice			DATE:
Section or Element	*Left hand*	*Right hand*	*Vision*	*Other Senses*	*Comments*
Select fish	Reach to trough- grasp fish with T and 1 2 3 4 around belly, p/u and bring forward to board	P/u knife with T and 1 2 3 4 around handle. With sharp edge of blade to right of filleter	Glance ahead for knife position on board	Touch LH on fish	
			Glance ahead for fish position on trough		
		Knife hold:			
Position fish	Place fish on board so that the dorsal fins fall to the edge of the board and the head lies to the right hand side of the filleter.	Hold knife handle against first and third joints of the fingers. Place upper part of T (1st joint) against lower blunt edge of knife and the lower part of T against upper edge of handle. Do not grasp knife tightly. Do not curl tip of fingers into palm of hand.	Check position of fish	Touch LH on fish	Knife is held in the RH during the complete filleting cycle. If knife is held correctly it should be possible to move the knife to the left and right by 'opening' and 'closing' the knuckles (when T is removed from handle).

LH = left hand
RH = right hand
p/u = pick up
T = thumb

1 = first finger
2 = second finger
3 = third finger
4 = fourth finger

Synchronous movements are recorded on the same line
Successive movements are recorded on succeeding lines

Figure 6.2

Manual skills analysis (Reproduced with acknowledgement to the former Food, Drink and Tobacco Industry Training Board.)

TASK BREAKDOWN: Interpersonal (Social) Skills

JOB: Manageress – Retail confectioner   TASK: Handling complaint (returned merchandise)

Stage	*Cues (eye, ear, etc.)*	*Responses (voice, eye, gesture, action)*	*Attention points*
1 Manageress (M) becomes aware of customer (C)	M sees/hears C enter shop	M (busy writing) puts pen down, makes eye contact with C and smiles M also tries to asses C. M decides course of action	M is prepared because she is facing shop entrance while working – stops working to impress C and to prepare for her. M smiles to make initial welcoming contact, M makes subjective judgement about type/mood of C and looks for signals
2 Manageress contacts and greets customer	Notes C's continuing stiffness and hostility	M comes round counter to C – gestures her further into shop. M smiles warmly with direct eye contact, greets C questioningly – by name	M removes barrier of counter to reduce anxiety – encourages C away from other customers. M's greeting designed to get C to talk, to relax and feel important
3 Manageress listens to complaint	Watches C's reactions. Hears complaint (that C's daughter had earlier been sold stale merchandise). M notes C's embarrassment by lack of eye contact. M detects that 'wind is slowly going from C's sails'	Keeps eye contact with C, nods when C makes valid point. M gives C her full attention – Allows C to talk until she has had her say	M knows danger of alienating C by interrupting her story M's attention makes C feel important – convinces her M is sympathetic not hostile
4 Manageress deals with complaint	Watches C's visible relief notes sincere thanks	Thanks C for her action. Smiles – offers money back immediately. Moves to till	M's actions dispels any remaining hostility/embarrassment
5 Manageress promotes possible future sale	Sees interest in C's eyes: notes enthusiastic response, hears C's daughter is soon to marry	While opening till, chats to C about daughter. Avoids too much eye contact to allow C to relax – hands over money with no reference to original problem	M responds to distract C from original problem and establish firm rapport – could shop cater for wedding?

relationship with other job holders or because of the demands of team work. Traditional analysis, looking inwards at the actual tasks of the job, has a tendency to ignore this important aspect. It is most likely to be revealed as the result of a problem-centred approach, where lack of co-ordination and understanding between colleagues or departments soon becomes apparent. It is only necessary to consider how much of a manager's or supervisor's time is spent in dealing with people to realize the importance of interpersonal skills.

Because of its complex interactive content, however, a sequence of behaviour cannot always be prescribed and special techniques of analysis are required. One such method is that of Rackham, Honey and Colbert (1971), who have devised a system of analysing face-to-face behaviour into categories, such as: 'suggesting', 'building' (on the suggestions of others), 'proposing', 'criticizing', 'seeking clarification', etc. Trained observers provide participants with a detailed breakdown of the behaviour they have exhibited during group task exercises, discuss this with them and provide opportunities for them to practise different behaviour categories. Prior to this, the trainers have conducted surveys throughout their organizations to take account of organizational climate and to ascertain which categories of behaviour appear to be associated with managerial success. This information is then fed back to their trainees.

Another method of analysing interpersonal skills is transactional analysis (TA). It is seen as a communications tool, the main purpose of which is to enable trainees to analyse their own interactions and develop insight and awareness, thus increasing their effectiveness. For further information, see Carby and Thakur (1976).

CARRYING OUT A JOB TRAINING ANALYSIS

The analyst

A line manager is ideally placed to identify the training needs of her subordinates, but she will not necessarily have the experience to carry out a full analysis. In most organizations it is the training officer, or one of her staff, who carries out the job training analyses. We saw in Chapter 3 that the assessment of an organization's training requirements can be a difficult process and the assessor must be technically competent and acceptable to those with whom she works. Similar qualities are needed by a job analyst, who requires an appreciation of learning difficulties, a logical mind, the ability to separate the important from the less significant parts of the job and an imaginative approach in providing training solutions. She also needs to be able to handle, at least initially, any difficulties exposed during an analysis. Motivation and discipline problems, misunderstandings caused by ill-defined responsibilities, and inappropriate organization structures can be uncovered, particularly when an organization first introduces job analysis. These kinds of problems adversely affect the business and therefore although concentrating mainly on training matters, the analyst has a responsibility to contribute to help solve such difficulties, where appropriate.

Steps in the analysis

Figure 6.4 shows the main steps in analysing a job for training purposes. The sequence shown in the figure illustrates a comprehensive job training analysis but the principles involved also apply to other forms of analysis.

Step 1: gain the co-operation of all concerned

A prerequisite for successful job training analysis is that those who are in any way concerned co-operate with the analyst, and that the general industrial relations climate in the department is favourable. The co-operation of the immediate superior, the job holder (and other managers, as necessary) and of staff or trade union representatives is essential, but cannot always be relied upon. Two typical problems which an analyst faces are that managers are too busy to spare the time to assist her, or that if the employee mistrusts the analyst's motives, inaccurate or incomplete data may result. An analyst has to exercise considerable interpersonal skill in explaining the purpose of the analysis, convincing those affected of its value and enlisting their support. Before carrying out any of the steps below it is necessary to inform everyone of the purpose of the investigation, or suspicions may be aroused when the analyst starts to ask questions. Consulting and involving people at the outset also ensures a better chance of obtaining their commitment to any training programme which might result, and constitutes the first step in a training intervention.

Step 1
Gain co-operation of all concerned.
↓
Step 2
Carry out pre-analysis investigation.
↓
Step 3
Decide appropriate analytical approach.
↓
Step 4
Analyse the job.
↓
Step 5
Write the job description.
↓
Step 6
Write the job specification.
↓
Step 7
Write the training specification.

Figure 6.4
The main steps in analysing a job for training purposes.

Step 2: carry out a pre-analysis investigation

A number of points are considered before an analysis is started to ensure that it is necessary and justified, since the activity of analysing a job can take many hours to complete. It is first necessary to establish that it is a training analysis that is wanted, because a problem which may appear to be due to a lack of training may have other causes, such as excessive workloads or poor organization (see Chapter 1). When it is agreed that the problem is a training one, the next step is to decide whether a training analysis is required. Questions, such as the following, clarify this point:

- What is the organization losing in terms of production or services because the employee has not been formally trained?
- Is sufficient information already available (e.g. from suppliers' manuals) to make a job training analysis unnecessary?

- How long does it take an average employee to learn the job without training? If a matter of hours or days then analysis may be unnecessary.

Having established that a training analysis is needed, a check is made to ensure that the job is unlikely to be changed significantly, e.g. as a result of the introduction of new work methods or performance standards, alterations to operational policies, or the restructuring of the organization. This check avoids the analysis of obsolescent jobs.

Step 3: decide the appropriate analytical approach

The criteria for selecting an appropriate approach to job training analysis have been discussed previously. At this stage, the techniques of analysis most likely to provide the necessary information are chosen. For example, a stages and key points analysis may be appropriate for most of the tasks within a job, with one task requiring a faults analysis in addition (see page 166). The choice of analytical techniques tends to be straightforward but care is needed to assess the real, as opposed to assumed, learning difficulties in a job. For example, the Engineering Industry Training Board (1971) has described how, in analysing certain craft jobs, manual skills analysis was thought to be an appropriate technique. Subsequently, it was realized that more importance needed to be attached to analysing the planning and decision-making activities rather than to the detailed job knowledge and procedures.

Step 4: analyse the job

The analyst needs to know the sources of information available, the appropriate methods of collecting it, and the depth of analysis required.

Sources of information include the following:

- the job holder, who can often provide the bulk of the data required;
- the job holder's superior, who will specify the purpose of the job and the necessary standards of performance; these points may be obvious for work where the content is largely prescribed, as in the case of most semi-skilled jobs, but it is often much less clear in other types of work, notably managerial jobs;

- service departments, such as O and M, work study, personnel and cost accounting, can assist the analyst working in a large organization;
- organization records, such as job descriptions/specifications, organization charts, policies, plans, procedures and sales and production records;
- suppliers' manuals are an essential source of information for training purposes, particularly when new equipment is introduced for the first time.

Methods of analysis

The analyst first identifies the job holder's responsibilities and tasks, and then finds out for each task what is done, why it is done and how it is done. This process involves analysing what plans the job holder follows, what cues she uses in initiating, controlling and completing a task or part of a task, and what skills and knowledge are required to respond effectively to the relevant cues at various stages in each task.

The choice of methods will depend upon the characteristics of the job to be analysed, but the following methods are commonly used (see also Talbot and Ellis 1969):

Observation by the analyst: in many cases watching an employee at work provides a great deal of information, particularly about what a job holder actually does and how she does it, and to a lesser extent why she does it. Very detailed and continuous observation is required when analysing the manual skill used by an operative in complex and short cycle repetitive work (see page 167). Continuous observation is not normally warranted for jobs in which tasks are repeated at irregular intervals, as sufficient information can usually be obtained by random sampling. For example, activity sampling of a manager's job can be an economic and effective means of determining the different activities in which she is involved during the course of a day, week or longer period of time. Observation by itself, however, is inadequate and at times not very informative: observing a supervisor standing looking down a conveyor belt, or a process operator reading a number of instruments on a control panel is of little help to the analyst.

Self observation: this can be a useful method of collecting data on the purpose and content of a job but relies entirely upon the job holder's willingness to keep a diary or record of her activities. The technique is used in the analysis of managerial and other work characterized by a high degree of discretion. Disadvantages of self-observation are that the observer may be too close to the job to see it objectively and that she may, for her own purposes, under- or over-emphasize certain aspects of her work at the expense of others. The job holder may be very busy and by the end of the day her recollections may not be strictly accurate. It is essential that the required record is as simple as possible, so that it can be kept up to date rather than becoming a chore to be completed later. One advantage of diary keeping is that it obliges the job holder to consider exactly how she is spending her time – a very salutory experience to anyone who has never done so! The majority of people tend to over-estimate what they should achieve within a given period and, by drawing attention to this fact, keeping a diary may well arouse interest in the management of time.

Questionnaire: this is a particularly useful technique if a significant number of analyses have to be made and should be used as a preliminary to an interview/discussion. It allows the job holder to think carefully beforehand and ensure that all relevant detail is included. The analyst must be skilled in questionnaire design.

Fact-finding interviews: discussions with the job holder and other relevant employees are an essential part of the job training analysis. The analyst should be competent in the use of interview techniques, such as the framing of questions and careful listening, to gain the maximum benefits from this method.

'Do-it-yourself': one way of learning about a job is to try to do it. By putting herself in the position of a trainee, the analyst experiences at first hand the difficulties involved in learning the job. While this may be impracticable or unnecessary, there are certain situations in which it is a useful method of collecting information. Tasks which are difficult to describe in words, such as those involving a high degree of manual dexterity, are amenable to this form of analysis.

Depth of analysis

Identifying the main responsibilities in a job is usually straightforward, identifying the tasks within a job is also relatively easy, but deciding how much detail is needed about a task and the skills and knowledge required to do it presents a problem. A solution is offered by Annett and Duncan (1968), see also Annett, Duncan, Stammers and Gray (1971), who argue that:

> a major difficulty, and one of the first to be encountered, is that a complete description of the execution of a task will include the information required for training, but will usually include much else as well. What is needed is some explicit rule or guide as to what to record for training purposes and at what level of description to operate. There is a danger that, without some rule as to what to include and what to exclude, essential training information will be buried in a plethora of detail.

The rule which Annett and Duncan propose is to: 'Begin with the most gross description of performance and ask two questions – what is the estimated probability, without training, of inadequate performance?, and what would be the estimated cost (in a general sense) to the system, of inadequate performance?' They suggest that the analyst should make a progressively more detailed investigation and description of the elements in a task until the limits of the training need are reached. This limit to the analysis will vary from task to task and is attained when it is considered that trainees would perform adequately without training, or should inadequate performance result, it would not be a serious matter. In other words, the task should continue to be broken down and described until the cost and probability of failure are negligible.

The use of Annett and Duncan's rule helps in a practical way to avoid unnecessary analysis. It also ensures that due consideration is given to such factors as safety problems, the trainee's ability to learn the job or task, and learning difficulties posed by the job. We might quote as an example the job of a waitress where one of the tasks identified might be to clear the tables in the restaurant. A subordinate operation might be to clean and polish the tables and another to stack and carry a pile of plates. It might be considered that a trainee waitress could wipe and polish tables without any tuition, but that stacking and carrying a pile of plates might require a little instruction, in order to avoid breakage and possible disturbance in the restaurant! Duncan and Kelly (1983) point out that in applying the 'stop rule', we are relying upon learning transfer to enable the trainee to perform certain tasks to an adequate standard (see page 141).

Finally, the analyst must investigate any learning problems which characterize the environment in which the trainee will eventually apply her skills and knowledge. For example, trainee bar staff may find it relatively easy to learn individual tasks off-the-job, but very hard to cope with the real work situation in a busy pub, when they have to be competent at serving rounds of drinks, pricing them correctly, chatting with the customers they are serving, and avoiding upsetting those they are not – all at the same time!

Step 5: write the job description

It is possible that this is already in existence in which case the analyst will have been able to use it as a guide. It is, however, useful at this point to check its accuracy. Jobs can change very rapidly; not every organization has a systematic updating procedure and the training officer may be the last to receive formal notification, if indeed she receives it at all. Much time and money can be wasted by training to standards and sequences which have been changed, and it is also extremely discouraging to the trainee. For this reason, it is helpful to mark the date at the top of the job description, and in fact of all job analysis documents at the time they are compiled.

Step 6: write the job specification

When the analysis has been completed and the data checked, the job specification is drawn up. The precise nature will depend upon the type of job. For instance, as we have noted, a managerial position will require different information from that of an operator. A job specification for training purposes gives much detail on skills and knowledge required and, as we have seen from the developments in core analysis, may reflect the environmental and 'job/role environment skills', as well as the tasks performed. It is good style, and useful for cross reference, to list the main tasks in the same order and with the same numbering as on the job description. The completed specification provides the yardstick against which a trainee's performance will be measured and any shortfall identified. It also provides the information required to design and run an appropriate training programme (see page 189). Before embarking upon the design of the programme, the training officer should verify the job specification with appropriate managers and obtain agreement by all relevant parties. It is particularly necessary to check the emphasis given to the different items. One of the important benefits of a detailed specification is that it clarifies the job, as frequently the incumbent's conception of her precise duties and responsibilities is different from that of her superior.

ASSESSING AN EMPLOYEE'S PERFORMANCE

We have examined the different approaches and techniques used in job training analysis and have explained that the end product of analysis is a statement of the expectations which an employer has of a particular job in the form of the skill and knowledge necessary for acceptable performance. This information provides the criteria against which to measure an employee's performance. Before an individual's training need can be determined, it is necessary to know her present level of competence. In this final section we consider briefly the ways in which this information can be obtained.

A new employee, selected against a personnel specification, should already have, in broad terms, the necessary ability, achievement and experience, and should require only limited training. It is, however, advisable to check this, either by discussion with the trainee, or, if appropriate, by administering a test (see page 202). Taking account of present knowledge and skill reduces the training time and therefore saves money and prevents boredom! It also serves a further purpose in that the new job may be very familiar in most respects but differs in one or two important aspects in which previous experience can hinder performance. This is known as negative transfer of learning. Possibly the only training which might be required would be to discuss the areas of difference and provide practice in them. With unplanned training, these areas would be found by trial-and-error but, particularly where safety controls are concerned, it is imperative to be aware of the dangers of negative transfer, since this is most likely to occur at critical times, or when the trainee has to concentrate on other matters.

A trainability test is 'a validated test designed to assess whether a job applicant has the potential to reach a satisfactory standard after training. The applicant is required to perform an appropriate, carefully designed, short task after being given prior instruction...' (Manpower Services Commission 1981). Downs (1977) suggests the use of trainability tests for a variety of jobs, including fork-lift truck driving, bricklaying, electronics, bottling, and in social skills such as interviewing a client for a mortgage with a building society. These tests are suitable for both young and older recruits and are generally regarded as more appropriate for older applicants than the traditional type of selection test.

A variety of methods can be used for the appraisal of existing employees, among which are:

- on-the-job coaching;
- periodic appraisal interviews;
- organizational audits and reviews;
- self assessment and employee's request for training;
- assessment centres;
- performance records, production and sales figures.

On-the-job coaching. The training needs of many employees are determined, and some can be met, during the guidance they receive from their manager in the normal course of their work (see Megginson and Boydell 1979).

Periodic appraisal interviews. Appraisal of an employee's work by her superior once a year, or as appropriate, enables a manager to take stock of strengths and weaknesses. While it is usually relatively easy for the appraiser to assess training needs necessary for the development of potential, it is often much more difficult to help staff to recognize and accept their limitations. Although there are some forms of training, for instance T Group training, which can help people to do this, an identified training need can only be considered fully 'valid', if the trainee agrees with it.

This is particularly important in the light of the findings of a survey by Gill (1978) which showed that companies perceived the main purpose of appraisal as assessing training needs to improve current performance. Emphasis appears to have shifted away from the development of future potential. Clearly, however, both aspects can be important when assessing training needs. Of the 288 companies which replied to the survey, only 2 per cent applied appraisal to shop floor level, 45 per cent had schemes for clerical staff, and about 90 per cent appraised their managerial staff. Gill concluded that appraisal systems seemed to be an accepted part of company life. Her findings, as to the purpose of staff appraisal, are supported by Randell, Packard and Slater (1984), who maintain 'Staff development aims to increase the performance of a person in their existing job and so to increase their satisfaction with that job.'

They suggest that planning for the individual's next job is a secondary objective. For a detailed review of the relationship between performance appraisal and career development, see Fletcher (1984), and Fletcher and Williams (1985).

Organizational audits and reviews. In Chapter 3 we described organizational audits of such matters as industrial relations, management potential, discrimination, and health and safety, and where these indicate shortfalls, individual needs are likely to be brought to light. Because of legal requirements, health and safety audits are of particular importance. A helpful publication in this field is produced by the Chemical and Allied Products Industry Training Board (1980).

Self assessment and employee's request for training. The onus for identifying training needs does not necessarily rest on management. In a sympathetic work setting, employees will tend to take the initiative and indicate their own needs for training (see Delf and Smith 1978). One possible difficulty of staff appraisal schemes is that superiors' judgement of their subordinates may suffer from bias. To avoid this, Fletcher (1984) suggests self-appraisal. He quotes evidence (Thornton 1980), which indicates that asking the appraisee to rate different aspects of her own performance in relation to each other, rather than in comparison with the achievements of her peers, results in more discriminatory judgements with fewer 'halo' effects (i.e. overall impressions influenced by one or two items) than those reached by superiors in the course of traditional appraisal schemes. The self assessment approach is consistent with the philosophy of 'continuing development' and in a supportive climate would provide a promising means of assisting subordinates to cultivate the skills of reviewing their own strengths and weaknesses and considering their own training needs.

Assessment centres. An increasing number of organizations are using assessment centres during the recruitment process and in the evaluation of individuals for promotion. The desired skills are determined prior to the assessment and 'simulations' (such as mock meetings, group exercises, role playing, in-tray exercises and report writing) are devised to test them. The candidates undertake the exercises, watched by trained assessors (usually members of senior management, or external consultants) who keep records on specially designed forms. The assessment lasts from one to three days, after which the appraisers discuss the candidates' strengths and weaknesses and supply detailed written reports. It is not always possible to determine promotability and training needs by evaluating an incumbent's performance in her current job, as it may contain only limited tasks, which do not offer appropriate scope for judging potential. Assessment centres can be a useful means of providing this opportunity and of exposing weaknesses which might be overcome by training before becoming a barrier to further progression.

Byham (1984) describes a way in which organizations in the USA have designed assessment centres to avoid the expense and inconvenience of candidates and assessors having to be away from their normal routine for a fixed period. Each candidate is instructed to make a series of appointments with the assessors, at mutual convenience and within a given time span. At each appointment, the candidate carries out an exercise similar to those given at a traditional assessment centre. When all the exercises are completed, the assessors meet for their discussion and evaluation and provide reports on each individual. The whole process is thus completed with minimal disruption to normal work. For a detailed discussion of the use of assessment centres, see Stewart and Stewart (1981).

Performance records, production and sales figures. Numbers of errors or complaints in a department, etc., provide information about an individual's work performance. However, these figures should be interpreted with caution as they may result from circumstances outside the control of the employee.

To summarize, job training analysis and assessment of performance play a critical role in planned training. They provide the basic information about what is required from an employee and what is inadequate in her performance. In the next chapter, we consider how training interventions and programmes can help to bridge this 'learning gap'.

BIBLIOGRAPHY

ANNETT J and DUNCAN K D. 'New media and methods in industrial training', (editors), Robinson J and Barnes N, London, British Broadcastng Corporation, 1968.

ANNETT J, DUNCAN K D, STAMMERS R B, and GRAY M J. *Task analysis*. Training Information Paper, No. 6, HMSO, 1971. (Reprinted 1979, Sheffield, Training Division, Manpower Services Commission).

ARGYLE M. *The psychology of interpersonal behaviour*. Harmonsworth, Middx. Penguin, 1983.

BOYDELL T H. *A guide to job analysis*. London, British Association for Commercial and Industrial Education, 1977.

BYHAM B. 'Assessing employees without resorting to a centre'. *Personnel Management*, October, 1984.

CARBY K, and THAKUR M. *Transactional analysis at work*. Information Report No. 23, London, Institute of Personnel Management, 1976.

CHEMICAL AND ALLIED PRODUCTS INDUSTRY TRAINING BOARD, *Assessing safety training needs*. Information Paper, No. 16, Staines, Middx. Chemical and Allied Products Industry Training Board, 1980.

DELF G and SMITH B. 'Strategies for promoting self development'. *Industrial and Commercial Training*, Vol. 10, No. 1, December, 1978.

DOWNS S. *Trainability testing*. Training Information Paper, No. 11, HMSO, 1977.

DUNCAN K D and KELLY C J. *Task analysis, learning and the nature of transfer*. Sheffield, Manpower Services Commission, 1983.

ENGINEERING INDUSTRY TRAINING BOARD. *The analysis of certain engineering craft occupations*. Research Report, No. 2, Watford, Engineering Industry Training Board, 1971.

FOOD DRINK AND TOBACCO INDUSTRY TRAINING BOARD. *How to use job analysis for profitable systematic training*. Guide No. 2, Croydon, Food Drink and Tobacco Industry Training Board, 1972.

FLETCHER C. 'What's new in performance appraisal'. *Personnel Management*, February, 1984.

FLETCHER C and WILLIAMS R. *Performance appraisal and career development*. London, Hutchinson, 1985.

GILL D. *Appraising performance, present trends and the next decade.* Information Report, No. 25, London, Institute of Personnel Management, 1978.

JONES S. *Design of instruction.* Training Information Paper, No. 1, HMSO, 1968.

MANSFIELD B. 'Getting to the core of the job'. *Personnel Management*, August, 1985.

MEGGINSON D, AND BOYDELL T, *A manager's guide to coaching.* London, British Association for Commercial and Industrial Education, 1979.

MANPOWER SERVICES COMMISSION. *Glossary of Training terms.* London, HMSO, 1981.

MANPOWER SERVICES COMMISSION. *Core skills in YTS: Part 1.* Sheffield, Manpower Services Commission, 1984.

RACKHAM N, HONEY P, and COLBERT M. *Developing interactive skills.* Guilsborough, Wellens Publishing, 1971.

RANDELL G, PACKARD P, and SLATER S. *Staff Appraisal.* London, Institute of Personnel Management, 1984.

SEYMOUR W D. *Industrial training for manual operatives.* London, Pitman, 1954.

SEYMOUR W D. *Industrial skills.* London, Pitman, 1966.

SEYMOUR W D. *Skills analysis training.* London, Pitman, 1968.

SINGLETON W T, (ed.), The study of real skills. Vol. 1, *The analysis of practical skills.* MTP Press, 1978.

STEWART A and STEWART V. *Tomorrow's managers today.* London, Institute of Personnel Management, 1981.

TALBOT J R and ELLIS C D. *Analysis and costing of company training.* Aldershot, Gower Press, 1969.

THORNTON G C. 'Psychometric properties of self appraisals of job performance'. *Personnel Psychology*, 33, 1980.

WARR P B and BIRD M W. *Identifying supervisory training needs.* Training Information Paper No. 2, London, HMSO, 1968.

WELLENS J. 'An approach to management training'. *Industrial and Commercial Training*, Vol. 8, No. 7, July, 1970.

WOODWARD J. *Industrial organization - theory and practice.* Oxford, Oxford University Press, 1980.

7: Determining and evaluating training strategies

INTRODUCTION

In Chapter 1, we defined the main stages in planned training, namely:

- determining whether training is the best answer to an organizational problem;
- identifying the training requirements;
- setting training/learning objectives;
- selecting the training strategy and planning the training;
- implementing the programme;
- evaluating the training.

We considered the first of these stages in Chapter 3, and in Chapter 6 we discussed the second stage, with an investigation into methods of determining individual training needs. We now consider the formulation of specific objectives, the choice of strategy, and the planning, implementation and evaluation stages of training.

TRAINING INTERVENTIONS

We use the term 'training intervention' to include any event which is deliberately planned by those responsible for training to assist learning to take place. It includes a wide range of activities from formal courses to structured work experiences and we refer to these activities as strategies.

The logical first stage is to determine exactly what it is hoped to achieve by training intervention, i.e. formulate the objectives. It is then necessary to decide the best means of achieving these objectives, select a strategy, plan the training accordingly, implement and evaluate it. There are thus four stages to consider:

– determination of the training objectives;

– determination of the appropriate training strategy;

– planning and implementation of the training; and

– evaluation of the programme

Although it is convenient to consider these stages in logical progression, it should be realized that they are not entirely discrete; for instance in determining the objectives, the training officer will be providing criteria which can be used as a basis for evaluation. It is sometimes necessary to employ training techniques, such as structured exercises, which will provide feedback of the learning which is taking place and which will thus form part of the evaluation. The final evaluation serves two purposes, it provides the trainer with feedback or knowledge of results, and draws attention to aspects of the objectives which have not yet been achieved. This involves a reconsideration of residual objectives and a return to the beginning of the cycle. In the interests of clarity, however, we shall deal with each of these activities in turn.

STAGE 1. DETERMINATION OF TRAINING OBJECTIVES

A learning objective may be regarded as an intent, expressed in the form of a statement, describing a proposed behaviour change in the learner. The term 'criterion behaviour' is used to define what the learner is expected to do at the end of the training. It specifies the tasks, procedures, techniques and skills that he should be able to perform, the standards of performance required and the circumstances in which the work will be carried out (see Mager 1984). There are therefore three stages in compiling a behavioural objective. These are:

– Specify the behaviour the learner is required to demonstrate for the objective to be achieved.

- Determine the important conditions in which the behaviour must be demonstrated. For example, the type or range of equipment to be used or the environmental constraints.

- Determine the standard to which the trainee must perform. This can vary from a precise production specification to criteria, such as absence of customer complaints. It is frequently the most difficult aspect to define, but it is usually possible although not always easy to find a way of describing what would be regarded as acceptable performance, even if in some instances it has to be 'to the satisfaction of the supervisor.

An example of a behavioural objective is 'On completion of the training, the word processor operator should be capable of typing *x* words per minute with no errors, using *y* system, under normal office conditions.'

It is worth noting that some words in the English language, such as 'understand', 'know', 'appreciate', are open to many interpretations. For instance if a person 'knows' how a refrigerator works, he might be able to design one, to assemble one, to repair one, or merely to describe its operation. Words such as these should not be used in compiling behavioural objectives. Preference should be given to more precise terms such as 'identify', 'differentiate', 'construct', or 'solve', which are capable of describing specific behaviour.

It should also be noted that there is a difference between 'learner' objectives and 'trainer' objectives. Examples of the latter might be 'to give an appreciation of...', 'to provide an adequate foundation for...'. These do not specify what the trainee is expected to do at the end of the training and should not be listed as behavioural objectives.

The training technique of 'behaviour modelling' is associated with a precise form of behavioural objectives based on a set of learning requirements drawn up after observation and discussion of those behaviours which distinguish a good performance from a bad one. Grant (1984) cites as examples of learning points for travel agency staff, when telephoning clients to inform them that their holidays have been changed:

1. Reassure the customer everything is going as planned and he/she is still going on holiday.

2. Convince the customer that he/she is special and has been singled out above all others...

The difference between this approach and skills analysis is that it is the objective which is defined, not the precise behaviour. By attempting to achieve each objective in sequence, the learner is 'modelling' his behaviour on that of the most competent members of staff.

It is not always easy or possible to structure an unambiguous behavioural objective in a training context, but the clearer the objective which results, the more likelihood there is of successful training. A trainee cannot be expected to know what he should be learning if the trainer's own objectives are uncertain! In some areas, such as management development, it is much more difficult to describe training objectives in strict behavioural terms, because they are often more like educational objectives (see page 7). The specific behaviour required may not be known at the time of training, or the possible behavioural outcomes may be too numerous to list. In such circumstances, one solution proposed by Gronlund (1970), is to state the general objective first, and then to clarify it by listing a sample of the specific behaviour which would be acceptable as evidence of the attainment of the objective. For example:

> At the end of the training programme, the manager will be able to take greater responsibility for the development of his own staff. Indicative activities will include:

- carrying out satisfactory appraisal interviews;
- enabling his subordinates to recognize and accept their own training needs;
- conducting effective coaching and counselling sessions;
- delegating successfully to his subordinate.

Objectives can also be formulated in this way without necessarily predicting the precise outcome. Many learning experiences raise open-ended questions, the answers to which have to be worked out when back on the job. It is unrealistic to set a behavioural objective that after a course on management styles, participants will change styles immediately on returning to work, but it is possible to determine indicative activities, such as demonstrating an interest in developing new interpersonal skills, or initiating discussions on management styles with colleagues.

In Chapter 5, we suggested that training can act as a catalyst for initiating change, and that it may be useful to make a distinction between training objectives and the ultimate outcome of an intervention. For example, a management conference might be called with the objective of arriving at some common agreement on the solution of a problem. A sub-objective might be that each manager would be able to identify the implications of the problem for his own department, and contribute to the solution by putting forward practical suggestions. A second sub-objective might be attitudinal in that although possibly not in entire agreement with the ultimate solution, each manager would have recognized the many facets of the problem and display some commitment to the final recommendations. In other words, the learning experience of discussion with colleagues holding varied viewpoints would give each manager a broader perspective and an understanding of the reasons for the decision, rather than an opinion based on his own narrower experience.

A record of conference proceedings including the contribution of each manager, and a subsequent follow up of the implementation of the proposals, would be methods of ascertaining the fulfilment of the objectives. What could not be specified beforehand, however, would be the nature of the conclusions reached, i.e. the ultimate outcome. Top management may well have had some desired solution in mind and the conference may have approved it, but if, in the course of debate, sound reasons emerged for adopting a different approach, top management's credibility would be lost if these findings were to be totally disregarded and the pre-determined solution imposed from above. In those circumstances such a conference may well have done more harm than good! Similarly, an intervention, such as a series of courses using Blake's Grid (Blake and Mouton 1981) may have as its purpose an examination and evaluation of the organization's management style, but the outcome of that review cannot be predicted.

It does not necessarily follow that the trainer alone should be formulating the objectives. The concept of continuing development implies that the trainee should be able to take increasing responsibility for his own learning, and therefore must be capable of drawing up his own objectives, although there may be some conflict between the desired objectives of the trainee and those of his employer (see page 10). Assisting in the determination of training objectives can be an important motivator, and indeed part of the learning process itself for any trainee, but in particular for young people undertaking a general basic training, either as employees or under the auspices of one of the Manpower Services Commission's schemes. The same principle applies to students from schools, colleges or universities who are undertaking work experience placements. The concept of 'transfer learning objectives' has been used to describe activities, the achievement of which would help young people to transfer their learning to unfamiliar situations, thereby helping them to cope with changing patterns of employment (Hayes *et al.* 1983); (see also page 227).

The term 'terminal behaviour' is used to denote the trainee's actual behaviour or abilities at the end of the training. Any difference between 'criterion behaviour' and 'terminal behaviour' indicates deficiencies in the training (see Mager 1984).

The link between job training analysis and behavioural objectives should now have been clarified. At this stage it becomes obvious whether the necessary knowledge and skills have been investigated and described in sufficient detail. For instance, 'communication skills' is too broad a description to be of much assistance; it could give rise to a wide range of objectives, for which appropriate training could range from report writing to learning how to chair a meeting. On the other hand, ability to give accurate and speedy information about train times to all telephone inquirers, gives a very clear indication of what is needed. Behavioural objectives are therefore essential to the design of a programme which requires specified behaviour as an outcome.

STAGE 2. DETERMINATION OF THE APPROPRIATE TRAINING STRATEGY

At this point, the training officer may be confronted with a range of choices, and selection of the most suitable strategy can be critical. We have classified the possibilities under five main headings:

- training on-the-job
- planned organization experience
- in-house courses
- planned experiences outside the organization
- external courses.

We shall shortly consider each of these in more detail.

The four 'decision criteria' to use in determining the appropriate training strategy are:

- compatibility with objectives
- estimated likelihood of transfer of learning to the work situation
- available resources (including time)
- trainee-related factors.

It is not possible to give specific rules which will hold good in every situation, not least because most cases are likely to result in a compromise between what is desirable and what is possible. The decision-making process is likely, therefore, to be one of 'best fit' and is exemplified in the following case. A training officer was requested, as a matter of urgency, to arrange team-building training for a group of managers about to embark on a new project, the success of which depended crucially upon group effort. There was little time to undertake the training.

Using the four criteria, the salient factors were:

- the objectives embraced knowledge (for example of group interaction) skills of group membership, as well as attitude formation;
- learning transfer to the work situation was essential; the organization climate was influenced by a practical 'down to earth' management style, which was likely to be supportive of training based on real, rather than theoretical issues;
- resources were very limited; time was short and there was little money left in the budget;
- trainee-related factors; the managers had family commitments and would not have welcomed being asked to stay away from home, although they might ultimately have been persuaded to do so. They could not be spared from their departments for long periods.

The training officer considered the possible strategies. He rejected on-the-job training as being unlikely to achieve the objectives because each manager was isolated in his own department. For a similar reason, he rejected planned activity outside the company. Planned activity inside the company satisfied the criteria of good learning transfer, acceptability and credibility to the managers concerned. He deliberated how it could be arranged. He then considered external courses and re-read a brochure for an adventure training course which he had previously thought looked useful. He knew this type of training was often effective in creating a team spirit and if all the managers were to go together there was a good chance the learning would transfer to the work situation. The timing was suitable, but the course lasted a full week. It would be difficult to arrange for all the managers to be absent from their departments so near the commencement of the project and the cost would use all his remaining budget: he recollected that one of the managers had a heart condition, which might cause difficulties. He considered other external courses and rejected them for similar reasons.

He then thought about the possibility of an internal course and decided that, because the objectives included attitudes and skill requirements, discussion sessions and group activities would be appropriate. There would be a better chance of learning transfer if it were possible to base sessions on real problems the managers would face in carrying out the project. From a resource viewpoint, the cost would be less than an outside course, and the timing could be arranged to suit the managers' availability. Although they might have to attend evening sessions they would not have to stay away from home; that could not be considered an advantage in achieving the objectives, but the training officer judged that in the circumstances it was the best compromise he could reach. A conference room and syndicate rooms were available.

The main difficulty was that time was short for him to prepare the programmes, but having considered his own commitments and those of his staff, he decided that it would just be possible, especially as it might be beneficial to arrange certain problem-discussion sessions after the project had actually started. This would enable the course to be based partly on 'real' material, which would help to ensure learning transfer similar to that provided by on-the-job training. He decided to consult senior management about the possibility of building some of the later sessions into the conduct of the project itself, and also to investigate what assistance he could obtain from his local college. In this way, he would be able to combine two strategies, an in-company course consolidated and made relevant by structured in-house activity. Training would thus be playing a direct and integrated role in implementing organization plans.

This example is not intended to demonstrate that an in-house course is necessarily superior to adventure training, which in other circumstances might have been more effective, nor does it illustrate that courses are always the answer, but that each decision as to the most appropriate training strategy is contingent on the circumstances and the resultant decision will reflect the 'best fit'.

We now turn to each of the five main forms of training strategies and the four 'decision criteria' in more detail and give examples of how they relate to each other.

The five main strategies

Training on-the-job

A full discussion of the merits and disadvantages of on-the-job training will be found in Chapter 5 (page 141). This training can include the traditional 'sitting with Nellie' (watching an incumbent at work) or as in the case of a night watchman or sales representative, accompanying him on his rounds. In management development, it may take the form of coaching and advice from immediate superiors, or, in some instances, merely seeing the example of a good superior's work practices, and trying to perform according to his standards (i.e. modelling), may suffice.

Humble (1973) maintains that 'management development is an important by-product of running a business efficiently'. He advocates a system of managment by objectives, which involves agreeing key areas and targets with individual managers, followed by discussion to assist achievement. Although the discussions may result in the provision of a variety of off-the-job training, the whole process may also be viewed as invaluable on-the-job training in such aspects as the management of time, work organization and planning. It is, however, a method of management, not a training technique and it is sometimes associated with a number of inherent disadvantages, notably that it can be costly, can require elaborate controls and needs a lengthy introduction.

Considered against the four 'decision criteria', the advantages of on-the-job training are that it is likely to be high in learning transfer and to appear inexpensive in terms of resources (but see examples of learning costs, page 55). The trainee may take longer to reach the desired objectives, because the environmental conditions may be unfavourable, but there can be some compensation in the fact that he may well be performing some part of the job during the training period. An important resource is the availability of a suitable on-the-job trainer. In Chapter 5 (page 145) we suggest that training can be likened to a game of skittles, where in order to achieve one target, it may first be necessary to aim at another, and before commencing on-the-job training, it may be necessary to provide training, for example in coaching skills for a senior manager, or instructor training for an operator instructor, in the case of manual tasks.

Planned organization experience

This can be designed within existing organizational processes and wherever possible as an integral part of mainstream developments. It can include, planned experience in other departments or within the same department, or the assignment of special responsibilities, problem-solving discussion groups, quality circles, special projects, developing fresh aspects of activity such as a new sales promotion, or a system of records. These are likely to provide positive transfer of learning, provided there is organizational support. On the other hand it is counterproductive to ask someone to undertake projects and special assignments when there is little hope of eventual implementation. Action learning (see page 261), involving learning 'by doing', provides a means whereby managers learn on the job, as well as acquiring awareness of their own developmental processes.

Opportunities for planned in-house activities are sometimes deliberately created, or may be planned to assist day-to-day running of departments. One organization arranges for its graduate trainees to take over a production section for four weeks, while the supervisor is on holiday. The graduate prepares for this by spending some time beforehand in the section, and actually takes over the week before the supervisor departs, continuing for a week after his return. This provides a challenging work experience for the graduate, while allowing the supervisor the privilege of taking his annual leave at a time other than the normal factory holiday.

Another form of training in this category which is growing in popularity is the use of mentors. It is suggested that mentoring originated in the concept of apprenticeship, and a mentor has been described as 'a role model... a guide, a tutor, a coach and a confidant' (Clutterbuck 1985). The mentor is usually eight to 15 years senior to the protégé, and may be the immediate boss, although this is not always satisfactory because the two roles can conflict. A more common arrangement, therefore, is that the mentor is a more senior individual above, and frequently to the side of, the protégé's boss. Mentoring has the advantages of inducting newcomers efficiently to the organization, of assisting them with organization problems and personal development, thereby increasing motivation and job satisfaction. The mentor can also pass on the organization 'culture'. A properly organized scheme of mentoring is an inexpensive and efficient method of employee development.

In-house courses

Many large organizations have a regular programme of in-house courses, for what might be regarded as 'maintenance' training. These can include updating courses in specific topics, or they may be general courses, such as those for junior, middle or senior managers, and attendance by those eligible for promotion is a routine practice. Other courses and conferences may be organized for specific needs, such as changes in legislation, company policy or industrial relations practice. Some internal courses may be consultative in nature, for instance conferences to discuss future organization development, or changes in structure or management style. Some of the longer part-time courses, such as NEBSS mentioned above, can also be organized on an in-house basis, usually with assistance from staff from a local college.

There is likely to be better learning transfer from internal, compared with external, courses, particularly if senior management are involved in some of the sessions. The training can be directed at real organizational problems which is likely to increase face validity and chances of effectiveness. Courses are useful when many employees require similar training at one time. A variation, is open access in-house training. Advances in information technology have enabled the provision of computer-based training programmes including the use of interactive video. For example, Austin Rover had the problem of training 600 engineers within a six week time-span, in a new specification system for vehicle components. With the help of a development grant from the Manpower Services Commission, the target was achieved on time, at half the cost of traditional training, by the use of computer-based learning. This type of training has a number of advantages in that it can take place very near the trainee's place of work, and progress can be at his own pace and convenience. Training times can be reduced by the use of pre-tests, which enable the trainee to omit any items with which he is already familiar, while intermediate and final tests ensure that the material has really been mastered. This type of intensive course is now being used by many other large organizations, such as Rowntree Mackintosh, Boots and Trust House Forte (see Manpower Services Commission 1981 and Chapter 9). For an amusing account of the effectiveness of *not* holding a formal training course, see Thayer and McGehee (1977).

Planned experiences outside the organization

Secondments and visits to suppliers, or to the premises of important customers in order to obtain external views of the organization's products and services can provide valuable experience. Visits are sometimes arranged to competitors or suppliers abroad, although these may be expensive. These experiences can, however, fulfil a number of objectives because, as well as imparting information, they often result in attitudinal change and can be used to provide a tangible reward or positive reinforcement for a recent job well done.

While training objectives are derived from organization needs, there can be circumstances when management is justified in encouraging employees to undertake self-developmental activities to progress their own careers, e.g. when promotion prospects are minimized and when current jobs afford little opportunity for challenge or development. Examples of such developmental activities include, undertaking a role within an appropriate professional body (resulting in contact and discussion with colleagues in other organizations), or experience in chairing or addressing meetings – or assisting in external projects for the local community. Peach (1981) has suggested that, in appropriate circumstances, members of management might be seconded for short periods to contribute their skills in the design and setting up of workshops for the disabled.

Learning transfer will depend upon the particular experience, but some attitudinal change is likely to result which will enable the incumbent to view his job in a different light. While accepting that there can be dangers in arranging learning activities of this kind, in that employees may gain useful experience which will enable them to move to other organizations, we stress the importance of mental activity and stimulation as a central feature of the process of continuing development (see page 137). There is therefore a case for making allowance for this factor when setting training objectives. It is necessary to balance the likely costs involved against the possibility of disillusioned employees who, having loyally carried out unchallenging tasks for the organization over a number of years, discover that they are unable to adjust to change and find it difficult and threatening to learn new techniques and methods.

External courses

A plethora of leaflets and brochures advertising external courses is constantly arriving on the desk of every training officer, and to send someone on a course appears an easy, although frequently expensive option. External courses are broadly of two kinds: the short full-time variety, run by consultants, colleges and universities, and longer (usually part-time courses) often leading to a qualification. There can be dangers in an organization becoming too inbred and it is useful for employees to find out what happens 'outside'. Furthermore, discussing the problems of others can often throw new light upon one's own situation. Where only one or two people require specialized knowledge an external course has traditionally been the best alternative, but the position may change with availability of open learning programmes.

Learning transfer is not likely to be high unless the organizational climate is supportive. For example, a survey undertaken by the Marks Group (1985), on the effectiveness of management training, found that nearly a quarter of the participants had made no attempt to apply anything they had learned from their courses to their own organizations. The most commonly quoted reasons for this lack of transfer were 'company power structure', 'entrenched attitudes', and 'lack of resources'. The majority of respondents had, however, been satisfied with their courses. None of the participants in the Marks' survey thought that attending the course would bring them any pay rise, 9 per cent saw it as a prerequisite for promotion, 7 per cent as a reward for past efforts and 42 per cent thought they had been offered the opportunity because of their status in the organization. It is significant to note that there is no specific mention of the fulfilment of a training need.

If external courses are to be effective, they must be chosen with care. The main factors to be considered are the precise objectives. Do they match those of the particular training need? Do the training methods accord with the course objectives? If the intention is to improve an employee's communication skills, what aspects of communication are covered and do they match the employee's requirements? Is there any opportunity for supervized practice and feedback? The acquisition of skill does not come through knowledge alone (see page 154). Is there any indication of the level of the course? Who are the organizers? What experience have they had in the field? Is there any information to indicate their competence? What other organizations have supported the courses? Sometimes feedback can be obtained from other organizations and evaluative details of courses are held by agencies who will provide information gleaned from former participants (see also Chapter 4).

There is a temptation to judge the merit of a course by its price but this can be extremely misleading. A considerable proportion of the price of a residential course is the cost of accommodation. Does the venue appear to be suitable? This may appear unimportant but if, for instance, a senior manager is asked to attend a course held in surroundings which he considers uncongenial, he may approach the learning material with negative attitudes. Training officers should satisfy themselves on these points before committing their organizations to the expenditure and opportunity cost of sending comparatively highly paid members of staff on expensive courses.

Part-time courses, particularly those leading to a qualification, constitute a relatively long-term commitment, sometimes extending over more than one academic year. It is important to ascertain that the employee is fully aware of his own required commitment and in particular, the amount of personal study time which might be demanded. Some courses require commitment from the organization, such as the provision of project work or time off to attend residential elements. It is important to ascertain the extent of the organization's commitment at the outset, and the willingness and ability of relevant managers to co-operate, so that money and time are not wasted by encouraging staff to follow courses which they cannot complete through lack of support. Many of these courses, such as the Diploma in Management Studies (DMS), the National Examination Board in Supervisory Studies courses (NEBSS), or those leading to membership of the Institute of Training and Development, or the Institute of Personnel Management, are normally regarded as a stage in career development, rather than a remedy for an immediate training need.

The decision criteria

Objectives

Although we have argued that objectives should be formulated in as precise terms as possible, it does not necessarily follow that each can be fulfilled by matching it exactly with a particular strategy. Indeed, more than one strategy may be necessary to achieve a single objective. For instance, a junior manager may be unskilled in presenting a persuasive case at committee meetings: one way of bridging this 'gap' might be for him to attend an appropriate course which incorporates suitable skill demonstration and practice sessions; another method might be for a more senior member of management to give him appropriate coaching, followed by on-the-job experience including attendance at specific meetings. In practice, probably a combination of both would be useful.

Questions such as the following, may assist in determining an appropriate strategy:

- Is the strategy consistent with the organization's training policy? (see Chapter 4).

- Is the objective mainly concerned with long term career development, or a short term need? For instance, seconding a manager to a part-time Master of Business Administration (MBA) programme would not be suitable for overcoming his immediate problem of inefficient management of time and might even exacerbate it!

- Is the main requirement theoretical knowledge, or is the real need that of a thorough understanding of the organization's policies and procedures? It has not been uncommon for managers to be sent to external courses on, for example, the principles and practices of marketing, when what is really required is a better understanding of company marketing policies, procedures and objectives. It is acknowledged, however, that a familiarity with general principles helps to set company practices in perspective (and possibly bring about an improvement in them), and that what is often required is a mixture of both theory and company practice.

- Is the main need really knowledge or practical skill? A course on computing which does not give 'hands on' experience, may help to change attitudes or arouse interest for further training, but is unlikely to help the participants with operational skills, or overcome possible anxieties about interacting with computers.

- Is part of the training requirement a general understanding and discussion of common problems? An important aspect of training can be an awareness and sensitivity to the total situation, and although this need might be partially met by dissemination of information, it will almost certainly require some kind of relevant experience, either a problem-solving discussion, or possibly brief secondments to other departments. Training can sometimes assume the form of consultation; an example might be when a conference is called with the dual purpose of consultation about the introduction of an appraisal scheme and possibly altering it as a result, as well as imparting the knowledge and skill required to carry out the appraisals and making the training more acceptable. It may be necessary to include general and theoretical material about appraisal, but the organization objective would not be met by sending staff individually on external courses.
- Does the objective involve introducing fresh ideas and new perspectives? Does it require contact with people from other organizations, either by external course or visits and secondments?
- Is the objective associated with a need for reinforcement, reward or prestige? Managers have sometimes claimed they have been offered the chance to attend a course as a reward. In the right circumstances this can be a valid training strategy. It is likely that the manager will approach the training with a favourable mental set and, if impressed, he may give more encouragement to his subordinates to attend courses.

Likelihood of learning transfer

In Chapter 5, we defined learning as a change in behaviour as a result of experience and demonstrated that it was an inevitable feature of organizational life. The provision of planned training is therefore considered as an intervention into an informal, continuous and powerful learning process, which affects the transfer of learning to the workplace in a way which should not be underestimated. It is not uncommon for staff returning from a course to be greeted with 'You've had your holiday, now get on with your work'. A backlog of problems awaits, and often there is not even an inquiry as to whether anything useful was learned, let alone a follow-up session about the implementation of new ideas. Sometimes in fact there might be direct opposition.

It is necessary, therefore, to be aware of the organizational barriers to the application of learning, which can assume many forms including sheer inertia, autocratic opposition, bureaucratic procedures, work overload, interpersonal relationships, vested interests, fear of change and insecurity. Such barriers must be taken into consideration when devising a training strategy, as must the overall climate, dominant management culture and style, and sophistication and previous training experience of the organization. For example, in an organization where there has been no previous planned training it might be unwise to start with a sophisticated form of interpersonal skills development for middle-aged supervisors, who have been employed there since leaving school. A short, practical course, where the job relevance is easy to determine would probably make a better beginning. They might then be encouraged to ask for further provision. Training might be regarded as the process of opening a door: when it is pushed ajar, it opens up vistas of other rooms and a corridor with more doors. The view often generates a desire to penetrate further, but before the first door was opened, it was not possible to realize that there was anything beyond.

As a general rule, the more the training officer can take part himself in mainstream organization activity and can involve the sources of power in the actual training, the greater the likelihood of learning transfer (see page 41). Examples might be:

- organizing learning sessions as an integral part of mainstream events (see example page 191);
- emphasizing the personal responsibility of managers in training their subordinates (see page 34), and assisting them to do this;
- assisting managers to coach their subordinates;
- ensuring that managers are directly involved in briefing and debriefing sessions for staff undergoing training;
- if the occasion is appropriate, arranging for top management to attend a course first; this is normally the pattern of attendance on courses leading to organization development programmes, such as Blake's Grid (Blake and Mouton 1981);
- developing managers and supervisors as trainers in their own departments;
- asking senior managers to lecture or lead sessions on in-house courses;
- the use of mentors (Clutterbuck 1985).

Some of these suggestions may involve training for superiors and achieving a particular objective may initially require an indirect approach.

Available resources

These include items such as:

- accommodation for running internal courses, or environmental constraints such as noise, space, for on-the-job training;
- equipment, or availability of money to purchase the hardware and software required for the use of new tehnology; in some organizations there is a microcomputer on every desk providing a ready made facility for the reception of in-house training programmes;
- staff expertise in training techniques such as coaching, writing programmes, delegating, acting as mentor;
- time span; how much time is available? Must the training be completed to particular 'deadlines'?
- finance; the length of training time may be governed by policy decisions on appropriate expenditure of staff time. Opportunity cost as well as the money involved in wages and salaries are relevant. For instance, if all senior management attend a training course for a week, or if a store closes for staff training for half an hour per week, what business is likely to be lost because of the absence of relevant managers or what sales might be missed by shoppers taking their custom elsewhere?
- available external help; are there good facilities and staff in local colleges? Is suitable help available from other organizations such as suppliers, or professional bodies?
- availability of relevant external courses; some expertise is specific to organizations and is therefore unlikely to be found externally;
- availability of external funding; in the shape of grants from bodies such as the Manpower Services Commission, European Social Fund.

For a further discussion on training resources, see Chapter 4.

Trainee-related factors

These include the following:

- the experience and current expertise of the trainee; superfluous training in aspects with which the trainee is already well acquainted can result in deteriorating performance through annoyance and boredom. Most computer-managed programmes incorporate pre-tests which enable learners to 'skip' aspects with which they are already familiar.

- learning style; the ultimate aim may well be to encourage employees to use a variety of different learning styles, but in the early stages of training, particularly if the content may be difficult for the learner, it is better to use a mode which appears to accord with his preferred or natural learning style. When attempting to convince trainees of the value of using different learning styles, it is advisable to start with content which is likely to be acceptable. For instance, many managers are interested in finding practical solutions to industrial relations problems. If training is required in this field, it may be useful to start with concrete examples and exercises which purport to find solutions, and subsequently progress to conceptual and theoretical aspects of the role of trade unions. On the other hand, a group of graduates with little or no experience of management, might well prefer the sequence reversed. It must also be noted that an overall objective should be to improve learning potential; an understanding of learning styles is one way of achieving this.

- age factor; (see also page 137 and page 205) older people, should not be made to feel inadequate in front of younger people, particularly if they are feeling insecure because they are being retrained on entirely new skills. If, for instance, they have a knowledge deficiency in arithmetic, they may find it more acceptable to undertake a computer-assisted programme or a distance learning course, where they can work in private at their own speed and convenience.

- size of group; the number of trainees has an obvious influence on the technique to be used. It is not practicable to organize a discussion for one person! Closely associated with group size is the availability of trainees because, although the number may be considerable, if they are separated by geographical location, or shift working, the effect may be to reduce numbers available at any one time, and computer-assisted learning or distance learning packages may be suitable. These have the additional advantage of standardizing instruction throughout a large organization. For instance, British Airways uses computer-based sales training, which is fully integrated with the training of booking clerks and includes such tasks as reservations, fare quotation and departure control (see Manpower Services Commission 1981).

- motivation; the likely attitude towards different styles of learning is relevant here, but other practical factors, such as the necessity to be away from home on a residential course should be taken into consideration.

STAGE 3. PLANNING AND IMPLEMENTATION OF THE TRAINING

Where practicable, it can be advantageous to consult those concerned about the design of their programme; in all circumstances, careful briefing of trainees and their superiors is essential, if learning is not to be inhibited by conjectures as to why the training is taking place. Exactly what is involved in planning and implementing will depend upon the form of training which has been chosen. As the most comprehensive preparation is likely to be required in planning an in-house course, we have selected this training strategy for fuller discussion. The steps in the design of a structured in-house course are shown in Figure 7.1.

Step 1
Review the training objectives

↓

Step 2
Determine appropriate sessions

↓

Step 3
Assess training times

↓

Step 4
Construct the timetable

↓

Step 5
Brief the trainers

↓

Step 6
Organize the preparation of material and equipment

↓

Step 7
Monitor and evaluate the training

Figure 7.1
Stages in the design of a structured training programme.

Designing and planning a structured internal training course

Step 1: review the training objectives

The objectives, and the knowledge, skill and attitudes required to achieve them, might be regarded as constituting the 'syllabus'. It is necessary to determine which objectives are the most important, and therefore where the emphasis of the programme should lie, and then to arrange the material into a suitable sequence. This may be determined purely by logic but attempts should be made at the outset to create interest and utilize the trainee's curiosity (see page 132). It is important to arrange the material in steps of suitable size for the trainee to master, and (unless structured discovery learning is intended) to ensure that the programme proceeds methodically from the known to the unknown, and that where appropriate, each session serves as preparation and introduction for those which follow.

Step 2: determine appropriate sessions

Decide what sessions will be necessary and set sub-objectives for each, anticipating how the attainment of each objective might be evaluated. Determine the most appropriate training technique (or method), bearing in mind that a particularly important objective might require several sessions using a variety of training techniques. For example, during a course on organizational change, one of the objectives might be that the participants should be able to identify the barriers to change. This could be introduced by syndicate discussion sessions, where each participant describes some change he has experienced, and indicates areas of concern. Syndicates could then discuss the origin and alleviation of those worries and whether they could have been avoided. A case study might then follow allowing participants to apply and reinforce some of their findings and, after discussion of the case, the session might conclude with a short lecture/summary of the whole topic, accompanied by a 'handout' of the salient points. The trainer would receive some evaluation of the learning which had taken place by listening to the trainees' contributions to the case study, but there are dangers in evaluating group performance. It might also be possible to use a self-administered test before the final summary session.

The criteria to determine the most suitable training technique for each session are similar to those for determining the strategy (see page 190), but a number of additional points might apply.

The following example helps to explain the need for care in the structuring of precise behavioural objectives. A group of craft trainees had to learn an electrical coding comprising nine colours and the job required instant association of a number (one to nine) with a particular colour. The objective would not be met if they learned the sequence of colours by rote, because each time they wanted to pair a colour and a number they would have to repeat the sequence, causing delay and allowing the possibility of error, which could have serious effects on safety. The training technique which was devised consisted of a visual presentation of well known objects associated with each colour, such as one brown penny, five green fingers. The use of vision and the association with previous knowledge quickly enabled the trainees to learn the information in the exact form in which it would be required: a green wire immediately bringing to mind the number five.

The age of the trainees can also influence the suitability of a technique. Belbin and Belbin (1972) discovered that certain methods were more effective than others with older trainees. Discovery learning, or forms of 'deductive' learning (i.e. where the requirement is to reason out the answer rather than learn it by rote) show the best results. Techniques which rely upon memory are not likely to be successful. Unlike older people, younger trainees enjoy a competitive approach, as in a quiz, and prefer frequent changes of topic. The former learn more effectively by concentrating on the same subject matter for longer periods; variety can be introduced by changing the training method.

If course participants are at different levels of ability in skill and knowledge and have differing degrees of practical experience, flexible methods, such as computer-assisted learning, or sometimes discussion groups and case studies, can be useful. Those with experience can be encouraged to assist but not dominate.

Step 3: assess training times

The time available for each session must be determined; participative methods may be the most effective in enabling learning transfer but they can be time-consuming, and it is therefore practicable to employ them for the most important aspects of the training. A further consideration is the time of day of each session; for instance, it may be considered wise to arrange a participative session straight after lunch, or after dinner during a residential course. Estimating the exact time required for each session is to some extent a matter of trial and error, and the requirements for the same programme can vary for different groups. An experienced trainer can usually gauge the timing reasonably accurately by consulting with those responsible for the various parts of the training, using the duration of similar programmes as a guide, and taking into account the age, experience and motivation of those to be trained.

Step 4: construct the timetable

The trainer should ensure that the timetable is flexible enough to be modified if required without affecting the whole programme, and determine the trainers for each session.

Step 5: brief the trainers

This is an important, and frequently neglected, step in the design process and misunderstandings can easily arise if the objectives for every section of the programme are not fully discussed and understood. The training technique to be used may well be discussed with the trainer but the final choice cannot be left to him entirely because of the need to obtain an overall balance. It is the course organizer who has to take this overall view. Otherwise, to quote the extreme case, it would be possible for each of several trainers to decide to show a film on the same day. Variety has to be planned, it cannot be left to chance. After briefing, the trainers then prepare the detailed material for their sessions.

Step 6: organize the preparation of material and equipment

Professionally prepared programmes, course manuals, log books and other references create a favourable impression. Unprepared or inadequate equipment suggests that the training is of secondary importance, and this can quickly affect the attitude of trainees.

Step 7: monitor and evaluate the training (see below).

STAGE 4. EVALUATION OF THE PROGRAMME

While it is generally accepted that there is a strong case for attempting to evaluate training, particularly in view of the very large sums of money which are spent on it (in 1980 it was estimated that employers spent about two and a half billion pounds a year on training: HMSO 1984), the attendant problems often appear insuperable. In fact, evaluation is one of the more difficult of the training officer's tasks, but it is not necessarily impossible.

The first difficulty is that it is necessary to know the exact knowledge and skill of each trainee before the start of the training. Without this information it would be impossible to assess what they have learned at the end. This would necessitate a pre-test, which is practicable in programmed or computer-assisted learning. It becomes more difficult when we consider an in-house course for managers. The first objective of every trainer in that situation is to establish rapport with the course members. Presenting them with a pre-test, especially if they are unlikely to be able to complete it, is hardly in accord with this aim, nor is it likely to inspire them with confidence and a favourable mental set. Even if a pre-test were to be arranged, it could be argued that participants had learned from the pre-test not the training, and it would therefore really be necessary to set up a number of control groups. This is unlikely to be practicable, and therefore the training officer will realize from the outset that he can only do the best which circumstances permit.

The questions which need to be answered in evaluating a particular training programme are as follows:

- Why is the evaluation required?
- Who is to do it?
- What aspects should be evaluated and when should this be done?
- What kinds of measurement will be used?

Why is the evaluation required?

A number of reasons can be given; in general terms the evaluation enables the effectiveness of an investment in training to be appraised and provides data which can justify expenditure on training. One of the difficulties in obtaining money for a training budget is that the results are usually regarded as intangible or an act of faith (page 59).

It also provides feedback to the trainer about his performance and methods and, if evaluation is ongoing, it can assist learning during the programme. It can also be used to improve subsequent programmes, although situations are seldom exactly alike. The evaluation also indicates the extent to which the objectives have been met and therefore whether any further training needs remain.

Who should carry out the evaluation?

Tracey (1968) makes the point that:

> evaluation must be co-operative. A one-man evaluation is little better than no evaluation, regardless of who does it, how competently he does the job, or how valid his findings may be. All who are a part of the process of appraisal, or who are affected by it, must participate in the process.

The main interested parties should be the trainee, his manager, his work group, his trainer, and his organization. To some extent the criteria used in determining the value of the training will be common among these individuals and groups, but there may also be differences:

- the training department's and line management's expectations from training will differ if inadequate communication exists between them and mistakes are made in the content of the programme;
- participants, particularly those on long programmes, can be critical of training, which in the view of the trainer is satisfactory; such differences of opinion may be due to inadequate provision of feedback on individual progress;
- training which is specific, in that it is useful only to the organization that provides it, may be less highly valued by a trainee.

What aspects of the training should be evaluated and when?

A number of different models have been suggested. The structure we describe below is after Whitelaw (1972) and Hamblin (1974), but for other alternatives see Warr, Bird and Rackham (1970) or Jones (1970). See Bramley and Newby (1984), for a useful framework of different concepts of evaluation, and a summary of appropriate techniques. Hamblin and Whitelaw suggest that training can usefully be evaluated at different levels each of which requires different techniques. An example of this type of model is given below.

Level 1: Reactions of trainees to the content and methods of training, to the trainer and to any other factors perceived as relevant. What the trainee thought about the training.

Level 2: Learning attained during the training period. Did the trainees learn what was intended?

Level 3: Job behaviour in the work environment at the end of the training period. Did the learning transfer to the job?

Level 4: Effect on the trainee's department. Has the training helped departmental performance?

Level 5: The ultimate level. Has the training affected the ultimate well-being of the organization, for example, in terms of profitability or survival?

It will readily be seen that these are sequential stages in the process: if it is found that behaviour on the job has not changed after training, unless evaluation has been carried out at Level 2, it will not be possible to ascertain whether the failure was due to lack of learning transfer or to the fact that the learning never took place at all. If the evaluation is to perform any of the functions we have outlined this type of detail is essential.

To facilitate evaluation, it is possible to set objectives at each of these levels. For instance, the objectives of a course providing an introduction to the organization's main frame computing facility, might be:

- that participants would recommend the course to their friends and wish to attend a further course themselves. This would involve a favourable reactions level evaluation (Level 1);
- that participants should be able to complete simple programmes in BASIC. This would involve objectives at Level 2;
- that participants should request terminals on their desks and suggest how they could be used to make daily work practices more efficient (Level 3);
- that the introduction of desk terminals for the course participants should result in increased output in the department (Level 4);

- that this increased productivity in the department should contribute to the profitability of the organization (Level 5).

It will be seen that the easiest levels to evaluate are 1 and 2 and that the process becomes increasingly difficult as Level 5 is approached. This is partly because of difficulties of measurement, but also because of the problem of establishing cause and effect. Organizational changes are multi-causal, for example it is usually impossible to determine how much of an increase in profitability is the result of a specific training intervention. There is also likely to be a time lag between the completion of the training and its effect on the organization, and the relevant learning may have arisen from a later source. It can be said, however, that the more successful the evaluation at the earlier stages, the more likely is the training to affect overall departmental or organizational performance.

What kind of measurement will be used?

Different techniques and yardsticks are appropriate for each level of evaluation.

At Level 1, where an attempt is being made to assess the recipients' reactions to their training, techniques such as questionnaires, interviews, group discussion, individual interview or asking trainees to write a report can be employed. Care must be taken with the timing of these methods. For example, if trainees have enjoyed a course, they may finish in a mood of euphoria which may not last after they return to work, and therefore a misleading impression might be conveyed if they are asked to complete a questionnaire at the end of the course (see Easterby-Smith and Tanton 1985).

Similarly, trainees may not be in a position to know immediately whether what they have learned will be useful. It may be necessary to wait some considerable time before being able to obtain informed opinion. Furthermore, although ideally learning should be a helpful experience, it can at times be painful, and trainees may encounter difficulty or criticism and attempt to divert this to the training activities. If such trainees happen to be the most vociferous during an evaluation discussion, the trainer may obtain a completely false impression. Experienced trainers learn to interpret this type of feedback, and to use a series of techniques to obtain their information. For instance, they might use a short questionnaire and/or hold a general discussion, or interview the participants separately after an appropriate length of time has elapsed. Another method is to issue a questionnaire, ask the trainees to complete it, hold their own discussion session and present what they consider to be the most salient points to the trainer.

A number of other indicators can also be used to provide evaluation at this level, including requests from participants for further training, their recommendation to others to follow the same course, or the return of past trainees for further help and advice. No single one of these can be taken out of context, but they can all assist to confirm or contradict an apparent trend.

At Level 2, the following techniques might be used:

Phased tests, as in craft training. These are beneficial in monitoring progress and providing feedback which can be used to modify the training as it proceeds. In addition they provide intermediate targets and knowledge of results to the trainees.

Final test or examination. This is still the most common type of evaluation activity in academic circles, although other types of assessment of learning have gradually been introduced. Final examinations have a number of disadvantages in that they are influenced by the trainee's ability to perform on a few chosen days and may therefore be affected by short-term memory, domestic circumstance or health. It is important that they are designed to incorporate a representative sample of the activities to be evaluated. One of the major difficulties is that some relevant and important items, such as skills, do not readily lend themselves to testing in this way. Written examinations are normally confined to theoretical types of courses.

Profiling. This has been introduced more recently in an attempt to ovecome some of the above difficulties (see page 233).

Projects. These allow trainees to apply what has been learned to the working situation, and provide feedback both as to what has been learned and the ability to apply it.

Structured exercises and case studies. Performance on these can give the trainer indications as to how well people are learning. Structured exercises, such as interviews using closed-circuit television, are particularly helpful as it is possible to watch performance improving as the training progresses and a record remains for comparison. Many of these activities, however, take place in groups and the trainer must beware of assuming that because a group has performed well, every member of that group has learned what was intended. One or two members can lead or inspire a group to the extent that it is difficult to realize that some people have contributed little.

Participation in discussions during training. This can be another indicator but requires skill in interpretation, as there can be a variety of reasons why trainees remain silent. They may feel overawed by prominent members of the group, or the entire group atmosphere may be alien to them. It is also possible that they have a different preferred learning style. These are all indicators which an experienced trainer tries to understand and manage.

Level 3 requires assessment of improved performance on the job. This is easiest in the area of manual or operator training where before and after measurements of output can often be made. It becomes more difficult to evaluate performance further up the organization hierarchy, where jobs are less prescribed and measurement imprecise. There is also likely to be a time lag between training and the appearance of indicators of performance improvement. For instance, upon returning to work after attending a course on sales techniques, a salesman may immedately practise what he has learned and sow the seeds of extra future orders. These may not materialize for some time, after which other factors in the situation may have changed – there may have been alterations to the product – and it is difficult, if not impossible, to attribute cause and effect (see page 59). The Stroud experiment (see Whitelaw 1972) was an attempt to provide feedback by asking colleagues of the trainee to note any change in behaviour on the job after the completion of training. This yielded some positive results, but must always be open to the criticism that if colleagues are asked to look for behaviour change, the implication has been made, and a mental set established, which would allow the perception (or imagined observation) of factors which otherwise might have passed unnoticed.

In general, it might be said that the more care that has been taken in the assessment of needs and the more precise the objective, the greater will be the possibility of effective evaluation. In the case of the salesman above, rather than an overall objective of increasing his sales, it might be possible to be more precise by using sub-objectives such as increasing second sales, or reducing customer complaints directed at staff.

The 4th and 5th Levels are the most difficult to evaluate for the reasons given, and also because departmental and organizational results depend upon many people and it is difficult to apportion improvements to the efforts of specific individuals. Evaluation is therefore often related in a more general way to the health of the organization. Evidence might be found in: overall profitability; lack of customer complaints; a favourable attitude to training; the standing of the training officer and the nature of requests made to him. (Is he, for example, included in discussions of matters which are central to the organization?); a system of staff appraisal which works; the availability of suitable people to promote from within and a proactive labour force which will accept change.

The majority of training in the private and public sectors takes place in a busy work environment and a rigorous scientific approach to evaluation, involving pre- and post-training tests, control and experimental groups, etc. although very desirable, is often not practicable. However, if adequate resources are not made available for evaluation purposes, the effectiveness of training will remain unchecked. This is the dilemma which faces the training officer in attempting to evaluate training.

This dilemma can be resolved to some extent by adopting the following pragmatic approach:

- set clear training objectives, expressed as far as possible in behavioural terms;
- include objectives for each level of evaluation;
- evaluate systematically at as many levels as practicable to obtain the total picture.

Together, these three steps will go a long way towards helping an organization maximize its benefit from investment in training. As Hesseling (1966) suggests:

> the main task of the trainer as evaluator is to test training effectiveness or to validate his professional claim that the selected training methods have brought about the desired result.

BIBLIOGRAPHY

AUSTIN ROVER. *Open learning*. Austin Rover Training Open Learning Unit.

BELBIN E and BELBIN R M. *Problems in adult retraining*. London, Heinemann, 1972.

BLAKE R R and MOUTON J S. *The versatile manager: a grid profile*. Irwin-Dorse, 1981.

BRAMLEY P and NEWBY A. 'The evaluation of training: clarifying the concept'. *Journal of European Industrial Training*, Vol. 8, No. 6, 1984.

CLUTTERBUCK D. *Everyone needs a mentor*. London, Institute of Personnel Management, 1985.

EASTERBY-SMITH M and TANTON M. 'Turning course evaluation from an end to a means'. *Personnel Management*, April 1985.

GRANT D. 'A better way of learning from Nellie'. *Personnel Management*, December, 1984.

GRONLUND N E. *Stating behavioural objectives for classroom instruction*. London, Macmillan, 1978.

HAMBLIN A C. *Evaluation and control of training*. Maidenhead, McGraw-Hill 1974.

HAYES C, FONDA N, POPE M, STUART R, and TOWNSEND K. *Training for skill ownership*. Sheffield, Manpower Services Commission, 1983.

HESSELING P. *Strategy of evaluation research*. Van Gorcum, 1966.

HMSO. *Training for jobs*. Government White paper, Cmnd 9135, London, HMSO, 1984.

HUMBLE J W. *Management by objectives*. London, British Institute of Management, 1973.

JONES J A G. *The evaluation and cost effectiveness of training*. London, Industrial Training Service, 1970.

MAGER R F. *Preparing instructional objectives*. California, Fearon, 1984.

MARKS GROUP. Reported in *Personnel Management*, August, 1985.

MANPOWER SERVICES COMMISSION. *Looking at computer-based training*. Sheffield, Manpower Services Commission, 1981.

PEACH L. 'A realistic approach to employing the disabled'. *Personnel Management*, January, 1981.

THAYER P W and McGEHEE W. 'On the effectiveness of not holding a formal training course'. *Personnel Psychology Inc*, 1977.

TRACEY W R. *Evaluating training and development systems*. American Management Association, 1968.

WARR P B, BIRD M, and RACKHAM N. *Evaluation of management training*. Aldershot, Gower Press, 1970.

WHITELAW M. *The evaluation of management training – a review*. London, Institute of Personnel Management, 1972.

8: The transition from education to work

INTRODUCTION

In this chapter we consider the role of training in helping young people overcome the problems in preparing for, and finding, employment to suit their abilities and aspirations. The progression from school to work has always constituted a major life change, with a number of attendant difficulties, which have been exacerbated in recent years by the fear of unemployment. We therefore begin by discussing youth unemployment and follow with a consideration of vocational guidance. We then review developments in the provision of youth training and initial full-time education, drawing particular attention to the type of provision which is now required to enable young people to compete with experienced workers in a constantly changing work environment. This is followed by an examination of relevant aspects of further and higher education. Finally, we turn to the process of induction, which although required by all new employees, is particularly necessary for young people as they enter work and as they move through each phase of their training.

YOUTH UNEMPLOYMENT

Young people represent an investment in the future. In these days of rapidly changing technology they can bring energy and ideas into an organization and rejuvenate an ageing workforce. They therefore represent an invaluable resource which the nation cannot afford to underutilize. The wider social effects of youth unemployment demand urgent solutions at the national level and a parallel response from individual organizations, and in the latter the training officer has an important role to play.

The Manpower Services Commission (1982), calculated that by the end of 1981 the number of those in employment had fallen to 20.4 million, a fall of 9 per cent in two and a half years, and was at its lowest level since the early 1950s. The problem was particularly acute for young people, as the number of unemployed school-leavers rose from 5,100 in 1973 (October), to 162,800 in 1983 (October) (Pearson, Hutt and Parsons 1984). It was estimated that, if no special provision were made, the number of unemployed school leavers in 1982/3 would be about 400,000 (Manpower Services Commission 1982). It was against this background that urgent steps were taken by Government and the MSC to alleviate the situation and the first Youth Training Scheme was started with minimum delay.

While the underlying cause was economic recession, a number of other features aggravated the situation. A long term upward movement in young people's susceptibility to unemployment had already been identified MSC (1976), the number of unemployed (aged under 20) as a proportion of total unemployed having risen from 12.5 per cent in 1970 to 27.8 per cent in 1976. Although still less than for any other age range, the duration of unemployment for young people had risen sharply. In addition, the MSC (1982), estimated that the number of young people leaving full time education would remain high until 1986, although it would gradually diminish towards the end of the decade.

The national unemployment figures disguise wide regional variations, the highest rate of decline in employment being in the West Midlands and the lowest in the South West. In some parts of the UK more than one in four of the labour force was out of work by the end of 1981. The burden is thus unevenly distributed and falls very heavily upon sectors of the population disadvantaged by factors such as geographical location, disablement or membership of a minority ethnic group.

The problem has been shared by the major EEC countries, all of which have suffered a steady annual increase in youth unemployment since 1970. The question of transition from education to working life was investigated by the Commission of the European Communities (1976), which reported that:

> finding employment is only the first step, making sure of congenial and suitable employment, adjusting to it, finding satisfaction in it and learning how to progress in a career are quite as important parts of the process of transition... The period of economic recession and the dramatic unemployment situation affecting young people have served to highlight in starker terms the problems for each generation of young people making effective transition from education to working life, and being sufficiently adaptable to meet changing circumstances later in life.

Some of the problems highlighted in the Commission's report are:

- the need for work experience, which is particularly important to help young people compete with adults in times of unemployment;
- the special help required for certain groups, such as girls (intensive guidance is needed for girls and their parents and teachers to combat the effects of stereotyped attitudes regarding suitable careers for women);
- migrants who may have linguistic or social and cultural difficulties;
- those who are ill-prepared for work because of lack of qualifications or low motivation;
- the need to strengthen relationships between education and employment and the necessity of obtaining information on the attitudes of young people leaving school.

Although this report was compiled some nine years ago, we quote it because it encapsulates the philosophy underlying our current national provisions and because these problems are likely to remain in force for a considerable time to come. Training cannot strike at the root causes of unemployment, it will not solve the problem, but it can alleviate some of the consequences and help to distribute the burden more evenly.

If we reflect on some of the considerations in Chapter 5 (see particularly page 138), the following picture emerges; in general, learning takes place more easily in youth and, as people grow older, those with lower cognitive ability show greater deterioration than those whose potential is above average. Age is not the sole determinant in the retention of mental ability. Previous learning experiences (including 'learning to learn') generally transfer and assist the acquisition of new knowledge and skills. Thus, unless some appropriate form of training is provided at the time when they are most able to take advantage of it, a considerable proportion of young people, particularly those at the lower end of the intelligence scale, may never have the chance of reaching their full potential. Seligman's concept of learned helplessness (see page 120), implies that those who unsuccessfully try to escape from the trauma of unemployment by the fruitless pursuit of work, will probably eventually learn that they are unable to control the situation, and activity will give way to depression. The learning and depression may persist long after the cause has been removed. It can therefore be seen that not only is there a great danger of insufficient skills for the nation's needs but also of the creation of underprivileged sectors of the population, low both in motivation to seek employment and in ability to learn new skills. The necessity for action is economic, social and moral.

VOCATIONAL GUIDANCE

Vocational guidance is described by Vaughan (1970) as the 'means of helping people to choose work in which they will be reasonably contented and successful within limits of their ability'. The considerable expansion in this field over the last few years has been due to the growing complexity of our educational system, the proliferation of job categories, the creation of new types of employment and the dissatisfaction felt by educationalists, young people and employers at the haphazard way in which the choice of a career is often made. In spite of this expansion, the amount of vocational guidance available to young people is still very limited.

Under the Employment and Training Act 1973, primary responsibility for placing school leavers in their first employment rests with the Careers Service of the local education authorities but young people may also use the Employment Service of the Manpower Services Commission. The main functions of the Careers Service are:

- to work with careers guidance teachers in schools and colleges and to provide students and their parents with information on education, employment and training opportunities; also to help with the planning of careers education programmes in schools;
- to help young people to find suitable training and employment, and employers to find suitable workers;

- to offer help and advice to young people on problems connected with their settlement in employment.

Pupils have individual interviews with careers officers, supplemented by self-report questionnaires, psychometric tests, and, where necessary, school and health reports.

Current levels of unemployment have brought about increasing demands on the careers services and considerable extra resources have been allocated. The problem is partially alleviated by the nature of some of the newer developments, such as the Youth Training Scheme, which aim to give a broad training, thus delaying specific careers decisions until experience has been gained. A further effect of such schemes has been to widen careers opportunities for some school-leavers, in that employers have found that young people who previously would not have been considered for interview can perform adequately when given a job (Institute of Personnel Management 1984). The officers of the Careers Service help careers teachers in drawing up programmes of activities and providing contacts. Training officers may well be asked for assistance in collaborative projects (see page 254), or to represent their branch of industry, or public sector at careers exhibitions. (For an example of schools industry liaison, see Robinson 1985). As the burden carried by the careers service officers has increased in that they now have the extra task of liaising between school-leavers and the YTS scheme organizers, the amount of time they can spend in schools or in giving direct vocational guidance is limited.

Careers education is firmly established in the curriculum of most secondary schools and starts in the fourth and fifth years. Good advice is essential because:

> these 13 to 14 year olds are expected to make decisions which frequently affect permanently the educational programme beyond the age of 16 and their career choices. (Avent 1984.)

At this stage they are assisted to assess their own strengths and weaknesses, sometimes by the use of computerized guidance systems, backed by detailed information contained in large job-banks, and to recognize the vocational relevance of the subjects they choose to take, or sometimes more significantly, those, such as mathematics or physics, which they choose to drop and which later may limit or delay their career choices.

Apart from the guidance they may receive from their tutors, careers help for students comes from two main sources. First, universities and colleges have appointment and careers advisory services to assist students find suitable employment. However, the large number of students in many colleges makes it very difficult for the appointments staff to give personal attention to them all, particularly as many students do not think seriously about the career implications of their degrees or diplomas until they are in their final year and faced with trying to obtain a job. At this stage, such guidance as is available may be too little and too late. In times of high unemployment, the considerable effort, worry and expense of job hunting can seriously interfere with the final year of study.

Secondly, the Department of Employment Professional and Executive Register (PER) offers a service for suitably qualified people over the age of 18, similar to that which the Youth Employment Service provides for school leavers. The initiative for seeking this rests with the student.

CURRENT PROVISION OF YOUTH TRAINING AND INITIAL FULL-TIME EDUCATION

Comparison with other EEC countries

Major trading competitors such as France and Germany place greater emphasis on youth training than does the UK. For example, it is claimed that in Germany 60 to 70 per cent of school-leavers take up apprenticeships (Johnson 1984) while in the UK the proportion has declined to little more than 5 per cent (Avent 1984), although plans are in hand to integrate craft training with the Youth Training Scheme. The aim in France is to provide all 16 year olds with the chance of vocational training to skilled worker standard, or encourage them to continue in full-time education up to university level.

It is difficult, and can be misleading, to make direct comparisons in this way because, as Johnson explains, in Germany the term 'apprenticeship' covers almost every kind of job open to 16 year olds, including those in commerce and the public service. Each country has different educational practices and traditions, including the extent to which vocational studies is provided in schools. For instance, in France, Luxembourg, Belgium, Ireland and the Netherlands, pupils can obtain a vocational certificate by the time they leave school at 16. Allowing for all these differences, however, it can be seen that the UK has fallen far behind its competitors in ensuring that all its young people are given the opportunity to reach their potential.

Johnson (1984), who gives a very useful account of youth training in Europe, points to the following problems common to all countries:

- relevance: reflecting dissatisfaction of employers with the work preparation provided by the education system;
- flexibility and choice: because in a rapidly changing situation it is necessary to provide training which would be useful in two or more occupations 'polyvalence', avoiding narrow career choices at too early an age;
- cost: each country has its own way of distributing the cost of training so that the state, the employer and the trainee each bear their share.

Developments in vocational training within the UK

In 1981, the Manpower Services Commission (1981) produced a discussion document, *A New Training Initiative*, which set out three major national objectives for training (see Chapter 10). Two of these relate to school-leavers:

> to develop skill training including apprenticeship in such a way as to enable young people entering at different ages and with different educational attainments to acquire agreed standards of skill appropriate to the jobs available and to provide them with a basis for progress through further learning [and] to move towards a position where all young people under the age of 18 have the opportunity either of continuing in full-time education or of entering a period of planned work-experience combined with work-related training and education.

The discussion document was widely supported and endorsed by a White Paper (HMSO 1981), which incorporated a 10 point programme of action including:

- the setting up of a youth training scheme;
- the development of an 'Open Tech' programme to make technical training more accessible to those who have the necessary ability;
- the drawing up of recognized standards for all the main craft, technician and professional skills to replace time-serving and age-restricted apprenticeships;

- the provision of initial full-time education giving better preparation for working life;
- the provision of more vocationally relevant courses for those staying on in full-time education;
- closer co-ordination of training and vocational education provision both nationally and locally.

Other proposals included an examination of an equitable means of sharing the cost of training, increasing the incentive for employers to provide better training for those in jobs, and the provision of a development fund for pilot schemes in particular localities or sectors.

THE YOUTH TRAINING SCHEME

The White Paper also recommended the setting up of a Youth Task Group (Manpower Services Commission 1982) to report on ways of developing the Youth Training Scheme to cover employed as well as unemployed young people. This group reviewed the long term needs of young people and concluded that not only would the decline in unskilled work necessitate laying a basis for higher competence, but the context of work was changing and there would be a requirement to be more involved with processes rather than repeated performance of a single task. In addition, because the labour market was highly competitive, young people would need a basic knowledge of the world of work, and the skills of job search, as well as personal and life skills, such as management of money matters, to help them survive and even benefit from change. The Task Group therefore proposed a comprehensive scheme to supersede the Youth Opportunities Programme which had been strongly criticized (see Chapter 10).

The YTS will ultimately include all young people aged 16 and 17 who have left full-time education and will offer them the opportunity of entering training or a period of planned work experience combined with work-related training and education. It is also thought desirable that 18 year olds with special needs (e.g. the disabled) should be covered. Initially, however, preference is to be given to minimum age school-leavers unemployed during their first year after leaving school. School leavers who obtained employment, including those undergoing the first year of an apprenticeship, could also be included. The current scheme is operated in two modes: Mode A whereby financial support is provided to employers for training both employed and unemployed young people and Mode B which embraces schemes such as training workshops and community projects solely for unemployed young people.

Mode A is operated by managing agents who arrange a programme of training and work experience for an agreed number of school-leavers and are also responsible for supervision and final certification. There is a wide variety of managing agents, including employers, local authorities, voluntary bodies, Chambers of Commerce and Industrial Training Boards. They receive a grant for each trainee from the Manpower Services Commission, which they retain if they undertake all the training themselves, but they can 'contract out' the provision of work experience for the trainees under their jurisdiction to a variety of different organizations. Similarly, they can arrange off-the-job training with a college or other institution and pay a fee accordingly. The managing agencies are approved and supervised by Area Manpower Boards (see Chapter 10), which assess each proposed scheme and are responsible for ensuring that the provisions meet the needs of the local community. At national level, the scheme is monitored by the Youth Training Board, representing employers, trade unions, local authorities, and education, voluntary and youth organizations.

The YTS programme was launched in 1983 and offers on-the-job training as well as a minimum of thirteen weeks off-the-job training linked with the work experience. The off-the-job element can be organized by a college of further education or other external organization, whilst in some cases the managing agent organizes it on employers' premises. It may be consecutive or interspersed with the work experience and may lead to vocational qualifications such as City and Guilds or BTEC (see page 230). The scheme allows for extremely flexible arrangements, provided that a number of salient features are incorporated.

Participants who are not employed by the organization will have the status of trainee, and will have a proper contract or traineeship agreement and, in cases of difficulty can ultimately have recourse to the MSC for fulfilment of the contract. Special attention must be given to Health and Safety: in Chapter 5, we emphasized that trainees, particularly those in strange surroundings, are more prone to accidents than experienced workers. In the early days of the scheme, insufficient attention was devoted to safety and several serious accidents occurred. Trainees are now protected by the Health and Safety at Work Act etc and, in this respect, are regarded exactly the same as employees.

Each element must be preceded by induction. There must be a planned programme of practical experience, as well as occupationally based training and a number of specified core areas must be incorporated. These are: number and its applications, communications, problem solving and planning, manual dexterity, and introduction to computer literacy and information technology.

Training should be provided in personal effectiveness skills to assist in the adjustment to adult life. Guidance and counselling must be available as well as a system of assessment, reviewing and recording of progress and final certification. Trainees should receive introductory programmes of training and skills related to a broad group of occupations and they should gain experience of sharing responsibility with adults, at the same time as learning about the world of work.

Assessment and final certification pose problems; if the scheme is to appear worthwhile to the participants and the training recognized by other employers, it must provide final accreditation. The flexibility which is such an essential feature and attraction, creates difficulties in the standardization and recording of achievement in a way which will be readily understood by the job market. The use of a system of profiling (see page 233), helps to overcome this and allows trainees to become involved in their own assessment.

Plans are under way for a two year YTS linked with craft training and a variety of other forms of vocational training, such as the Certificate of Pre-vocational Education (see page 257). It is suggested that there is a need for a vocational qualifications system which:

> provides a single coherent framework within which learning – however acquired – is assessed; and clearly identifies where responsibility for the establishment of standards and assessment procedures lies. It should be supported by a register of information on arrangements for the assessment and testing of vocational competence. (Manpower Services Commission and Department of Education and Science 1985).

It is intended that YTS certification will be integrated into an improved structure of vocational qualifications (see Chapter 10).

Manpower Services Commission officers and representatives of training bodies such as the Construction Industry Training Board and the Retail Consortium are developing 'skeletal modules' which categorize occupational skills in a particular job area, with a view to providing validating bodies, such as City and Guilds, Royal Society of Arts and the Business and Technician Education Council with a basis for the award of qualifications relating to standards of competence. There will be about 20 modules and each trainee will receive a final certificate summarizing those in which she has attained the required standard of achievement. It is hoped that the certificate will constitute a recognized qualification with credibility to employers (BACIE 1985). For practical advice on setting up and running Youth Training Programmes see Singer and Johnson (1983).

Learning transfer

An essential concept of YTS is skill ownership or the 'privatization' of skills; in other words they should be of such nature, and learned in such a way, that they are not specific to one organization or situation, but become more of a lifelong asset to the trainee in finding and keeping different types of employment. This approach is in sharp constrast with much previous training which was 'employer controlled' in the sense that the trainee was exposed only to those aspects of skill and knowledge which met the specific organization needs. The employer paid for the training, and saw no merit in enabling employees to obtain skills which were not only beyond requirements but might assist them to obtain jobs elsewhere, or demand higher salaries.

One way of assisting the 'ownership of skills' is by grouping the types of job experience the trainees are likely to acquire into broad occupational categories or occupational training families (Hayes *et al.* 1983) (see also page 140). Examples include administrative, clerical and officer services, manufacturing and assembly, and technical and scientific. This may be seen as a useful way of organizing training, but it has been subject to criticism; in the absence of sufficient research and experience there is no evidence of greater transfer of learning between jobs in the same occupational family than between those in different families, other than can be ascertained by determining common elements empirically (Annett and Sparrow 1985). Indeed it is suggested that the concept might have a 'blinkering effect' if people who trained in one family of skills restricted their opportunities by considering themselves unsuited for employment in another.

The use of core analysis also assists learning transfer by defining core skills, using a recognized reference list which will be readily understood in a variety of organizations (see page 161). A training officer must understand these techniques, not only to prepare programmes for her own organization, but also to to enable her to assess the training needs of a new employee trained elsewhere under the YTS.

A further means of achieving this 'privatization' is by the use of transfer learning objectives, described by Hayes *et al.* (1983) as 'objectives the achievement of which can help young people cope effectively with new and unfamiliar situations within the occupational training family'. They give as an example of a traditional objective, 'able to answer customer questions about products' and a corresponding learning transfer objective 'able to find out the characteristics of unfamiliar products which potential customers might want to know'. The concept of 'being able to find out', is one which could be taken into many other forms of training, as it is a prerequisite of learning to learn, or continuing development. Its application could be extended beyond knowledge, for instance in interpersonal skills training a frequent implicit objective is to develop means of finding out the effect of one's actions and attitudes upon others.

Motivation

Most unemployed young people want a job. Many see YTS training as a palliative to unemployment and, if there is no likelihood of permanent work becoming available, it is difficult to create enthusiasm for the virtues of skills for their own sake. One approach is to interest trainees in their own learning, and find out what they feel they need to know and to be able to do. 'It is important that the school leaver should have learned to set goals for learning and to recognize and use a variety of learning resources to achieve these goals.' Institute of Personnel Management (1983). The design and ethos of the YTS scheme entails: involvement of the participants; consultation on all aspects including course content; personal assessment; counselling sessions and where practicable, careers guidance. In other words, it is essentially a learner-centred scheme, which calls for special skills on the part of supervisors and instructors, for whom training courses are available at accredited centres throughout the UK. Ultimate success, however, is still likely to depend on the extent to which YTS can embrace the employed, as well as those without a permanent job.

The extension to two years, and the inclusion of craft training could go a long way towards making YTS a recognized form of training for all minimum aged school-leavers, and one from which it is possible to emerge with a variety of qualifications. The motivation to attend such a course is likely to be greater than to be involved in what might be seen merely as a substitute for a 'proper job'. Much, however, will depend upon the quality of the two-year programme. The attitude of employers to the new final certificate and the success rate of previous trainees in gaining permanent employment will also be important motivators. Some of the problems associated with the YTS are noted on page 299).

Some measure of the effectiveness of the scheme and also of the role of education in reducing youth unemployment, may be seen in the figures supplied by Upton (1985), which show that in 1983/4, 43 per cent of 16 year olds remained at school or went into further education, 14 per cent were unemployed, 22 per cent entered YTS and 21 per cent obtained employment.

DEVELOPMENTS IN INITIAL FULL-TIME EDUCATION

The White Paper (HMSO 1981) contained the outline of a programme to provide more vocationally relevant courses for those staying on in full-time education. Current provision includes the following:

Certificate of Pre-vocational Education (CPVE). This one-year course is aimed at pupils who wish to stay on at school but do not want to take A levels, or a specialized vocational qualification. The course includes core studies as well as vocational studies. The latter should take at least a quarter of the programme and involve a minimum of 15 days' work experience. There are five occupational categories – business and administrative services, technical services, production, distribution and services to people. These vocational groups are taught at three different levels:

- introductory, which enables pupils to determine if they have any aptitude for the particular occupational group, and allows them to sample different groups;
- exploratory level which allows the acquisition of transferable job skills;
- preparatory level which prepares pupils to start on a particular vocational route.

The CPVE course aims to provide a universally recognized grounding for jobs, or for a variety of vocational courses, or to afford a route back to more academic studies leading to A levels or BTEC awards (see page 230). This course obviously fulfils the requirement mentioned earlier in this chapter of not forcing career decisions too early and it is also an example of the way in which basic education and training can be used to supplement career guidance.

The Technical and Vocational Education Initiative (TVEI) was set up in 1983 as a five year experiment. It aims to 'open to young people within education, across the whole range of ability, a technical and vocational route to recognized national qualifications' (HMSO 1984). It is for 14 to 18 year olds within a wide range of ability, from the very bright to the less able. It is a very flexible concept with no closely defined objectives or curricula and individual local education authorities can submit their own schemes. The Manpower Services Commission, in close liaison with the Department of Education and Science, is in control of this initiative. Each TVEI programme must fulfil a number of criteria which include: the provision of a four year curriculum to prepare the student for employment in a rapidly changing society, the development of problem solving skills, technical and vocational aspects, planned work experience, equal opportunities for young people of both sexes, regular written assessment and counselling. These are educational programmes, which attempt to strike a balance between practical work and related study and thereby begin the construction of the bridge between school and work. The programmes will lead to nationally recognized qualifications.

The City and Guilds of London Institute (CGLI) has designed pre-vocational courses which were undertaken by some 98,000 candidates in 1983/4. These courses are designed for young people within a wide range of abilities, who are in their final year of full-time education, but have have not yet committed themselves to a specific vocation. There are nine foundation courses including construction, agriculture and community care, and they can be used as guides for schools to develop their own courses. The CGLI and the teachers are jointly responsible for assessment.

The Royal Society of Arts (RSA) run vocational preparation courses in areas such as distribution, clerical work and basic receptionist/telephone skills. In 1983/4 over 5,000 students between 14 and 18, including some on YTS schemes, took these vocational preparation courses.

The Business and Technical Education Council (BTEC) awards are also important qualifications for young people. These awards were developed from the recommendations of the Haslegrave Report (1969). This Committee had been set up to investigate the education of technicians and had concluded that although the term was traditionally applied to the technical sector only, there is a wide range of occupations in the business sector to which this term can also be applied. On the recommendation of this report, the Technician Education Council (TEC) was set up in 1973 with responsibility for technician courses in the technical sector and the Business Education Council (BEC) in 1974, for those in the business sector. The two have since merged to become BTEC. A parallel organization exists in Scotland.

All the BTEC courses are modular in design and they are of three levels: General, National and Higher National. General or first level awards are suitable for trainees starting work at 16 and include core areas of study as well as option modules. Examples of core areas for the business studies area are, communications, human relations, organizational structures and environment, office services and clerical skills. National awards are for students who have attained credit standard in BTEC first level awards, or the required number of GCE 'O' level passes. Higher National awards have an entry qualification of BTEC National award, or a required number of GCE 'A' and 'O' level qualifications or the equivalent. Many of the subjects studied are similar to those in the lower level courses, but are taken to a higher standard.

BTEC is committed to collaborating with other bodies such as the City and Guilds of London Institute and the MSC, and has:

> contributed significantly to the recent national move towards a more explicit pre-vocational stage being the norm in most young people's education. The Council believes that this can lead to a major

> improvement in preparing young people for working life and in motivating them to seek vocational development after they leave the pre-vocational stage. (BTEC 1984.)

The Council has always been particularly mindful of the necessity to integrate employment needs and education. For example, business studies courses are designed to provide rungs on the ladder for those who are aiming at professional qualification, and foster knowledge and skills for those planning careers in business or public administration (Business Education Council 1976). Students can study for the awards on a full-time, part-time or sandwich basis and, if successful, they can obtain some exemptions from the examinations of appropriate professional bodies, for example purchasing and accountancy.

The Government is concerned that there should be compatibility between the different schemes YTS, TVEI and CPVE (HMSO 1985), but the variety of vocational qualifications is still wide and adds a new dimension to the assessment of training needs for young entrants. If young employees are not to be bored by unnecessary repetition, the training officer will require a good knowledge and understanding of the objectives, content and standard of the various schemes in order to arrange programmes of training which will follow and build on what the young entrants have already learned. Where external courses are undertaken as part of in-house training schemes (such as YTS) they must be carefully integrated with the work experience. The training officer may also be asked to collaborate closely with colleges by taking part in informal discussions or as a member of advisory boards. In addition, she needs to realize the implications of some of the newer features. Two developments which could be particularly far reaching are work experience and systems of profiling.

WORK EXPERIENCE

Many of the programmes described, for example CPVE, and TVEI, require short term work experience placements. Schemes which are experimental at the moment may be successful but if they were to be widely replicated, so that every school were to seek this type of work experience, there is some doubt as to whether industry and public sector employers could cope. Of practical importance is whether the placements could be spread over the teaching year, or must be concentrated in the summer term only. Training officers would be in danger of receiving requests from many sources simultaneously and there would be a strong argument for some form of local co-ordination, in terms of the numbers to be placed. Much greater co-ordination would also be required between the school teacher and the work supervisor in setting realistic objectives and time-scales for placements, as well as evaluation and discussion with the young people. Large organizations might ultimately find the necessity to appoint a work experience tutor or co-ordinator.

Work experience is a commendable addition to the school curriculum, but it is not an easy option; to be successful it demands careful planning, time and resources from the host organization. Unless pupils have a very clear idea of what they are trying to gain, there is a great danger that within the short time available they will obtain a superficial impression or that they will not take the opportunity seriously. The attitude and commitment of teaching staff is of prime importance, as was found in earlier years with the introduction of placements and sandwich courses in higher education (see Chapter 10). Liaising with organizations over student placements and joint assessment of progress is extremely time-consuming and therefore proper time allowances must be available. For a discussion of the criteria for successful planned work experience see Hollingshead, Kelly and Bagenall (1984), and Heywood (1984).

The Institute of Personnel Management (1984) is urging its members to offer work experience placements, and to manage them professionally, by taking the following steps:

- finding out about the programme of which the work experience will form a part;
- setting learning objectives for work experience in collaboration with the young person's teacher;
- reviewing the work experience against the learning objectives at the end of the placement;
- bringing young people together for common work experience sessions, e.g. induction;
- producing written material to avoid duplicating verbal instructions;
- updating the work programme continuously in the light of experience.

The Institute suggests that the demands for work experience should come from a single co-ordinating source in the locality and that a survey of the availability of local work experience placements should be carried out annually. Furthermore, if work experience is to be an important part of new-style practical learning programmes, the Department of Education and Science should formulate a policy clarifying the place of work experience in educational courses, and outlining minimum criteria for control and evaluation.

PROFILING

Profiling is not a method of assessment, but a means of recording achievement which is increasingly incorporated in the progammes for young people, including YTS and TVEI. Many traditional forms of assessment might be described as 'norm-referencing', because the results would be expected to conform more or less according to a normal curve of distribution (where the majority cluster around the average, with small numbers obtaining either very high or very low marks). Although these systems afford the facility of comparing trainees with each other, or with a given standard, they provide a global grading rather than a clear picture of what the trainee can actually do. The extreme case might be where one student obtains a first-class honours degree and another student obtains a third-class degree – an employer might judge the first student to be brighter than the second. It is, however, still not apparent what either student can actually do. For instance, the second student might have other attributes such as self-presentation skills, which would make her a better choice for an appointment in sales management than the student with first-class honours.

Criterion-referenced assessment, on the other hand, involves assessing performance on a number of specified competencies, such as ability to use a micrometer or to operate a duplicating machine. The assessment may consist of a grading system for each competency or, alternatively, a behavioural objective approach may be adopted and the exact standard and conditions under which the performance takes place defined. The trainee's standard of performance on each competency is then recorded as a 'profile'. Singer and Johnson (1983) suggest that the trainees should be involved in monitoring their own progress and assist in drawing up their own profiles, which should be completed by 'more than one tutor in more than one context (e.g. shop floor, classroom)'. In this way the technique is used not just for recording assessment, but as a learning tool. The ability to evaluate one's own strengths and weaknesses might be regarded as one of the essentials of self-development. One dimension of the assessment profile might be 'the ability to learn new competencies', which is of interest to any prospective employer.

The definition of a standard by which to determine whether a competency has been achieved, and which will be readily understood and accepted by different employers, is still a matter of difficulty. Hayes *et al.* (1983) refer to the concept of 'experienced worker standard' and suggest that in reality supervisors have an awareness of what constitutes acceptable performance and that they should be involved in the assessment. This is a very practical solution, but still leaves a problem for potential employers because what is acceptable in one organization may not be so in another, and knowledge of the host organization will have to be taken into consideration when recruiting those who have received the training, and attempting to evaluate their profiles. It must be recognized, however, that most young school-leavers will seek jobs locally and that this might not therefore pose too many difficulties. In the interests of uniformity, the way in which the information is presented will be of crucial importance and it might be helpful to reach some common standards, for example with respect to the language used. (Institute of Personnel Management 1984).

One approach might be a dual format consisting of a summary profile in a standardized presentation, which would enable employers to make shortlisting decisions, and a detailed profile in a more flexible form to allow for more diverse information, which would be useful during interviews and final selection procedures. The profile should highlight the trainee's strengths but, if it is to be really useful, it should expose weaknesses. How best to achieve this is a matter which has not yet been resolved, most consideration having so far been devoted to the recording of positive aspects. For further discussion on profiles see Further Education Curriculum Review and Development Unit (1982).

The use of profiling has applications to other areas of training. For instance, the various activities at an assessment centre for managers result in a profile of each manager's performance on the selected dimensions (see page 179). Profiling also provides a useful and clear basis for vocational guidance and assessing further training needs.

While considerable time and energy is being devoted to appropriate and more informative ways of recording achievement, the ultimate success of profiling will depend upon employers. If they regard educational qualifications mainly as indicators of ability on which they will be able to superimpose their own training, and if they continue to demand a specific number of 'O' and 'A' levels for entry to their organizations, then profiling, and in fact the vocational aspects of the new programmes for young people will not bring the anticipated results. It is therefore important for personnel officers and training officers to be aware of the responsibilities they carry and to make informed, unprejudiced judgements about the new schemes. There is encouraging evidence of enterprising attempts at collaboration between the education system and industry and commerce. For further information on profiling see Holmes (1984), Robinson (1985) and Mortimore (1984).

While these signs are encouraging there is a strange paradox in the situation: as the opportunities for employment become fewer, and the estimated years of working life diminish, there could be a good argument for maintaining that the prime function of education is to produce good citizens who, as well as being employable, can use their leisure wisely, and if need be, can stand back and indulge in healthy criticism of organizations and institutions. This is not to deny that mistakes have been made in the past, and that some spheres of education have tended to isolate pupils from industry instead of encouraging them to take part in wealth creation, nor to overlook the fact that school-leavers need skills to compete with adults in the labour market. The danger is the familiar one of throwing out the baby with the bath water, in that tomorrow's citizens will require more than the sum of a collection of transferable competencies.

FURTHER AND HIGHER EDUCATION

Employment and training at 18-plus

Since 1945 there has been a major increase in the number of young people who go into the sixth form at school (or transfer to a college of further education) and so do not start work until they are about 18 years old. These school leavers normally have one or more GCE 'A' level passes (or increasingly in future, one of the new vocational qualifications under TVEI) and leave full-time education for one of three reasons. First, their examination grades are not good enough for them to continue their studies; secondly, there is a growing number who, although qualified for a place at college or university, want a job straight away, if possible, rather than face the prospect of waiting three or four years; or, thirdly, they have been selected to follow a sandwich degree or diploma course.

These school and college leavers have spent 13 years in full-time education and a high proportion of them look for employment which offers good career prospects. Those who have already had some vocational training may obtain jobs immediately as, for example, junior secretaries, while others who have followed science-based courses may obtain posts in industry as trainee technicians and technologists, sometimes taking part-time BTEC courses (see page 230). Still others will use their general education as a background and start a professional career in, for example, accountancy, insurance or banking.

Eighteen and 19 year olds are realizing the importance of receiving good training and rightly expect their employers to provide planned programmes. These should be designed to take into account variables such as the following: the fact that these trainees are usually well motivated and prepared to work hard; that they tend to be self starters; that they are potentially very capable young people and need to be given work which challenges their abilities; and that education will probably play an important role in their training and development programmes.

It is from this group of school-leavers that organizations recruit young men and women with potential and sponsor them on sandwich courses. These are available in a wide variety of disciplines, such as mechanical and electrical engineering, business studies, chemical technology, computing, food science and applied physics, and lead to a first degree of the Council of National Academic Awards (CNAA), or of a university or, in some cases, to a National or Higher National Diploma or Certificate.

Sandwich courses are vocationally orientated and designed so that the student spends time in industry and at college before graduating. The in-company part of the programme requires careful planning on the part of the training officer to ensure that it is effective, in phase with the academic curriculum and is paced to match the maturation of the student. Project work and job rotation through different departments and sometimes in different companies or industries are features of many sandwich courses. Projects provide a very useful learning experience for students, but a great deal of preparatory work is needed on the part of the training officer and the college lecturers in selecting and defining a project which is feasible from the employer's point of view and of value to the individual trainee and to the organization. Job rotation is also a useful method of learning and contrasts with the traditional 'tour' approach, although the latter method is still followed by some organizations.

Fifty one per cent of polytechnic graduates entered permanent employment in 1982, but there was considerable variation in the different subject groupings: the statistics relating to management science and to business and commerce being 81 and 74 per cent respectively (Committee of Directors of Polytechnics 1984). 'For all subjects combined, polytechnic graduates were significantly (at the one per cent level), more likely to have obtained permanent employment by the end of their graduating year than university graduates', although the reverse was true for accounting graduates (see Bourner 1984).

Some major companies and a growing number of small organizations sponsor suitably qualified 18 year old school-leavers on sandwich courses in preference to employing graduates straight from full-time courses. The advantages of the former approach are that during the three or four years of the sandwich course, students receive formal education and practical training and, on qualifying, are familiar with the sponsor's ways and capable of doing a job with the minimum of further training. As trainees progress through their courses, their talents for particular work can be spotted and developed. Both employers and trainees are then in a strong position to select the most appropriate field for eventual employment and steps can be taken to plan ahead for their first job.

However, one survey (see Boys 1984), found little evidence of employers regarding the more vocationally relevant courses, specially designed by polytechnics to prepare students for industry and commerce, as compensation for the perceived 'A' level deficiencies in the polytechnic undergraduates. There was still a tendency to regard 'quality', however defined, as something innate, which enabled a person to be developed on taking up employment rather than an attribute engendered by the educational system. An applicant's personality was extremely important and could override academic considerations. The study described by Boys suggests that:

employers use higher education primarily as a useful screen in which the academic qualifications of potential recruits and the type of institution attended are more influential than the type of course studied.

Could there be a slight note of warning here for the new vocationally-orientated courses for younger school-leavers?. It is also suggested, however, that even large scale recruiters have considerable knowledge gaps about the education system which cast doubt upon whether they are obtaining full value from it (see also Chapter 10).

Employment at 20-plus

Young men and women who have taken full-time or sandwich courses leading to a degree or diploma are between 20 and 22 years old before they start their first permanent job. While some final year students have a clear idea of the careers they will follow, others, and in particular those who have taken non-vocational courses, have considerable difficulty in deciding the kind of employment they would wish to pursue.

Unfortunately, careers in industry or commerce have tended, in the past, to be regarded by many students, and their advisers, as second-best to university research, the civil service or teaching, and concern has often been expressed about the need to attract more graduates into business. Many companies, especially large ones, offer graduates excellent training opportunities and promotion prospects, and this has helped to create a better image of commercial and industrial organizations. These companies have shown that they can offer graduates careers which compare well with some of the traditional fields of employment historically reserved for highly educated young men and women.

The rapid growth in the number of young people obtaining degrees and diplomas has not been matched by a parallel increase in the number of jobs required by graduates. There has been a gradual change in the pattern of graduate employment and there can be problems in helping them find job satisfaction and to feel that their talents are being utilized.

Rogers and Williams (1970) divide the pattern of demand for graduate employees into three periods: the pre-1950 era, when graduates tended to be recruited by the public service and the armed forces; the 1950s when hostility to graduates as theorists diminished and enlightened employers, particularly the larger companies, recruited their 'crown princes'; and the 1960s when graduates were being accepted generally and in increasing demand: the decade of the 'taut' and brief training programme. To this must be added a fourth period: the 1970s and 1980s, characterized by a buyer's market. Recent evidence, however, suggests that the employment prospects for graduates are rising and that there is a growing interest in recruiting graduates by small businesses and other organizations which have never done so before (*Personnel Management* 1985). This emerging pattern will apply particularly to graduates in 'shortage' subjects, such as electronics, but there will also be openings in general management training in industry and commerce. The evidence indicates the importance of aspects such as 'numeracy, the ability to present effectively information in meetings and reports, a working familiarity with computers and the ability to work in collaboration with others'.

The employment and training opportunities in industry and commerce which are open to graduates depend on a number of factors, including the discipline they have studied, their personality and interests, and the job market. There are, however, basically three categories of new graduates seeking employment: those with qualifications which are vocational, semi-vocational, or non-vocational.

Graduates with vocational qualifications. Students who have completed vocational courses in subjects such as production engineering, computer technology, industrial design or business studies, have qualifications which are relevant to specific fields of employment. They have acquired sufficient skills and knowledge during their courses to be able to do a responsible job after only a few weeks of induction and job familiarization training, particularly if they have followed a sandwich course.

However, many vocational first degrees and national diplomas provide students with a broad-based education and relatively little specialization. As a result, graduates in, say, business studies who specialize in accountancy in their degree courses are not qualified accountants. Similarly, mechanical engineering graduates are not immediately eligible for membership of a professional body. These students may be exempted from certain professional examinations, but they will have to study further and gain relevant practical experience at work to qualify for full membership. The early part of their employment is, in effect, further training, being the practical experience needed by the graduate seeking a professional qualification.

Graduates with semi-vocational qualifications. These students have certain expertise of potential use to an organization but they need to acquire commercial or technological skills before they can be gainfully employed. Examples include: graduates in physics, chemistry or pharmacy being prepared for technical sales or research and development positions; graduates in English, for journalism and advertising; and those in foreign languages for export-import business, or travel agency work.

Assuming that these graduates have the personality, drive and other qualities required by an employer, they will need training to induct them into the organization, to provide them with a general background to the industry or the field of employment, and to enable them to acquire the business or technological knowledge and expertise they need for their work. This expertise may be in such fields as manufacturing technology, selling or computing. On-the-job training and practical work experience is a major part of their training. Training programmes for these graduates vary in length: six to eight months is an average time, and they are thus much longer than those for graduates with vocational degrees or diplomas.

Graduates with non-vocational qualifications. Students who have studied subjects such as sociology, history or politics, find that the currency of their qualifications in the commercial job market is very limited, as they cannot offer employers any technical skills or knowledge that they can profitably use. Their degrees indicate academic ability, but this by itself is not enough to obtain employment, since employers will only be willing to provide the necessary lengthy job training (possibly of a year or more) if this investment seems prudent.

A greater number of graduates in non-vocational subjects are recognizing that they need to improve their qualifications by studying for examinations leading to membership of professional bodies such as the the Institute of Training and Development and the Institute of Personnel Management or one of the accountancy bodies. Others may read for higher degrees on an evening or day-release basis in, say, management studies.

INDUCTION TRAINING

The process of induction begins with the initial contact between the new employee and the organization, as this is when first impressions are formed. It can therefore be considered as including the whole of the recruitment process. The main aims of induction training are to welcome new employees into the organization or department, and to ensure that they understand certain basic information about the job and its environment. Thus induction is the one type of training necessary for all trainees, whether young or old, whether they are newcomers or have changed their work within the organization. Labour turnover is frequently highest among those who have recently joined an organization. The term 'induction crisis' is used to describe the critical period when new starters are most likely to leave. A well planned induction course can help to decrease labour turnover by ensuring that new starters settle quickly in their jobs and reach an efficient standard of performance as soon as possible. However it must be recognized that faulty selection can be a contributory factor to the 'induction crisis'.

Legislation, for example in the fields of industrial relations and health and safety, has caused companies to review the content and effectiveness of their induction arrangements and these reviews have led to two major conclusions. First, an awareness that the traditional induction course which all employees attend disregards the particular needs of special groups, such as school leavers, Youth Training Scheme trainees, immigrants, the disabled, or adults being retrained for new jobs. While such staff will share some common induction needs, their programmes must also reflect the differences and, as a result, will vary both in content and duration from one category to another. Secondly, companies recognize that the wider induction objectives cannot be achieved in an initial short course of training. This position is illustrated in the context of school leavers by the following quotation from the Manpower Services Commission (1975) study on the vocational preparation for young people but also applies to other categories:

> What is needed...is a personnel policy specifically for young entrants which recognizes the special problems they face in the transition to the new environment of adult working life, at a time when they are also experiencing the personal problems of growing up. Such a policy would reflect awareness of the teaching methods in use nowadays in schools, the common attitudes of young people towards work and the

community; their ideals and expectations; the difficulties faced by young people in growing up; in adapting to working life, in working with older people, and in understanding and accepting the discipline of the workplace. Particular attention would also be given to trying to see that those close to the entrants, particularly their supervisors and workmates were able to guide them in their development, both as individuals and as capable members of the working community, and that the young people themselves know where they can go to get advice, whenever they need it.

From this it follows that induction cannot be carried out by the training officer alone, but must be an overall managerial responsibility. Many induction needs are concerned with the immediate working environment and therefore a most important part is played by the supervisor and those working in the vicinity. For these reasons, induction must be regarded as an integral part of the organization's training plan and its importance should be stressed in the training given to all employees and especially to managers and supervisors.

Induction training should not be regarded as a requirement for new employees only. Young trainees need a short induction period for each phase of their programme, particularly if they are progressing through different departments. It should include a discussion of the objectives and expectations of trainee and organization or department, as well as any necessary knowledge about the new environment. Students or pupils on work experience placements also require induction although their programmes may be different in emphasis and depth of detail from those designed for permanent employees.

The following list indicates the points which may need to be covered during the induction period:

- *Conditions of employment*: the contract of employment, payment procedures, holiday arrangements, Factories Act, absence and sickness procedures, meal and tea breaks, disciplinary procedures;

- *Welfare*: pension and sickness schemes, welfare and social activities, medical services;

- *The organization*: foundation and growth, products, standards, market;

- *Introduction to workplace*: meeting the supervisor and fellow employees, geography of department (e.g. canteen, toilets), the job, who's who, future of the organization;

- *Safety*: hazard areas, fire alarm procedure, fire points and exits, no smoking areas, first aid and accident procedures, safety rules, security arrangements, safety committees, safety representatives;
- *Training arrangements*: person(s) responsible for training, content of training programmes, further education;
- *Organization facilities*: clubs, discount schemes;
- *Pay system*: how to read a pay slip, overtime and incentive payments, pension schemes, income tax and other deductions;
- *Trade unions and staff associations*: the role of trade unions, grievance procedures.

The content and approach to induction training should be planned around the needs of the trainee. In some cases a few hours' induction is adequate but in others it may last for several weeks. It is preferable to split the content of longer induction programmes into several sections, providing the trainee with the information as she needs it. As an extreme instance, a school leaver is unlikely to be interested in details of the pension scheme the minute she has arrived in the organization. Her first concerns are likely to be; 'Will I be able to do the job?' and 'What will my supervisor and co-workers be like?' In Chapter 5 we discussed the value of curiosity, and the appropriate timing of the sessions on an induction course can be a decisive factor in effectiveness. For a full discussion of induction, see Fowler (1983) and ACAS (1982).

In this chapter, we have considered ways of training and educating young people so that not only will they be competitive in the immediate job market, but they will also have learned how to learn. Competence in one type of job is unlikely to ensure employment during a whole working life; our rapidly changing technology will necessitate frequent acquisition of new knowledge and skills. In Chapter 9, we consider some of the issues surrounding retraining and continuing development.

BIBLIOGRAPHY

ANNETT A and SPARROW J. *Transfer of learning and training, basic issues: policy implementation: how to promote transfer*. Research and Development No. 23, Sheffield, Manpower Services Commission, June, 1985.

ADVISORY, CONCILIATION AND ARBITRATION SERVICE, *Induction of new employees*. Advisory Booklet No. 7. London, Advisory, Conciliation and Arbitration Service, 1982.

AVENT C. 'Transition from school to work'. *BACIE Journal*, July/Aug, 1984.

BRITISH ASSOCIATION FOR COMMERCIAL AND INDUSTRIAL EDUCATION. 'Skeletal modules'. *Transition*. BACIE, 1985.

BOURNER T. *Handbook for the graduates' first destinations transbinary database*. London, Council for National Academic Awards, 1984.

BOYS C. 'Are employers making the most of higher education?' *Personnel Management*, September, 1984.

BUSINESS EDUCATION COUNCIL. *First policy statement*. London, Business Education Council, 1976.

BUSINESS AND TECHNICIAN EDUCATION COUNCIL. *Policies and priorities into the 1990s*. London, BTEC, September, 1984.

COMMISSION OF THE EUROPEAN COMMUNITIES. 'From education to working life'. In *Bulletin of the European Communities, Supplement 12/76*, 1976.

COMMITTEE Of DIRECTORS OF POLYTECHNICS. *Press information sheet. No. 6*, November, London, 1984.

COUNCIL FOR NATIONAL ACADEMIC AWARDS. *Graduates' first destinations. Project conducted by Brighton Polytechnic*. London, CNAA Development Services Publication 4, 1984.

FOWLER A. *Getting off to a good start: successful employee induction*. London, Institute of Personnel Management, 1983.

FURTHER EDUCATION CURRICULUM REVIEW AND DEVELOPMENT UNIT. *Profiles*. London, FEU, 1982.

HASLEGRAVE REPORT. *Report of the committee on technician courses and examinations*. HMSO, 1969.

HAYES C, FONDA N, POPE M, STUART R, and TOWNSEND K. *Training for skill ownership*. Sheffield, Manpower Services Commission, 1983.

HEYWOOD M. *Planned experience – a survey and synthesis of criteria for work experience*. London, Further Education Unit, 1984.

HMSO. White paper, *A new training initiative: a programme for action*. Cmnd.8455, London, HMSO, 1981.

HMSO. White paper, *Training for jobs*. Cmnd 9135, London, HMSO, 1984.

HMSO. White paper, *Education and training for young people*. Cmnd 9482, London, HMSO, 1985.

HOLLINGSHEAD B AND OTHERS. *Planned experience – a survey and synthesis of criteria for work experience*. London, Further Education Unit, 1984.

HOLMES S. 'Are schools and industry getting each other's message?' *Personnel Management*, December, 1984.

INSTITUTE OF PERSONNEL MANAGEMENT. *A positive policy for training and development*. A policy statement prepared by the IPM National Training Committee, London, IPM, 1983.

INSTITUTE OF PERSONNEL MANAGEMENT. *TVEI recommendations on improved school/work liaison*. London, IPM, 1984.

JOHNSON R. 'Youth training in Europe'. *Personnel Management*, July, 1984.

MANPOWER SERVICES COMMISSION. *Manpower review*. Sheffield, Manpower Services Commission, 1982.

MANPOWER SERVICES COMMISSION AND DEPARTMENT OF EDUCATION AND SCIENCE, *Review of vocational qualifications in England and Wales, Interim report*. Sheffield/London, September, 1985.

MANPOWER SERVICES COMMISSION. *Vocational preparation for young people*. Sheffield, MSC, 1975.

MANPOWER SERVICES COMMISSION. *Towards a comprehensive manpower policy*. Sheffield, Manpower Services Commission, 1976.

MANPOWER SERVICES COMMISSION. *A new training initiative; an agenda for action*. Sheffield, MSC, 1981.

MANPOWER SERVICES COMMISSION. *Youth task group report*. Sheffield, MSC, 1982.

MARKS GROUP. 'Feedback from management courses'. Editorial comment on survey. *Personnel Management*. August 1985.

MORTIMORE J. *Profiles in action*. London, Further Education Unit, 1984.

PEARSON R HUTT R, and PARSONS D. *Education, training and employment*. Institute of Manpower Studies, Series No. 4, Aldershot, Gower, 1984.

PERSONNEL MANAGEMENT. 'Good news for graduates. Reference to annual assessment of employment prospects by Association of Graduate Careers Advisory Services, the Standing Conference of Employers of Graduates and the Central Services Unit for Careers and Appointments Services'. Editorial comment, *Personnel Management*, March, 1985.

ROBINSON A. 'Schools industry liaison – a partnership at Slough'. *BACIE Journal*, July/Aug, 1985.

ROGERS T G P and WILLIAMS P. *The recruitment and training of graduates*. London, Institute of Personnel Management, 1970.

SINGER E J and JOHNSON R. *Setting up and running youth training programmes*. Surrey, Centre for Learning and Development in association with the Institute of Personnel Management, 1983.

UPTON R. 'What next for youth training?' *Personnel Management*, April, 1985.

VAUGHAN T D. *Education and vocational guidance*. London, Routledge and Kegan Paul, 1970.

9: Continuing development – some issues

INTRODUCTION

In this chapter, we first consider the range of activities which may be involved in the continuing development process and the way in which they can be influenced by personal and organizational factors. Secondly, we examine the implications for the training officer of some specific retraining situations. The third section is devoted to the national background and the effect of government policy, which is exemplified by two case histories. Fourthly, we outline proposed changes in craft training which provide opportunities for late entry and updating. Finally, we describe open learning facilities. This section focuses on learning to learn, within the setting of organizations.

THE UPDATING, CONTINUING DEVELOPMENT AND RETRAINING SPECTRUM

Continuing development and retraining are terms with such considerable overlap of meaning that it is hardly fruitful to draw a fine distinction between them. Collectively, they are associated with a variety of activities which might be regarded as a continuum ranging at one end from every-day experience such as giving and receiving advice; reading articles in journals; obtaining information from the media or from educational publicity; to attending organized events such as meetings, discussions, conferences, seminars; participating in the affairs of professional bodies; and at the far end of the continuum, more formalized training such as in-house courses, external courses (part-time and full-time), release for longer periods of study or planned experience, e.g. job rotation.

The frequency and effectiveness of these occurrences may be influenced by two factors. First, the climate and attitude of the organization, which can range from complete inactivity and lack of concern, through varying degrees of allowing, supporting, facilitating and providing resources, to the stage of planning and carrying out mandatory training programmes.

Secondly, the predisposition of the individual who may only contemplate undertaking training when told to do so, and when facilities are explicitly provided. On the other hand, he may be willing, but needs encouragement and help and sometimes needs to be 'pushed' by his organization, or exhorted by his professional body. For instance, the Law Society and the Institute of Personnel Management are becoming increasingly interested in the continuing development of their members. At the far end of the scale, are those who take the entire initiative upon themselves. (Taking responsibility for one's own learning is becoming a popular concept, but is not incompatible with the suggestion that people may still benefit from some imposed discipline such as target dates and deadlines!)

These activities are not new. Some of them, such as part-time courses, have a history which can be traced back to the early industrial revolution and the era of the Mechanics' Institutes (see Chapter 10). However, the accelerating rate of technological development and the organization change it necessitates, have focused attention on the need for all employees to be up to date, flexible and adaptable. This requirement has become an essential factor in enabling companies to be competitive in world markets and in attempting to achieve national economic recovery.

SOME SPECIFIC CIRCUMSTANCES IN WHICH RETRAINING TAKES PLACE

While it is recognized that development is a constant and lifelong process, there are a number of circumstances which necessitate sudden change and an intensive form of retraining. Each of these situations can have different implications for the trainer and trainee. It is therefore appropriate to consider them in turn.

The first situation is that of acquiring new skills or knowledge in one's own field. An example would be a typist who learns word processing, or the personnel officer who learns to manage a computerized record system. The second relates to retraining for promotion as part of career progression. This may include learning a completely new set of skills to be applied within the same, or a similar, environment, for example, an operative or craftsman, who becomes a chargehand or supervisor. A third aspect is retraining in the same skills and knowledge on the same job for those whose performance has deteriorated, while a fourth occurs when redundancy in the original job is followed by retraining for entirely different work within the same organization. The final set of circumstances comes about when the incumbent is made redundant, leaves, or is dismissed from the organization, cannot get a job using his existing expertise, and has to find his own retraining opportunity elsewhere, perhaps involving an entirely different type of work.

Although in designing training programmes, much attention is paid to what new knowledge and skills will be required, it is frequently the attitudinal aspect which causes most problems. For instance, updating training may involve upgrading and the job incumbent may be unwilling to undertake it without adequate remuneration in recognition of his enhanced value to the organization. On the other hand, there may be union opposition to the training (for example of multi-skilled craftsmen) based on fear that fewer people will ultimately be required and that management is 'selling jobs'. Another possibility is that the training will be resisted because those in influential positions have a vested interest in maintaining the status quo (see page 147).

Retraining for promotion may take place gradually over a period of time, possibly in the form of planned experience or attendance at relevant courses, but the attitude of management may be such that no formal training is provided at all, on the assumption that the incumbent will 'grow into the job'. Stewart (1975) points out that, although technical training may be provided in these circumstances, interpersonal skills are frequently ignored. For instance a sales representative, whose contact has been mainly with customers outside the organization boundaries, may require a new range of interpersonal skills if transferred to line management with responsibility for subordinates.

Retraining within the same organization because the original job has ceased to exist, may generate feelings of resentment, loss of status, worry and insecurity. Providing retraining may be viewed by management as a generous gesture, and much may be expected of trainees in this situation. Retraining is sometimes used as an extended selection process when there are insufficient new jobs for all the internal candidates. Those who make the best progress are retained, those whose performance is inferior being declared redundant. This system may appear advantageous to the organization, ensuring that the most able candidates are eventually selected, but is likely to contribute to strain and anxiety during training, particularly for less able trainees.

Retraining after performance has declined requires highly skilled tuition. It is necessary to determine the cause of deterioration which which may include physical, emotional, interpersonal factors, or merely a collection of inferior working practices. Environmental aspects should be examined, carefully and tactfully, as faulty materials or equipment (which may indicate training needs in other parts of the organization) or apparently imperceptible changes in the job, can result in lower standards of performance, which may not be entirely attributable to the job holder's incompetence. In these circumstances any suggestion that retraining is likely to be needed may add insult to injury. For further discussion of analysing performance problems see Mager and Pike (1970).

Retraining for a different job in a new organization involves the initial problem of finding opportunities for training. This may cause worry, disillusionment or even depression: commencement of retraining may be accompanied by anxiety to succeed. The longer a period of unemployment continues, the more difficult it can be to find a retraining opportunity, and some would-be-trainees never manage to cross this hurdle, and join the hard core of long-term unemployed.

These situations have many features in common, none of which are new, but are aggravated by the speed and continuity of change, which allows little time for attitudes to adapt. An efficient trainer will consider each case carefully to diagnose and investigate potential problems. Easy solutions may not be forthcoming but an understanding approach and willingness to discuss and listen will create a helpful environment.

THE NATIONAL BACKGROUND

Retraining issues relating to individuals and organizations are affected by national policies, particularly those concerned with the resources available. In the 1960s, in times of full employment, the Council of Ministers of the European Economic Community formulated the ideal of offering to:

> everyone in accordance with his aspirations, skills, knowledge and working experience and by permanent means for vocational improvement, eligibility for a higher occupational level or instruction for a different activity at a higher level'. (EEC 1963.)

Attempts were made through a system of grants under the Training Opportunities Scheme, introduced in 1972 (see page 280), to provide individuals with opportunities to undertake training or retraining courses with a view to enriching their own career satisfaction, as well as fulfilling the requirements of the labour market. A person already in a job could, in certain circumstances, and on his own initiative, obtain a TOPS grant to undertake a full-time course leading to professional qualifications thus enabling him to advance to a more highly skilled occupation.

Times have changed and these ideals now stand in sharp contrast to the policy expounded by the Manpower Services Commission in their Adult Training Strategy (MSC 1983), that retraining for adults must be related to the current needs of the economy, and therefore demands for retraining should be primarily instigated by employers. There is some logic in the argument that directing the training effort and investment towards making British industry more competitive in international markets should help to stimulate the economy, and lead to more jobs and more opportunities for employment. A second argument is that the future is largely unpredictable, and motivation is difficult to sustain for learning apparently non-existent jobs. Training 'for stock', in order to produce a pool of skilled or qualified people ready for future needs, would be impracticable and a misuse of scarce resources.

The following case history illustrates the effect of this policy on an unfortunate individual who, through no fault of his own, becomes unemployed and is unable to find another job.

Case history 1

Jim, a graduate in his late 20s, became unemployed when the building company, in which he worked as purchasing officer, went into liquidation. A resourceful and enterprising person, he applied himself energetically to the task of finding another job. As he lived in a rural area, some distance from the public library, he soon found that he had invested a considerable amount of money in buying newspapers and periodicals to search for job advertisements, and in stamps and notepaper to write hundreds of applications. It was all to no avail and he began to realize that perhaps his best hope lay in finding an organization which would accept him on a scheme to retrain for some different kind of work. After a considerable outlay his efforts came to nothing. Most organizations offering traineeships wanted recent graduates, and had recruited up to their requirements during the university 'milk round'. At 29 he was too old. The other possibility he explored was that of attending a full-time vocational course at his nearest polytechnic, but he was unable to obtain a grant to do so, and would have lost his right to social security, his only source of income, had he become a full-time student. He considered trying to borrow the money to fund him while taking the course, but felt this was an unwise option, as, if it did not lead to a job, his position would have been worse than ever.

There are many people in Jim's position, and while sound economic arguments may be made for present government policies, attention must be drawn to the fact that a nation also has social objectives. In Chapter 8, we pointed to the dangers of long-term unemployment and the threat of having a sector of young, unemployable citizens. Government actions to assist young people go a considerable way to alleviate the situation. But although the trend towards more vocational education in schools allows young people to compete favourably in the job market, and provides a broader foundation to make future retraining easier, the main thrust of their education is increasingly orientated towards work preparation. This must ultimately result in increased frustration if work is not available. Having obtained a job and then finding themselves unemployed, like Jim, they require some help other than a prospective employer, who may not immediately materialize. Approximately one billion pounds of government funding was allocated to training in 1984 (HMSO 1984), but only about one quarter of this total (£250 million) was directed to adult training, in the hope that employers would provide whatever additional resources were necessary.

The Secretary of State for Employment urged employers to set aside five per cent of their payroll for training and retraining (Institute of Personnel Management 1985). The actual position was described by the Chairman of the Manpower Services Commission. He disclosed that in West Germany employees receive two and a half times as much off-the-job training as in Britain, where private sector employers currently devote 0.15 per cent of their turnover to in-service training (Tank 1985). History demonstrates that in their struggle to keep down costs during difficult and uncertain times, employers will view training as an area suitable for pruning. Indeed, two of the main reasons for the Industrial Training Act in 1964 were the lack of investment in training by employers and the uneven distribution of responsibility and cost: some organizations contributing the lion's share and others nothing. The training levy raised by the Engineering Industry Training Board was higher than that of the other ITBs and at 2.5 per cent of turnover was considered by some to be excessive.

While investment in retraining is essential if a nation is to prosper, when should it take place? There can be disincentives in employing trainees who are surplus to requirements. During a downturn in the economy, the very legislation introduced to enhance employment conditions (relating, for example, to redundancy and unfair dismissal) could exacerbate a company's difficulties to the point of bankruptcy. The policy of using overtime to cope with increased demand, particularly if it might be temporary or seasonal, appears financially safer. The result is to sharpen the inequalities between those who are working long hours and earning more than ever before and those who, like Jim in the case above, are unable to re-enter the mainstream of work activity, and become impoverished.

The Youth Training Scheme provides a very necessary alleviation for young people and at the same time takes considerable numbers of teenagers off the labour market. Unless, however, there are adequate preparations for dealing with adult unemployment, these measures could well be storing up problems for the future. If, during their formative years, young people are to be exposed to an education, the content of which is directed more than ever before to the needs of employment, they may experience correspondingly greater frustration at finding themselves without work early in life; a frustration which will be compounded if their retraining depends upon the unobtainable sponsorship of an employer. This is most likely to happen to ethnic minority groups, women, or those living in areas of high unemployment, such as the West Midlands or North East, resulting in communities of long-term unemployed; thus posing a threat to the stability of our society.

In addition, the fear of becoming long-term unemployed, and the difficulties of obtaining retraining, affect the attitudes of the employed. It can be argued that rapid acceptance of new technology will hasten economic recovery but this necessitates an accelerated rate of change. There will always be some suspicion of new proposals but it can be aggravated by workers' fears that, although rapid change may ultimately be good for the nation in general, it will be quite the reverse for those who lose their jobs and are unable to gain access to retraining. Currently this problem is being partially resolved by the increase in early retirement and a growing, passive acceptance that many people will be unemployed for a considerable part of their working lives. Many young and middle-aged are learning to accept that they will never work at all. Could this be described as learning that the trauma is uncontrollable? (see page 120). It is certainly not a favourable climate in which to foster active enthusiasm for continuing development, a theme to which we will return (see page 262).

There is, however, a counter argument: the following case history illustrates how present government policy can result in the provision of resources to assist an organization to effect the change and increased efficiency which is necessary for its long term survival.

One of the features of the case is a local collaborative project. This is part of a programme set up by the Department of Education and Science and the Manpower Services Commission:

> to help firms, colleges, skill centres, trade unions and other organizations to work together to investigate the training needs and problems of industry and commerce in their area and decide how best to tackle them. (Department of Educaton and Science 1984.)

The programme offers 'financial support to help employers define and tackle skill needs at the local level, working in collaboration with colleges, polytechnics, universities, skill centres and other training organizations' (DES 1984). In this way, scarce resources can be directed, in a cost-effective manner, towards a common effort. It is also hoped that 'working with employers will help colleges and other providers of training to respond quickly and flexibly to new demands, as skills and work practices change' (Joseph 1984).

However, finding the resources and providing training in knowledge and skills is only part of the process of effecting change; one of the main difficulties can be attitudinal, as the case described demonstrates.

Case history 2

A clothing manufacturing company, having already experienced considerable redundancy problems, has an urgent need to increase profitability. The target of a 30 per cent increase in sales is necessary if the essential improvement in return on capital is to be achieved. This situation has arisen because of foreign competition in both home and overseas markets. The new target can only be attained by exporting, which involves raising standards to capture specialist markets, and reducing costs to a competitive level.

Three corporate objectives have therefore been formulated by the directors, and three related projects (each funded by a separate government grant) are being initiated. The first objective is to improve profitability by reducing labour costs through the introduction of new equipment and technology on the production line, as well as the use of laser beams in the cutting room.

To obtain the best use of the new equipment it is necessary to alter some of the production methods and to retrain the staff involved. The local PICKUP officer knows of a company in another sector of the clothing industry which has similar training needs, and the two parties have been brought together. The colleges in the area have organized themselves into a consortium and are able to provide two students, one an undergraduate from the textiles department of a university, and one from a college of further education, to investigate the needs, prepare the training material and run a pilot training scheme. This task will form an integral part of the students' own course work. A grant was obtained from the Manpower Services Commission and the Department of Education and Science for this collaborative project.

The second corporate objective is to reduce costs by the introduction of more effective computer-assisted control procedures which will enable each department to set targets and monitor performance. A grant has been obtained for the necessary retraining which is to be carried out with the help of expertise from private agencies and from colleges.

The third corporate objective is to raise quality standards, and a government grant has been made available to retrain staff responsible for design and inspection, so that they can formulate procedures to guarantee high quality. Training in the area of product quality awareness is also to be provided for supervisors and operatives.

The directors recently called a meeting to explain the projects in advance to supervisors and workforce. So far, the reception has been cool. There is a noticeable lack of enthusiasm from a few of the key production staff, who have offered no public criticism, but fail to display the positive leadership required to motivate their staff. The training officer's analysis is that a number of senior staff are aware that their careers are blocked until retirement and resent the extra effort involved in the change. They also realize that the new approach will necessitate departmental reorganization and fear they may be subordinated to younger supervisors with a better understanding of the new methods. Their first reaction is to discourage the change, not by overt criticism, but by apathy and passive resistance which readily spreads to the workforce. As in many retraining situations, the most difficult task is not the imparting of knowledge and skills, but that of changing entrenched attitudes.

This situation is reminiscent of the quotation from Greiner (page 146), where key executives attempted to maintain an outdated structure because their power was derived from it. It is also a reminder of the fact that retraining is frequently associated with organization change and development, which can have consequences which reach far further than the acquisition of new knowledge and skills. In the short term at least, some employees may see a vested interest in maintaining the status quo. To render training ineffective does not necessarily require active opposition: passivity and indifference on the part of a few influential people can cause problems in arousing the enthusiasm and motivation needed for a successful outcome. The irony of the situation is that there is frequently a mismatch between the provision of retraining and the motivation to undertake it. Those who are unemployed and eager to obtain a retraining opportunity find it difficult and, for a variety of reasons, those in employment may resist it.

OPPORTUNITIES FOR RETRAINING IN CRAFT SKILLS

Two of the objectives of the *New Training Initiative; an Agenda for Action* (Manpower Services Commission 1981) are of relevance to the training or retraining of adults.

Objective 1 stated:

> we must develop skill training, including apprenticeship, in such a way as to enable people entering at different ages and with different educational attainments to acquire agreed standards of skill appropriate to the jobs available and to provide them with a basis for progression through further learning.

This objective is closely related to retraining opportunities, as craft training in many industries was denied to those over a certain age. This was a consequence of history, in that the period of apprenticeship or craft training coincided with the number of years between starting work at minimum school-leaving age and eligibility for a full adult pay rate at 21: craft training therefore became known as 'time serving'. Applicants older than the minimum school leaving age were often refused because they could not be 'fitted in' to the wages system. The proposal to define precise standards as a basis for the period of training, rather than the concept of a fixed time, is by no means new and it is claimed (HMSO 1984) that considerable progress has already been made in this respect, particularly in engineering, electrical contracting, printing and construction industries. It is hoped to link foundation training with a flexible structure of modules, with clearly defined and assessable standards (see also page 225).

The proposed new arrangements would appear to have the merit of simplifying the assessment of future training needs; the more clearly the attained standards of competence have been defined, the easier it will be to identify new areas of knowledge and skill required and to determine where learning transfer is likely to take place. The new approach is also likely to facilitate the acquisition of skills which cross traditional craft boundaries, in accordance with the requirements of new technology. It is, however, not a simple matter to arrange; it involves not only the meticulous defining of standards, but negotiations between employers and unions about new pay structures, craft boundaries and the status of skilled men and that of 'dilutees'. The employment of adults retrained in the government-sponsored Skillcentres has frequently foundered on this rock. There has always been the practical difficulty of wage payment during training: time rates are normally based on age, and while employers have been willing to pay a school-leaver's rate to a new craft trainee, it is a more expensive operation to pay an adult rate for a lengthy period of training. The adoption of a modular system may assist towards this end, as it may be possible for adults to learn only those modules which are essential for the particular job. But a modular scheme requires a generally accepted and effective foundation training, and this is currently lacking for many occupations.

THE OPEN TECH PROGRAMME

Objective 3 of the *New Training Initiative* stated:

> we must open up wide opportunities for adults, whether employed, unemployed or returning to work, to acquire, increase or update their skills and knowledge during the course of their working lives.

In pursuit of this objective came the recommendation for the creation of the Open Tech Programme. The Open Tech is not an academic institution which runs its own courses. It is managed by a steering group which supervises a fund provided by the Manpower Services Commission to 'pump prime' projects which will result in open learning opportunities, overcoming the traditional constraints. This is done by using new 'methods of delivery'. Although the Open Tech Programme is here discussed in the context of retraining, the open learning approach is also relevant to the training of young people. For example, learning material from Open Tech projects has been incorporated into some YTS schemes and aspects of craft training, and the volume of open learning courses for young people administered by colleges is now very considerable. In Scotland, in particular, where travelling distances to the nearest college might make regular attendance impracticable, it is now possible to study for a wide range of recognized qualifications through open learning programmes.

Among the barriers to learning identified in the Open Tech Programme Consultative Document (MSC 1981) are:

- limited availability of courses in a particular locality;

- fixed starting dates, location, and times of attendance usuitable for many people;
- inappropriate learning methods or group composition, such as managers attending the same course as school-leavers;
- overt and hidden costs and inconvenience in attending a fixed location, for example travelling expenses, tiredness, travelling time, money spent on baby sitters;
- unwillingness or inability of employers to sponsor training.

The same consultative document (MSC 1981) distinguishes three main features of open learning:

- it is centred on the needs of trainees rather than the limitations of educational institutions and their administrative systems;
- it is problem-centred, incorporating whatever mix of learning methods, materials or support is necessary to overcome the barriers to learning;
- it is concerned with the learning process itself, i.e. how people learn and determination of appropriate and cost effective methods.

Open learning materials now exist in a range of industries including agriculture, footwear, hotel and catering, and printing. They cover aspects such as supervisory/management skills, technician training and office technology. It is possible to combine course material, media facilities, tuition and other supportive arrangements to suit the specific situation. Regional provision has been co-ordinated by projects such as the Midtech scheme, which operates through colleges of further and higher education in Bedfordshire, Hertfordshire and Cambridgeshire and offers a wide range of packages in telecommunications, electrical engineering, retailing, chemicals, mechanical engineering and developing small businesses.

These regional developments are changing and extending the range of available retraining opportunities. For example, colleges can perform the role of learning resource centres, for the use of students who manage their own learning. Already there are 'drop in and learn' units, where the role of the trainer is not to instruct in the traditional sense, but to assist learners to identify their needs and find suitable material to help them. Seen in this light, the Open Tech Programme has enormous potential to encourage a philosophy of learning, which takes it away from the traditional trainer-managed situation, to one where the responsibility and initiative lies with the trainee. This approach could have far-reaching effects on the role of trainers and teachers as well as of the institutions to which they belong. The trainer is likely to become more of a provider of flexible learning resources as emphasis shifts from formal sessions (see page 104). It is suggested (Worthington 1985) that there will be greater cross-industry contact between trainers as more information about what is available is provided by MARIS (Materials and Resources Information Service).

The development of open learning has been accelerated by the urgent need for rapid change and updating, particularly in areas such as computing, robotics and electronics and the accompanying advances in information technology which have facilitated and enriched the provision of innovatory learning methods. Worthington (1985) gives an example of a Trust House Forte programme covering computer technology, supervisory management, improving profitability, marketing, personnel management and employment law, and food and beverages. Open learning is particularly suitable for the 'split shift' system and long hours of the catering industry and it was reported that some chefs were working into the night, while others were getting up two hours early in the morning to finish a programme! Where appropriate, students were given the option of recording their exercises on cassette, as opposed to written work. Many of them wanted to continue to other areas of learning.

Most Open Tech projects are producing material in modular form which allows individuals to select those sections of the total package they really need. A directory has been produced by the National Extension College giving information on all Open Tech projects listed by module.

The following quotations illustrate some industrial companies' evaluation of the importance of the development of open learning:

- 'Open learning has proved to be cost effective in comparison with other forms of training'. GKN.
- 'The fact that open learning is industry based and driven is giving it credibility and filling a training gap that was seen to have been growing'. Vickers.
- 'Open learning could add several new dimensions to training efforts'. Rowntree Mackintosh. (Manpower Services Commission 1985.)

Distance learning is a form of open learning which allows trainees to learn away from a centre; using media such as television, microcomputers, telephones, audio/video cassettes, tapes, books and specially written programmes.

LEARNING TO LEARN

Many of today's difficulties in retraining can be laid at the door of yesterday's training schemes, in that the emphasis was often on learning specific skills and knowledge within as short a time span as possible. The methods used, which were mainly trainer led, were designed to meet predetermined outcomes which did not usually include enhancement of the ability to learn. Although it can be claimed that any learning assists future learning, it can also be argued that the present generation has been ill prepared for the rapid and continuous retraining which has to take place. Attention is now being paid, particularly in the vocational training of school-leavers, to methods which not only assist transferability of learning to a variety of jobs, but also improve the capacity to learn (see Chapter 5). Very importantly, the confidence acquired by successful learning transfers and helps the trainee to tackle new learning challenges. Success breeds success!

A number of approaches are being tried to assist future generations to overcome this difficulty, including drawing up checklists of core skills (see page 161), grouping skills into occupational training families (see page 226), the use of task analysis to determine basic skills which may transfer to other competencies, and the use of transfer learning objectives (i.e. learning to find out, see page 227). Yet another approach is for trainees to be involved in consideration of the learning process itself. This can be achieved in a variety of ways, such as the study of learning styles, and in particular, the Kolb Learning Cycle (see page 126); by self development groups; individual or group exercises using every-day experiences as learning material; keeping log books to record learning processes.

An important contribution is made by action learning, an approach originated by Revans (1971 and 1983). He distinguishes between the acquisition of traditional, or programmed knowledge which he calls 'P', and questioning insight, described as 'Q'. He does not reject 'P', but sees it as only one aspect of learning. Action learning is concerned with 'Q', and an essential feature is the social aspect incorporated in the role of 'sets' or learning groups. Revans (1982) describes action learning as:

> a means of development, intellectual, emotional or physical, that requires its subject, through responsible involvement in some real, complex and stressful problem to achieve intended change sufficient to improve his observable behaviour henceforth in the problem field.

The main learning vehicle is an individual project, based on a real and significant organization problem: it must involve action and implementation as well as recommendation and thus the problem of learning transfer to the work situation is avoided. The 'sets' meet regularly to discuss their projects and assist each other. Revans describes the 'set' members as 'comrades in adversity'. Their role is to help each other to learn from experience. Attention is therefore drawn to the learning process itself, and the members are usually required to keep log books recording their observations and personal development. For further information, see Boddy (1981) and Pedler (1983).

CONTINUING DEVELOPMENT

The Institute of Personnel Management's (1984) *Code on Continuous Development* stresses that successful continuing development:

> requires that responsibilities are understood by everyone; that priority operational needs are communicated quickly and effectively; that each learner can feel that he/she shares ownership of any collective learning plans; that he/she can feel confident of his/her ability to create some personal learning plans; and that appropriate facilities and resources are available as a normal part of working life.

Continuing development concentrates on learning within an organization setting and requires corporate commitment and the creation of an appropriate climate. This will only arise when:

> Every manager, every trainer, every supervisor, every experienced worker has a responsibility for guiding and helping others to learn from every-day experiences. (Manpower Services Commission 1980.)

BIBLIOGRAPHY

BODDY D. 'Putting action learning into action'. *Journal of European Industrial Training*, Vol. 5, No. 5, 1981.

COUNCIL OF THE MINISTERS OF THE EUROPEAN ECONOMIC COMMUNITY. *General principles for the implementation of common vocational training policy*. 63/266 OJ, No. 63, April, 1963.

DEPARTMENT OF EDUCATION AND SCIENCE. Press release, *Colleges and firms join forces in seven local training projects*. Notice 182/84, London, November, 1984.

HMSO. White paper, *Training for Jobs*. London, HMSO, 1984.

INSTITUTE OF PERSONNEL MANAGEMENT. *Continuous development: people and work*. London, Institute of Personnel Management, 1984.

JOSEPH, SIR KEITH. Reported in Department of Education and Science, press release, *Colleges and firms join forces in seven local training projects*. Notice 182/84, London, November, 1984.

KING T. 'Minister stresses the role of training'. Report of CBI conference, *Personnel Management*, September, 1985.

MAGER R and PIKE P. *Analysing performance problems*. California, Fearon Publishers, 1970.

MANPOWER SERVICES COMMISSION. *Second report of the Training of Trainers Committee*. Sheffield, Manpower Services Commission, 1980.

MANPOWER SERVICES COMMISSION. *A new training initiative; an agenda for action*. Sheffield, Manpower Services Commission, 1981.

MANPOWER SERVICES COMMISSION. *An 'Open Tech' programme: a consultative document*. Sheffield, Manpower Services Commission, 1981.

MANPOWER SERVICES COMMISSION. *Towards an adult training strategy – a discussion paper*. Sheffield, Manpower Services Commission, 1983.

MANPOWER SERVICES COMMISSION AND DEPARTMENT OF EDUCATION AND SCIENCE. *Review of vocational qualifications in England and Wales, Interim Report*. Sheffield/London, Manpower Services Commission and Department of Education and Science, 1985.

PEDLER M. *Action learning in practice*. Aldershot, Gower, 1983.

REVANS R W. *Developing effective managers*. London, Longmans, 1971.

REVANS R W. *The origins and growth of action learning*. Chartwell Bratt, 1982.

REVANS R W. *The ABC of action learning*. Chartwell Bratt, 1983.

STEWART R. 'Classifying different types of managerial jobs'. *Personnel Review*, Vol. 4, No. 2, 1975.

TANK A. 'Training to compete'. *New Technology*, May, 1985.

WORTHINGTON M. 'Changing course'. *Open Tech Programme News*, No. 8, July, 1985.

10: The evolving national training scene

INTRODUCTION

An analysis of the UK national training scene yields a complex situation. This complexity is the product of interactions among three major groups:

- employers, and in particular the degree of priority which the majority of organizations give to training their staff;
- employees and their trade unions, and the often ambivalent attitudes they have adopted towards training;
- the State, which had traditionally left responsibility for training in the hands of employers but at times intervened through legislation and, in the 1980s, itself became a major provider of funds for training through the Manpower Services Commission.

In this chapter we begin our review of the national training scene by taking an historical perspective of employers' and trade unions' attitudes towards training and note their influence on the availability and quality of training in this country. We then describe in some detail the major interventions made by the State through legislative measures.

We have adopted this approach because we believe that by understanding how the present systems of industrial training have evolved, the reader will be able to develop an informed view of their strengths and weaknesses, become familiar with the major bodies which have (or have had) responsibility for training in this country, and be able to appreciate the difficulties which face those seeking to make further reforms.

THE INFLUENCE OF EMPLOYERS

The best training practices in the UK compare very favourably with those anywhere in the world. Progressive firms and employers' federations have long argued that it is industry's responsibility to provide training for their employees and that appropriate training can only be provided by the industry itself. But unlike other major industrial nations, the majority of employers in this country provide neither the quantity nor the quality of training that is needed. They tend to have an indifferent, or possibly a paternalistic, approach to training and, as we see later in this chapter, they generally regard legislative attempts to reform industrial training as unwarranted interference in the operation of their businesses. Indeed, it was largely due to pressure from employers that the activities of the Industrial Training Boards were at first restricted (by the 1973 Act), and, following the 1981 Employment and Training Act, that most of the Training Boards were disbanded.

A *laissez-faire* attitude towards training on the part of the typical employer is not a new development. It appears to have its roots in the nineteenth century with the emerging division of responsibilities for general education, vocational education, and training. Over the past 150 years, the State has gradually accepted responsibility for the extension of primary and secondary education (with a non-vocational bias) but during much of this period it was left to voluntary groups to provide technical education in support of the country's expanding industries. This latter tradition began in the 1760s with the establishment of the Mechanics' Institutes (funded by philanthropists and voluntary contributions) and continued in the nineteenth century with the creation of technical schools or colleges, some by employers but most by private subscription, which offered part-time technical education. Responsibility for these technical institutions was later assumed by local education authorities and, under their guidance, the present system of further and higher education establishments has evolved.

With the exception of the few enlightened firms which ran their own in-company schools, technical education (outside the universities) was a voluntary and usually an evening class activity, in which employers played little part except perhaps to encourage attendance. This typical employer's view of vocational education persists today not only in technical fields (such as engineering) but in other areas such as clerical, sales and management education. It is worth noting that it was not until the 1950s that apprenticeship agreements began to include provision for craft trainees to attend day release classes at a technical college (see Perry 1976).

This inheritance of divided responsibilities has unfortunately, but perhaps inevitably, led to much friction between industry and education. Typical criticisms made by employers are that teachers are 'out of touch' with the real world and as a result schools and colleges fail to provide young people with the kinds of skills and attitudes towards work required by industry. Counter criticisms from educationalists are that employers are unsympathetic towards educational aims and values which are not work related, that dialogues with industry are difficult to establish and in any case show that employers have divided views about, for example, curriculum content. The record shows that support from industry is often poor, even for educational developments which it has endorsed.

An example of employers' attitudes to vocational education is the failure (in times of economic boom and recession) of industry and commerce to provide sufficient, good quality training placements for sandwich course students. The sandwich course model of vocational education was developed by colleges and polytechnics, and by some universities, in response to the demands of employers' organizations for technicians and graduates whose diploma or degree courses had included both theoretical studies and practical work experience. Industry is keen to employ the products from sandwich courses (see Department of Education and Science Report 1985) but the number, and in particular the quality, of industrial and commercial placements has not kept pace with the number of students wanting to study vocational subjects via a sandwich course. Some 20 years after the Council for National Academic Awards first validated business studies undergraduate sandwich courses, only on one such course in the UK are all students fully sponsored by employers (see Simpson and Kenney 1985).

There appear to be four main reasons for this widespread attitude of employers. First, for centuries, employers regarded training as coterminous with craft apprenticeships. Non-craft jobs were not deemed to be skilled, so why should young employees or adults employed to do such 'unskilled' work, require training? Workers were expected to learn a job without formal assistance from their employer: if they failed to do so they were replaced. There is therefore an absence of a tradition to provide such training. As Thomason (1981) aptly expresses it:

> Training was just not a habit of employing organizations, and where it was undertaken it was usually treated as a charitable donation which would be suspended when times were harder.

Secondly, because training evaluation is often difficult (see Chapter 7) and many companies have no direct experience of carrying it out successfully, they remain unconvinced that it can be a worthwhile investment. There is, therefore, a widely held view that the economic case for training is at best 'not proven': despite evidence to the contrary, such as that provided by the National Economic Development Council Manpower Services Commission Report (1984) which compared training and education provision in West Germany, the USA, Japan and the UK.

Thirdly, with the increased mobility of labour, coupled with the decline of the tradition that employees spend their working lives with the one employer, training is often seen by employers as adding to an individual's market value and so potentially encourages staff turnover, especially in times of skill shortages. In this situation, it appears to make good business sense *not* to train.

Fourthly, organizations regularly review and, where possible, reduce their expenditure budgets, especially in times of recession. Problems which may result from cutting the training budget are often perceived to be less critical (at least in the short term) than those occurring from reduced expenditure on other facets of the business, such as sales or production. In difficult trading conditions, companies argue that they cannot afford to spend money on 'luxuries' such as training. Training expenditure is therefore a prime candidate for severe cuts, as recent history has demonstrated only too clearly. There is evidence which argues that this practice is ill advised. The MSC commissioned a survey of 500 UK companies to investigate the relationship between business performance (indicators such as output and new products) and adult training provided by firms. The investigation concluded that 90 per cent of the top performing companies in the survey had extensive adult training programmes and moreover had increased their investment in training by 25 per cent over the previous five years. In contrast, the unsuccessful businesses only provided training for a small minority of their employees and had reduced by a fifth their training investment over the same period (MSC 1985). This is an important lesson which has still to be learned by many UK organizations.

To summarize, many UK employers tend not to be persuaded by the economic arguments for investing in training and see no need to provide it, except possibly for strictly limited categories of employee such as managers. Nor do many employers generally accept that they have a social responsibility to offer training, although this view is susceptible to change if, as in the case of the Youth Training Scheme, supporting grants are available (see Chapter 8). Many employers take the view that the responsibility for acquiring skills and knowledge rests firmly with employees who are expected to learn on the job and, if necessary, by studying in their own time. People not yet in employment or who are unemployed are expected to use local and national government training facilities. Thus the typical human resource strategy of an organization which requires skilled or professional staff is to recruit them from the labour market. Training existing employees is not often a preferred option.

THE INFLUENCE OF TRADE UNIONS

In discussing the influence of trade unions on the development of industrial training in this country we must distinguish between their activities at national and local levels. At a national level trade union officials have largely played an important role in raising the consciousness of their members, of employers and of the country as a whole, to the humanitarian and economic benefits of training. In addition to the traditional areas of union concern (such as craft apprenticeship issues, health and safety training, shop steward training and industrial relations training for managers), the Trades Union Congress and the national unions have persistently argued the case for more and better training in general and especially for young people. Trade unions' motives have not always been of a reforming nature. There are examples of refusal to recognize so-called 'dilutees', resistance to training for flexible working practices, adherence to out-dated training times for apprentices, and non co-operation with the YTS programme.

Yet because of the higher priority which the membership have given to pay and other conditions of employment, training has rarely figured as a central issue in negotiations with employers: it is difficult to find examples of industrial action in support of training! But in times of economic prosperity, when their influence and power are at their greatest, the trade unions have not always backed their rhetoric with strong action at the workplace in support of training. As might be expected in times of recession, their capacity to influence is much reduced.

For many years, strong arguments have been made in support of more training for the less skilled worker. For example, in 1963, Cousins, General Secretary of the Transport and General Workers' Union, insisted that:

> for the purpose of our export trade, it is as essential to have a skilled docker, or a skilled freight handler, certainly a skilled operative in the chemical industry or the new industries based on oil derivatives, or skilled miners, or a skilled distributive worker, as it is to have any other people... the easiest way to break down in a modern civilization is for the sewage workers to be ineffective. They are the basis of modern industry. (Quoted by Perry 1976.)

But the efforts of the non-craft, or general, trade unions to improve training and vocational education opportunities for their members have been hampered by the 'training is only required for skilled work' attitude of many employers referred to above, an attitude which is also often prevalent among many employees themselves. In representing the interests of semi-skilled or so called 'unskilled' workers, union officials have also been handicapped by the almost complete absence of planned training in these occupations, although, as explained in Chapter 6, training for short-cycle manual skills work attracted much attention for a period after the Industrial Training Act came into force. In a society which is generally apathetic towards training of any kind, it is not surprising that little progress has been achieved by the unions, not least because of the costs that employers would incur in training the very large number of people engaged in the less skilful occupations.

The trade unions had a strong influence on the work of the Industrial Training Boards, an influence much helped by their statutory representation at board level (see page 275). The impact of the trade unions' values and industrial experience is, along with others, reflected in the training policy statements, training recommendations and other publications of the ITBs. Although most of the Boards have now been disbanded, their training guidelines in many cases remain as bench marks of good training practice.

Similarly, the trade union commissioners on the Manpower Services Commission (see page 279) have been influential in shaping national policies for training and other manpower functions. The trade unions have been strong advocates of initiatives such as the principle of a national Youth Training Scheme (although disagreeing with the manner of its implementation) and of the extension of training opportunities to members of society (women and girls, ethnic minorities, the disabled) whether in work or unemployed whose career prospects are blighted by traditional attitudes, by prejudice or because higher than average costs might be incurred by employers if training were to be provided. Yet, despite such advocacy, training in the UK continues to be concentrated on a relatively narrow range of jobs and this 'inheritance' is as much to do with trade union custom and practice and collective bargaining priorities as with the intrinsic training needs of the occupation. In particular it is women, unskilled workers and ethnic minorities who continue to be disadvantaged (see *Central Policy Review Staff Report* 1980).

While the public statements of national trade union officers (see Chapple 1980), and indeed the published national policies of unions may indicate a willingness to accept reforms of traditional training practices, a very different situation often prevails at plant level. Local and lay trade union officials work in an environment dominated by pay, job security, alleged vicitimization and similar problems: issues which have immediate implications for their members (and for employers). It is exceptional for priority to be accorded to training matters. However, mention should be made of the large volume of trade union officer training which is undertaken by the TUC, much of it in colleges of further education, and of the courses run by the individual unions in their own training centres, including joint union and management training.

Trade unions have been much criticized for their resistance to apprenticeship reform. For centuries craft unions have jealously guarded their control over entry to apprenticeship, and the duration of the training period, as a means of upholding the status and regulating the pay of craftsmen. But by limiting the numbers of craftsmen in the system, trades unions were acting against the national interest since industrial output was constrained by the perennial shortages of skilled people, even in periods of high unemployment. The picture has been further complicated by the technological advances which, from the trade unions' point of view, have threatened the jobs of craftsmen as, for example, in the printing industry.

Although some progress was made by the Industrial Training Boards in reducing the duration of apprenticeships and in improving their content, continuing problems with apprenticeships led the Manpower Services Commission to give priority to 'training for skills' in their national review, *A New Training Initiative* (1981). High unemployment, the associated decline in union membership and power, the dramatic reduction in the number of apprentices taken on by industry, the growth of new technology-based 'skilled' work for which there are no traditional apprenticeships, the two-year Youth Training Scheme 'apprenticeship' for all school-leavers, and the linking of some traditional apprenticeships with YTS schemes, all suggest that further reforms may be less difficult to achieve than in the past. However, the problems should not be underestimated: for example, as Cross (1985) points out, the developing 'hybrid' maintenance engineering craftsmen 'do not fit easily into existing craft union representative structures'.

In summary, the influence of the trade unions in promoting training has been limited. They were unsuccessful in stopping the disbanding of most of the ITBs and had to settle for what in their perception are less than satisfactory training arrangements for both young and older worker in times of recession and major technological change.

STATE INTERVENTION

In the remainder of this chapter we outline and evaluate how State intervention has influenced industrial training in this country. We consider the effects of the three pieces of legislation which in their different ways had far-reaching results: the Industrial Training Act, 1964; the Employment and Training Act, 1973; and the Employment and Training Act, 1981.

We first examine the major events which led to the 1964 Act, and then consider its implementation and that of the 1973 Act during the period 1964 to 1981 'the ITB era'. We then review the period 1981 to 1985 – 'the MSC era', which was characterized by the paradox of on the one hand companies being made responsible for their own training and on the other by a movement in government strategy from industry-based policies for training to national policies and interventions achieved through an increasingly powerful MSC.

THE BACKGROUND TO THE INDUSTRIAL TRAINING ACT 1964

Perry (1976) has described how the Statute of Artificers of 1563, by making a seven year apprenticeship compulsory and by restricting entry to certain craft trades, provided the legal framework for vocational training in this country until the deregulation, *laissez-faire* philosophy of the industrial revolution led to the statute's repeal in 1814. Yet, as we have already noted, nearly two centuries later, the protective and élitist purposes of the statute persist in two important aspects of industrial training. First, despite some progress, the restrictions on access to craft training and the 'time served' basis of the apprenticeship remain unresolved. Secondly, the related and equally unfortunate legacy persists that training is only required to learn 'craft' skills.

Perry (1976) has also described how at frequent intervals over the last 100 years Parliament established commissions or committees of inquiry in response to public concern about the greater technological, scientific and commercial progress of our industrial competitors. Report after report was produced on different aspects of the UK's manpower policies and practices. Major reforms were introduced in the educational sphere, e.g. the Forster 1870 Education Act, the 1918 Fisher Education Act and the 1944 Butler Education Act. Apart from the Industrial Organization and Development Act 1947, which sought to set up co-ordinated patterns of industrial training but led to little progress, no specific action was taken by the State to improve training until 1964.

By the early 1960s a widely based view emerged that the inadequate provision of training in the UK could no longer be tolerated. The country's prosperity depended on its skills rather than its natural resources and, it was claimed, the lower productivity of certain UK industries compared with, for example, their counterparts in the USA, was due to the less efficient British management. The *laissez-faire* approach to training in the UK had consistently failed to supply adequate numbers of skilled workers, and concern was especially prevalent about the impact of these difficulties on the engineering industries in view of their great importance for the national economy. Dissatisfaction was expressed at the inability of the country's craft-orientated training systems to meet the needs of the changing economic conditions and to cope with the post war birth rate 'bulge'. Attempts to improve the general situation by persuasive methods, such as those recommended in the Carr Committee Report (1958), had only a minimal effect. In addition there were shortages of technologists and technicians while, as the Robbins Committee (1963) reported, the provision for management education in this country was inadequate.

Also in the early 1960s, there was growing interest in the UK joining the European Economic Community, and it became clear that much of our industrial training compared unfavourably with that in countries such as Germany and France. Section Three of the Treaty of Rome, which deals with the free movement of persons, services and capital, posed problems for the UK, as did the EEC directives for the national recognition of diplomas and other qualifications.

Thus, for a variety of reasons, pressures for the reform of the country's industrial training led to the consensus view that legislation for training was necessary, a view that was uncontroversial in party political terms because training was a politically neutral issue at that time. Whitehall's response to these pressures was contained in the White Paper *Government Proposals: Industrial Training* (HMSO 1962). This marked the beginning of a new era by officially recognizing that exhortation had failed and that legislation was necessary to meet the UK's training needs. The (Conservative) Government argued that the shortage of skilled manpower was retarding the rate of industrial expansion, that the quality of much of the country's training was inadequate, and that the cost of training should be more equitably distributed. These three points formed the cornerstone of the Industrial Training Act 1964. For detailed accounts of the developments which led to the passing of this legislation, see Page (1967), Hansen (1967), Perry (1976).

THE INDUSTRIAL TRAINING ACT 1964

The main objectives of this legislation are described in an official guide to the Act (1964) as follows:

- to ensure an adequate supply of properly trained men amd women at all levels of industry;
- to secure an improvement in the quality and efficiency of industrial training;
- to share the cost of training more evenly between firms.

The Act laid down that these objectives would be achieved on an industry basis through the establishment of Industry Training Boards. Each ITB would be responsible for the development of training recommendations, the approval of standards and facilities, and the encouragement of research into training problems. Each ITB would have an independent chairman, an equal number of employer and employee members, and a lesser number of educationalists. Members would be appointed on a part-time, unpaid basis and in their personal capacities, not as delegates of their organization.

Under the Act an ITB had a duty to levy employers in its industry and provide companies with financial incentives to carry out training. The levy income was also to be used to finance the Board's administrative costs. ITBs were given the authority to: pay training grants; assess the industry's training needs; and require companies coming within scope to supply information about the numbers, categories and training of their employees.

Despite these provisions, the Act was basically enabling or permissive, in that although an ITB had to levy companies in-scope, employers had no legal obligation to train their personnel. They could if they wished regard the levy as a tax and decline to carry out any training. The Act was therefore perhaps typically British in seeking a compromise between the two extremes of *laissez-faire* and compulsion to train.

A Central Training Council (CTC) was established under the Act to advise the Secretary of State for Employment on the exercise of his functions under the Act and on any other training matters about which either he or the ITBs required advice. The Council had some severe critics and it was abolished with the advent of the Employment and Training Act, 1973. The criticisms of the CTC mainly focused on its lack of executive authority but it should be noted that the Council published basic recommendations for training in various functional areas many of which have stood the test of time.

During the six years following the introduction of the Act, 29 Boards were established and they sought to meet their objectives imposed upon them by the Act in a number of ways:

- they raised a levy and paid a grant to those companies whose training satisfied the ITB's requirements;
- they offered firms a training consultancy service;

- they published training recommendations for their industry which could be adapted, with minimum alteration, to suit a company's training requirement;
- some Boards established their own training centres in which they offered facilities, normally restricted to trainees from in-scope companies e.g. the Road Transport ITB's Multi Occupational Training and Educational Centres (MOTECs);
- they developed special training programmes in collaboration with public and private sector course providers.

Initially, the ITBs made slow progress. They had first to organize themselves before they could start influencing training in their industries. The requirement that Boards had to be self-financing within 12 months of their formation, made more difficult their already formidable task of assessing the volume and quality of training taking place, determining training priorities, and designing levy-grant schemes. A not insignificant task was the compilation of a register of names and addresses of all companies within scope. For example, the Chairman of the Distributive ITB reported – nearly three years after his Board had been established – that there were still probably 250,000 small firms within its scope which had not been registered (Spencer 1971).

Between 1964 and 1972, an ITB generally required all companies within its scope to pay a levy, but only those firms which carried out training approved by the ITB received grants. In this way an attempt was made to distribute the training costs more fairly within their industry. Companies that did no training received no ITB grant and so paid their levy (in effect) to those firms which trained according to ITB standards. This meant that a company undertaking an above average amount of approved training received more money from its ITB in training grant than it paid in levy. There was, however, an upper limit to the amount of grant which a company could claim in any one year, usually expressed as a percentage of the amount paid in levy.

The first six years after the 1964 Industrial Training Act became law saw the evolution of a network of ITBs covering, with a few important exceptions, most industries of any size in the country. This was itself a major development in the British training scene and was achieved, in spite of its radical nature, with the continued support of the Confederation of British Industry, the Trades Union

Congress and the further education system. There were, however, very considerable difficulties.

PROBLEMS ASSOCIATED WITH THE INDUSTRIAL TRAINING ACT 1964

Soon after they were created the ITBs began to attract criticisms from some employers (for attempting too much and for being excessively bureaucratic) and from unions and educationalists (for not moving fast enough in reforming training practices). For a variety of reasons (see below) by the end of the 1960s neutral observers and even former protagonists of the Industrial Training Act strategy were expressing serious concern about the achievements of the ITBs. Criticisms from pressure groups, such as the electrical engineering industry and interests representing small business, became increasingly strident and it became clear that changes would have to be made.

In 1972, the Department of Employment issued a discussion document, *Training for the Future*, which assumed that there had been a permanent shift in the attitude of industry towards training and so proposed radical changes to the ITB system. It is interesting to note that the government's assumption was not shared by the Confederation of British Industry or the Trades Union Congress (see Richardson and Stringer 1981). The following reasons were amongst those given in the discussion document for a change in the legislative framework for industrial training:

- A substantial number of people worked in occupations which were not covered by Training Boards.

- The ITBs did nothing for the unemployed and little for the declining industries. In the early 1970s, the number of unemployed had grown sufficiently to pose social and political problems for government, while companies' views on training (and ITBs) changed as full employment gave place to unemployment.

- Determining equitable criteria by which to judge the standard and quantity of training caused many problems. For instance, firms with a high labour turnover could claim to be undertaking a great deal of training, although there was no guarantee that those who had left would be re-employed within the industry.

- It was an impossible task to ensure that statistical returns made by firms were accurate. Extensive inspections would have required large numbers of ITB staff, which in turn would have raised administrative expenses, so reducing the money available to be repaid to industry in grant. Moreover, it was difficult for ITB staff to adopt the dual role of inspector and adviser.
- The payment of levy at the beginning of the year (especially a high levy such as Engineering ITB's 2.5 per cent of payroll) caused cash flow difficulties to some firms, since training grants were not paid by ITBs to eligible companies until months later.
- It was felt that the training activities of ITBs should be co-ordinated and manpower planning implemented.

Other criticisms of the operation of the Act at that time were that different ITBs approached the same problem in different ways, thus presenting difficulties for companies in-scope to more than one Training Board; that the ITBs put forward as 'best practice' training activities which may have worked well in large organizations but not necessarily in smaller ones; and there was an excessive emphasis given to off-the-job training.

On the credit side, the 1964 Act had many beneficial effects which will be discussed later. However, it is probably best viewed as the means by which companies were induced to give training a trial, and in this respect the first ITBs carried a greater responsibility than they may have realized. The Training Boards had few excuses for failure; they had access to top management and if ITBs could not convince employers that training was a sound business proposition, then it could not be bolstered up permanently as an activity to which lip service had to be paid in order to retrieve a levy. It is a matter of debate as to whether the ITBs were given enough time to implement successfully the 1964 Act, but in the event the deficiencies in the 1964 Act led to the changes contained in the Employment and Training Act, 1973.

THE EMPLOYMENT AND TRAINING ACT 1973

This Act had four main functions:

- it set up three bodies, the Manpower Services Commission, the Employment Service Agency (ESA) and the Training Services Agency (TSA), subsequently renamed as Divisions of the MSC;

- it conferred upon the Secretary of State for Employment the power to provide temporary employment for 'persons in Great Britain who are without employment';
- it laid upon each local authority the duty to provide career services;
- it amended the Industrial Training Act (1964), notably in the following ways: the statutory duty on ITBs to raise a levy was removed; the amount of levy that could be raised was effectively limited to one per cent of the payroll; ITBs were enabled to issue Levy Exemption Certificates to companies whose training is 'in accordance with proposals published by the Board'; and the Treasury assumed responsibility for the funding of the ITBs' administrative costs.

The Manpower Services Commission

The MSC has 10 members: a chairman, three members appointed after consultation with the TUC, three after consultation with the CBI, two after consultation with Local Authority Associations, and one with professional education interests. It is responsible to the Secretary of State for Employment, and the Secretaries of State for Scotland and for Wales. In the words of the Act, it is the duty of the MSC:

> to make such arrangements as it considers appropriate for the purpose of assisting persons to select, to train for, obtain and retain employment suitable for their ages and capacities and to obtain suitable employees....

Very significantly, in contrast to the 1964 Act, the 1973 legislation acknowledged a social responsibility for the individual, as well as providing for the needs of business organizations.

THE INDUSTRIAL TRAINING BOARD ERA: 1964–1981

This period began in an economic boom and with considerable optimism that the country's longstanding industrial training problems would be largely resolved by the radical 'carrot and stick' interventions to be provided by the Industrial Training Act. It ended in a severe economic depression with the dismantling of much of the ITB system and a return, for many employers, to the status quo of *laissez-faire* practices. In the following section we describe how the grand design for industrial training developed and declined.

The primary purposes of the 1964 and 1973 Acts were to increase the quantity and quality of training at all levels in industry and commerce, and to share the costs more equitably. To what extent were these three aims met?

The increase in the quantity of training

It would be wrong to attribute the substantial increase in training that took place in the years after 1964 exclusively to the work of the ITBs, but there can be little doubt that their advice and incentives played a major part in this expansion. Government and ITB statistics, and research projects (see Giles 1969, and Mukherjee 1970) provide evidence of the rapid growth in the quantity of training, particularly in those industries covered by Industrial Training Boards. Between 1964 and 1968, for example, there was an increase of 15 per cent in the number of employees under training in the manufacturing industries alone. Much of this growth was in operative and craft training, which were then perceived as high on the list of the nation's training priorities. The number of group training schemes rose from 60 in 1965 to 700 in 1975, an indication that small firms were involved in the expansion. There was also a slow but steady increase in the proportion of young people under 18 on day release courses: from 19 per cent in 1964 to 22.6 per cent in 1973. The introduction of the Training Opportunities Scheme (TOPS) in 1972 provided people who were not in employment with the opportunity to acquire skills and qualifications and receive a grant to assist with living expenses.

However, despite all the progress there were disturbing features. For example, the operation of the TOPS scheme, which cost £226 million in 1977, was criticized by the Comptroller and Auditor-General: the trainee drop-out rate of 27 per cent was high, and the proportion of TOPS training in commercial and clerical skills was considered unlikely to give the necessary boost to the manufacturing industries (see Perry 1978).

More serious was the indication contained in the CBI Industrial Trends Surveys from 1960 to 1978 that, even in times of unemployment, almost a quarter of Britain's manufacturers reported shortages of skilled labour which limited their output. In the capital goods industries, just over a third of firms faced this constraint, in machine tools the figure was 50 per cent, while in spinning and weaving it was 58 per cent. These surveys showed a consistent gap, each year since 1960, between the percentage of companies which stated they were working at full capacity (used as a barometer of the state of economic demand), and the percentage of those which reported that the shortage of skilled labour limited output. In 1978, while almost 40 per cent of employers claimed to be at full capacity, between 20 per cent and 25 per cent claimed they had a shortage of skilled labour.

It is, of course, possible to contest these figures (a lack of skilled people is a convenient explanation for not achieving production targets), but this data appears to be backed by a substantial amount of other evidence, ranging from that of the Engineering Construction Economic Development Council's estimate of a shortage of 500 draughtsmen, to the NEDC working party's report of:

> a chronic shortage of high calibre design engineers and draughtsmen, to the cancellation by ICI of a major investment at Wilton, because of the lack of sufficient skilled instrument artificers. (Carvel 1978.)

The Manpower Services Commission (1976) reached a similar conclusion:

> There is good reason to believe that taking all employers together, industry has never provided as much training in vital skills as the economy requires. Since recruitment is cut back heavily in periods of recession, and training in transferable skills takes some years to complete, the effects of the cut back tend to become apparent just as demand is increasing with economic upturn. By definition, the gap between supply and demand cannot be plugged rapidly by long-term training.

However, these problems were partly a reflection not only of company recruitment and training policies but also of their traditional promotion and pay policies which at times were contradictory: for example, the regular 'loss' of skilled craft, technician and technologist staff through their appointment to supervisory and management jobs. Another important problem at the time was the lack of incentive to spend years of training on an apprenticeship when the status and pay differentials between qualified and unqualified employees were low and declining. This problem, as Harrison (1984) has noted, has a long history:

> In Victorian times the skilled man's wage rate was normally twice that of the labourer, by 1914 the difference was only 50 per cent, and in 1952 it was 16 per cent.

But the major problem seemed to stem from the cyclical nature of the economy, when insufficient training during a recession resulted in shortage of skilled labour during the ensuing boom. For instance, the total number of trainees fell by 400,000 from 1.6 million in 1970 to 1.2 million in 1971.

It is tempting to take a macro view and point to national shortages but from a company's standpoint the answer is not simple. Constantly rising wage rates at that time, as well as increases in the cost of training, made it expensive for a company to maintain surplus labour either of trainees or its own longer serving personnel, in anticipation of a possible upturn in the economy. Some measures which improved training may ironically also have proved to be a deterrent to firms. For instance, the Engineering ITB's (1978) proposals for craft training helped employers to balance their supply and demand for skilled labour more quickly because training time was reduced but it also inhibited them from recruiting apprentices they did not need at that time as they had to pay a full craftsman's wage at age 18, a much more expensive form of investment than the traditional apprentice, who would 'fetch and carry' on the factory floor for several years at a low rate of pay.

This is not a plea for a return to old training methods, nor a criticism of planned training, but a reminder that training interventions, however desirable, can have undesirable side effects. Furthermore, motivation and morale play a vital part in training, and the brightest recruits are unlikely to be attracted to an industry which is in recession. If learning is to be really effective, skills require consolidation, practice and experience immediately after acquisition. But this would take production work from the existing labour force and so be unacceptable to unions and employees worried about job security. These difficulties appear to make a strong case for State responsibility for training, so that in a recession expenditure can actually be increased (counter-cyclical training), but it is very difficult to predict exactly the skills that will be required in the boom, when or if there is to be one, particularly in view of variations in regional labour markets, and there would still be motivational problems for many trainees (see Chapter 5).

What constitutes an adequate supply of skilled labour is a complex question. Employees are not a disposable commodity and, if there is ample supply of skilled people to cope with any upsurge of the economy, they must either be made redundant or retained at a loss during a slump: both alternatives are costly to a company.

Understandably organizations, for reasons of caution or even for sheer survival, deliberately take a middle of the road approach, and rarely recruit or train to the peak of their requirement.

The Manpower Services Commission (1976) suggested two solutions to the continuing problem of skill shortages. One involved a public subsidy for training in transferable skills above a norm, and the other involved collective funding to encourage relevant employers to increase their recruitment for training by repaying them the whole or part of the cost of their initial stages of this training. The funding of the latter approach would be geared to regular decisions about the level of intakes into training for the occupations selected. But, as we have seen above, companies are not only concerned with the costs of training: they may decide to limit production rather than risk enlarging their labour force beyond their permanent needs. Clearly, a range of national policies affect company decisions about the training of skilled manpower.

Unemployment rose during, and especially towards the end of, the 1970s although paradoxically many job vacancies remained unfilled. It became obvious that the Industrial Training Boards had not succeeded in bringing about the volume of required 'transferable skills' or 'across industry' training necessary to avoid either the classic skill shortages of the post-war years (shortages which had been the prime stimulus for government and industry to move towards State intervention in training) or to bring about an adequate supply of skills needed by the growing new technology-based industries.

The mid-1970s also saw the beginnings of the very serious social problem of youth unemployment and the attempt to counter it by providing work experience and some training for young people: the introduction of the MSC's Youth Opportunites Programme (YOP). But by the end of the 1970s the volume of training undertaken within companies was being reduced drastically as the recession deepened. Criticisms of the YOP mounted as it became clear that many youngsters were being used as cheap labour and were receiving neither planned work experience nor formal training. The failure of the YOP programme led to its replacement in 1983 by the Youth Training Scheme.

Thus the evidence showed that the ITBs had been unable to bring about the quantity of training required by industry either in times of boom or recession. The hoped-for change in employers' attitude towards training, regarding it as an investment, had not taken place.

On the contrary, company training budgets had been among the first to be cut as the recession deepened: many organizations had closed their training departments by the beginning of the 1980s. Even in the engineering industry, with its better than average tradition of training, the number of full-time training staff fell from 12,305 in 1969/70 to 9,688 in 1979/80 (Engineering Industry Training Board 1981). Taking the manufacturing industries as a whole, compared with the peak year of 1968, the number of trainees had fallen by nearly 50 per cent (Department of Employment 1980). This dramatic decline was partly due to the reduction in the number of people employed in these industries, partly to the shorter apprenticeships, but also represented a real fall in the proportions of those receiving training.

It could be argued that the strategy of stimulating industry-based training through the ITB system had largely failed because the training expertise that had been built up in companies was being dispersed and that the aim of the 1964 Act 'to ensure an adequate supply of properly trained men and women', had not been achieved and could never be achieved without a radical change in the employers' perception of training as an investment.

Improvement in the quality of training

To what extent did the general quality of training improve in this country in the period 1964 to 1981? This is not an easy question to answer for three main reasons. First, what is meant by 'quality' is a matter of judgement or opinion. Secondly, it is very difficult to isolate from other actual or possible causes of change, the particular contribution that training legislation may have made to a specific or a general improvement. Thirdly, although during the period there were many improvements in the quality of training activity, in part related to the direct and indirect effects of legislation, such a statement needs very considerable qualification. For example, improvements were not necessarily adopted universally within organizations let alone across whole industries. A further and very important caveat is that in times of economic prosperity employers were prepared to accept the argument that 'quality pays in training matters', but the same argument was quickly discounted when trading conditions deteriorated. While it could be argued that there was an underlying improvement in the best training practice in the UK, its adoption was more frequently short term than permanent.

The ITBs had a difficult role in creating better quality training within a client organization since companies rightly decided for themselves what training their employees needed and how best to provide it. An ITB's influence over training standards in its industry was (and continues to be) therefore, indirect. Nonetheless, as a result of Training Board efforts, managements became more conscious of the costs involved in learning and as a result more critical of inefficient training. But the process of raising the general standards of training is a lengthy one.

We noted in Chapter 1 that the ITBs placed a great deal of emphasis on the use of systematic methods and that this helped to bring about a new approach to training. A major factor here was the application of job training analysis, which undoubtedly counteracted loose thinking in determining objectives and relevant content for company training programmes. The advice given by ITBs on the criteria to use in selecting external courses certainly stimulated colleges and commercial organizations to set more precise training objectives and to meet these with appropriate course design.

During the 1964 to 1981 period a vast amount of job training analysis was completed and the results published by ITBs (see Chapter 6). This stimulated training officers to find a basic job or task analysis in their own ITB's publications, which they could adapt for many of the jobs within their organizations. The ITBs provided the focus for the modernization of the country's training systems, for example the Engineering ITB's training modules for craft apprentices. Training Boards took the initiative in working through joint examination committees, examination councils, BEC and TEC (subsequently merged as BTEC), to improve the standardization and integration of in-company and college elements of training programmes.

The orientation of job training analyses changed significantly through this period. In the 1950s, the emphasis was on the analysis of what were basically motor and perceptual skills (Seymour 1966). Gradually, as these types of job were analysed or replaced by automation, the emphasis changed towards the analysis of problem-solving and decision making skills, which in turn stimulated the study of intellectual and social skills (see Youngman *et al.* 1978). Researchers, such as Argyle (1970), were working on methods of analysing interpersonal skills, and while this research proceeded independently of the ITBs, the latter were able to encourage its practical application. Much of the early work of the Training Boards was understandably concerned with relatively mechanistic aspects of analysing jobs but later drew more heavily upon the wider findings of the behavioural sciences. A good example of this is the study of career development by the Food, Drink and Tobacco ITB (see Chadwick and Hogg 1978). Some of the contributions which helped improve the quality of training came from research projects financed originally by the Central Training Council, and subsequently by the Manpower Services Commission's Training Division, which maintains a register of research activities connected with training.

Another noticeable development during the expansion phase of the ITBs' activities was the increase in the quality of appointees to training officer positions. Because of the poorly developed state of training before 1964, there were few high calibre training specialists and this shortage of appropriately qualified personnel led to major problems both in companies and in ITBs. Many of the appointments made to company training officer posts, in response to the 1964 Act, reflected the very low status in which the training function was often held. The post was not infrequently filled by a former craft instructor or by someone nearing retirement or 'unwanted' elsewhere in the organization. In the decade after the ITBs were formed the general calibre of company training staff greatly improved, but as the economy deteriorated, so did the general quality of training staff. The MSC (1978) expressed concern that 'the level of status and influence of many training staff was (still) relatively low'. It was understandable and inevitable that given a choice, the more able managers would seek careers in priority functions, such as information technology or marketing.

An increased awareness of training issues was achieved through the wider recognition given to the policies and activities of bodies in the field of training and development, notably the Institute of Training and Development, the British Association for Commercial and Industrial Education (BACIE), and the Institute of Personnel Management. Training and development practice was also assisted through the improved content and standards of the examination schemes and other educational activities of the professional bodies. All of these developments stimulated a rapid growth in training literature, ranging from documents published by Training Boards, the Department of Employment, the MSC, to training journals and publications of many kinds.

Thus the ITBs should be recognized as having contributed significantly to the general improvement in the quality of training systems and practice that took place in the 1960s and 1970s.

Sharing the cost of training more equitably

This aim was included in the 1964 Act primarily to compensate those companies which trained staff and then had them poached by another employer, often, it was said, by smaller firms which did not, or could not, train their own employees. Whether this was as common a problem as had been suggested is now open to doubt, as many small firms are known to have a negligible labour turnover and so have little need to poach. Another issue here is that in some industries (e.g. electricity supply) an ITB was established but there was no tradition of significant movement of skilled personnel between employers in that industry and therefore in this respect a levy-grant incentive scheme had no significance.

Nonetheless it remained broadly true that some companies trained and others did not, and that ITBs designed levy-grant schemes in an attempt to correct this imbalance (see Kenney and Donnelly 1972). Boards were in a dilemma in trying to keep their schemes as simple as possible and yet making them flexible enough to accommodate the variety of conditions within their industries. For example, it was argued that although smaller companies were helped by the expansion of ITB-sponsored group training schemes, there was a tendency for grant proposals to benefit the medium or large company (see Confederation of British Industry 1971).

It should be noted that a levy-grant scheme was designed to meet the industry's training needs, which were unlikely to be similar to those of an individual company. A firm could therefore be in the position of having to choose between training to meet the national guidelines as laid down by the ITB, and so maximizing grant, or training to meet its own needs and, as a result, possibly being eligible for a smaller, or zero, grant.

Companies reacted differently to the levy-grant incentive. Some paid the levy, trained to meet their own needs and tended to look upon grant payments as of secondary importance. Others saw the levy as a tax, paid it and did no training. Still other companies were motivated to train for the wrong reasons. They believed that by maximizing grant they retrieved their levy but, as Forrester (1968) points out, this ignored the fact that levy and grant were not the only elements in the training cost benefit equation. He expresses this equation:

cost of training + levy – grant – benefits of training = net cost.

Hence, significant though the amounts of levy and grant may have been, what really mattered was the net cost that the company had to pay for its training. Obtaining a high percentage return of levy was only to the net advantage of a company if the costs of training involved were not excessive. Looking at levy-grant in isolation from other costs and benefits did not, and could not, give a true picture of the training costs, but many companies were slow to realize this fact.

The objective of cost-sharing through the medium of a levy-grant scheme proved very difficult to achieve, and in the light of experience the validity of the argument that training costs could, and should, be more equitably distributed was seriously doubted. The Confederation of British Industry regarded the sharing of the cost of training more evenly between firms as an impracticable and undesirable objective. It argued:

> that no employer should be expected to bear more than his fair share of training costs in his industry, but the conception that one employer should be subsidized by others when he does more than his fair share should be approached with great care. Experience indicates that the use of levy and grant schemes to this end may create as much inequity as it resolves. (Confederation of British Industry (1971.)

The Department of Employment (1972) also concluded that:

> In practice the idea of full cost redistribution has been largely abandoned by Boards...in general the employer who trains beyond the needs of his own business receives little compensation for his extra costs from the levy-grant system, and equally firms who rely on recruiting workers trained by others do not contribute substantially to the cost of their training.

Thus the evidence indicates that the aim of the 1964 Act to share the costs of training more equitably, was not achieved by the ITBs.

THE BACKGROUND TO THE EMPLOYMENT AND TRAINING ACT 1981

As we have seen, the introduction of the 1964 Act was characterized by a high degree of agreement and enthusiasm among employers, unions and government: it was assumed that the industry-wide approach to training set out in the legislation would solve many of the country's skill shortages. But this consensus and enthusiasm soon began to fade. By the end of the 1960s, employers were demanding, without the support of unions or educational interests, a review of the operation of the Act. Training had become a party political issue, sharpened by the passing of the 1973 Employment and Training Act, which, *inter alia,* led to a reduction in the autonomy of Industrial Training Boards, particularly as far as levy-grant policies were concerned.

However, far from being impressed by the provisions of the 1973 Act, many employers and Conservative politicians continued to criticize the ITBs throughout the 1970s: a decade in which trading conditions were severely affected by two downturns in the economy (1972, 1975) and by the beginning of the worst depression that the country had experienced since the 1930s. The dramatic change in the labour market – from near full employment to rapidly growing unemployment – and the ever greater emphasis which firms placed on business activities that demonstrably improved the 'bottom line' of balance sheets, was matched by employers cutting expenditure on in-company training and demanding release from what was now viewed as the irrelevance of ITB bureaucracy. The Manpower Services Commission had also attracted criticism for not having consulted adequately with industry, for not being sufficiently assertive in leading and co-ordinating the Training Boards (for example, in tackling the cross-sector skills training problem, which was assuming new proportions with the rapid development of computer-related skilled work common to many industrial processes), and for the failure of the ITBs to address the problems of local labour markets. These demands and criticisms were sympathetically received by the incoming (1979) Conservative Government.

The MSC had been aware of these criticisms and in 1977 had announced its intention to mount a formal review of the working of the 1973 Act. It was not until early in 1979 (i.e. before the general election) that the MSC established a review body to report on the:

> ...working of the Employment and Training Act 1973 so far as it relates to arrangements for the promotion of training for employment, together with the provision of further education closely associated with training, and the links between them, and to recommend how those arrangements should be altered or developed for the future,

> having particular regard to: the future needs of the economy for trained manpower of all kinds; the needs of workers, including young people entering employment; the efficient working of the labour market nationally and locally, (and) the need to ensure the economical and effective use of public funds.

In July 1980, the Review Body produced its report and recommended that:

> Public policy towards training should in future concentrate on: ensuring there is an effective training contribution to the profitable exploitation of new technology, increased productivity, and faster economic growth; extending vocational preparation for young people; increasing opportunities for adults to enter skilled occupations, or to update or upgrade their skills through retraining; introducing efficient training methods more widely, and ensuring that appropriate standards are set and attained.

As we shall see, these recommendations were to form the basis of the MSC's national training policies for the 1980s. The report, which contained 27 detailed proposals, broadly accepted the criticisms of the MSC and ITBs referred to above but recommended no radical changes to the national training arrangements. The report included the following proposals:

- funding of the ITBs' operating costs should be returned to industry (so as to give industry more control of the ITBs' activities);
- there should be no statutory limit on the size of the levy which could be introduced by Training Boards (the Confederation of British Industry representatives reserved their position on both these matters);
- the MSC should examine the scope of the ITBs and the boundary between industries in-scope and those not in-scope;
- a clearer definition was required of the roles and responsibilities of the MSC and industry training organizations, and the MSC should develop a better information system.

The outcome of the consultative period which followed the publication of *Outlook on Training* (1980) confirmed that the days of consensus in training were over. The Report was criticized as being complacent and protective of the 'training industry', effectively arguing for the continuation of the *status quo*. These criticisms came not only from employer organizations. The Institute of Personnel Management (1980), for example, expressed the view that:

> too much attention had been focused in the Report on the ITB sector of the national training system;... Only half the total workforce is employed by organizations in scope to an ITB, a declining proportion too; the percentage of exempted organizations shows that, in fact, far fewer than 50 per cent of the workforce is thus represented. Small firms, many public organizations, much of the service and commercial sector are excluded from ITB coverage altogether.

The IPM regretted that the review body had not investigated the merits and demerits of the voluntary joint training bodies which covered about a third of the UK workforce. The IPM commented that 'levies may well be an obstruction not an incentive to more and better training in the future', and that 'the IPM would support an MSC initiative to establish voluntary training boards in place of the ITBs, employing the resources of the latter, able to concentrate on training rather than inspection'. Many employers, argued the IPM, would use a training consultancy service, the voluntary training board, if fees were modest and the board did not represent a threat.

In line with the political philosophy of the new (Conservative) Government and the views of industry and of others such as those expressed in the previous paragraph, the Secretary of State for Employment announced in November 1980 that he wished to extend the area of reliance upon voluntary arrangements. He asked the MSC to carry out a sector-by-sector review of industry to determine those Training Boards which should remain as statutory bodies and those which should move to a voluntary basis i.e. be discontinued as statutory bodies. The Secretary of State also announced the Government's intention to have powers to abolish an ITB where it (the Government) considered it necessary (at that time the Government could only do this on the recommendation of the MSC). Two months later a Bill was introduced into Parliament and in July 1981 the Employment and Training Act was passed.

THE MANPOWER SERVICES COMMISSION ERA: 1981–1985

The Employment and Training Act 1981

The Act has the following main provisions:

- the Secretary of State for Employment is empowered, after consultation with the MSC, to set up, abolish or change the scope of an Industrial Training Board;

- the Secretary of State for Employment can direct ITBs to publish information which they hold, subject to safeguards concerning confidentiality;
- an ITB is enabled to finance its operating expenses from a levy on employers;
- an ITB is empowered to use past levy income to finance its operating expenses;
- an ITB has the power to widen the scope of levy exemption;
- establishments within enterprise zones are exempt from paying levy and from providing information to an ITB.

Employers did not welcome all the provisions in the Act. They were very reluctant to accept that the operating costs of the ITBs should once again be the responsibility of industry: these costs had been met by the Treasury for the previous eight years. The sugar on the pill was, as Pocock (1982) pointed out:

> the employers' representatives on the Boards have virtually complete jurisdiction over the levy imposed, since levy proposals must be supported, not only by a majority of trade unionists and employers, but also by a majority of the employers' representatives (educationalists have never been able to vote on the levy). The net result of this change is that the balance of power on Training Boards now rests firmly in the hands of the employers' representatives.

The Act, among other things, gives the Secretary of State for Employment very considerable powers to change the ITB system and its funding. These powers were used to abolish 16 of the remaining Industrial Training Boards which had been established under the 1964 Act. The Training Boards which survived the Secretary of State's review cover some 30 per cent of the country's workforce and are those for agriculture, engineering, construction, clothing and allied products, hotel and catering, road transport, off-shore petroleum, and plastics processing. The scope of some of these ITBs was altered. The reasons given by the Government for this return to voluntarism were that training in those 16 sectors of industry whose ITBs were to be abolished could be organized with less cost, less bureaucracy and more commitment by employers under voluntary training arrangements, i.e. non-statutory training organizations (NSTOs) – a view that was supported by most of the employers concerned but rejected by the trade unions and most educationalists. There are currently some 170 NSTOs.

The future of the remaining ITBs is not certain. The Engineering ITB's abolition was sought, unsuccessfully, by 13 major companies (all with first-class records of training) on the grounds that the Board's standard-setting role should be undertaken by the Engineering Council and the City and Guilds (see *Personnel Management* 1984). The Engineering Employers' Federation in 1984 called for a major restructuring of the Board and argued, for example, that the Engineering ITB should discontinue training grants except for short-term 'pump priming'.

The Manpower Services Commission: 1974-81

Within 10 years of its formation the MSC had become and has since remained the dominant force in the UK national training scene, despite a slow start in making its mark and notwithstanding a period during which its continued existence was seriously questioned. The direct and indirect influence which the MSC has on many training and education decisions at national, regional, company and individual levels justifies further consideration of its development and of its plans. For a discussion of the rationale for State provision of training and an evaluation of State interventions, see Ziderman (1978).

When the 1973 Act was being debated there was a widely held view that a national body should be formed to give overall direction to the work of the ITBs – a role which the Central Training Council had not performed – and to bring under the same central control the training services which were then provided by the Department of Employment, e.g. the Government Training Centres and, from 1972, the Training Opportunities Scheme. It was envisaged that the strategic objective of improving the co-ordination of the training and the employment policies of government with those of industry and commerce would be achieved by this approach. These were the objectives which the MSC was given on its creation in 1974 and there were high expectations that this novel, national approach to the UK's human resource problems would achieve benefits which the previously tried *laissez-faire* and industry-based policies had failed to produce.

Initially, the MSC's influence on the UK's training was limited. The ITBs resented the constraints placed on them by the 1973

Employment and Training Act and resisted MSC 'interference' in their activities. This opposition was effective in the short term in preserving much of the autonomy of the individual ITBs but, as we have seen, the MSC's slow progress in co-ordinating the work of Boards led to a mounting criticism of the MSC by employers and increasing concern within government. Employers and government were trying to cope with the intractable problems of the economic recession and the MSC's (including the ITBs') contribution to help solve these problems was perceived to be limited. Shortages in traditional skills still caused difficulties for some employers but a more significant problem was that the growth of the high technology industries was being handicapped by the scarcity of the new skills, while investment in training was declining and company training departments and budgets were being cut.

Through its Training Services Agency (TSA) and Employment Services Agency (ESA), the MSC was set the task – never before attempted in peace time – of linking the problems of manpower planning and supply with an integrated national training provision. Following a review in 1978 of the MSC, its operations were combined to form a single manpower services organization and, as noted above, both the ESA and the TSA became operational divisions of the reorganized MSC. Greater emphasis was placed on the provision of all manpower services at regional level. A third division was also formed to take charge of special programmes, including those for young people and those providing temporary employment for adults. During the 1970s, as the number of unemployed increased, this aspect of the MSC's work became of central importance – in political as well as social terms.

At the time of its reorganization the MSC, through its Training Services Division, was responsible for 23 ITBs and the non-ITB sector, and for the Training Opportunities Scheme (TOPS), under which over 100,000 people had been trained in 1977. The TSD also had direct training services of its own, including the Training Within Industry Unit (TWI), now disbanded, the Skill Centres (now operating under the Skillcentre Agency), and a mobile instructor service.

In the period up to 1981, the TSD sought to help provide the training needs of industry largely through the work of the ITBs which covered firms employing rather less than two thirds of the working population (MSC 1977). Since the 1973 Act, the ITBs had been required to discuss their arrangements for training levies and exemptions with the Training Services Division. TSD subsidies were also available to ITBs to encourage key training activities in their industries. It was claimed that under this structure, the ITBs were able to play a major part in training programmes of national importance by relating wider national requirements to the needs of particular industries. While each industry had its specific requirements, and the MSC helped each ITB with its own priorities, there was, nevertheless, considerable overlap in areas such as management development and clerical training.

The TSD sought to establish relationships with relevant organizations and contributed to the analysis of the training needs of a number of priority areas such as banking, insurance, finance and the National Health Service, to assist the non ITB sector of the economy. In addition, the Division produced a set of multi-industry training needs of national importance such as those for young entrants, women, management development, and health and safety at work.

Attempts to meet the training needs of individuals were made by improving training provision through the ITBs, for example in supporting craft and technician apprentices whose employers could no longer offer training, and through the expansion of the Training Opportunities Scheme to assist adults who needed retraining to take up new employment. TOPS courses were provided in the Skillcentres, at colleges or employers' establishments and a wide range of programmes was offered.

Activities aimed at improving the effectiveness and efficiency of training included: co-ordinating the research and information work of the ITBs, sponsoring external research and development projects, and providing advice and information, including publications. For a review of the MSC's work, five years after its establishment, see Cooper (1978).

We have already seen that in 1979, in response to mounting public pressure, the MSC set up a review body to examine the activities of the ITBs and by inference its own performance. The election of a Conservative government later that year and its declared dislike of quangos (quasi autonomous government organizations), as the MSC had been often described by its critics, raised doubts as to the continued viability of the MSC. However, the worsening economic situation and especially the rise in the number of young unemployed created very strong pressures for government intervention in the training and employment fields. But how was this to be achieved?

Clearly the Training Boards could not be used. The government had sympathized with employers' generally highly critical, view of the ITBs and had signalled its intention to minimize statutory training obligations for industry.

The MSC, which is essentially a government-funded body, provided a suitable vehicle to demonstrate government concern and to channel expenditure in directions consistent with its overall economic strategy. Hence as a matter of government policy the budget and influence of the MSC has grown dramatically since the beginning of this decade. The Commission's dominant position in the national training scene (and increasing influence in secondary and further education) is a direct result of government funds being made available for training on an unprecedented scale. The expenditure for the Training Divison, which does not include the Skillcentre Training Agency or the TVEI programme, was £498 million in 1980/81 and is estimated at £1,143 million in 1988/89 (expressed in 1984/85 cash prices). In addition to its income from government, the MSC receives grants from the European Community's Social Fund (£220 million in 1983/4) for training initiatives to help particular areas and groups with special employment problems, such as young people. The MSC also receives income from its services to employers.

The Manpower Services Commission: 1981-85

In 1981 the MSC published a consultative paper, *A new training initiative*, which proposed three strategic training objectives for the nation in the 1980s: developing skill training; equipping young people for work; and widening opportunities for adults. The MSC's proposals received wide support and in its document, *A new training initiative – an agenda for action*, MSC (1981), the MSC outlined what action should be taken and by whom to achieve the three objectives. The MSC's national training priorities were accepted by government in the White Paper, *A new training initiative – a programme for action* (HMSO 1981), which expresses the objectives in the following way:

> Objective One: to develop skill training including apprenticeship in such a way as to enable young people entering at different ages and with different educational attainments to acquire agreed standards of skill appropriate to the jobs available and to provide them with a basis for progress through further learning;

> Objective Two: to move towards a position where all young people under the age of 18 have the opportunity either of continuing in full-time education or of entering a period of planned work experience combined with work-related training and education;
>
> Objective Three: to open widespread opportunities for adults whether employed or returning to work, to acquire, increase or update their skills and knowledge during the course of their working lives.

These objectives have formed the corner stone of Government and MSC policies for training in the 1980s, and are in accordance with the Government's commitments as a member State of the European Community. The scale and speed of their implementation are based on expectations of financial aid from the European Social Fund (HMSO 1984). As we shall see, the three objectives have been accorded differing degrees of priority. Details of the programmes and initiatives which have been developed in the fields of youth and adult training under the auspices of the New Training Initiative (NTI) are described in numerous publications from government (see, for example the White Paper, *Training for Jobs* (1984)) and from the MSC, (see, for example, the Commission's Annual Reports and Corporate Plans). For an independent review of the New Training Initiative, two years after its introduction, see Ryan (1984).

In the remainder of this chapter we comment briefly on the salient developments in training resulting from the White Paper (HMSO 1981) and conclude with some observations on the functioning of the MSC. Developments in the training of young people and adults are discussed more fully in Chapters 8 and 9.

In implementing the NTI, the MSC has moved away from the former proactive policy, variously described as 'training for stock', 'speculative' or 'countercyclical' training, i.e. training undertaken in anticipation of an increased demand for skills following an upturn in the economy. The current conventional wisdom accepts the long-standing criticisms of the human resource planning approach as a secure basis for predicting national long-term skill requirements and acknowledges that it is impossible to make accurate predictions about future national manpower needs. There are so many relevant variables such as technical change, capital, stocks, output, prices, etc. that:

> ... the task of forecasting how much change there will be in demand at any date in the future and to what extent there may be a shortfall of excess of supply is so formidable as to verge on the impossible. (Mukherjee 1974.)

The MSC, as we explain below, now follows two different policies in seeking to meet future demands for skills. Its approach for young people has been to provide broadly based training and vocational education which will give youngsters ownership of 'portable skills', skills which it is hoped will be transferable within and to a lesser extent outside a particular 'occupational training family' (Hayes *et al.* 1983), but for a critique of this approach, see Annett and Sparrow (1985). However, the extension of the YTS from one to to two years may mean that it will have to become more job-specific.

The thrust of the MSC's policies for adults has been to encourage training in skills for which there are current shortages. Having discarded the long term, detailed, human resource planning approach to tackling national skills shortages, the MSC has based its policies for its adult training strategy on a 'react to real demand' model which has three main features. First, that the monitoring of demands for skills is best done at a local or regional level (the MSC's Area Manpower Boards, see page 224, help to provide this intelligence); secondly, that success in meeting real demands for skilled and otherwise qualified people depends upon the capacity of the providers to respond quickly through flexible and efficient systems of delivering training; and thirdly, constraints on access to training or retraining (and on the skills being used subsequently) must be minimized.

In 1983, the MSC set up a network of 55 Area Manpower Boards (AMBs) to help in the implementation of the New Training Initiative. Each AMB provides local machinery which advises the Commission on the planning and implementation of its programmes locally, including special types and quantities of training required in the area, and approves and assists in monitoring MSC projects. The AMBs were very closely concerned with the introduction of Youth Training Scheme programmes, and are expected to play an important role in providing employers and unions with information about training and education opportunities available in the area.

The Institute of Personnel Management (1985) called for an expansion in the role of the AMBs, noting that the heavy demands placed on them in the early years of the YTS Programme meant that the boards had not been able to 'fulfil their role as local focusing agents for the whole range of training and development activities'. The expanded role of the AMBs should include 'establishing training and devlopment as an essential, and normal, feature in the lives of each individual in the UK' and 'the priority task for each

AMB over the next few years is to make itself and its role and purposes known in its locality'.

An important advantage claimed for the AMB system is that the human resource problems of organizations of all sizes can be more readily identified and tackled. This is of particular significance since smaller firms are seen as being the locus for many of the new opportunities for employment.

The training of young people

Most progress has been made in NTI Objective Two. The Unified Vocational Preparation (UVP) programme, the Work Experience on Employers' Premises (WEEP) Programme, and the Youth Opportunities Programme (YOP) (which had received damming criticisms because some employers used YOP youngsters as cheap labour and did not give them adequate preparation for work or planned work experience), were all replaced by the Youth Training Scheme (see Chapter 8). Initially the YTS was a 12 month work-based programme of basic vocational training and experience which included 13 weeks off-the-job training or further education. The duration of the YTS was extended to two years from 1986, with the support of the CBI, although not without reservations by some employers (see Bevan and Hutt 1985).

The introduction of the YTS in 1983 was a remarkable advance in the training of young people both in its objectives and in the scale of its provision. The rising numbers of unemployed young people, exacerbated by the 'bulge' in the birth rate reaching school-leaving age, together with the failure of the Youth Opportunities Programme, put great pressure on the MSC to introduce the YTS as a matter of urgency. In its first year, some 300,000 young people received training under the scheme and MSC expenditure on YTS (with YOP) amounted to £600 million in 1983/84. According to the MSC's corporate plan, this will rise to £765 million in 1988/89 (MSC 1985).

But the YTS programme has not been without its problems. These have included:

- young people mistakenly regarding YTS as an extended, low wage, YOP placement and hence rejecting it, even though for some youngsters this meant unemployment and disadvantageous social security benefit;

- some employers selecting the better qualified school leavers and discriminating against girls, the less able youngsters, and ethnic minorities;
- criticisms of the further education courses as being costly, irrelevant to the needs, abilities and interests of many trainees;
- trade union opposition to the Government's insistence that YTS trainees should receive a training allowance rather than a working wage;
- refusal by major public service unions to accept YTS schemes;
- complaints from employers about the unnecessary complexity and jargon-ridden requirements of the MSC and its cumbersome administration;
- concern about the quality of the training being offered, and inadequate MSC monitoring of managing agents;
- criticisms of the occupational training families' approach (see Johnson 1984, Singer 1984, Annett and Sparrow 1985).

The YTS, with all its problems, has, from the employers' point of view, brought considerable benefits to those organizations which take part in the scheme. As Upton (1985) observes, in addition to enabling employers to demonstrate their concern for the plight of unemployed young people living in the neighbourhood, YTS provides employers with a means of making far better recruitment decisions. Nearly a quarter of trainees were subsequently engaged by the employer with whom they trained, but more than a third of all YTS trainees had no job to go to when they left the scheme in 1984.

The MSC is also pursuing three other major policies which will have a long-term impact on young people and their preparation for employment: the Technical and Vocational Education Initiative (TVEI); the purchase of work-related, non-advanced further education; and the review of vocational qualifications.

The TVEI programme began as a five-year pilot project in 1983. It aims to stimulate the provision of technical and vocational education for the 14 to 18 age group and so help young people to be better prepared for the world of work. The Manpower Services Commisssion is funding the development of a voluntary, four-year course, based in schools and colleges of further education, which leads to a nationally recognized qualification. This initiative is regarded with circumspection by some educationalists but the funds available (£30 million per annum) to schools, hard pressed as a result of public sector expenditure controls, have helped to ensure that TVEI projects are well resourced. Further funds have been allocated for the TVEI-related in-service training of teachers in schools throughout the UK.

The Government's decision to transfer a quarter of the budget for work-related, non-advanced further education from local education authorities to the MSC by 1986/87 was not well received by educationalists. The Government argued that by pursuing this policy the public sector providers of vocational training and education would be more responsive to employment needs both locally and nationally.

The MSC review of vocational qualifications in England and Wales followed the White Paper, *Education and Training for Young People* (HMSO 1985). The White Paper expressed concern that the present system:

> does not generally provide adequate opportunity for individual achievement certified by one body or part of the system; testing of skills and competence as well as knowledge and understanding; recognition of learning achieved outside formal education and training situations; and flexible patterns of attendance and learning.

The MSC, in consultation with interested bodies, will recommend a structure of vocational qualifications, which:

> is more relevant to the needs of people with a wide range of abilities; is comprenhensible to users; is easy of access; recognizes competence and capability for progression to higher education and professional qualifications; and allows for the certification of education, training and work experience within an integrated programme.

The outcome of this review will have immediate relevance for the qualifications to be awarded to trainees who have completed a two year YTS programme but the implications for adults are equally significant.

Training for occupational skills

Changes in the training arrangements for occupational skills, the first objective of the NTI, have proved very difficult to achieve. This is not surprising since the reforms being sought are among those which the 1964 legislation tried to address, e.g. that training for all work containing significant skills should not be based on 'time serving' but on the achievement of agreed standards, and that access to skilled jobs and training (either initial or updating) should be available to those able to benefit from it, irrespective of their age or sex.

The MSC (1984), in reviewing developments in the modernization of occupational training, pointed to progress in some industries, for example in engineering, electrical contracting, and printing, and in the linking of the YTS with craft training programmes. But developments in this field depend primarily upon employers and unions; the role of the MSC is to influence and encourage reforms.

Adult training and retraining

Adult Training Strategy – Proposals for Action (MSC 1983), makes clear that the role of the MSC in meeting NTI objective number 3 (see page 297) is primarily to act as a catalyst in promoting changes of attitude, and approaches to adult training and education by working in collaboration with employers and the major providers of adult training and education; for example, in promoting the Department of Education and Science's Professional, Industrial and Commercial Updating Programme (PICKUP), which encourages continuing education for adults. The Commission's role as a direct provider of training is marginal.

The strategy includes the following initiatives (see the White Paper *Training for Jobs* (HMSO 1984):

- Recognition that the country's economic prosperity depends upon a supply of people capable of meeting the present demands of the new technologies and of the changing skills and knowledge which these technologies will require. The MSC mounted a long-term, national campaign to improve employers' awareness of the critical importance of retraining and continuing education in providing the competencies needed.

- Action at a national level to improve the efficiency of the adult education and training market, by clarifying the objectives and requirements of the different interests involved for the benefit of employers, individual users, and the providers, including who should pay for training and in what circumstances.

- Secure improvements in the access to training and to jobs, based on individuals' abilities and competence throughout their working lives. This requirement is linked with NTI Objective One.

- Encouraging collaboration between employers and providers of education and training at local level so as to improve both the specification of local skill needs and the supply of local training provision.
- Improving the collection of, and access to, information about labour markets and training provision nationally and, especially, locally.
- Encouraging the development of new, cost-effective methods of training which are flexible and accessible to employers and to individuals.
- Providing support for these initiatives through two main MSC programmes: the Job Training Programme (JTP), which focuses on the supply of skills known to be in demand, and the Wider Opportunities Training Programme (WOTP) which 'helps unemployed adults to improve their basic skills, retain employability and cope with changes in jobs and work. (Bacon 1985.)

In seeking to meet this objective the MSC has, as we have already noted, adopted a market-orientated approach, that is it encourages (and to some extent itself provides) training which equips people with skills that are required now (see page 251). The responsibility for the updating training or retraining of employed adults is placed squarely with the employer, although some MSC grants are available to them under JTP, for example to help meet what are considered to be key skill requirements. The MSC's funds are also used for pump priming training projects, notably through the Open Tech Programme. The MSC provides restructured TOPS training, linked basic training, work preparation and work experience within the Community Programme, and a range of other schemes for the unemployed (see MSC 1983). For a discussion of the policy options in the use of vocational training to reduce unemployment, see Belbin (1981).

Ryan (1983) argues that the government is unjustified in using different criteria in its approaches to adult and youth training. Commercial criteria, which emphasize short term costs and benefits, are applied more rigorously to adult training, as is illustrated by the relatively limited training opportunities which the MSC provides for adults. What justification is there in training adults for jobs which do not exist? This differs markedly from the approach adopted in respect of youth training. The government promises a YTS place to all school-leavers, even though many trainees will have no jobs on the completion of YTS or will find work but will not use the skills they have learnt.

As an indication of the MSC's priorities, the expenditure on TOPS and the Open Tech Programme was £156 million in 1983/84 and is estimated to be £260 million in 1986/87, while that for YTS is £774 million and £1137 million respectively. (*Corporate Plan*, MSC (1984)). One interpretation of these figures is that training is used to provide an alternative to unemployment for one sector of the workforce but not the other.

The Manpower Services Commission – the national training authority?

In its White Paper *Training for Jobs* (HMSO 1984), the government referred to the MSC as a 'national training authority' bearing in mind the clause in the 1973 Act which states that it is the duty of the MSC:

> to make such arrangements as *it* (our italics) considers appropriate for the purpose of assisting persons to select, to train for, obtain and retain employment.

This designation conveys notions of technical expertise, of independence, and of a status earned by achievement.

The MSC has introduced, often at short notice, a series of major training programmes which have benefited hundreds of thousands of people, in many cases at a critical stage in their lives. Some of the programmes, such as the Open Tech, have been conceptually and technically highly creative. But YOP, TOPS and YTS have all been beset by serious problems. It is difficult to assess the extent to which these problems are the result of ideas not being fully thought through by training and education specialists at the MSC, or of the latter's advice not being accepted by the MSC's 'civil service' administrators, or of policies stemming from short-term expediency under pressure from government.

'He who pays the piper calls the tune' is a fact of life which can present difficulties even when there is a broad consensus as to which tune should be played. The sharp differences which now exist between the human resource policies of the major political parties inevitably mean that the MSC's activities, which are funded by the government of the day, are interpreted rightly or wrongly as embodying party political doctrines, as, for example, in the YTS pay-versus-allowance debate. This state of affairs undermines, some would say destroys, the MSC's status as a public body independent of political bias. It also has implications for the continuity of policies with a change of government.

Reforms are rarely achieved easily, and bearing in mind the magnitude of the changes in the systems of training and vocational education implemented by the MSC since 1981, opposition has in the main been muted. This is partly because the interested parties have in different ways had to face difficult decisions and the outcome has been a compromise. The YTS illustrates this point. The trade unions' dilemma is that of balancing their reservations about the scheme against the knowledge that for many school leavers the certain alternative would have been unemployment. For the MSC the dilemma is weighing the benefits of raising the standards of training and work experience expected from trainees by employers against the effects this would have on the supply of YTS places in firms. The dilemma of educationalists is whether to support the scheme, with its narrow educational aims, at a time when college resources are declining.

In the context of the continuing high levels of unemployment, national training problems and interventions have become party political issues. The MSC, not least because of its enormous and growing budget, is attracting increasing criticism for not having produced training programmes which worked in practice, for not having maintained sufficient autonomy from government, and for not having achieved a solution to skill shortages in key industries (Institute of Personnel Management 1985).

BIBLIOGRAPHY

ANNETT J and SPARROW J. *Transfer of learning and training. Basic issues: policy implications: how to promote transfer*. Research and Development No. 23. Sheffield, Manpower Services Commission, 1985.

ARGYLE M. *Psychology of interpersonal behaviour*. London, Penguin, 1970.

BACON J. 'The adult training strategy'. *Industrial and Commercial Training*, Vol. 17, No. 3, May/June, 1985.

BELBIN R M. 'Some policy options in reducing unemployment, an experimental approach'. *BACIE Journal*, October, 1981.

BEVAN S, and HUTT R. *Company perspectives on YTS*. IMS Report No. 104. Brighton, Institute of Manpower Studies, 1985.

CARR COMMITTEE REPORT. *Training for skill, recruitment and training of young workers in industry*. London, National Joint Advisory Council, HMSO, 1958.

CARVEL J. 'Where have all the skilled men gone?' *The Guardian*, 15th August, 1978.

CENTRAL POLICY REVIEW STAFF REPORT. *Education, Training and Industrial Performance*. London, HMSO, May 1980.

CHADWICK D and HOGG Y. *Career planning and development for managers*. Croydon, Food, Drink and Tobacco Industry Training Board, 1978.

CHAPPLE F. 'Employment and training in the next twenty years'. *BACIE Journal*, Nov/Dec 1980.

CONFEDERATION OF BRITISH INDUSTRY. 'Operation of the Industrial Training Act', statement by the CBI, *Supplement to the Education and Training Bulletin*, February, 1971.

COOPER K. 'Review of the Employment and Training Act'. *BACIE Journal*, Vol. 32, No. 3, March, 1978.

CROSS M. *Towards the flexible craftsman*. London, The Technical Change Centre, 1985.

DEPARTMENT OF EDUCATION AND SCIENCE. *An assessment of the costs and benefits of sandwich course education. A report by a committee on research into sandwich education*. London, DES, 1985.

DEPARTMENT OF EMPLOYMENT. *Training for the future: a plan for discussion*. London, HMSO, 1972.

DEPARTMENT OF EMPLOYMENT. *Employment Gazette*. September, 1980.

ENGINEERING INDUSTRY TRAINING BOARD. *Review of craft apprenticeship in engineering*. Information Paper, No. 49, Watford, Engineering Industry Training Board, 1978.

ENGINEERING INDUSTRY TRAINING BOARD. *EITB Annual Report and Accounts*. Watford, Engineering Industry Training Board, 1980/81.

FORRESTER D, quoted by HARLEY J in 'How to assess your training costs'. *British Industry Week*, 22nd. November, 1968.

GILES W J. 'Training after the Act'. *Personnel Management*, Vol. 1, No. 2, June, 1969.

HANSEN G B. *Britain's Industrial Training Act, its history, development and implications for America*. Washington D.C., National Manpower Policy Taskforce, 1967.

HARRISON J E C. *The common people – a history from the Norman conquest to the present*. London, Flamingo. 1984.

HAYES C, FONDA N, POPE M, STUART R, and TOWNSEND K. *Training for skill ownership – learning to take it with you*. A report to the Manpower Services Commission, Brighton, Institute of Manpower Studies, 1983.

HMSO. White paper: *Government proposals, industrial training*. London, HMSO, 1962.

HMSO. White paper: *A new training initiative: a programme for action*. London, HMSO, 1981.

HMSO. White paper: *Training for jobs*. London, HMSO, 1984.

HMSO. White paper: *Education and training for young people*. London, HMSO. 1985.

INDUSTRIAL TRAINING ACT, 1964. *General guide, scope and objectives*. London, HMSO, 1964.

INSTITUTE OF PERSONNEL MANAGEMENT. *Comments to the Manpower Services Commission*. London, Institute of Personnel Management, October, 1980.

INSTITUTE OF PERSONNEL MANAGEMENT. *Submission in response to the Manpower Services Commission's discussion paper Review of the Area Manpower Boards*. London, IPM, 1985.

INSTITUTE OF PERSONNEL MANAGEMENT. *Survey of skill shortages*. London, IPM, 1985.

JOHNSON R. *Occupational training families: their implications for FE*. London, Further Education Unit, Department of Education and Science, 1984.

KENNEY J P J and DONNELLY E L. *Manpower training and development*. London, Harrap, 1972.

MANPOWER SERVICES COMMISSION. *Training for vital skills: a consultative document*. London, Manpower Services Commission, 1976.

MANPOWER SERVICES COMMISSION. *Review and plan*. London, Manpower Services Commission, 1977.

MANPOWER SERVICES COMMISSION. *Training services agency – a five year plan*. London, Manpower Services Commission, 1978.

MANPOWER SERVICES COMMISSION. *Training of trainers. First report of the Training of Trainers Committee*. Sheffield, Manpower Services Commission, 1978.

MANPOWER SERVICES COMMISSION. *Outlook on training: review of the Employment and Training Act 1973*. Sheffield, Manpower Services Commission, 1980.

MANPOWER SERVICES COMMISSION. *A new training initiative: an agenda for action*. Sheffield, Manpower Services Commission, 1981.

MANPOWER SERVICES COMMISSION. *Adult training strategy – proposals for action*. Sheffield, Manpower Services Commission, 1983.

MANPOWER SERVICES COMMISSION, *A new training initiative, modernization of occupational training: a position statement*. Sheffield, Manpower Services Commission, 1984.

MANPOWER SERVICES COMMISSION. *MSC corporate plan 1984–1988*. Sheffield, Manpower Services Commission, 1984.

MANPOWER SERVICES COMMISSION. *MSC corporate plan 1985–1989*. Sheffield, Manpower Services Commission, 1985.

MANPOWER SERVICES COMMISSION. *Adult training in Britain*. IFF Research Ltd. Report. Sheffield, Manpower Services Commission, 1985.

MUKHERJEE S. *Changing manpower needs: a study of Industrial Training Boards*. Broadsheet 523, Political and Economic Planning, 1970.

MUKHERJEE S. *There's work to be done*. Manpower Services Commission, London, HMSO, 1974.

NATIONAL ECONOMIC DEVELOPMENT OFFICE AND MANPOWER SERVICES COMMISSION. *Competence and competition, training and education in the Federal Republic of Germany, the United States and Japan*. London/Sheffield, NEDO and MSC, 1984.

PAGE G T. *The Industrial Training Act and after. A. Deutsch*, 1967.

PERRY P J C. *The evolution of British manpower policy, from the Statute of Artificers 1563 to the Industrial Training Act 1964*. London. British Association for Commercial and Industrial Education, 1976.

PERRY P J C. 'Is TOPS tops?' *BACIE Journal*, Vol. 32, No. 7, July, 1978.

PERSONNEL MANAGEMENT. Editorial report. London, April, 1984.

POCOCK P. 'Whither what's left of the Training Boards?' *Personnel Management*, July, 1982.

RICHARDSON J J and STRINGER J. 'The politics of change.' *Industrial and Commercial Training*. February, 1981.

ROBBINS COMMITTEE REPORT. *Report of the committee on higher education*. London, HMSO, 1963.

RYAN P. *'Government employment and training policies: an evaluation'*. Talk given to the annual conference of the Manpower Society. London. The Manpower Society, September, 1983.

RYAN P. 'The New Training Initiative after two years'. *Lloyds Bank Review*, No. 152, April, 1984.

SEYMOUR W D. *Industrial skills*. London, Pitmans, 1966.

SIMPSON M F J and KENNEY J P J. *A wholly sponsored undergraduate business programme – a twenty year perspective*. Proceedings of the World Council and Assembly on Co-operative Education, Edinburgh, 1985.

SINGER E. 'Occupational training families – a breakthrough or a diversion'. *BACIE Journal*, Nov/Dec. 1984.

SPENCER G A. Letter to *The Times*. 3rd March, 1971.

THOMASON G. *Textbook of personnel management*. London. Institute of Personnel Management, 1981.

UPTON R. 'What next for youth training?'. *Personnel Management*, April, 1985.

YOUNGMAN M B. et al. *Analysing jobs*. Aldershot, Gower Press. 1978.

ZIDERMAN A. *Manpower training: theory and policy*. Macmillan studies in economics, London, Macmillan Press, 1978.

11: Developments since 1986 – a review

INTRODUCTION

The 1986 edition of this book was written in the shadow of unemployment and recession. There has since been an up-turn in the economy and a number of issues have emerged which have important implications for national and organizational training and development policies. A serious deficit in education and training compared with our competitors is compounded by certain demographic factors and is likely to have a detrimental effect on our international trading position. Despite the fact that unemployment, although reduced in comparison with 1985, still features, shortages of special skills are ever present. The first part of this chapter is concerned with these issues, whilst in the second part we investigate recent national developments such as the reorganization of the Manpower Services Commission (first into the Training Commission and now the Department of Employment: Training Agency), and other important government measures. Finally we consider developments in training philosophy.

NATIONAL ISSUES

Demographic factors

The latest projections show a fall of 1.2 million between 1987 and 1995 in the number of people in the labour market under 25 (HMSO 1988). Employers will have to tap new sources for their recruitment and pay particular attention to unemployed people, older workers, ethnic minorities and women. For every ten school leavers in 1988 there will be only seven in the very near future. It is feared that by the early 1990s the number of girls leaving school with five 'O's and one 'A' level may be no more than the normal intake of young people into the Civil Service administrative grades and nursing (Faux December 1987). This has major implications for employers who may face increasing competition in recruiting and retaining young staff. The situation is now very different from the decade up to 1986, when the number of people of working age increased by almost two million. There will be an actual reduction in numbers completing degrees and diploma courses; employers will find more difficulty in recruiting those who have already completed their vocational training and may only be able to obtain the skills they need if they are prepared to remove unnecessary age and qualification barriers and develop opportunites for those who have been out of work.

There is a danger that school leavers will try to satisfy short term employment goals in industry rather than build long term careers. They could be attracted to poorly paid low calibre work instead of taking qualifications leading to rewarding skilled jobs.

Foreign competition

There is rapidly increasing competition from Third World countries, as well as from the projected common European market in 1992. The position is exacerbated by the fact that in many Third World countries the population is rising – in India the rise is as much as one million a month – and because of the ample supply of labour even qualified people expect comparatively low rates of pay. British school leavers with no qualifications cannot expect to be paid wages several times higher than those in the Third World. Unless something is done very quickly we will become extremely vulnerable to competition. Third World countries are advancing rapidly in the use of new technology which is easily transportable across the world. It is no longer true that the western world has technological supremacy. We are faced with the problem of making our goods competitive in both quality and price.

Technology and raw materials are no longer the crucial factor: trained people are the key to success. Companies will need to consider investment in people in the same way as any other asset and the development of a competitive workforce must be part of every business plan. When we enter the single European market in 1992, our competitors will already have made a bigger investment in the skills and competence of their workforce. As our population has ceased to increase, it will no longer suffice to train young people only; employers will need to recruit and train workers of all ages. The European market will have advantages in opening up new opportunities for us, but in order to reap the benefit we require not only the right skills but the right attitudes to change.

The changing nature of work

The majority of new jobs in the 1990s will be in small businesses or in self-employment. By 1995, the service sector will account for 70 per cent of employment. The main growth areas will be small businesses and financial services, catering and hotels, distribution and recreation and leisure. The current number of part-time workers has already risen to over 5 million and this will increase, as well as the practice of contracting temporary work and home work; the wider use of new systems of technology will increase the possibilities of distance working; there will be a greater demand for highly trained people, particularly those in managerial and professional occupations (HMSO 1988).

Inadequate training

Seven out of ten of the people who will be employed in the year 2000 are already in the workforce. Many of them left school at the minimum age and have had little or no systematic education or training since then. Continuous development (see page 336) will become more and more important to widen and deepen employees' experience and to equip them with specialist skills.

Training and education in Britain still lag behind those of competitors. A study conducted by the National Institute of Economic and Social Research demonstrated that in the 45 firms in Britain and Germany included in the survey, there was no significant difference in the age and type of machinery, but productivity was 10 to 130 per cent higher in the German plants. The firms were mainly metal manufacturers but also machine-tool suppliers and service agents with 50 to 500 employees. Two-thirds of the German workers were qualified craftsmen, compared with less than one-third of the British. All the German foremen had passed examinations as craftsmen and had been given additional training, whilst in Britain most had risen to their positions purely through their experience on the shopfloor. The German production managers were qualified engineers, whilst in Britain they often had a finance or sales background and their lack of technical knowledge led to delays in installing complex equipment because they were too cautious in judging its capability. Most of the German workforce could undertake routine maintenance of machines, whilst in the UK breakdowns had to be rectified by a special team of trained men. It is suggested that almost half the machines in Britain are not used effectively because their full capacity is not understood. Lack of technical expertise and training was the main explanation for the difference in productivity between the British and German companies. Studies of building tradesmen and office workers reached similar conclusions, namely that inadequate training in Britain is the main factor in poorer performance.

A series of enquiries produced by NIESR into the comparative education and training of West Germany, France and Japan discovered some depressing facts for Britain. At graduate level Britain is comparable with West Germany, but in the lower half of the ability range British children seem to lag two years behind. Only 10 per cent of pupils in Germany leave school without a certificate in a broad range of subjects, and there are strict requirements in the 'core' subjects, such as mathematics. In Britain the bottom 40 per cent obtain no qualifications. At the age of fifteen pupils' attainments in core subjects in Japan are higher than here. The average English school leaver has a CSE pass (grade 4), whilst the average Japanese pupil attains the equivalent of a good 'O' level. In West Germany 60 per cent of the workforce attained apprentice qualifications compared with 30 per cent in Britain. The NIESR (1988) report on office workers shows that training of office workers in France is well ahead of that in Britain. This is of increasing importance as simple routine clerical jobs give way to electronic office equipment, which requires the ability to undertake a broader range of tasks. Private sector and public sector spending on training is £5.5 billion compared with £9.2 billion spent in West Germany (Handy 1987).

Skills shortages

The most predictable shortages are for professional engineers and computer staff, whilst there are indications that manufacturing jobs will decline. History shows, however, that when there is a boom in the economy, a shortage of properly qualified people in many areas of industry and commerce may be a limiting factor on growth. For instance, *The Employment Gazette* for August 1987 showed unfilled vacancies at Jobcentres as 234,900 – up 22 per cent in a year. The White Paper *Training for Employment* (DoE 1988) revealed that there were 700,000 job vacancies in any one month in Britain, compared with only 250,000 available at Jobcentres.

A survey conducted in 1987 by the Institute of Directors showed that labour supply had overtaken cash flow as the greatest boardroom worry, with senior executives in the North and Midlands reporting skill shortages in engineering, electronics, high technology and construction, and a demand for more heavy goods vehicle mechanics, chefs, qualified accountants, display printers and sewing machinists. A company which had obtained a large aviation contract from the United States had to send some of the work to a Canadian firm because of lack of skilled machinists. A company making elevators had to spread the net widely all over the North of England to recruit 40 specialist machinists (Beresford 1987). Liverpool in particular suffered from the paradox of heavy unemployment and jobs urgently waiting to be filled (Faux August 1987), whilst the London building boom led to a severe shortage of skilled construction workers, to the extent that they were being 'bussed' into the capital each week from the Midlands and the North and forced to stay in caravans and portable cabins.

A Quarterly Survey from the Association of British Chambers of Commerce (1987) revealed that in the Thames Valley, 70 per cent of companies complained of shortages of skilled manual staff. Reported shortages in Merseyside rose from 33 to 37 per cent in three months and the pattern was similar in Greater Manchester, West Midlands and Yorkshire. In the microchip industry business confidence was high, but most organizations were seeking technicians, designers and production and process engineers. Two-thirds of the construction contractors were short of carpenters and bricklayers, and in Birmingham there was an urgent need for skilled shopfloor workers. Many firms which closed their apprentice schools during the recession now find that the flow of potential skilled staff has dried up. There is now no-one to replace trained staff who are retiring. There are also reports of skill shortages in information technology, particularly for manufacturing systems engineers and computing and factory automation skills on the shop floor. An Incomes Data Survey Report (1989) highlights shortages of skilled staff in the public sector and asserts that core workers are being sought in the private sector.

NATIONAL MEASURES

The Training Agency

Following the outright opposition of the TUC to the Employment Training Schemes, the government abandoned the tripartite basis of the Training Commission (formerly the Manpower Services Commission), and in the autumn of 1988 transferred all rights directly to the Department of Employment. The Training Commission was formally abolished in the Employment Bill (December 1988), and the body which replaced it is now called the Department of Employment: The Training Agency. The five major fields of the Training Agency's activity are:

- vocational education;
- initial vocational training;
- training for unemployed people;
- training for employed people;
- building a responsive training infrastructure.

The agency now has six main tasks:

- to encourage employers to develop the skills of their employees;
- to provide and encourage appropriate training for young people when they leave full-time education;
- to help the long-term unemployed acquire the skills and experience that will help them find regular employment;
- to help the education system become more relevant to working life;
- to ensure that the training, counselling and other support needs of small businesses and the self-employed are met.

The Agency will set standards, and will lead the national training initiative, retaining control over TVEI, Enterprise and Education and 'compacts' between schools and industry (see below), but will hand down the delivery of programmes to others, mainly the new Training and Enterprise Councils (TECs). In principle, where an activity relates to the whole country, such as the reform of the vocational qualifications system or National Training Awards, the responsibility will lie with the Training Agency centrally.

National Training Task Force

The Government White Paper 'Employment for the 1990s' (HMSO December 1988) outlined the government's belief that a local employer-led training system provides the best model for the future. The White Paper set up a Task Force composed of the chairpersons and chief executives from leading private companies, as well as one representative each from the TUC, education, the voluntary sector and local authorities, to assist the Secretary of State to develop new local training arrangements.

Training and Enterprise Councils (TECs)

These were set up under the White Paper 'Employment for the 1990s' and launched in March 1989. They are loosely based on the American model of Private Industry Councils to encourage economic growth. Their remit will include executive responsibility for local delivery of the government enterprise training programmes, researching local labour-market needs, overseeing the Small Firms' Service Counsellors, liaison with local bodies concerned with enterprise and encouraging more private-sector investment in training initiatives.

The New Training System

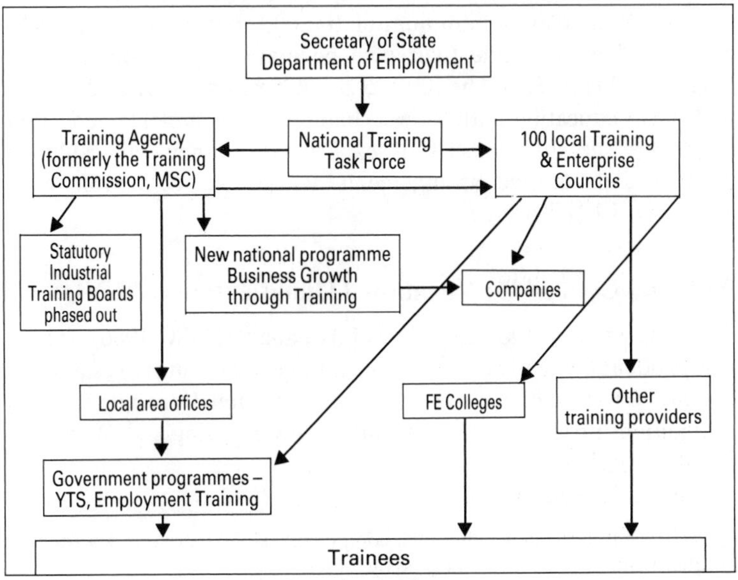

(Adapted from Financial Times, 6 December 1988)

Two-thirds of the Board members are to be chief executives, or the equivalent, from the private sector of the business community; the remainder will be from such areas as education, local authorities and the unions. They have 9 to 15 members (but can draw on extra people if required) and are to be independent of any particular institution. The Training Agency staff are to be seconded to the new Councils which will have a budget for the government training programme, but they will be expected to raise extra cash from local employers (to be matched with government funds) to support their own initiatives. Three billion pounds is currently available for the TECs, to be spent on Employment Training and YTS, the new Business Growth Training Programme, the Enterprise Allowance Scheme and local initiatives. About £100 million has been allowed for the management of the TECs. Each Council will get £250,000 in the first year for a local Initiative Fund, to be topped up by annual grants and bonuses. The TECs will be performance-related and payments will be linked to achieving specific targets. The Training Agency will set standards for YTS and Employment Training for the TECs to achieve. The latter in turn will sub-contract the delivery of training to local providers such as Managing Agents and will make direct contact with them without any Training Agency involvement.

Each Council is to cover an area with a working population of around 250,000 and a minimum of 100,000, but potential Councils will be asked to define their own geographical boundaries. It is envisaged that there will be 100 TECs. They will need to develop links with local education authorities, chambers of commerce and other employers' organizations. It is expected that they will build on existing collaborative arrangements within the community (see section on LENs) below.

National Council for Vocational Qualifications (NCVQ)

This was set up in 1987 after the White Paper (HMSO 1986). It is an independent company limited by guarantee. The aim is to establish a comprehensive national vocational qualification framework for all occupations up to about Higher National level, in England, Wales and Northern Ireland.

The Council was set up to:

- secure standards of occupational competence and ensure that vocational qualifications are based upon them;

- design and implement a new national framework for vocational qualifications;
- approve bodies making accreditation awards;
- obtain comprehensive coverage of all occupational sectors;
- secure arrangements for quality assurance;
- set up effective liaison with bodies awarding vocational qualifications;
- establish a national database for vocational qualifications;
- undertake any necessary research and development;
- promote vocational training and qualifications.

The system is targeted to be in place by 1990/91, by which time the Council is expected to be self sufficient, charging a fee for each student or trainee award endorsed. The aim is also to make learning and qualifications open to everyone regardless of age, sex, race or disability. NCVQ will accredit but will not award the qualifications. There are to be four levels of National Vocational Qualifications (NVQs), ranging from the most basic to those concerned with technical and managerial skills, and the well known qualifications, such as City and Guilds, will be allocated a place within the framework. Conditional accreditation has so far been given for certain qualifications in agriculture, electrical contracting, heating and ventilation, hotels and catering, motor vehicle repair, retail and travel.

NCVQ's definition of competence is 'the ability to perform work activities to the standards required in employment'. The qualification consists of a statement of competence in performing a variety of work-related activities, as well as the skills and knowledge required. It is intended that these will be much more detailed than existing certificates so that intending employers will be given a clear idea of what the holders can do. The NCVQ will not specify what particular type of assessment should be adopted, other than that it should be under conditions as close as possible to those under which a competence would normally be practised. These may include practical demonstration and/or a written answer. Questions as to how the assessment in the workplace can be made in an objective way, or standards judged and comparisons made, remain at present unanswered, but clearly monitoring and reviewing of the processes involved will be necessary.

Open access is an essential feature, and those who have acquired competence through open learning or work experience outside formal programmes may request to be assessed. There are to be no upper or lower age limits, except those demanded by legal constraints, and emphasis will be given to providing equal opportunities for those with special needs. Positive action will be required and the Council has a brief to monitor the policies of awarding bodies.

By the provision of a national system of credit accumulation, it is intended to provide a progressive ladder to different levels of award within the same competence, to give accreditation for what has already been achieved and where possible to facilitate transfer of competence from one area to another. Discussions take place between awarding bodies, the Training Agency and the training boards, to establish a system whereby units can be accumulated by differing methods of study, over varying periods of time, and incorporated in a record of competence. The NCVQ will establish a database of qualifications which may be awarded by validating bodies, examining bodies or professional bodies. The aim is to build on existing expertise and to increase both the volume and quality of awards. The NCVQ has now approached the government for agreement to bring degree and postgraduate qualifications, as well as the vocational awards of professional bodies, within the new framework. A number of professional bodies have expressed concern at this projected change.

NCVQ claims that there will be the following benefits for employers:

- improved profitability and economic performance;
- development of a workforce more able to adapt to new situations;
- increased co-operation between employers, training organizations and awarding bodies. The statement of competence will be understood and accepted by employers, training providers and employees;
- increased individual motivation and awareness of standards. Employees will be able to see a path on which to progress should they choose to do so;
- easier recruitment of competent employees through NVQs. Employers will know what NVQs stand for and be able to judge the competence of award holders;
- clear goals set for continued learning and staff development, providing the opportunity for improvement in corporate performance (NCVQ January 1988).

Awarding bodies currently number approximately 300 and there is no doubt that an arrangement which brings structure and order to qualifications and allows accreditation for what has already been accomplished is long overdue. In averting unnecessary duplication of effort it will encourage people to climb up the ladder to obtain the qualifications so much needed by the British workforce. The TUC supports NCVQ strongly, but is concerned that competencies should not be linked to narrow job specific training, and affiliated trade unions have been advised to resist any attempt by employers to do so. We need to be sure that the concept of 'national standards' does not lead us to a 'lowest common denominator' strategy that would reduce overall performance. Criteria are unlikely to reflect the highest level of performance to which an individual may strive or a particular employer need. Assessment in conditions related to employment may also be subject to the constraint of context; whether the conditions in which the assessment is carried out reflect the entirety of contexts in which an individual may be asked to perform. Additional evidence may therefore have to be sought through the use of simulations or more traditional methods of assessment. However, the value of standards would be greatly diminished if emphasis was given to those aspects for which criteria for assessment can be easily defined, rather than to the essentials of the task.

The consultative process is of paramount importance, as relevance to the needs of employers and improvement in job performance will only be possible if employers within occupations and sectors are involved in defining acceptable standards and determining, along with the validating bodies, how they can be incorporated into qualifications. Training officers should keep themselves well informed of developments and make their organization's views known to industrial training bodies, Chambers of Commerce and/or their Local Employer Network (see pages 331-2). By April 1989 over 80 qualifications had been accredited and most of the relevant validating bodies were fully involved.

Youth Training Scheme

Two-year YTS began in April 1986 and by September 1987 large numbers had progressed into the second year. In 1987, 430,000 young people took part in YTS and there are currently approximately 3300 managing agents in private industry and local government. The Government now guarantees that every 16/17-year-old school leaver will be able to find a place on the scheme. YTS has helped to restructure the youth labour market and reduced unemployment, and will have important long term consequences.

The impact of YTS on skill shortages is however open to question. A survey undertaken by Deakin B M and Pratten C F (1987) showed that by reducing the cost of employing young people, YTS had induced extra jobs, as organizations were encouraged to create an internal reserve of youth labour. Firms facing labour shortages were more likely to recruit and train YTS trainees to fill their vacancies. Thirty per cent of the sample firms indicated that they had skill shortages, which fell into three categories:

- advanced skills where YTS trainees were likely to have little impact;
- those generally acquired by apprenticeship, such as toolmaking and welding. Many first-year and some second-year apprentices now come wholly or partly under YTS funding, but would probably have been recruited without YTS;
- specialist skills and experience where YTS had little impact.

The researchers concluded that many YTS trainees were being trained for skills which are not in short supply, such as retailing (25 per cent of all trainees), hotels (7 per cent), hairdressing (6 per cent), and clerical tasks (10 per cent). Together these categories account for almost 50 per cent of YTS trainees. Managers were asked if they had noticed any general increase in the supply of skilled or experienced workers which could be attributed to YTS apart from the effects of their own programme. There were 217 negative replies as against 19 positive answers. About 42 per cent of companies said that the scheme had encouraged them to improve the training offered to young people in the form of a review and sharpening of training programmes, the addition of extra elements such as health and safety, extra expenditure on equipment, widening training programmes to cover more skills, providing experience to trainees in more departments.

It is accepted that the initial focus of YTS was on training and obtaining places for young people during a time of high unemployment. In this respect it has been successful. The researchers acknowledge that the transferable skills acquired, and the work experience, will improve the trainees' chances of obtaining other employment. The suggestion is, however, that the next development should concentrate on training placements to fill skill shortages and an expansion of facilities for the acquisition of advanced skills.

The Training Agency and other appropriate bodies, working with NCVQ, are developing a wider range of qualifications so that trainees can become accredited in different levels of competencies. The results of a survey of 4000 trainees (TC 1987) showed that almost 98 per cent of second year trainees said that they went in for a qualification in their first year, and over half actually obtained a qualification. Forty per cent said the thing they most liked was the work, 23 per cent said they particularly liked the people with whom they worked. The main complaint was low pay. The types of work where most young people on YTS gained training and eventual employment included metal and electrical processing, repair and manufacture, clerical work, catering, hairdressing and other personal services, selling, construction, mining and related work.

Because of demographic changes, the bargaining position of young people will change dramatically in the 1990s. One consequence might be the conferment of Employed Status on all YTS trainees, who would be paid competitive rates whilst in receipt of the required vocational training. It is expected that employers will increasingly take over responsibility for YTS and shoulder a greater and greater part of the cost. Large employers are already doing so.

Approved Training Organizations (ATOs)

The Training Agency assess and approve organizations which deliver and arrange YTS and ET (see below) training programmes, with the intention of moving to a position where only ATOs are admitted to the scheme; virtually all managing agents have now achieved this status. The following criteria are used for YTS:

- the ability to design and operate a two-year programme;
- previous record of training;
- resources in the organization;
- competence of staff;
- premises and equipment;
- assessing trainees;
- effective programme review;
- financial viability;
- positive commitment to equal opportunity;
- positive commitment to health and safety.

Long term,this should ensure the control of quality and standards in training, but the concept could pose problems in that the principle of joint development and consultation has been one of the real strengths of the programme and any attempt to impose conditions may prove detrimental.

The granting of status to participating organizations coupled with the linking of the programme with qualifications and, in many cases, first and second year apprenticeships, should enhance the image of YTS and answer many of the criticisms which were levelled at the earlier YOPS scheme and one year YTS. There has been a gradual shift of attention from processes to outcomes in the form of qualifications and profiles. Some larger organizations now undertake all their school leaver recruitment through YTS. An important question for the future is: to what extent will this become the general practice, and involve employed as well as unemployed young people?

Adult training

On 18 November 1987, the Secretary of State for Employment stated that the priority must now be to provide training for the unemployed, who lack the basic skills workers now need. It was felt that the Community Programme gave valuable experience, particularly of the discipline of work, but little training, whilst the Job Training Scheme provided good training but for a variety of reasons had a low take-up rate. In February 1988 the White Paper, 'Training for Employment', was published and accepted in full the MSC (subsequently the Training Commission) recommendation for a new Employment Training Scheme (ET). This was to be developed substantially out of the Job Training Scheme and the Community Programme. It was started in September 1988, with a target of providing training for up to 600,000 adults a year, but by May 1989 the total of participants had reached only 175,000. A report commissioned by the Department of Employment (Atkinson 1989) indicates that many employers are critical of the inflexibility of the Training Agency and indifferent towards ET. The shortage of skills had forced employers to train workers for new jobs, but none of the employers interviewed felt they could find potential employees through ET. It displays the following features:

- a single new programme for adults to provide both work experience and high quality training;
- continuing involvement of managing agents;
- up to twelve months training for people out of work more than six months;
- individual assessment leading to individual programmes of training/practical experience;
- attention to the needs of particular groups, e.g. disabled, ethnic minorities, women returning to work and inner city residents;
- participants will enjoy the same protection as YTS trainees in matters of health and safety, equal opportunities and protection against discrimination;
- employers will make a contribution and participants will receive an allowance plus an additional payment and expenses;
- the scheme will be voluntary.

Places are guaranteed to those aged 18 to 24 who have been unemployed for six to twelve months, with the possibility of further places for those aged between 18 and 50 who have been out of work more than two years. At least 40 per cent of the programme must be allocated to training.

The initial assessment period should last two and a half days for each person entering the programme. This is provided by Training Agents who are competent to offer advice. Together the individual and the adviser work out needs and objectives and agree an Action and Personal Training Plan, consisting of a tailor-made training package. The action plans are supposed to identify the units of competence taken from NCVQ-endorsed qualifications, or those which have been nationally or locally agreed. Those who might find difficulty in coping initially with the full pressures of a working environment begin with project work. There is an opportunity to acquire skills and, in some cases, a qualification. The White Paper cited evidence that 25 per cent of long term unemployed adults have literacy and numeracy problems and that half of those out of work for more than six months had no educational qualifications. On the other hand, one in five of the long term unemployed between the ages of 18 and 24 have at least one 'A' level. Questions have already been raised as to whether one scheme can be sufficiently flexible to cope with such a diverse range of people. It is claimed that training provided will range from basic skills to hi-tech. Certainly the initial individual assessment stage appears essential.

The White Paper also reveals that 40 per cent of the long term unemployed had been in semi-skilled or unskilled manual occupations, and that where they have skills they are not relevant to the jobs available. This raises the question of whether the programmes are long enough or sufficiently rigorous to bring people up to the required skills level. The original Job Training Programme was criticized as 'slave labour' and there was initial unfavourable trade union reaction to the new proposals. Schemes which provide work experience must always tread the fine line between value to the recipient and cheap labour for employers, because the only way one can really gain experience of a job is to do it.

Business Growth Training Programme

Launched in April 1989, this will be warranted by the TECs and aims to improve the quality and effectiveness of training by British companies. It is particularly aimed at helping managers to cope with the challenge of the 1992 European Single Market. It is a practical programme directed at all types of business. Companies are offered a choice of five schemes:

- kits for better business training plans;
- better business skills for owner-managers;
- using consultants to manage change;
- tackling your skill needs jointly with other companies;
- help in implementing their own innovative training solution.

The Training Agency proposes to link it with the National Training Awards Competition (see below).

Open College

The Open College started in September 1987 with a remit to provide training and reskilling opportunities for those at work and those seeking new jobs. It offers an ever-broadening range of courses, selecting the best of those currently available elsewhere, including material from 'Open Tech' (now disbanded), and collaborates with employers to develop and commission courses of its own. It also works with individual companies to develop courses tailored to their specific training needs.

The College has open access: there are no entry qualifications and open learning allows students to proceed at their own pace. No degrees or diplomas will be awarded, but some courses will count as credits towards recognized qualifications. The College works very closely with the National Council for Vocational Qualifications, 75 per cent of programmes being accredited to NCVQ standard, and the approach is competency-based. Courses for companies are divided into five areas:

- 'getting started', for those needing a basic grounding in numeracy and literacy;
- business and management at differing levels, from simple office, commercial and supervisory skills to more advanced professional training for senior managers. These can be used for new entrants or for retraining and updating;
- industry and technology, including engineering, manufacturing, electronics and other related areas;
- service skills relating to a range of the service sector including selling, marketing, customer care, hotel and catering and the caring occupations;
- 'Training and Trainers', including nationally acccredited training in open learning delivery.

More than 80 learning packages have been devised on vocational subjects such as understanding information technology, running a public house, basic numeracy, looking after children and becoming a successful negotiator. The average course takes about 30 hours to complete. Course materials consist of some, or sometimes all, of the following: workbooks, resource books, practical kits, computer software, video and audio tapes. An example of an Open College programme is that on 'Making Presentations'. It contains a humorous video, which it is suggested would make a useful starting point, and covers such items as use of visual aids, body language, how to cope with nerves. The programme is in five units concerned with specific aspects and each unit is split into sections. Units 1 and 2 deal with planning presentations, and 3, 4, and 5 with techniques. Attractive illustrated workbooks are provided, with exercises and spaces to write answers, and an audio cassette follows the progress of learners through voice training and ways of overcoming problems such as nerves, poor diction and talking too quickly. There is a tutors' guide as well as notes of guidance for trainees which include a self assessment exercise to help them identify their main needs by grading their own past performance, a table to help them determine priorities and plan their work and an evaluation questionnaire to complete and return at the end of the programme.

There are assessed assignments, including a multiple choice computer-marked exercise, as well as a written assignment on preparation and a practical presentation, the latter being assessed either by the tutor or an appropriate person from the workplace, using the comprehensive check-list from which a profile of the trainee's ability can be derived. The programme is designed to lead to one and a half units of a BTEC Certificate of Achievement. Some programmes are designed to be linked to distance learning materials and courses at colleges and polytechnics. The college also has access to the broadcast networks, and currently broadcasts on Channel 4, S4C, TV AM and BBC. Television material is regarded as enriching and supporting the programmes, which are in themselves self contained.

The Open College was launched with a £15 million grant from the MSC and is expected to break even in three years. After a difficult start mainly due to the shortness of the preparation and lead time, it was confidently reported that over 40,000 students had enrolled within the first year of its existence.

An Employers' Advisory Group meets regularly to advise the College on what products and services to develop, and the College Corporate Services Division exists to co-ordinate the full range of services it provides for organizations, and to adapt them to specific needs. Services include consultancy and analysis of requirements, programme development and implementation as well as overall assessment and evaluation. Advice is also given on integrating open learning with traditional training, and on setting up In-House Centres, which may take a variety of forms from an open learning workshop to a library and lending resource base or a central distribution point for courses. Organizations are invited to take up corporate membership of the College, entitling them to discounts, promotional copies of courses, hotline support and information about activities. Organizations may also sponsor programmes, such as the one on Managing Change sponsored by the Independent Television Association.

National Training Awards

This scheme was launched in 1987, backed by the CBI, TUC and Channel 4's *Business Programme*. The aim is to stimulate a closer sharing of ideas and co-operation by identifying and publicly recognizing excellence in training development and practice as a means of demonstrating the link between training and improved business performance. Awards are made annually by the Training Agency, entries being judged first by regional panels and the best submitted to a national panel.

Categories for entry include:

- training organized by employers (from any or all parts of the workforce);
- training designed and delivered by training providers;
- innovation and/or developments in training methods and/or media.

Each category is further divided in terms of the size of the organization, to ensure that comparisons are not unduly influenced by the scale of the operation or the available resources. Consideration is given to six key elements: organization need, training objectives, training design, training delivery, training outcome, and organization benefit. The link between training objectives and training outcomes is considered crucial as well as that between organization need and organization benefit. In its first year the competition fulfilled its aim of attracting a wide and representative range of entries, 1143 being eligible for award consideration.

Technical and Vocational Education Initiative (TVEI)

The Government announced in the White Paper *Working together – Education and Training* (HMSO 1986) that this initiative would be extended nationally from a small number of pilot projects and by the late 1990s the education of the majority of students in higher education will have been influenced by TVEI. It is not a course or a syllabus but a programme for developing new ways of managing the education of all 14-18 year olds so that their curriculum will be wider, richer, and more relevant to working life. Schools and colleges often work in consortia to develop a wider range of educational opportunities than could be provided by one institution, and a number of courses not traditionally associated with secondary schools are now more widely available.

New teaching and learning styles directed towards active learning have been developed and students are encouraged to take more responsibility for their own learning. They undertake studies with a significant technological content and gain practical experience of enterprise through problem solving activities. They have planned work-related experience and apply the knowledge and skills they learn to solving 'real life' problems. They have access to self-study and open learning techniques and are assisted to develop qualities such as self confidence and resourcefulness as well as communication skills. All projects offer four year programmes which are run in existing schools and colleges, providing equal opportunities for boys and girls across the ability range. They include a broad framework of general education, including relevant work experience, and lead to nationally recognized qualifications. Career and educational counselling is also provided.

As well as the enhancement and broadening of existing provision, TVEI has also encouraged the development of new examinations and combinations of qualifications, and most students receive records of achievement in the form of profiles, which will cover all aspects of their attainments including those not assessed by traditional examinations. It will help to advance the Government's objectives for a national foundation curriculum. Local authorities are responsible for the operation of programmes, but the Initiative as a whole will be administered by the Training Agency through its Directorate of Education programmes. A National Steering Group is composed of members drawn from education, industry and local government and works closely with Her Majesty's Inspectorate and the Education departments.

Enterprise programmes

From 1988 onwards support and assistance is available from the Training Agency for the implementation of Enterprise Programmes within Higher Education Institutions. These are designed to encourage students to be self-reliant, enterprising, and aware of economic issues and to equip them to be effective in the world of work.

Compacts

This idea orginated in the USA and was aimed specifically at inner-city public high-schools, an example being the Boston Compact in Massachusetts. Local schools and industries collaborate to define goals and targets young people should attain. The employers then make a commitment to offer a job with training, or training which will lead to a job, to pupils reaching the defined standards. Martineau (1989) gives the following examples of goals set by employers to improve school/industry collaboration in the London compact:

- provide places for work experience;
- take teachers on secondment;
- release staff to work in schools;
- guarantee jobs for pupils who achieve compact goals;

For their part, young people will:

- reach agreed targets for attendance and punctuality;
- secure qualifications in English and maths;
- show commitment and satisfactorily complete two weeks of work experience.

Compacts can also embrace pupils' records of achievement, work shadowing, TVEI and efforts to identify and meet local skill shortages. The first year of the London scheme has shown a remarkable increase in the numbers staying on at school and an 8 per cent improvement in attendance. The government is now providing funding for the development and follow up phase of thirty compacts.

The PICKUP scheme

The Department of Education and Science's Professional, Commercial and Industrial Updating Programme (PICKUP) in universities, polytechnics and colleges is now calculated to be reaching one in thirty of the nation's workforce, the numbers on updating courses having increased by almost 40 per cent over the first two years. It is targeted to reach one in ten by the early 1990s, and is to be strengthened by the provision of £3 million PICKUP allocation to universities for 127 projects in 47 institutions and £4.9 million to polytechnics and colleges for the forthcoming year (see also pages 111, 255 and 302).

An example of a PICKUP project can be found in the study by a team from the Institute of Personnel Management which examined 127 employer-college training partnerships to find the key factors for success, and found the following six basic requirements:

- top management sees training as important and links it directly to the firm's operating performance;
- defines its training strategy, demonstrates its importance by its actions and communicates the strategy throughout the firm's management structure;
- personnel and training specialists completely understand and are committed to the firm's operational objectives;
- college, polytechnic and university staff are respected for their competence by the firm's senior management and by the company's training staff;
- line managers, trainers and college staff work jointly on producing tailor-made materials to meet specific training needs;
- line managers define specific objectives for the training, monitor progress during the project and measure results against objectives at the end.

Local Employer Networks (LENs)

The LENs project was launched in February 1987, with the intention of having 132 networks in place by June (one for every local education authority), but by September contracts had been agreed with only 55. The idea grew out of a proposal from a group of engineering companies during the review of industrial training boards in the early 1980s, to the effect that 'local employer forums' should be set up to look at training in the neighbourhood. In 1986, the MSC and the Association of British Chambers of Commerce (ABCC) proposed that the chambers should have a more prominent role in education and training, following the precedent of West Germany.

The CBI, TC and ABCC suggested that networks should provide relevant labour market material for planning in local vocational education and training as well as advice and consultancy to local employers on education and training. Each network has a 'base organization' such as a chamber of commerce, a group training association or local action group, and has a governing body, with a known person in the business community as its chairperson and a full-time co-ordinator. Members of the governing body are drawn from a cross section of local employers.

By September 1988 there were some 120 networks in operation, involving over 2000 employees. They were just beginning to get off the ground when the White Paper (HMSO December 1988) established the Training Enterprise Councils. Some of the networks, particularly those centred on well established chambers of commerce, may provide a good basis for the new TECs, although these will be different bodies with a wider range of interests. (For further discussion see Wright 1989.)

Management development and education

The fact that Britain lags behind its international competitors in management development and education has been highlighted by Handy (1987). This report demonstrates that British managers are amateurs compared with their counterparts in the United States, West Germany and France. Only 20 per cent of senior company executives have degrees or professional qualifications compared with 63 per cent in West Germany and 85 per cent in the US. Only one in ten managers entering industry in Britain has had any management training compared with nine out of ten in the US.

Handy puts forward a ten point agenda which includes the recommendation that the educational base should be expanded by educating people more broadly for more years (there should be a framework for early business education to give all those likely to have management or business responsibilities a grounding in the core subjects) and the suggestion that leading corporations should ensure that their managers should have five days off-the-job training each year. He suggests a two part qualification in the form of an MBA Part 1 (or a Business Diploma or Certificate) followed by MBA Part 2 which would concentrate on the application of the core areas of knowledge and skill in business and management. He suggests a Development Charter setting out a code of good practice in management development, endorsed by a Charter Group of companies who would commit themselves to the aims of the Charter, and also sponsor research into new developments and support conferences and seminars for the exchange of information.

A commitment of five days' training or education per manager per year would necessitate more collaboration between business schools and colleges and more managers prepared to act as teachers. Handy suggests that the Local Employer Networks (see page 331) might initiate courses for developing the educational skills of managers to assist them to act as mentors, as in Japan.

In 1988 the 'Management Charter Initiative' began under the auspices of the Council for Management Education and Development (CMED 1988) and the Charter Group was formed. Introducing the initiative, the Secretary of State for Trade and Industry urged chief executives to make the following pledge:

> that their organization recognizes that the professionalism and enterprise of their managers at all levels is a key to their business success; that they will develop the talents of their managers as a central part of their business strategy; and that they wish to add their organization's name to those prepared to back an initiative to improve management standards in Britain today.

A code of practice was drawn up committing participating organizations to the following main items:

- to encourage and support managers in continuous development of management skills and leadership qualities in themselves and those with whom they work;
- to ensure that the development of managerial expertise is a continuous process and is integrated with the work flow of the organization;
- to provide a coherent frame for self development within the context of organizational goals;
- to provide ready access to learning and development opportunities with support and time release;
- to encourage and help managers to acquire relevant recognized qualifications;
- to participate in appropriate networks of the Management Charter Initiative, thereby sharing information, ideas, experience, expertise and resources;
- to strengthen links with sources of management education to ensure that the training offered matches corporate needs and future requirements;
- to contribute to closer links with educational establishments to promote a clearer understanding of the role of management;
- to appoint a Director or equivalent to oversee the fulfilment of these undertakings.

By April 1989 some 180 employers had subscribed to the Charter Initiative, which is seeking:

- the restructuring of qualifications associated with management education, particularly by defining and enhancing the competence elements;
- the establishment of a national forum to carry the movement forward.

One of the original proposals was to create a professional 'chartered' managers' qualification. This met with criticism on the grounds that it might lead to a restrained and bureaucratic environment and was abandoned. CMED is now regarded as a standard-setting body, leaving the production of new qualifications to others such as the British Institute of Management – which is developing a new Management Certificate, to be followed by a Diploma, with the eventual target of establishing a new Masters Degree.

An important feature of the new qualifications is to be the recognition of previous management awards and experience. Much controversy centres around the notion of 'competences', or essential managerial skills and abilities. It can be argued that the essential competences will vary according to the level of management, size and culture of organization and type of industry; the question of assessment also raises difficulties. Moreover, management may be regarded as a total process which is greater than the sum of prescribed competences.

The Council for National Academic Awards was commissioned by CMED and funded by the Training Agency to produce a report (CNAA 1989) on a national framework of assessment arrangements. CNAA is developing a system of credit and transfer to enable collaboration between employers, polytechnics and universities. For instance, certain employers may now have their in-house training validated for credit towards CNAA awards. It is also reported (Devine 1989) that CNAA is developing more formal relationships with the Management Charter Initiative.

The White Paper (1988): 'Employment for the 1990s'

In summary, this resulted in:

- Training and Enterprise Councils (TECs);
- the National Training Task Force;
- Business Growth through Training Programmes;
- the privatization of the Skills Agency;

Emphasis was given to the qualifications developed by the NCVQ and to TVEI, which will be comparable with the new national curriculum being introduced by the DES.

The Industrial Training Act came into force in 1964 because employers were failing to train, preferring to alleviate their skills shortage problems by competing for each others' labour. Twenty-five years and many pieces of legislation later, we are still suffering from skills shortages and placed low in the international league table for training.

The abolition of the MSC and the provisions in the White Paper (1988) might be considered to have come round full circle; the tripartite co-operation of government, unions and employers set up in 1964 has been swept away and training is once more in the lap of employers. Government funding and encouragement is being provided, but will need to be augmented. Critics point to the political bias of the current provisions and cite history as evidence that employers will not adequately shoulder the burden. Questions arise about the social responsibility for individual needs such as those of the handicapped and minority groups, which were acknowledged by the legislation in 1973. It is pertinent to enquire whether long-term national needs can adequately be met by local networks considering local requirements. Traditionally, employers have taken a short-term view and stopped or reduced training at the beginning of a recession, with the result that skills shortages have hindered progress at an upturn in the economy. The Training Agency is designated to address national issues; much will depend upon the strength of its influence.

There is, however, a view that training is an integral part of management; managers are only so-called because they have more to do than they can personally accomplish; training others to work for them is an inescapable responsibility and there is justification in linking training to outcomes and business development. Employers have complained in the past that the education and training provided nationally is not relevant to their needs. The TECs might be seen as representing a significant shift in initiative from a national body to a network of local ones. They could open up a major opportunity for a fresh approach to training, one which is employer-led with decision-makers from the private sector rather than civil servants. Individual employers will have to consider carefully the future needs of their organizations and local communities and develop a coherent education and training policy, to which the various schemes will apply in greater or lesser degree. Each scheme attempts to deal with a specific problem by aiming at preparing different groups of people for work.

DEVELOPMENTS IN TRAINING PHILOSOPHY

Continuous development

Recognizing the overriding importance of self-directed lifelong learning in today's rapidly changing environment, the Institute of Personnel Management has produced a code entitled *Continuous Development, People and Work,* to help senior managers broaden their views about learning and training and relate their learning activity to the organization's business activities. The code emphasizes that learning within the organization must be managed on a continuous basis. Important conditions for learning activity to be beneficial to the organization and employees include:

- spelling out the implications of the strategic plan in terms of the knowledge and skills of relevant employees;
- integration of learning and work: encouragement must be given to all employees to learn from the problems and challenges of their day to day activities;
- the impetus must come from the chief executive and other members of the top management team, and investment in continuous development must be seen as being as important as investment in research or new product development.

The code has seven key headings: policies, responsibilities and roles, the identification of learning opportunities and needs, learner involvement, the provision of learning resources, benefits, and results. It will be seen that everyone in the organization must be involved in continuous development, and it has implications for all stages of the learning and training process. The ultimate aim is for continuous development to become fully integrated into work, with managers instigating most of the learning for themselves and everyone contributing to the identification of learning opportunities. The major benefits are first, improved operational performance, and second, the joint development of people and work. For further discussion and examples of continuous development see Barrington (1986), Mumford (1986) and Wood (1988).

Planned training

We traced the development of training models from the four stages of systematic training in vogue during the sixties into the many different forms of planned training and the systems models to the problem centred approach. But as Donnelly (1987) has pointed out:

> One of the major difficulties with models in the sphere of training is that they can quickly become outdated oversimplifications in an area which is becoming increasingly diverse and complicated. It is therefore essential that we continually analyse, question and, where necessary, modify what may be viewed as received truths within the area of training: time can have a halo effect on the ineffectual.

He draws attention to the importance of pre-assessment factors, such as the availability of budgets, cultural values, policies and responsibilities, a consideration of which is necessary before the decision to train is taken. At this stage it is only one of a series of options. He also emphasizes that evaluation activities are a part of all stages; for example, there is a need to develop initial evaluation requirements and criteria at the development stage. There is no doubt that the model he suggests represents an advance in thinking, particularly in situations where the desired outcomes can be prescribed, and the trainer is the organizer, or at least the catalyst, of training.

Current theories of continuous development and 'managing one's own learning' can appear to lack congruence with the concept of planned training, which by its very nature implies that 'somebody else' is planning it for the trainees, and that training is 'doing things to people'. The concept of the trainer as a learning resource rather than instructor has been gathering momentum for some years, but if as trainees we are to manage our own learning, is not the logical consequence that we will turn to assessing our own needs? These may or may not coincide with predetermined organization objectives, or fit neatly into a model. The question also arises as to who owns such a model, the organization or the trainees?

Current trends are towards a more open approach, where the assessment of need becomes an integral part of the learning experience, rather than one stage of a four-step process conducted by the trainer. One such approach is embodied in the philosophy of action learning (see pages 261 and 262), which has made considerable strides in popularity, and is wholly consistent with managing one's own learning and learning to learn. Typical action learning questions are:

- What am I, or what is my organization, trying to do?
- What is stopping us from doing it?
- What can we try to do about it?
- Who knows about the problems we have?
- Who can help solve them?

These questions can be raised by individuals, or by groups of individuals in an organization. In the latter case, training becomes a group activity and a typical approach might be to define the problems which arise and identify what the group or 'set' needs to know in order to solve them. In this way training is still occurring in a logical and purposeful way, and the stages of the model are valid, but the planning evolves from the training activity itself rather than having been predetermined.

BIBLIOGRAPHY

ATKINSON J, MEAGER N. *Employer Involvement in Adult Training Initiatives*. IMS, University of Sussex, Brighton, 1989.

BARRINGTON H A. 'Continuous development: theory and reality'. *Personnel Review*. Vol 15, No 1, 1986, pp 27-31.

BERESFORD P. Report on the survey by the British Chamber of Commerce in *The Sunday Times*, 6 September 1987.

BURGOYNE J. 'Management development for the individual and the organization'. *Personnel Management*. June 1988.

CNAA. *Feasibility Study on a National Framework of Assessment Arrangements for Management Education*. CNAA, London, 1989.

CNAA. *Towards a new certificate in management*. CNAA Development Services, Published by the Training Agency, Sheffield, 1989.

CONSTABLE J and McCORMICK R. 'The making of British managers'. A report for the BIM and CBI into management training, education and development. April 1987.

COUNCIL FOR MANAGEMENT EDUCATION AND DEVELOPMENT. *Management Charter Initiative*. London, CMED, 1988.

DEAKIN B M and PRATTEN C F. Report in *Employment Gazette*, October 1987.

DEPARTMENT OF EMPLOYMENT. *Training for employment* (Cm 316). London, HMSO, 1988.

DEVINE M. 'The best that we can manage?' *The Times*, 12 April 1989.

DONNELLY E L. 'The training model: time for a change?' *Industrial and Commercial Training*. Vol 19, No 3, 1987.

FAUX R. Report in *The Times,* 17 August 1987.

FAUX R. Report in *The Times,* 15 December 1987.

HANDY C. *The making of managers*. London, National Economic Development Office, April 1987.

HMSO. *'Working together – education and training'* (Cm9832). London, HMSO, 1986.

HMSO. *White Paper: Employment for the 1990s*. London, HMSO, December 1988.

INCOMES DATA SERVICES. *Public Sector Pay Review of 1988; Prospects for 1989*. IDS, London, 1989.

INSTITUTE OF PERSONNEL MANAGEMENT. *Continuous development: people and work* (IPM Code). London, IPM, 1987.

MARTINEAU R. 'First term report on the London "compact"'. *Personnel Management*, April 1989.

MUMFORD A. 'Self development: missing elements'. *Industrial and Commercial Training*. Vol 18, No 3, May/June 1986. pp 6-10.

MUMFORD A and others. *Developing directors – the learning processes*. MSC, January 1987.

NATIONAL COUNCIL FOR VOCATIONAL QUALIFICATIONS. *What's in it for employers?* London, NCVQ, 1988.

NATIONAL INSTITUTE OF ECONOMIC AND SOCIAL RESEARCH (NIESR), Report in *The Sunday Times,* 31 May 1988.

SECRETARY OF STATE FOR EMPLOYMENT, quoted in *The Times,* 13 April 1988.

TRAINING COMMISSION. *Postal survey of young people entering their 2nd year of YTS*. Sheffield, Training Commission (formerly MSC), 1987.

WOOD S, ed. *Continuous development*. London, Institute of Personnel Management, 1988.

WRIGHT D. 'LENs in the light of TECs'. *Personnel Management,* May 1989.

Appendix I

LIST OF ABBREVIATIONS

AMB	Area Manpower Board
ATS	Adult Training Strategy
BACIE	British Association for Commercial and Industrial Education
BEC	Business Education Council (now BTEC)
BTEC	Business and Technician Education Council
CBA	Cost Benefit Analysis
CBI	Confederation of British Industry
CGLI	City and Guilds of London Institute
CNAA	Council for National Academic Awards
CPVE	Certificate of Pre-Vocational Education
CRAC	Career Research Advisory Centre
CSE	Certificate of Secondary Education
CTC	Central Training Council
DBA	Diploma in Business Administration
DE	Department of Employment
DES	Department of Education and Science
DETA	Department of Employment: The Training Agency
DMS	Diploma in Management Studies
EEC	European Economic Community
ESA	Employment Services Agency (later Employment Division of the Manpower Services Commission)
ESD	Employment Services Division (later Employment Division of the Manpower Services Commission)
IPM	Institute of Personnel Management
ITB	Industrial Training Board
ITD	Institute of Training and Development
ITeC	Information Technology Centre
JTP	Job Training Programme
LCP	Local Collaborative Projects

LEN	Local Employers' Network
MA	Managing Agents
MARIS	Materials and Resources Information Service
MBA	Master of Business Administration
MBO	Management by Objectives
MOTEC	Multi-Occupational Training and Education Centres (of the Road Transport ITB)
MSA	Manual Skills Analysis
MSC	Manpower Services Commission
NAFE	Non-Advanced Further Education
NCVQ	National Council for Vocational Qualifications
NEBSS	National Examination Board for Supervisory Studies
NSTO	Non-Statutory Training Organization
NTA	National Training Awards
NTI	New Training Initiative
OD	Organization Development
OTF	Occupational Training Families
PER	Professional and Executive Register
PICKUP	Professional Industrial and Commercial Updating Programme
RSA	Royal Society of Arts
SCOT-VEC	Scottish Vocational Education Council
TA	Training Agent
TA	Transactional Analysis
TEC	Technician Education Council (now BTEC)
TEC	Training Enterprise Council
TOPS	Training Opportunities Scheme
TSA	Training Services Agency (later Training Division of the MSC)
TSD	Training Services Division (later Training Division of the MSC)
TVEI	Technical and Vocational Education Initiative
TWI	Training Within Industry
UVP	Unified Vocational Preparation Programme
WEEP	Work Experience on Employers' Premises
WOTP	Wider Opportunities Training Programme
YOP	Youth Opportunities Programme
YTS	Youth Training Scheme

Appendix 2

LIST OF TRAINING ACTIVITIES

Reproduced with the permission of the Local Government Training Board, from Training Recommendation 17, *Training and Development of Training Officers* (1976).

The following list of activities is not intended to be exhaustive.

1 Training policy:

- make recommendations on the authority's training policy and assist in its formulation.

2 Identify training needs and priorities:

- participate in the identification of future manpower needs and in decisions on ways of meeting these;
- liaise with other training staff in the authority and with management;
- identify the long and short-term training needs of the authority, departments and sections, job categories and individual employees;
- define overall training objectives to meet the training needs within the confines of the authority's training policy;
- estimate the resources required to meet the objectives;
- recommend areas of training priority, taking into account the authority's training policy and limited resources available;
- advise individuals on training problems.

3 Plan training:

- formulate a training plan taking account of the overall manpower plans for the authority;
- liaise with other staff in the authority with a responsibility for training;
- liaise with colleges and other outside organizations concerned with training (e.g. Training Boards and Provincial Councils);
- evaluate various ways of meeting training needs;
- set objectives for training programmes;
- prepare training programmes to meet the long and short-term training needs of the authority, departments and sections, job categories and individual employees;
- prepare training estimates and budgets;
- prepare any necessary training controls, records, and validation procedures.

4 Implement training:

- advise on the preparation of man specifications for recruitment and selection purposes and assist in selection of staff, if required;
- organize and supervise internal courses to meet the planned objectives;
- make and supervise practical training arrangements;
- select, train and brief instructors;
- prepare training material for internal courses, and operate and maintain training equipment;
- participate in internal courses;
- select external courses; advise management on the suitability of external courses to meet planned objectives, supervise the operation of externally conducted training programmes and the associated on-the-job training;
- maintain records of training;
- carry out evaluation and validation procedures, amending training plans accordingly.

5 Management of training:

- set objectives of training section to meet the authority's training policy;
- plan work load and priorities of the training section; organize the staff to meet the objectives;
- ensure an effective utilization of the authority's training resources (staff, premises, equipment, etc.); operate within the approved budget;
- keep management informed of the progress of training;
- organize and carry out the training and development of all the authority's training staff;
- liaise with senior managers on the future objectives of the authority and the need for development of particular categories of staff;
- help to establish the best conditions for learning in the authority.

Appendix 3

A BRIEF GUIDE TO TRAINING TECHNIQUES

Based on Paper No. 5 of the former Ceramics, Glass and Mineral Products Industry Training Board.

The following is intended only as a general guide to some of the more common techniques.

METHOD: WHAT IT IS	WHAT IT WILL ACHIEVE	POINTS TO WATCH
Lecture		
A talk given without much, if any, participation in the form of questions or discussion on the part of the trainees.	Suitable for large audiences where participation of the trainees is not possible because of numbers. The information to be put over can be exactly worked out beforehand — even to the precise word. The timing can be accurately worked out.	The lack of participation on the part of the audience means that unless the whole of it, from beginnning to end, is fully understood and assimilated the sense will be lost.

METHOD: WHAT IT IS	WHAT IT WILL ACHIEVE	POINTS TO WATCH
Talk		
A talk incorporating a variety of techniques, and allowing for participation by the trainees. The participation may be in the form of questions asked of trainees, their questions to the speaker, or brief periods of discussion during the currency of the session.	Suitable for putting across information to groups of not more than 20 trainees. Participation by the trainees keeps their interest and helps them to learn.	The trainees have the opportunity to participate but may not wish to do so. The communication will then be all one way and the session will be little different from a lecture.
Job (skill) instruction		
A session during which a job or part of a job is learned to the following formula: (a) the trainee is told how to do the job; (b) the trainee is shown how to do the job; (c) the trainee does the job under supervision. Each of these parts may be a complete session in itself. (a) talk (b) demonstration (c) practice	Suitable for putting across skills. The job is broken down into small stages which are practised. The whole skill is thus built up in easily understood stages. This gives the trainees confidence and helps them to learn. More suitable when the skill to be learned is one which depends on a lot of knowledge first being learned. Many clerical skills are of this sort.	The skill to be acquired may best be learned as a 'whole' rather than as parts. It is difficult for trainees to absorb large chunks of information and then to be shown what to do at some length before they get the opportunity to put the learning into practice.

METHOD: WHAT IT IS	WHAT IT WILL ACHIEVE	POINTS TO WATCH
Discussion		
Knowledge, ideas and opinions on a particular subject are freely exchanged among the trainees and the instructor.	Suitable where the application of information is a matter of opinion. Also when attitudes need to be induced or changed. Trainees are more likely to change attitudes after discussion than they would if they were told during a talk that their attitude should be changed. Also suitable as a means of obtaining feedback to the instructor about the way in which trainees may apply the knowledge learned.	The trainees may stray from the subject matter or fail to discuss it usefully. The whole session may be blurred and woolley. Trainees may become entrenched about their attitudes rather than be prepared to change them.

METHOD: WHAT IT IS	WHAT IT WILL ACHIEVE	POINTS TO WATCH
Role-play		
Trainees are asked to enact, in the training situation, the role they will be called upon to play in their job of work. Used mainly for the practice of dealing with face-to-face situations (i.e. where people come together in the work situation).	Suitable where the subject is one where a near-to-life practice in the training situation is helpful to the trainees. The trainees can practise and receive expert advice or criticism and opinions of their colleagues in a 'protected' training situation. This gives confidence as well as offering guidelines. The trainees get the feel of the pressures of the real life situation.	Trainees may be embarrassed and their confidence sapped rather than built up. It can also be regarded as a 'bit of a lark' and not taken seriously.
Case-study		
A history of some event or set of circumstances, with the relevant details, is examined by the trainees. Case-studies fall into two broad categories: (a) those in which the trainees diagnose the causes of a particular problem; (b) those in which the trainees set out to solve a particular problem.	Suitable where a cool look at the problem or set of circumstances, free from the pressures of the actual event, is beneficial. It provides opportunities for exchange of ideas and consideration of possible solutions to problems the trainees will face in the work situation.	Trainees may get the wrong impression of the real work situation. They may fail to realize that decisions taken in the training situation are different from those which have to be made on the spot in a live situation.

METHOD: WHAT IT IS	WHAT IT WILL ACHIEVE	POINTS TO WATCH
Exercise		
Trainees are asked to undertake a particular task, leading to a required result, following lines laid down by the trainers. It is usually a practice or a test of knowledge put over prior to the exercise. Exercises may be used to discover trainees' existing knowledge or ideas before further information or new ideas are introduced. Exercises may be posed for individuals or for groups.	Suitable for any situation where the trainees need to practise following a particular pattern or formula to reach a required objective. The trainees are to some extent 'on their own'. This is a highly active form of learning. Exercises are frequently used instead of formal tests to find out how much the trainee has assimilated. There is a lot of scope in this method for the imaginative trainer.	The exercise must be realistic and the expected result reasonably attainable by all trainees or the trainees will lose confidence and experience frustration.

METHOD: WHAT IT IS	WHAT IT WILL ACHIEVE	POINTS TO WATCH
Project		
Similar to an exercise but giving the trainee much greater opportunity for the display of initiative and creative ideas. The particular task is laid down by the trainer but the lines to be followed to achieve the objectives are left to the trainee to decide. Like exercises, projects may be set for either individuals or groups.	Suitable where initiative and creativity need stimulating or testing. Projects provide feedback on a range of personal qualities of trainees as well as their range of knowledge and attitude to the job. Like exercises, projects may be used instead of formal tests. Again there is a lot of scope for the imaginative trainer. Used to help evaluate candidates in assessment centres.	It is essential that the project is undertaken with the trainee's full interest and co-operation. It must also be seen by the trainee to be directly relevant to his needs. If the trainee fails, or feels he has failed, in the project there will be severe loss of confidence on his part and possible antagonism towards the trainer. Trainees are often hypersensitive to criticism of project work.

METHOD: WHAT IT IS	WHAT IT WILL ACHIEVE	POINTS TO WATCH
In-tray		
Trainees are given a series of files, papers and letters similar to those they will be required to deal with at the place of work (i.e. the typical content of a desk-worker's in-tray). Trainees take action on each piece of work. The results are marked or compared one with another.	Suitable for giving trainee desk-workers a clear understanding of the real-life problems and their solutions. The simulation of the real situation aids the transfer of learning from the training to the work situation. A valuable way of obtaining feedback on the trainees' progress. Also useful for developing attitudes towards the work, e.g. priorities, customers' complaints, superiors, etc. Used to help evaluate candidates in assessment centres.	It is important that the contents of the in-tray are realistic. The aim should be to provide trainees with a typical in-tray. The marking or comparison of results must be done in a way which will not sap the confidence of the weaker trainee.

METHOD: WHAT IT IS	WHAT IT WILL ACHIEVE	POINTS TO WATCH
Business and management games (simulations)		
Trainees are presented with information about a company — its financial position, products, market, etc. They are given different management roles to perform. One group may be concerned with sales, another with production and so on. These groups then 'run' the company. Decisions are made and actions are taken. The probable result of these decisions in terms of profitablility is then calculated.	Suitable for giving trainee managers practice in dealing with management problems. The simulation of the real-life situation not only aids the transfer of learning but is necessary because a trainee manager applying only broad theoretical knowledge to the work situation could cause major problems. Also a valuable way of assessing the potential performance of trainees. It helps considerably in developing many aspects of a manager's role.	The main difficulty is in assessing the probable results of the decisions made. A computer is often used for this purpose. The trainees may reject the whole of the learning if they feel the assessment of the probable outcome of their decisions is unrealistic. There is also a risk that the trainees may not take the training situation seriously.

METHOD: WHAT IT IS	WHAT IT WILL ACHIEVE	POINTS TO WATCH
Group dynamics		
Trainees are put into situations in which: (a) the behaviour of each individual in the group is subject to examination and comment by other trainees; (b) the behaviour of the group (or groups) as a whole is examined. (The trainer is a psychologist, or a person who has received special training.)	A vivid way for the trainee to learn of the effect of his behaviour on other people and the effect of their behaviour upon him. It increases knowledge of how and why people at work behave as they do. It increases skill at working with other people and of getting work done through other people. A valuable way of learning the skill of communication.	Difficulties can arise if what the trainee learns about himself is distasteful to him. Trainees may 'opt-out' if they feel put off by the searching examination of motives. It is important that problems arising within the group are resolved before the group breaks up.

Consolidated bibliography

ADVISORY CONCILIATION and ARBITRATION SERVICE. *Induction of new employees*. Advisory Booklet, No. 7, London, ACAS, 1982.

ANDERSON A and TOBBELL G. *Costing training centres*. IMS Report, No. 72, Brighton, Institute of Manpower Studies, 1983.

ANNETT J and DUNCAN K D. *New media and methods in industrial training*. Robinson J and Barnes N (eds), London, British Broadcasting Corporation, 1968.

ANNETT J, in *Psychology at Work*. Warr P (ed.), Harmondsworth, Penguin Education, 1974.

ANNETT J, DUNCAN K D, STAMMERS R B, and GRAY M J. *Task Analysis*. DEP Training Information Paper, No. 6, London, HMSO. (Reprinted Sheffield, Training Division, Manpower Services Commission, 1979.)

ANNETT J. *Skill loss*. Sheffield, Manpower Services Commission, 1983.

ANNETT J and SPARROW J. *Transfer of learning and training. Basic issues: policy implications: how to promote transfer*. Research and Development, No. 23, Sheffield, Manpower Services Commission, 1985.

ARGYLE M. *Psychology of interpersonal behaviour*. Harmondsworth, Penguin, 1970. (reprinted 1983).

ARMSTRONG P and DAWSON C. *People in organizations*. Kings Repton, Cambridge, Elm Publications, 1983.

AUSTIN ROVER. *Open learning*. Austin Rover Training Open Learning Unit.

AVENT C. 'Transition from school to work'. *BACIE Journal*, July/Aug, 1984.

BACON J. 'The adult training strategy'. *Industrial and Commercial Training*, Vol. 17, No. 3, May/June, 1985.

BANK J. *Outdoor training for managers*. Aldershot, Gower Press, 1985.

BARON B, in *Managing human resources*. Cowling A G and Mailer C J B. (eds), London, Arnold, 1981.

BARRINGTON H A. 'Continuous development: theory and reality'. *Personnel Review*, Vol 15, No 1, 1986. pp 27-31.

BASS B M and VAUGHAN J A. *Training in industry — the management of learning*. London, Tavistock Publications, 1966.

BELBIN E and BELBIN R M. *Problems in adult retraining*. London, Heinemann, 1972.

BELBIN R M. *Employment of older workers*. No. 2, Training Methods, Paris, OECD, 1969.

BELBIN R M. 'Some policy options in reducing unemployment, an experimental approach'. *BACIE Journal*, October, 1981.

BENNETT R and LEDUCHOWICZ T. *What makes for an effective trainer?* Bradford, MCB University Press Ltd, 1983.

BERESFORD P. Report in *The Sunday Times,* 6 September 1987.

BEVAN S and HUTT R. *Company perspectives on YTS*. IMS Report, No. 104, Brighton, Institute of Manpower Studies, 1985.

BLACHERE M. *Role of training in setting up new economic and social activities*. 2nd. edition. Berlin, European Centre for the Development of Vocational Training, (CEDEFOP), 1980.

BLAKE R R and MOUTON J S. *The versatile manager: a grid profile*. Irwin-Dorse, 1981.

BODDY D. 'Putting action learning into action'. *Journal of European Industrial Training*, Vol. 5, No. 5, 1981.

BORGER R and SEABORNE A E M. *The psychology of learning*. Harmondsworth, Penguin, 1982.

BOURNER T. *Handbook for the graduates' first destinations transbinary database*. London, Council for National Academic Awards, 1984.

BOYDELL T H. *A guide to job analysis*. London, British Association for Commercial and Industrial Education, 1977.

BOYDELL T H. *A guide to the identification of training needs*. London, British Association for Commercial and Industrial Education, 1983.

BOYS C. 'Are employers making the most of higher education?' *Personnel Management*, September, 1984.

BRAMHAM J. *Practical manpower planning*. London, Institute of Personnel Management, 1982.

BRAMLEY P and NEWBY A C. 'The evaluation of training: clarifying the concept'. *Journal of European Industrial Training*, Vol. 8, No. 6, 1984.

BRIDGE J. *Economics in personnel management*. London, Institute of Personnel Management, 1981.

BRITISH ASSOCIATION FOR COMMERCIAL AND INDUSTRIAL EDUCATION. *Report writing*. London, BACIE, 1981.

BRITISH ASSOCIATION FOR COMMERCIAL AND INDUSTRIAL EDUCATION. 'Skeletal modules'. *Transition*, BACIE, 1985.

BRITISH CHAMBER OF COMMERCE SURVEY, Reported by P. Beresford in *The Sunday Times,* 6 September 1987.

BROMLEY D B. *The psychology of human ageing*. Harmondsworth, Pelican, Penguin Books, 1975.

BURGOYNE J. 'Management development for the individual and the organization', *Personnel Management,* June 1988.

BURNS T and STALKER G N. *The management of innovation*. London, Tavistock Publications, 1966.

BUSINESS AND TECHNICIAN EDUCATION COUNCIL. *Policies and priorities into the 1990s*. London, BTEC, 1984.

BUSINESS EDUCATION COUNCIL. *First policy statement.* London, Business Education Council, 1976.

BYHAM B. 'Assessing employees without resorting to a centre'. *Personnel Management*, October, 1984.

CANNON J. *Cost effective decisions.* London, Institute of Personnel Management, 1979.

CARBY K and THAKUR M. *Transactional analysis at work.* Information report No. 23, London, Institute of Personnel Management, 1976.

CARBY K and THAKUR M. *No problems here.* London, Institute of Personnel Management, 1977.

CARR COMMITTEE REPORT. *Training for skill, recruitment and training of young workers in industry.* London, National Joint Advisory Council, HMSO, 1958.

CARROLL S J. 'The relative effectiveness of training methods — expert opinion and research'. *Personnel Psychology*, 1972.

CARVEL J. 'Where have all the skilled men gone?' *The Guardian*, 15th August, 1978.

CASSELS J. 'Education and training must be geared to match the demand for more skills in British industry today'. *The Times*, 13th June, 1985.

CENTRAL POLICY REVIEW STAFF REPORT. *Education, training and industrial performance.* London, HMSO, 1980.

CENTRAL TRAINING COUNCIL. *Industrial training and further education.* London, HMSO, 1966.

CHADWICK D and HOGG Y. *Career planning and development for managers.* Croydon, Food, Drink and Tobacco Industry Training Board, 1978.

CHAPPLE F. 'Employment and training in the next twenty years'. *BACIE Journal*, Nov/Dec, 1980.

CHAPPLE F. 'A report on the Electrical, Electronic, Telecommunication and Plumbing Union's retraining programme'. *The Times*, 13th March, 1984.

CHEMICAL AND ALLIED PRODUCTS INDUSTRY TRAINING BOARD. *Information paper on productivity agreements.* Chemical and Allied Products Industry Training Board, 1970.

CHEMICAL AND ALLIED PRODUCTS INDUSTRY TRAINING BOARD. *Assessing safety training needs.* Information Paper, No. 16, Staines, Middx. Chemical and Allied Products Industry Training Board, 1980.

CLOTHING AND ALLIED PRODUCTS INDUSTRY TRAINING BOARD. *Levy exemptions and key training grants.* Leeds, Clothing and Allied Products Industry Training Board, 1977.

CLUTTERBUCK D. *Everyone needs a mentor.* London, Institute of Personnel Management, 1985.

COMMITTEE OF DIRECTORS OF POLYTECHNICS, Press information sheet. 6th November, 1984.

COMMISSION OF THE EUROPEAN COMMUNITIES. 'From education to working life', in *Bulletin of the European Communities Supplement*, 12/76, 1976.

CONFEDERATION OF BRITISH INDUSTRY. 'Operation of the Industrial Training Act'. Statement by the CBI, *Supplement to the Education and Training Bulletin*, February, 1971.

CONSTABLE J *and* McCORMICK R. 'The making of British managers'. A report for the BIM and CBI into management training, education and development. April 1987.

COOPER K. 'Review of the Employment and Training Act'. *BACIE Journal*, Vol. 32, No. 3, March, 1978.

COUNCIL FOR EDUCATIONAL TECHNOLOGY. *Open learning*. Information Sheet No. 5, Southampton, Council for Educational Technology, 1984.

COUNCIL FOR MANAGEMENT EDUCATION AND DEVELOPMENT. *Management Charter Initiative*. London, CMED, 1988.

COUNCIL OF THE MINISTERS OF THE EUROPEAN ECONOMIC COMMUNITY. 'General principles for the implementation of common vocational training policy'. 63/266 OJ No. 63, April, 1963.

CROFTS P. 'Distance learning's broader horizons'. *Personnel Management*, March, 1985.

CROSS M. *Towards the flexible craftsman*. London, The Technical Change Centre, 1985.

CUMING M. *A manager's guide to quantitative methods*. Kings Repton, Cambridge, Elm Publications, 1984.

DAVIES A T. *Industrial training — an introduction*. London, Institute of Personnel Management, 1956.

DEAKIN B M *and* PRATTEN C F. Report in *Employment Gazette*, October 1987.

DELF G and SMITH B. 'Strategies for promoting self development'. *Industrial and Commercial Training*, Vol. 10, No. 1, December, 1978.

DEPARTMENT OF EDUCATION AND SCIENCE. 'Colleges and firms join forces in seven local training projects'. Press release notice 182/84, November, 1984.

DEPARTMENT OF EDUCATION AND SCIENCE. *An assessment of the costs and benefits of sandwich course education, a report by a committee on research into sandwich education*. London, Department of Education and Science, 1985.

DEPARTMENT OF EMPLOYMENT. *Glossary of training terms*. London, HMSO, 1971.

DEPARTMENT OF EMPLOYMENT. *Training for the future: a plan for discussion*. London, HMSO, 1972.

DEPARTMENT OF EMPLOYMENT. *Employment Gazette*. September, 1980.

DEPARTMENT OF EMPLOYMENT. *A new training initiative: a programme for action*. London, HMSO, 1981.

DEPARTMENT OF EMPLOYMENT. *Training loans. A proposal from the Secretary of State for Employment for an experimental training loans scheme for adults*. Department of Employment, 1984.

DEPARTMENT OF EMPLOYMENT. *Training for employment* (Cm 316). London, HMSO, 1988.

DONNELLY E L and BARRETT B. 'Safety training since the Act'. *Personnel Management*, June, 1981.

DONNELLY E L. 'Training as a specialist function — an historical perspective'. *Working Paper*, No. 9, London, Faculty of Business Studies and Management, Middlesex Polytechnic, 1984.

DONNELLY E L. 'The training model: time for a change?' *Industrial and Commercial Training*. Vol 19, No 3, 1987.

DOWNS S. *Trainability testing*. Training Information Paper, No. 11, London, HMSO, 1977.

DUNCAN K D and KELLY C J. *Task analysis, learning and the nature of transfer*. Sheffield, Manpower Services Commission, 1983.

EASTERBY-SMITH M and TANTON M. 'Turning course evaluation from an end to a means'. *Personnel Management*, April, 1985.

ENGINEERING INDUSTRY TRAINING BOARD. *The analysis of certain engineering craft occupations*. Research report, No.2, Watford, Engineering Industry Training Board, 1971.

ENGINEERING INDUSTRY TRAINING BOARD. *Review of craft apprenticeship in engineering*. Information Paper, No. 49, Watford, Engineering Industry Training Board, 1978.

ENGINEERING INDUSTRY TRAINING BOARD. *Annual report and accounts 1980/81*. Watford, Engineering Industry Training Board, 1981.

ENGINEERING INDUSTRY TRAINING BOARD. *Summary of annual report 1982/3*. Watford, Engineering Industry Training Board, 1983.

EQUAL OPPORTUNITIES COMMISSION. *Code of practice for the elimination of sex and marriage discrimination and the promotion of equality of opportunity in employment*. London, Equal Opportunities Commission, 1985.

ESTES W K. *Learning theory and mental development*. New York, Academic Press, 1970.

EUROPEAN ECONOMIC COMMISSION. *Preliminary guidelines for a community social policy programme*. Sec (71), 6000 Final, 17th March, 1971.

FAUX R. Report in *The Times,* 17 August 1987.

FAUX R. Report in *The Times,* 15 December 1987.

FESTINGER L. *A theory of cognitive dissonance*. Evanston, Ill., Row Peterson, 1957.

FLEISHMAN E A and HEMPEL W E. 'The relationship between abilities and improvement with practice in a visual discrimination task'. *Journal of Experimental Psychology*, 49, 1955.

FLEISHMAN E A. *A leadership climate, human relations training and supervisory behaviour*. Studies in Personnel and Industrial Psychology. Homewood, Ill. Dorsey, 1967.

FLETCHER C. 'What's new in performance appraisal'. *Personnel Management*, February, 1984.

FLETCHER C and WILLIAMS R. *Performance appraisal and career development.* London, Hutchinson, 1985.

FOOD DRINK AND TOBACCO INDUSTRY TRAINING BOARD. *How to use job analysis for profitable training*. Systematic training guide, No. 2, Croydon, Food Drink and Tobacco Industry Training Board, 1972.

FORRESTER D. quoted by HARLEY J. in 'How to assess your training costs'. *British Industry Week*, 22nd. November, 1968.

FOWLER A. *Getting off to a good start – successful employee induction*. London, Institute of Personnel Management, 1983.

FURTHER EDUCATION CURRICULUM REVIEW AND DEVELOPMENT UNIT. *Profiles*. London, Department of Education and Science, 1982.

GARBUTT D. *Training costs with reference to the Industrial Training Act*. Gee and Company Ltd, 1969.

GILES W J. 'Training after the Act'. *Personnel Management*, Vol. 1, No. 2, June, 1969.

GILL D. *Appraising performance, present trends and the next decade*. Information Report, No. 25, London, Institute of Personnel Management, 1978.

GLASER R. *Training research and education*. New York, Wiley & Sons, 1965.

GOLDSTEIN I L. 'Training in work organizations'. *Annual Review Psychology*. 31:229-72, 1980.

GRANT D. 'A better way of learning from Nellie'. *Personnel Management*, December, 1984.

GREINER L E. 'Evolution and revolution as organizations grow'. *Harvard Business Review*, July-August, 1972.

GRONLUND N E. *Stating behavioural objectives for classroom instruction*. London, Macmillan, 1978.

GUEST D and KENNY T. *A textbook of techniques and strategies in personnel management*. London, Institute of Personnel Management, 1983.

HALL N. 'Cost effective analysis in industrial training'. *Manchester Monographs*, No. 6, University of Manchester, 1976.

HAMBLIN A C. *Evaluation and control of training*. Maidenhead, McGraw-Hill 1974.

HANDY C. *The making of managers*. London, National Economic Development Office, April 1987.

HANSEN G B. *Britain's Industrial Training Act, its history, development and implications for America*. Washington DC, National Manpower Policy Taskforce, 1967.

HARRISON J E C. *The common people – a history from the Norman conquest to the present*. London, Flamingo. 1984.

HASLEGRAVE REPORT. *Report of the committee on technician courses and examinations*. London, HMSO, 1969.

HAYES C, FONDA N, POPE M, STUART R, and TOWNSEND K. *Training for skill ownership — learning to take it with you*. A report to the Manpower Services Commission, Sussex, Institute of Manpower Studies, 1983.

HAYES C *et al*. 'International competition and the role of competence'. *Personnel Management*, September, 1984.

HESSELING P. *Strategy of evaluation research*. New York, Van Gorcum, 1966.

HILGARD E R and others. *Introduction to psychology*. New York, Harcourt Brace Jovanovich, 1983.

HMSO. *Industrial Training Act, 1964, General guide, scope and objectives*. London, HMSO, 1964.

HMSO. *White paper: Government proposals, industrial training*. London, HMSO, 1962.

HMSO. *White paper: A new training initiative: a programme for action*. London, HMSO, 1981.

HMSO. *White paper: Training for jobs*. London, HMSO, 1984.

HMSO. *White paper: Education and training for young people*. London, HMSO, 1985.

HMSO. *'Working together – education and training'* (Cm 9832). London, HMSO, 1986.

HOLDING D H. *Principles of training*. Oxford, Pergamon Press, 1965.

HOLDING D H. 'Knowledge of results' in *Skills*. Legge D. (ed.), Harmondsworth, Penguin, 1970.

HOLLAND D. 'Strategic benefits from computer integrated manufacture'. *The Production Engineer*, June, 1984.

HOLLINGSHEAD B *et al. Planned experience – a survey and synthesis of criteria for work experience*. London, Further Education Unit, Department of Education and Science, 1984.

HOLMES S. 'Are schools and industry getting each other's message?' *Personnel Management*, December, 1984.

HONEY P and MUMFORD A. *Manual of learning styles*. Maidenhead, Honey, 1982.

HONEY P and MUMFORD A. *Using your learning styles*. Maidenhead, Honey, 1983.

HOWELLS R and BARRETT B. *The Health and Safety at Work Act, a guide for managers*. London, Institute of Personnel Management, 1975.

HUCZYNSKI A. 'Training methods — fads and fancies?' *BACIE Journal*, March/April, 1984.

HUMBLE J W. *Management by objectives*. London, British Institute of Management, 1973.

INDUSTRIAL SOCIETY. *Survey of training costs*. New Series, No. 1, London, The Industrial Society, 1985.

INSTITUTE OF PERSONNEL MANAGEMENT. *Comments to the Manpower Services Commission*. London, IPM, October, 1980.

INSTITUTE OF PERSONNEL MANAGEMENT. *A positive policy for training and development*. London, IPM, 1983.

INSTITUTE OF PERSONNEL MANAGEMENT. *Continuous development: people at work*. London, IPM, 1984.

INSTITUTE OF PERSONNEL MANAGEMENT. *TVEI: Recommendations on improved school/work liaison*. London, IPM, 1984.

INSTITUTE OF PERSONNEL MANAGEMENT. *Submission in response to the Manpower Services Commission's discussion paper Review of the Area Manpower Boards*. London, IPM, 1985.

INSTITUTE OF PERSONNEL MANAGEMENT. *Survey of skill shortages*. London, IPM, 1985.

INSTITUTE OF PERSONNEL MANAGEMENT. *Continuous development: people and work*, (IPM code). London, IPM, 1987.

IRON AND STEEL INDUSTRY TRAINING BOARD. *The management of health and safety*. Iron and Steel Industry Training Board, 1976.

JACKSON K F. *The art of solving problems*. Bulmershe-Comino Problem Solving Project, Bulmershe College of Higher Education, Reading, 1984.

JAMES R. 'The use of learning curves'. *Journal of European Industrial Training*, Vol. 8, No. 7, 1984.

JANNE H and SCHWARTZ B. *The development of permanent education in Europe*. Brussels, Commission of the European Communities, 1980.

JENKINS D, in *A textbook of techniques and strategies in personnel management*. Guest D and Kenny T (eds), London, Institute of Personnel Management, 1983.

JENNINGS S and UNDY R. 'Auditing managers' I R training needs'. *Personnel Management*, February, 1984.

JENSEN A R. *Educability and group differences*. London, Harper and Row, 1976.

JOHNSON R. 'Youth training in Europe'. *Personnel Management*, July, 1984.

JOHNSON R. *Occupational training families: their implications for FE*. London, Further Education Unit, Department of Education and Science, 1984.

JONES J A G and Moxham J. 'Costing the benefits of training'. *Personnel Management*, Vol. 1. No. 4, 1969.

JONES J A G. *The evaluation and cost effectiveness of training*. Seminar, London, Industrial Training Service, August, 1970.

JONES J A G. *Training intervention strategies – making more effective training interventions*. ITS Research Monograph, No. 2, Industrial Training Service Ltd. London, 1983.

JONES S. *Design of instruction*. Training Information Paper, No. 1, London, HMSO, 1968.

JOSEPH, SIR KEITH, reported in Department of Education and Science press release. *Colleges and firms join forces in seven local training projects*. Notice 182/84, November, 1984.

KAY H. 'Accidents: some facts and theories' in *Psychology at Work*. Warr P (ed.), Harmondsworth, Penguin Education, 1983.

KEARSLEY G. *Costs, benefits and productivity in training systems*. London, Addison-Wesley, 1982.

KENNEY J P J and MARSH P J. 'Management schools and industrial training'. *Industrial and Commercial Training*, Vol. 1, No. 2, December, 1969.

KENNEY J P J and DONNELLY E L. *Manpower training and development*. London. Harrap, 1972.

KENNEY J P J, DONNELLY E L, and REID M. *Manpower training and development*. London, Institute of Personnel Management, 1979.

KING D. *Training within the organization*. London, Tavistock Publications, 1964.

KING T. 'Minister stresses the role of training. Report of CBI conference'. *Personnel Management*, September, 1985.

KOHLER W. *The mentality of apes*. London, International Library of Psychology, Routledge, 1973.

KOLB D A, RUBIN I M, McINTYRE J M. *Organizational psychology, a book of readings*, 2nd edn. 1974. Englewood Cliffs N J, Prentice Hall, 1974.

KOLB D A, RUBIN I M, McINTYRE J M. *Organizational psychology – an experiential approach*. Englewood Cliffs N J, Prentice Hall, 1974.

LAIRD D. *Approaches to training and development*. London, Addison-Wesley, 1978.

LATHROPE K. 'Stop your workforce standing still'. *Personnel Management*, October, 1985.

LOCAL GOVERNMENT TRAINING BOARD. *Training and development of training officers*. Training recommendation, No. 17. Luton, Local Government Training Board, 1976.

MAGER R and PIKE P. *Analysing performance problems*. San Francisco, Fearon Publishers, 1970.

MAGER R. *Preparing instructional objectives*. San Francisco, Fearon Publishers, 1984.

MANPOWER SERVICES COMMISSION. *Vocational preparation for young people*. Sheffield, MSC, 1975.

MANPOWER SERVICES COMMISSION. *Towards a comprehensive manpower policy*. Sheffield, MSC, 1976.

MANPOWER SERVICES COMMISSION. *Training for vital skills: a consultative document*. Sheffield, MSC, 1976.

MANPOWER SERVICES COMMISSION. *Review and plan*. Sheffield, MSC, 1977.

MANPOWER SERVICES COMMISSION. *Training Services Agency — a five year plan*. Sheffield, MSC, 1978.

MANPOWER SERVICES COMMISSION. *Training of trainers. First report of the Training of Trainers Committee*. Sheffield, MSC, 1978.

MANPOWER SERVICES COMMISSION. *Outlook on training: review of the Employment and Training Act, 1973*. Sheffield, MSC, 1980.

MANPOWER SERVICES COMMISSION. *Direct trainers. Second report of the Training of Trainers Committee*. London, HMSO, 1980.

MANPOWER SERVICES COMMISSION. *Glossary of training terms*. 3rd edition. London, HMSO, 1981.

MANPOWER SERVICES COMMISSION. *A new training initiative*. Sheffield, MSC, 1981.

MANPOWER SERVICES COMMISSION. *A new training initiative: an agenda for action*. Sheffield, MSC, 1981.

MANPOWER SERVICES COMMISSION. *An 'Open Tech' programme, a consultative document*. Sheffield, MSC, 1981.

MANPOWER SERVICES COMMISSION. *Looking at computer based training*. Sheffield, MSC, 1981.

MANPOWER SERVICES COMMISSION. *Youth task group report*. Sheffield, MSC, 1982.

MANPOWER SERVICES COMMISSION. *Manpower Review*. Sheffield, MSC, 1982.

MANPOWER SERVICES COMMISSION. *Towards an adult training strategy. A discussion paper*. Sheffield, MSC, 1983.

MANPOWER SERVICES COMMISSION. *Adult training strategy — proposals for action*. Sheffield, MSC, 1983.

MANPOWER SERVICES COMMISSION. *A new training initiative, modernisation of occupational training: a position statement*. Sheffield, MSC. 1984.

MANPOWER SERVICES COMMISSION. *MSC corporate plan 1984–1988*. Sheffield, MSC, 1984.

MANPOWER SERVICES COMMISSION. *Core skills in YTS: Part 1*. Sheffield, MSC, 1984.

MANPOWER SERVICES COMMISSION. *MSC corporate plan 1985–1989*. Sheffield, MSC, 1985.

MANPOWER SERVICES COMMISSION. *Adult training in Britain*. IFF Research Ltd. Report, Sheffield, MSC, 1985.

MANPOWER SERVICES COMMISSION AND DEPARTMENT OF EDUCATION AND SCIENCE. *Review of vocational qualifications in England and Wales, Interim Report*. Sheffield/London, MSC and DES, 1985.

MANSFIELD B. 'Getting to the core of the job'. *Personnel Management*, August, 1985.

MARKS GROUP. 'Alfred Mark's Group quarterly survey'. *Personnel Management*, August, 1985.

McGEHEE W and THAYER P W. *Training in business and industry*. Chichester Wiley, 1961.

McGREGOR D. *The human side of the enterprise*. Maidenhead, McGraw-Hill, 1960.

McILWEE T. *Personnel management in context: the 1980s*. Kings Repton, Cambridge, Elm Publications, 1982.

MEGGINSON D and BOYDELL T. *A manager's guide to coaching*. London, British Association for Commercial and Industrial Education, 1979.

MILLER V A. *The guide book for international trainers in business and industry*. NY, Van Nostrand Reinhold/American Society for Training and Development, 1979.

MORTIMORE J. *Profiles in action*. London, Further Education Unit, Department of Education and Science, 1984.

MUKHERJEE S. *Changing manpower needs: a study of Industrial Training Boards*. Broadsheet 523, Political and Economic Planning, 1970.

MUKHERJEE S. *There's work to be done*. London, Manpower Services Commission, HMSO, 1974.

MUMFORD A. *Making experience pay*. Maidenhead, McGraw-Hill, 1980.

MUMFORD A. 'Review of action learning in practice'. *Industrial and Commercial Training*, Vol. 16, No. 2, 1984.

MUMFORD A. 'Self development: missing elements'. *Industrial and Commercial Training*. Vol 18, No 3, May/June 1986. pp 6-10.

MUMFORD A *and others*. *Developing directors – the learning processes*. MSC, January 1987.

NATIONAL COUNCIL FOR VOCATIONAL QUALIFICATIONS. *What's in it for employers?* London, NCVQ, 1988.

NATIONAL ECONOMIC DEVELOPMENT OFFICE and MANPOWER SERVICES COMMISSION, *Competence and competition, training and education in the Federal Republic of Germany, the United States and Japan*. London, NEDO/MSC, 1984.

NATIONAL INSTITUTE OF ECONOMIC AND SOCIAL RESEARCH (NIESR), Report in *The Sunday Times,* 31 May 1988.

NELSON J. 'The criteria inventory'. *Industrial Training International*, Vol. 1, No. 8, 1966.

NICHOLSON B. 'Managing change in education and training'. *BACIE Journal*, March/April, 1985.

NORD W R. 'Beyond the teaching machine: the neglected area of operant conditioning in the theory and practice of management'. *Organisational Behaviour and Human Performance*, Vol. 4, 1969.

OTTO C P and GLASER R O. *The management of training*. London, Addison-Wesley, 1970.

PAGE G T. *The Industrial Training Act and after*. London, André Deutsch, 1967.

PASK G. 'Styles and strategies of learning'. *British Journal of Educational Psychology*, 46, 1976.

PEACH L. 'A realistic approach to employing the disabled'. *Personnel Management*, January, 1981.

PEARSON R, HUTT R and PARSONS D. *Education, training and employment.* Institute of Manpower Studies, Series No. 4, Aldershot, Gower Press, 1984.

PEDLER M. *Action learning in practice*. Aldershot, Gower Press 1983.

PEPPER A D. *Managing the training and development function*. Aldershot, Gower Press, 1984.

PERRY P J C. *The evolution of British manpower policy from the Statute of Artificers 1563 to the Industrial Training Act, 1964*. London, British Association for Commercial and Industrial Education, 1976.

PERRY P J C. 'Is TOPS tops?' *BACIE Journal*, Vol. 32, No. 7, July, 1978.

PERSONNEL MANAGEMENT. Editorial report. *Personnel Management*,April, 1984.

PERSONNEL MANAGEMENT. 'Good news for graduates'. Editorial comment, *Personnel Management*, March, 1985.

PETTIGREW A M, JONES G R and REASON P W. *Organizational and behavioural aspects of the role of the training officer in the UK chemical industry : a research study in two phases*. Chemical and Allied Products Industry Training Board, 1981.

PETTIGREW A M, JONES G R, and REASON P W. *Training and development roles in their organizational setting*. Sheffield, Manpower Services Commission. 1982.

POCOCK P. 'Whither what's left of the Training Boards?' *Personnel Management*, July, 1982.

POWELL L S. *A general guide to the use of visual aids*. London, British Association for Industrial and Commercial Education, 1981.

PRASHAR U. 'Evening up the odds for black workers'. *Personnel Management*, June, 1983.

PRESTON F. Report in *The Times*, 6th March, 1985.

RACKHAM N, HONEY P, and COLBERT M. *Developing interactive skills.* Guilsborough, Wellens Publishing, 1971.

RANDELL G, PACKARD P and SLATER S. *Staff appraisal.* London, Institute of Personnel Management, 1984.

REDDIN W J. 'Training and organizational change'. *BACIE Journal*, Vol. 2, No. 1, March, 1968.

REID M. Unpublished paper, 1976.

REVANS R W. *Developing effective managers*, Longmans, 1971.

REVANS R W. *The origins and growth of learning.* Chartwell Bratt, 1982.

REVANS R W. *The ABC of action learning.* Chartwell Bratt, 1983.

RICHARDSON J J and STRINGER J. 'The politics of change'. *Industrial and Commercial Training*, Vol. 13, No. 2, Feb, 1981.

RICHARDSON J and BENNETT B. 'Applying learning techniques to on the job development, Part 2'. *Journal of European Industrial Training*, Vol. 8, No. 3, 1984.

ROBBINS COMMITTEE REPORT. *Report of the committee on higher education.* London, HMSO, 1963.

RODGER A, MORGAN T and GUEST D. *A study of the work of industrial training officers.* Staines, Air Transport and Travel Industry Training Board, 1971.

ROGERS T G P and WILLIAMS P. *The recruitment and training of graduates.* London, Institute of Personnel Management, 1970

RYAN P. *Government employment and training policies: an evaluation.* Talk given to the annual conference of the Manpower Society. London, The Manpower Society, September, 1983.

RYAN P. 'The new training initiative after two years'. *Lloyds Bank Review*, No. 152, April, 1984.

SECRETARY OF STATE FOR EMPLOYMENT, quoted in *The Times,* 13 April 1988.

SELLIN B. *Youth unemployment and vocational training.* Berlin, CEDEFOP, 1983.

SELIGMAN M E P. *Helplessness.* San Francisco, Freeman, 1975.

SEYMOUR W D. *Industrial training for manual operatives.* London, Pitman, 1954.

SEYMOUR W D. *Skills analysis training.* London, Pitman, 1966.

SEYMOUR W D. *Industrial skills.* London, Pitman, 1966.

SIMPSON M F J and KENNEY J P J. 'A wholly sponsored undergraduate business programme — a twenty year perspective'. *Proceedings of the World Council and Assembly on Co-operative Education*, Edinburgh, 1985.

SINGER E J. *Training in industry and commerce.* London, Institute of Personnel Management, 1977.

SINGER E J. *Effective management coaching.* London, Institute of Personnel Management, 1979.

SINGER E J and JOHNSON R. *Setting up and running youth training programmes.* Surrey, Centre for Learning and Development in association with the Institute of Personnel Management, 1983.

SINGER E J. 'Occupational training families – a breakthrough or a diversion?' *BACIE Journal*, Nov/Dec, 1984.

SINGLETON W T. (ed.), *The study of real skills. Vol. 1*, The analysis of practical skills. MTP Press, 1978.

SKINNER B F. *Science and human behaviour*. London, MacMillan, 1965.

SKINNER B F. *Walden two*. London, Collier MacMillan, 1976.

SPENCER G A. Letter to *The Times*, 3rd. March, 1971.

STAMMERS R and PATRICK J, *The psychology of training*. (Essential Psychology Series, General editor, Heriot P), London, Methuen, 1975.

STEWART A and STEWART V. *Tomorrow's managers today*. London, Institute of Personnel Management, 1981.

STEWART R. 'Classifiying different types of managerial jobs'. *Personnel Review*, Vol. 4, No. 2, 1975.

STEWART R and SMITH P. *Review of the national administrative training scheme. National Health Service*. Oxford, Oxford Centre for Management Studies, 1984.

STRINGFELLOW C D. 'Education and training'. *Industrial Training International*, Vol. 3, No. 2, August, 1968.

SYKES A J M. 'The effect of a supervisory training course in changing supervisors' perceptions and expectations of the role of management'. *Human Relations*, 15, 1962.

TALBOT J P and ELLIS C D. *Analysis and costing of company training*. Aldershot, Gower Press, 1969.

TANNEHILL R E. *Motivation and management development*. London, Butterworths, 1970.

TANK A. 'Training to compete'. *New Technology*, May, 1985.

TAVERNIER G. *Industrial training systems and records*. Aldershot, Gower Press, 1971.

TAYLOR N. *Selecting and training the training officer*. London, Institute of Personnel Management, 1966.

THAKUR M, BRISTOW J and CARBY K. *Personnel in change — organisation development through the personnel function*. London, Institute of Personnel Management, 1978.

THAYER P W and McGEHEE M. 'On the effectiveness of not holding a formal training course'. *Personnel Psychology*, 1977.

THOMAS L F. 'Perceptual organization in industrial inspectors'. *Ergonomics*, Vol. 5, 1962. Quoted in *Experimental Psychology in Industry*, Holding D H (ed.) Harmondsworth, Middx. Penguin, 1969.

THOMASON G. *Textbook of personnel management*. London, Institute of Personnel Management, 1981.

THORNTON G C. 'Psychometric properties of self-appraisals of job performance'. *Personnel Psychology*, 33, 1980.

TRACEY W R. *Evaluating training and development systems*. American Management Association, 1968.

TRAINING COMMISSION *Postal survey of young people entering their 2nd year of YTS*. Sheffield, Training Commission (formerly MSC), 1987.

TRAINING SERVICES AGENCY. *An approach to the training of staff with training officer roles*. Sheffield, Training Services Agency, 1977.

TRESSELL R. *The ragged-trousered philanthropists*. London, Panther Books, Granada Publishing, 1984.

TURRELL M. *Training analysis: a guide to recognizing training needs*. Plymouth, Macdonald and Evans, 1980.

UPTON R. 'What next for youth training?' *Personnel Management*, April, 1985.

VAUGHAN T D. *Education and vocational guidance*. London, Routledge and Kegan Paul, 1970.

VERNON P E. *Intelligence and attainment tests*. London, London University Press, 1960.

VOGT O. 'Study of the ageing of the nerve cells'. *Journal of Gerontology*, No. 6, 1951.

WALTERS B. In *A textbook of techniques and strategies in personnel management*. Guest D and Kenny T (eds), London, Institute of Personnel Management, 1983.

WARR P B and BIRD M W. *Identifying supervisory training needs*. Training Information Paper, No. 2, London, HMSO, 1968.

WARR P B, BIRD M and RACKHAM N. *Evaluation of management training*. Aldershot, Gower Press, 1970.

WELFORD A T. 'On changes in performance with age'. *Lancet*, Part 1, 1962.

WELLENS J. 'The exploitation of human resources'. *The Times*, London, 26th August, 1968.

WELLENS J. 'An approach to management training'. *Industrial and Commercial Training*, Vol.8, No.7, July, 1970.

WHITELAW M. *The evaluation of management training — a review*. London, Institute of Personnel Management, 1972.

WOOD S, *ed. Continuous development*. London, Institute of Personnel Management, 1988.

WOODWARD J. *Industrial organization — theory and practice*. Oxford, Oxford University Press, reprinted 1980.

WOODWARD N. 'A cost benefit analysis of supervisor training'. *Industrial Relations Journal*, Summer, Vol.6, No.2, 1976.

WORTHINGTON M. 'Changing Course'. *Open Tech Programme News*, No. 8, July, Sheffield, Manpower Services Commission, 1985.

WRIGHT D S and TAYLOR A. *Introducing psychology — an experimental approach*. Harmonsworth, Middx. Penguin Education, 1970.

YOUNGMAN M B, et al. *Analysing jobs*. Aldershot, Gower Press, 1978.

ZIDERMAN A. *Manpower training: theory and policy*. MacMillan studies in economics, London, MacMillan Press, 1978.

Index